49°
124°
123°
Georgia Strait
Semiahmoo Bay
Blaine
49°
122°

Vancouver Island
Sidney
San Juan Islands
Bellingham Bay
Bellingham
Rosario Strait
Anacortes
Swinomish Slough
Skagit River
Victoria
La Conner
Mount Vernon
Deception Pass
Whidbey Island
Race Rocks
Canada
United States
Smith Island
Strait of Juan de Fuca
Camano I.
Saratoga Passage
Ediz Hook
Sequim Bay
Port Discovery
Admiralty Inlet
Whidbey Island
Dungeness
Port Townsend
Port Gardner
Everett
Port Angeles
48°
Snohomish
Snohomish River
Port Ludlow
Puget Sound
Port Gamble
Poulsbo
Port Madison
Liberty Bay
Seattle
Lake Washington
Hood Canal
Bremerton
Sinclair Inlet
Colvos (West) Pass
Vashon I.
East Pass
Commencement Bay
Carr Inlet
Tacoma

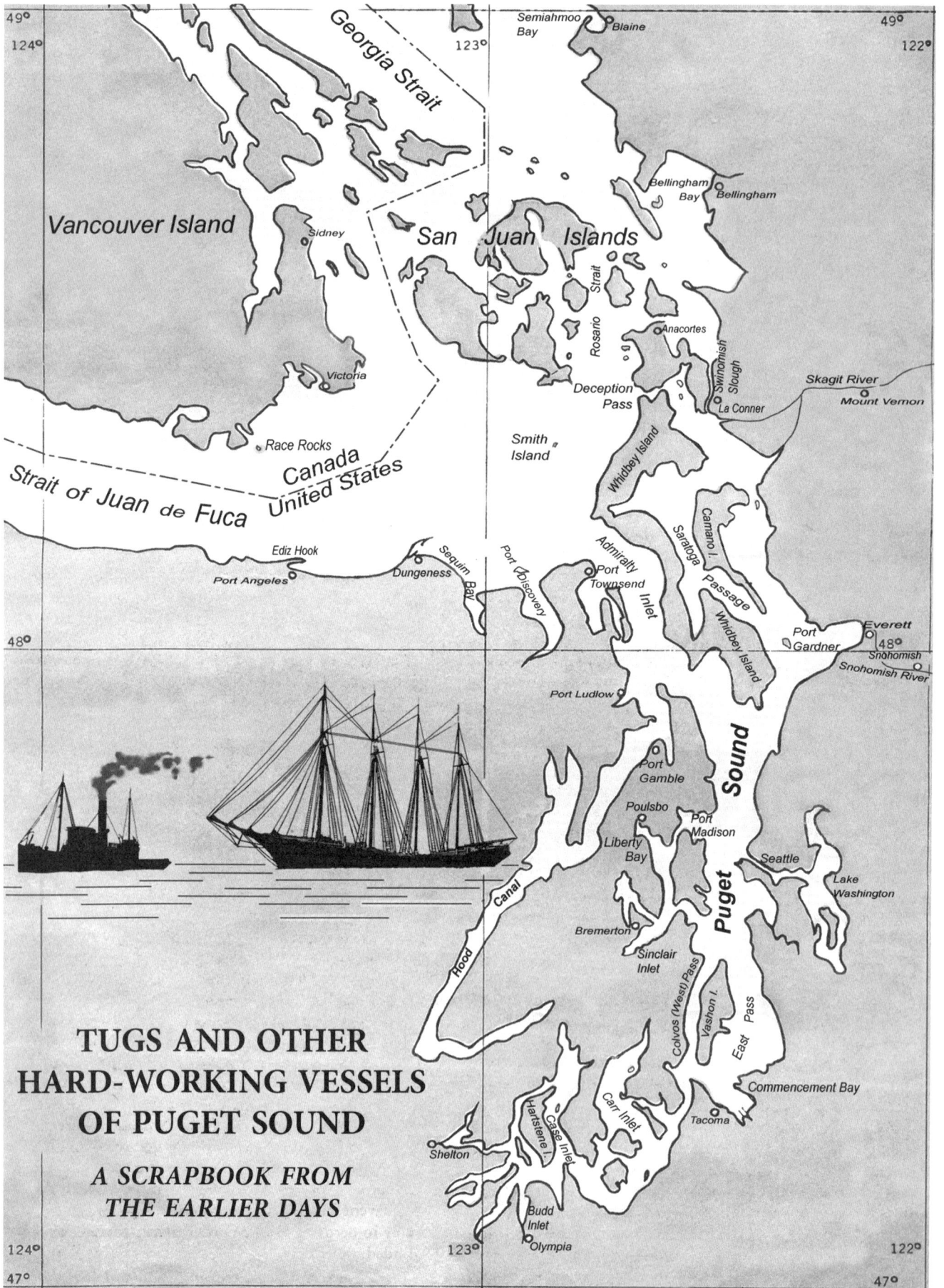

TUGS AND OTHER
HARD-WORKING VESSELS
OF PUGET SOUND

A SCRAPBOOK FROM
THE EARLIER DAYS

Hartstene I.
Case Inlet
Shelton
Budd Inlet
Olympia
124°
47°
123°
122°
47°

TUGS AND OTHER HARD-WORKING VESSELS OF PUGET SOUND

A SCRAPBOOK FROM THE EARLIER DAYS

Book Publishers Network
P.O. Box 2256
Bothell • WA • 98041
PH • 425-483-3040

10 9 8 7 6 5 4 3 2 1

Printed in the United States of America

LCCN   2010910121
ISBN10 1-935359-41-X
ISBN13 978-1-935359-41-8

Cover Design: Laura Zugzda

Permission has been requested but not yet granted for illustrations on pages 119, 270, 271, and 328

PUGET SOUND
A COMMENT ON THE FRONTISPIECE

Fjord-like Puget Sound stretches more than 80 nautical miles, in a north-south direction, from Deception Pass to the southern most point at Olympia. A vessel making a passage between those two locations by following the meandering channels, however, would travel a considerably greater distance. At mean high water, Puget Sound has a water surface area in excess of 1000 square miles that is lined by more than 1300 miles of beautiful, forested shoreline. Under Puget Sound's surface, more than 26 cubic miles of water are contained with depths varying up to 150 fathoms.

Two tide changes occur each day in Puget Sound, the difference between high and low water ranging up to 15 feet or more at Olympia and Shelton in the southern sound. Most of this tidal flow moves through Admiralty Inlet in northern Puget Sound, while a much smaller quantity of water flows through narrow Deception Pass where the current runs at a swift velocity of up to 10 knots at mid-tide. The water in Puget Sound is basically salt water, of course, but fresh water flowing into the sound from numerous rivers contributes about 20 percent to the total volume.

This picture does not depict a scene on Puget Sound; the photo was actually taken in Saginaw, Michigan, and shows log rafts being assembled on the Saginaw River in the late 1800s. Log rafts such as these were assembled by lumbermen who worked throughout Michigan and Wisconsin felling the pine and spruce trees that grew in the forests there.

When the timber played out in those areas, these men moved westward and settled in the Pacific Northwest where the stands of trees covered the land as far as the eye could see. Maritime commerce on Puget

Log rafts at Saginaw, Michigan, late 1800s.
(Courtesy of Ralph Stroebel)

Sound also began to flourish in the 1800s, the primary attraction for the wind ships of that era being the hauling of lumber and poles cut from the abundant timber available in the forests surrounding Puget Sound.

CONTENTS

Towing Companies (continued):

PREFACE

Tugs and Other Hard-Working Vessels of Puget Sound: A Scrapbook from the Earlier Days is intended to provide an account of Puget Sound tugboating and other marine activities, as well as a description of some typical industries that were dependent upon Puget Sound marine transport, in the earlier part of the last century. In general, the time span selected is from the 1920s to the 1960s, although a portion of the material is from years before and after that era. Perhaps this book could be thought of as a scrapbook and, in fact, that is the way I view it.

The chosen period includes the early years of my life, and therefore, I was witness to most of the picture portrayed here, an image that is still quite vivid in my own mind. This account applies to various areas of Puget Sound, but considerable attention is given to Olympia and the southern sound. Because I was born in Olympia and lived there in my younger days, I was well acquainted with the waterfront in southern Puget Sound. The firms in that area were similar to those that existed elsewhere on Puget Sound, also.

It is doubtful that a book such as this could ever be complete, for it seems that there are always more questions looking for answers. Accounting for all of Puget Sound shipping would probably be impossible, too, but most of the marine transportation companies and vessels that I was especially familiar with are depicted. A number of marine towing companies, ranging from modest size to large, are described. In addition, attention is paid to other working vessels, such as those involved with freight, passengers, fishing, and other occupations.

The record provided here was not initiated as an effort to write a book, but rather, it simply began with an intent to list, with notes, my collection of photos. Most of the photos in the book are snapshots that were taken by myself starting in 1939 at the age of ten and continuing, off and on, into the 1960s. I like snapshots, even those with defects. Snapshots are personal and spontaneous and, frequently, were taken by persons now unknown, which creates a mystery about who took the pictures and what the circumstances

were. To supplement the pictures from my own collection, other photos and original design drawings, as well as recollections, were contributed by members of my family, other individuals, and museums and archives.

All locations given are in the state of Washington unless noted otherwise. Throughout this book, data, such as length, tonnage, or horsepower, may be given for a particular vessel. These data are recorded in *Merchant Vessels of the United States* as published by the U.S. government. Hull lengths listed here are register, or document, lengths rounded to the nearest foot.

The register length is taken from the fore part of the hull planking or plating at the bow to the after part of the rudderpost, or rudder stock for most of the types of vessels described in this book. To arrive at a hull length overall, a portion of the stem forward of the planking or plating at the bow and the distance from the reference point on the rudder post, or rudder stock, to the aft end of the hull must be added to the register length.

A vessel's gross tonnage is derived from calculations and measurements of the ship's total internal volume in which 100 cubic feet is equal to one ton. Net tonnage is based on the gross internal volume but with the volume of certain spaces that have been defined as nonrevenue producing, such as living spaces and machinery spaces, deducted. Gross tonnage, then, gives an impression of ship size while net tonnage is an indicator of cargo carrying capacity and earning ability.

Weight and displacement (weight of the water displaced by the hull) bear no relationship to gross and net tonnage but, instead, are in long tons of 2240 pounds for vessels based in salt water or in short tons of 2000 pounds for vessels operating in fresh water, such as the Great Lakes.

A ship, then, will have several "tonnages." A tanker, for example, will have values for gross and net tons based on internal volume. In addition, a tanker will have a weight in tons, equal to the weight of the water displaced by the hull. The tanker will also be identified by the weight, known as "deadweight" tons, of cargo the ship is capable of carrying, in this case petroleum products.

Audrey and the author at Olympia, circa 1948.
(From the author's collection)

As stated previously, I was born in Olympia and, along with three siblings, sisters Annette and Louise and brother Morris Jr., grew up at 1802 East Bay Drive on the eastern edge of Olympia's harbor. For a time, my father, Morris Sr., worked with steam powered donkeys which were used for yarding logs in the woods. In this occupation, he rode the steam powered logging train into the hills early in the morning and back down in the evening. Not only were the days long at the logging show, but also quite a bit of time was needed for the commute to and from the work site. Later, my father operated steam locomotive cranes in the sawmills for many years. As Morris Sr. worked at his career for the family, so the author's mother, Anna, provided well for the needs of the family in the home, a full-time calling.

As a youngster at home, I had much to watch when the tugs were handling barges and log rafts in the East Bay area at Olympia. I also spent a lot of free time hanging out around the harbor and tug moorages. In those days, Olympia was an industrial town, and there was a great deal to see.

Later on, school vacations provided me with opportunities to work along the Olympia waterfront, including longshoring at the Port of Olympia, scraping and painting the bottoms of Delta V. Smyth Tugs and Barges' floating equipment, working as a deckhand aboard Smyth's tug *Nile,* and decking aboard Weyerhaeuser Logging Company's towboat *R. A. McDonald* at their log dump in Henderson Inlet (locally known as South Bay) when the crew was shorthanded. In addition, I decked aboard a power scow in the fishing industry at Bristol Bay, Alaska, the salmon fishing seasons in that area occurring during the summer.

Although continuing to work on the water would have been a good life, I instead received a degree in engineering, naval architecture and marine engineering, at the University of Michigan, which was followed by an equally rewarding career in ship design.

Norm Knutsen 2010

The view from 1802 East Bay Drive in Olympia, the author's boyhood home, as it was in the earlier days.

A BRIEF LOOK AT EARLIER TIMES

The importance of marine transportation was described elegantly by E. W. Wright in his preface to *Marine History of the Pacific Northwest* of 1895: "The vanguard of civilization for centuries has been led by the mariners, and their achievements from the days of Columbus mark the beginning of history in every new country which has become a portion of the known world."

And so it was with the Puget Sound country. Around the year 1500, explorers, including John Cabot and Gaspar Cortereal, searched the northern seas for an eastern entrance to a shorter route that was thought to exist between the Atlantic and Pacific Oceans. About 20 years later, Ferdinand Magellan, who had renounced his Portuguese citizenship over disagreements with the monarchy, set sail under the Spanish flag and discovered the passage at Terra del Fuego that now bears his name. The Straits of Magellan at the southern end of South America then opened the way for further exploration along the west coast of South America and North America.

Initially, the first sailors to navigate along the North Pacific Coast were not seeking commercial gain but, instead, were looking for a western entrance to this alleged northern passage between the Atlantic Ocean and Pacific Ocean that would have provided a shorter route between Europe and the Orient. During these voyages, though, an entrance to the rumored passage in that icy part of the world never came into view. Eventually, however, the English, French, and Spanish navigators developed trade with the indigenous people of the North Pacific Coast, and goods, principally furs, were carried on the return voyage.

Captain George Vancouver is believed to be the first explorer to spend a considerable amount of time on Puget Sound, so named, in 1792, after his lieutenant Peter Puget. Others followed, including Captain Charles Wilkes, who arrived at Seattle in 1841 aboard the sloop-of-war *Vincennes*. Captain Wilkes represented the U.S. government on a mission to examine the rivers and harbors of the Pacific Coast, and a comprehensive survey was made of Puget Sound during that voyage. It was during the early 1800s, also, that commerce had begun to flourish in the Puget Sound area. Sailing vessels appeared on the sound carrying all manner of goods that were needed by the early settlers.

Below is an illustration of a bark, flying the flag of Norway, from a painting by the author's uncle, Samuel N. Knutsen, in 1894. At the time the painting was created, Sam was 10 years old and living in Bergen, Norway, his country of birth. Later, as a teenager, Sam went to sea in sailing ships.

At the end of a voyage to America, he signed off the ship and remained in the United States, eventually settling in the Puget Sound area. Later, Sam made violins and was proficient in playing the instrument. He also pursued his education at the college level, a most remarkable person indeed.

From a painting by Samuel N. Knutsen, age ten at the time, 1894. (Courtesy of Anna J. Knutsen)

At the time when sailing ships were first appearing on Puget Sound, the only other vessels in the area were the Indian canoes, each carved from a single log, most commonly western red cedar. The hull shape and method of construction were guided by knowledge that was handed down from generation to generation.

Such craft were of various sizes and configurations, depending upon intended usage. The most beautiful canoes were sleek of line with sculptured images, representing birds, whales, and other wildlife, carved at the bow. Some boats were given pram-shaped bows. Other water craft were more barge-like in form and cumbersome for carrying heavy loads of goods.

Ships visiting from other ports, after unloading cargo that had been carried to the Pacific Northwest, loaded logs and poles, cut from the vast stands of timber, for transport on the return voyage. The poles were required for construction activities in California, particularly to support the rapid development in San Francisco. Wind ships also appeared from ports in other parts of the world to transport logs to those faraway places.

The increase in commercial enterprise on Puget Sound continued. Sawmills were established at any cove that had sufficient space and water depth for the full-rigged ships, barks, barkentines, brigs, and schooners to moor and load lumber.

With the production of lumber added to the ongoing shipping of logs and poles, the Puget Sound economy was growing more rapidly, and ships were calling in ever-growing numbers. Eventually, too, with the abundance of timber, shipbuilding took hold on Puget Sound.

Marine steam power was introduced to the Pacific Northwest when the sidewheeler *Beaver*, built on the Thames in 1835, arrived. As time went on, other steam-propelled vessels, including sidewheelers, sternwheelers, and eventually, propellers, were built and entered trade on Puget Sound. Prior to this time, local transportation around Puget Sound had been supplied mostly by Indians and their canoes. The steamers provided faster and more comfortable transportation for the growing population of people in the area.

Many sailing vessels, particularly the square riggers, entering and leaving harbors on the West Coast required a tow by a tug through the harbor entrances since their maneuverability in confined waters was limited. Steamships were able to negotiate the entrance to a harbor under their own power but still needed a pilot on board who knew the harbor channels well and could avoid a grounding. In the early days of steamships, pilots were often transported by sail boats to ships standing offshore in need of this type of assistance.

In the photo at left, the elegant and classic 83-foot schooner *Gracie S* was sojourning in Elliott Bay. The vessel, originally named *Wanderer*, was built of wood at San Francisco, California, in 1893 as a pilot schooner. Later in life, after *Wanderer*'s working days were over, the schooner was placed in yachting service as *Gracie S* by movie actor Sterling Hayden. The end arrived when, at 70 years of age, *Gracie S* was lost after stranding on a reef northeast of Tahiti at Rangiroa.

***Gracie S* in Elliott Bay, 1950.**
(From the author's collection)

There was no particular point in time when these steam-powered vessels completely replaced windships or when propeller driven vessels replaced sidewheelers and sternwheelers in the Pacific Northwest; rather, they all existed together for a good many years during this evolution. In turn, steam plants were gradually replaced by internal combustion engines for ship propulsion.

The first internal combustion engines utilized spark ignition and volatile gasoline, and it was not unusual to suffer explosions and fire. Later, semi-diesel engines, utilizing a glow plug or a hot portion of the combustion chamber that was not in contact with the cooling water (producing what is known as surface ignition) to assist combustion, were developed. Still later, full-diesel engines, having a compression ratio sufficiently high to ignite the fuel without other aid, replaced the lower compression semi-diesel engines. These types of engines were derived from a design developed by Rudolph Diesel in Germany in the 1890s and burned oil instead of gasoline to provide economical operation and to improve safety.

Gradually, as propellers replaced paddle wheels, the design of propellers changed, also, evolving from forms featuring wide blade tips, much like early cooling fan blades, to later configurations incorporating aerodynamically contoured blades. Propellers proved more efficient than paddle wheels for ship propulsion.

Some of these early vessels were still in service until the middle of the last century and so, for a time in the first part of the author's life, ships propelled by sail, paddle wheels, and propellers, ships and boats of various types powered by steam, and vessels powered by internal combustion engines were all plying their trade on Puget Sound. During this period, too, many smaller boats were still propelled by oars in the ancient way. Without a doubt, these years were unique in the history of Puget Sound maritime commerce.

The photo at right shows the sternwheel and the starboard crank arm and connecting rod, duplicated by a similar assembly out of sight on the port side, that propelled the large U.S. Army Corps of Engineers steam powered, shallow draft snag boat *W. T. Preston*.

A familiar sight around Puget Sound for many years and the last of sthe sternwheelers on the sound, *W. T. Preston* was eventually retired, hauled out, and placed on a dry land perch next to the water at Anacortes. The sternwheeler is open for viewing by the public.

Most of the Puget Sound companies in those days were engaged in the business of producing wood products, firms that included pulp mills, lumber mills, shingle mills, plywood plants, and wood-preserving operations. There were numerous boat-builders in the area supplying the demand for much needed water transportation. In addition, marine freight transportation companies and towing firms were in the business of moving logs, lumber, wood chips, sand, gravel, and other cargo. There were companies that produced and sold concrete made from sand and gravel that were mined at locations such as Steilacoom and Mats Mats. Other companies were at work in metal fabrication, marketing petroleum products, and even manufacturing explosives.

During the last years of this time period, the world was changing, and the demand for the products manufactured by Puget Sound wood-processing companies was fading away, with resultant dampening effects upon marine transportation as well. Creating a product requires the movement of raw materials and the transportation of the finished goods; hence, manufacturing and transportation are interdependent. When the fortunes of many of these industries declined and operations ceased, the need for transportation was affected, and as a result, many firms that were engaged in waterborne commerce went away.

W. T. Preston's sternwheel, 1950s.
(From the author's collection)

Pleasure boats built in the early part of the last century bore little resemblance to the streamlined, speedy yachts of today. At right is the outboard profile for a wooden motor boat designed by Wm. H. Hand Jr. from the book *Motor Boat Building* of 1929. Just below that drawing is an illustration from a postcard showing wooden boats moving through the large lock at Ballard. The wooden yachts of the day were works of art, inviting to the eye.

Boatbuilding slowly began to taper off in the mid 1950s because of a gradual decline in commercial fishing and a reduced requirement for other types of work boats, as well. When new working vessels were needed, many of them were delivered from shipyards on the Gulf Coast of the United States, where costs were lower. The construction of pleasure boats continued, but many of the smaller boatbuilders eventually went out of business, unable to compete with the larger firms with their mass-production lines. The use of wood in boat

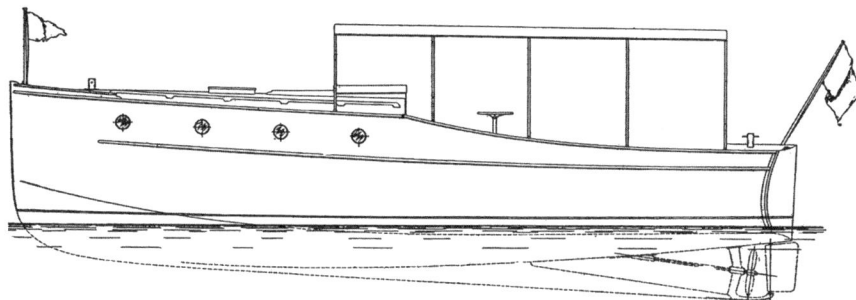

30-foot wooden cruiser designed by Wm. H. Hand Jr. (From *Motor Boat Building*, 1929)

Wooden boats outbound in the large lock at Ballard, circa 1940. (Courtesy of Anna J. Knutsen)

construction was eventually displaced by the economy of steel and fiberglass.

In the 1950s, more logs were being shipped from Puget Sound ports instead of finished lumber. Because of a slowdown in business, many marine towing firms disappeared or changed hands through acquisition by larger firms. Most of the earlier wooden towboats were gradually retired, replaced by those built of steel. Some of the elderly tugs survived, though, and continued on in private ownership. The photo at left shows a large group of retired tugs assembled during a Harbor Days celebration at Percival Landing in Olympia.

Retired tugs at Percival Landing in Olympia during a Harbor Days celebration, 1989. (Courtesy of Anna J. Knutsen)

13

SOUTHERN PUGET SOUND WATERFRONT INDUSTRY

Southern Puget Sound, with a myriad of inlets, passages and islands, is very scenic. In the earlier days, much of the shoreline was covered with dense forests and was still relatively undeveloped. As viewed from the water, fewer homes and other signs of civilization could be seen as compared with the scene today.

A large, deep draft ship making a passage south to visit Olympia would enter the southernmost region of Puget Sound by rounding the eastern side of Anderson Island past Nisqually Reach. A smaller vessel would usually head west through Balch Passage between McNeil Island and Anderson Island, then southwest through Drayton Passage. Upon reaching Devil's Head, a point off to starboard on the Key Peninsula, the light at Johnson Point, pictured below, would be in view.

The light at Johnson Point.

In this illustration, the light at Johnson Point is shown as viewed from the northeast, and a swing around the point with the light off to port will take a vessel southwest through Dana Passage, which separates Hartstene Island and the mainland. This light, at 22 feet above the water, flashes green at six-second intervals. Also mounted on the platform is a horn that sounds at 30-second intervals when conditions are foggy.

At left in the picture, just beyond Johnson Point, is the entrance to Henderson Inlet (also known locally as South Bay). At right in the distance, the Itsami Ledge marker shows a light that flashes green at four-second intervals. This light indicates a shoal in Dana Passage that deep draft vessels must stay well clear of.

After making a turn to port at Johnson Point and continuing on for about four and a half miles through Dana Passage, a vessel will have the Dofflemyer Point light, shown below as viewed from the south, off the port beam. Before reaching this light, a vessel could make a starboard turn around Brisco Point, shown at left in the background of this picture, at the southern end of Hartstene Island and proceed on a westerly heading through long and narrow Hammersley Inlet to the city of Shelton. A port turn at Dofflemyer Point light will take a vessel south into Budd Inlet and on to Olympia, six miles in the distance.

At the top of the Dofflemyer Point structure, 30 feet above the water, a white light flashes at six-second intervals, and in foggy weather, a horn sounds at 15-second intervals. The Brisco Point light is 40 feet above the water and flashes red at four-second intervals.

The light at Dofflemyer Point.

14

Legend

1 Buchanan Lumber Co.
2 Delson Lumber Co.
3 West Side Log Dump
4 Olympia Towing Co.
5 Hardel Plywood Co.
6 Reliable Welding Works
7 Panama Shingle Co.
8 Tumwater Lumber Mills
9 Olympia Harbor Lumber Co.
10 H. A. Long Boat Shop
11 Olympia Boat Works
12 Percival Landing
13 Capital City Tug Co.
14 Union Oil Co. of California
15 Olympia Sand and Gravel Co.
16 Delta V. Smyth Tugs and Barges
17 Standard Oil Co. of California
18 Port of Olympia
19 The Texas Co.
20 Puget Sound Shipbuilding Co.
21 Associated Plywood Mills
22 Olympia Wood Preserving Co.
23 Washington Veneer Co.
24 Graystone
25 Springer Mill
26 Olympia Shingle Co.
27 Olympia Veneer Co.
28 Joe Ritner Boat Shop
29 Log Raft Storage Area
30 Barge Storage Area

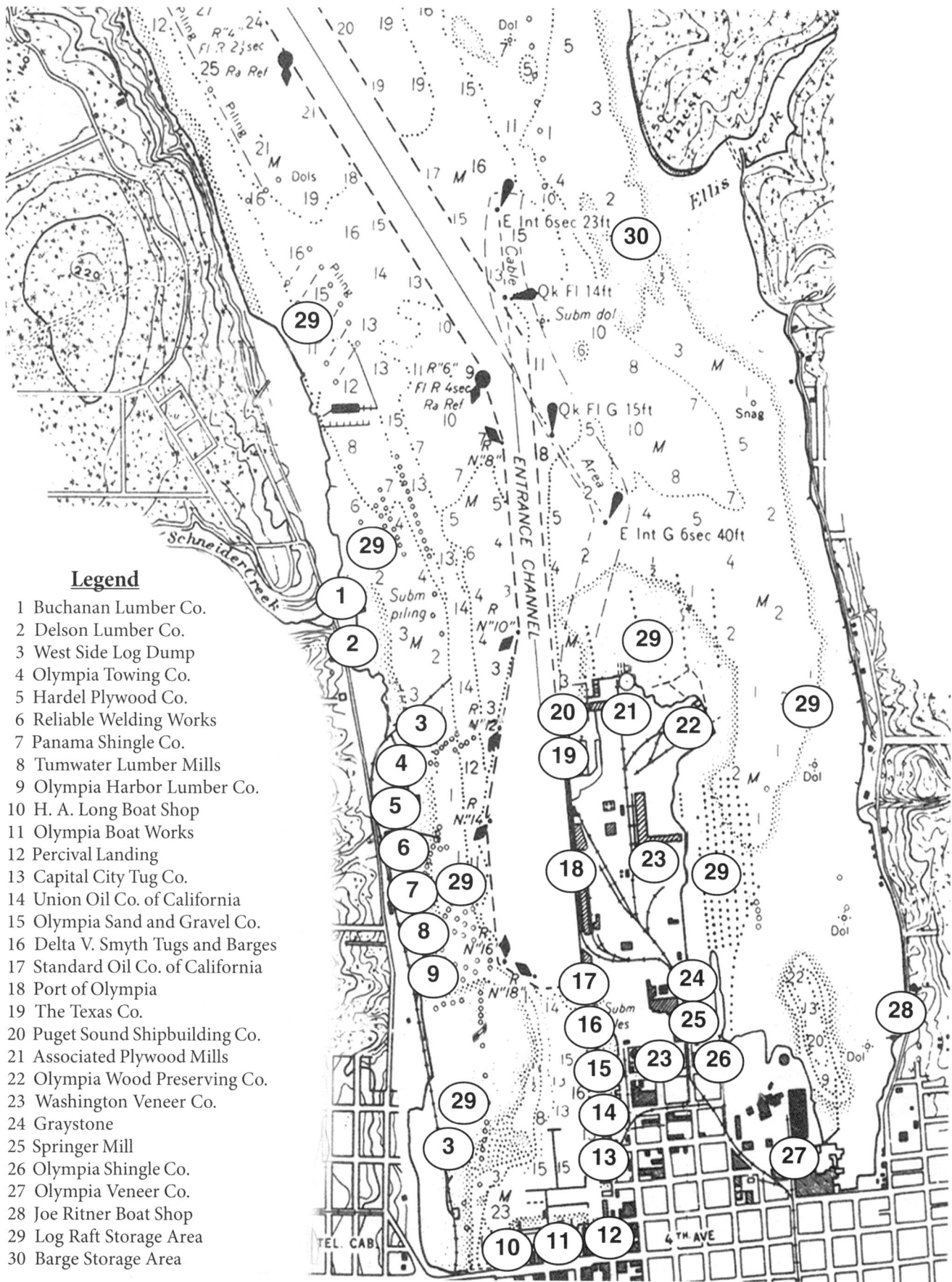

Waterfront industry at Olympia, 1940s.

15

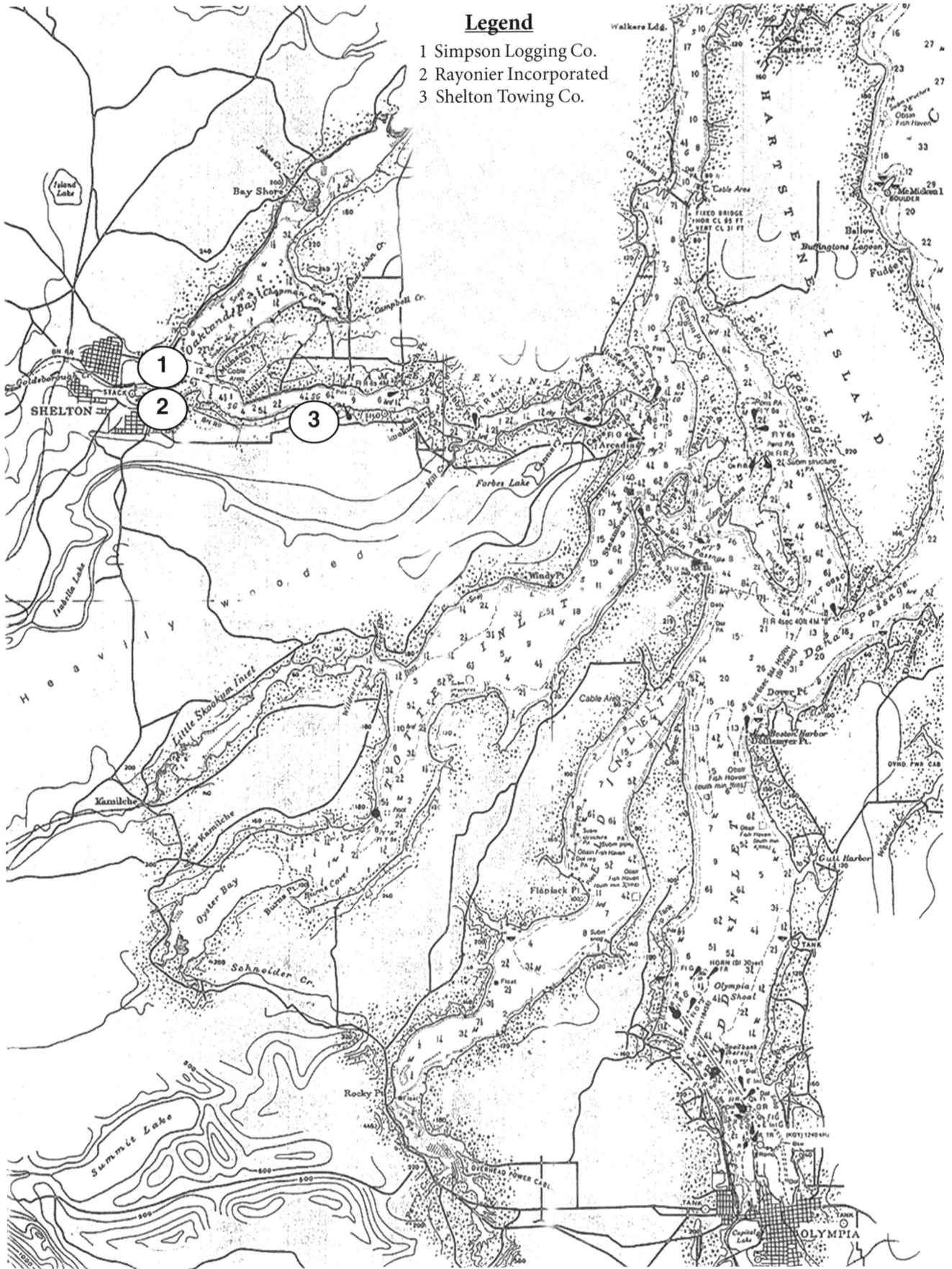

Legend
1 Simpson Logging Co.
2 Rayonier Incorporated
3 Shelton Towing Co.

Waterfront industry at Shelton, 1940s.

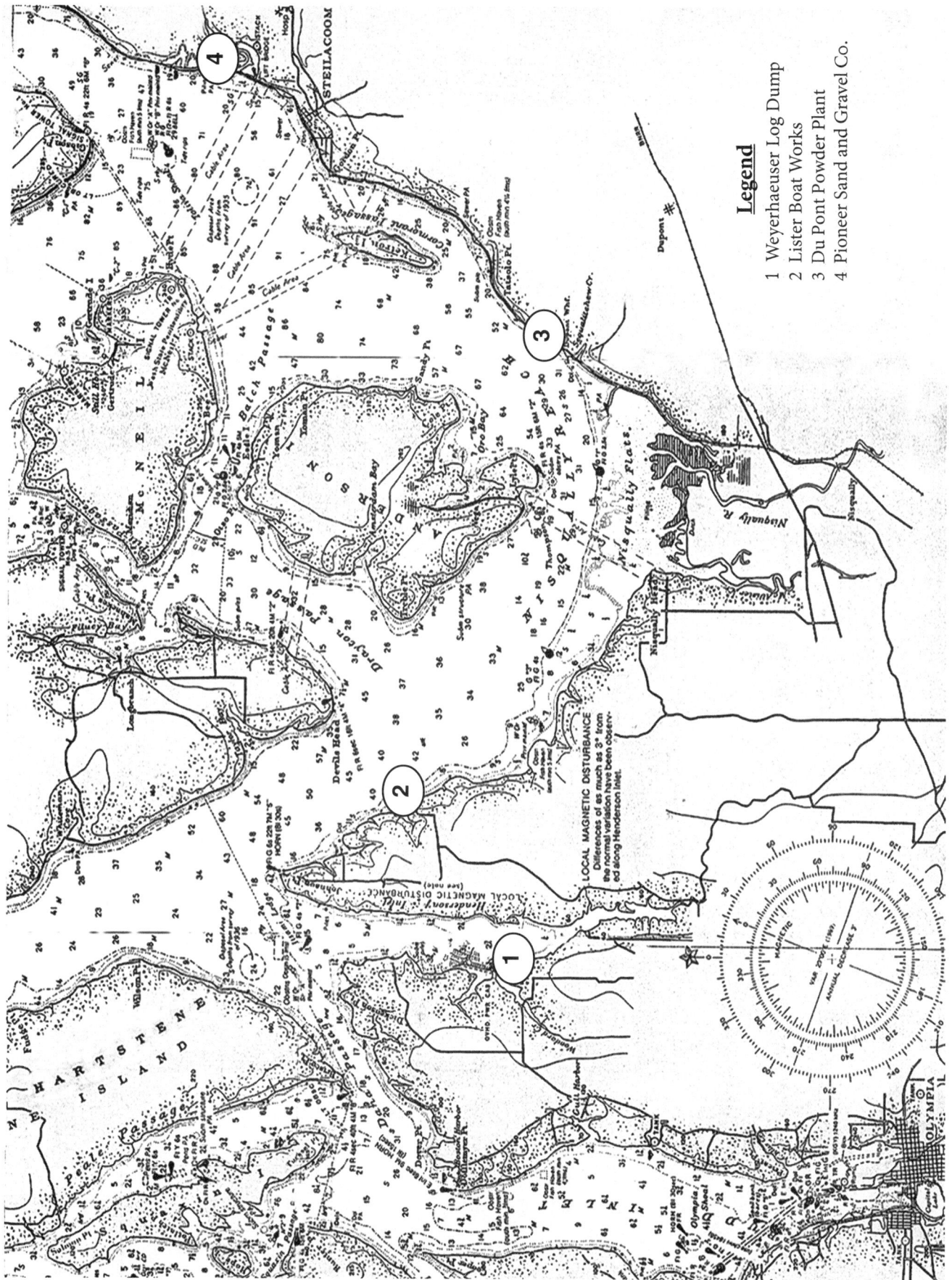

Legend
1 Weyerhaeuser Log Dump
2 Lister Boat Works
3 Du Pont Powder Plant
4 Pioneer Sand and Gravel Co.

Waterfront industry Henderson Inlet to Steilacoom, 1940s.

During the period covered by this narrative, Olympia was not only the seat of government for the State of Washington, as it is today, but was also extensively industrialized. Along the shoreline of Olympia's harbor, mills and plants were busy converting logs into lumber, shingles, and plywood, while other facilities built ships, produced concrete, and supplied treated poles and piling as well as petroleum products. Three marine towing companies were also located in Olympia.

A view of Olympia harbor looking north from the Capitol dome, 1940.
(Courtesy of Anna J. Knutsen)

The photo above, taken from the Capitol Dome, gives an overview looking north over what is now known as Capitol Lake to Olympia's harbor and Budd Inlet extending beyond. At left in the photo is the Fourth Avenue Bridge. It can be seen that the Budd Inlet tides swept through under the bridge so that the water in the foreground was brackish, that is, salt water but with fresh water from the Deschutes River mixing in. The mud flats were revealed twice a day when the water level dropped with the ebb tides. Later, however, a dam was constructed at the location of the bridge to exclude the salt water, thus forming what is known today as the fresh water Capitol Lake.

Several sawmills operated in Olympia during the period covered in this book. At the north end of West Bay Drive, which ran along the shore at left in the above photo, was Buchanan Lumber Company (1, page 15). This firm was named after the company's original owner, J. C. Buchanan. The mill employed more than 70 people and produced over 30,000,000 board feet of lumber per year, this product then being shipped to points both in the United States and overseas.

Just south of Buchanan's sawmill, a lumber mill, Delson Lumber Company (2, page 15), was owned and operated by members of the Delta V. Smyth family. This mill's name was a derivative of a portion of Smyth's first name, Delta, combined with a reference to his son.

At left in the photo above, there is a dark line running along the shore. This was the Northern Pacific Railroad track that ran north along West Bay Drive and extended to the West Side Log Dump (3, page 15). The log dump consisted of a wooden pier, jutting out into the bay, upon which the track had been laid. A Northern Pacific 0–6–0 switch engine moved a string of logging cars to the dump, these cars having been split out of a longer train that had been brought into Olympia from the woods. When the dumping operation was finished, the string of empty cars was moved out and replaced with a group of loaded cars.

A length of the log dump pier was constructed with "super elevation" so that the track sloped laterally, and when a logging car was at that location, the car was also tilted laterally. A pair of wire ropes, attached to the trestle, was fed under the logs that were resting on the car's bunks. The wire ropes were then pulled taut causing the logs to lift and roll off of the car and into the water.

Care had to be taken so that the engine never entered the section of track that was sloping laterally or the locomotive might topple over. To avoid such an occurrence, two empty cars were coupled between the engine and the last logging car to act as a spacer. Logs were usually carried on flat cars or on what were known as "skeleton cars," each consisting of two four-wheeled trucks connected longitudinally with a long timber. Logs, unloaded by a hoist, were also carried in gondola cars.

Hoisting a rail car out of the water at Olympia's West Side Log Dump, 1940.
(Courtesy of Anna J. Knutsen)

Along with the super elevation of the rails at the log dump site, which caused the rail car to tilt sidewise, occasionally a railroad car would tip too much if the logs dragged on the car, and it would follow the logs into the water. To recover the logging car, my father Morris N. Knutsen would be called from Olympia Harbor Lumber Company, where he was the operator of that sawmill's Ohio steam locomotive crane, to run the crane north along the Northern Pacific track to the log dump and hoist the car out of the water and back onto the track.

The photo above shows the crane, being operated by the my father, hoisting a flat car that had tumbled into the bay. As the photo indicates, it was a cool, damp, gloomy day in Olympia, but even though the crane cab was partially open at the front and sides, warmth would have found its way to the operator from the boiler and oil-burning firebox located at the rear of the crane.

In addition to the log dump near the north end of West Bay Drive, another log dump was lo-

cated just north of the Fourth Avenue bridge on the West Side of Olympia (also indicated as 3 on page 15). The rails at this log dump were not tilted, but instead, a traveling steam-powered log dumper was used to hoist the logs from the cars and drop them into the water. This log dumper had a wood-burning, vertical fire tube boiler.

During the first half of the 1900s, Northern Pacific steam engines brought trains of 80 or more logging cars into Olympia from the southwest Washington woods several times a week. As noted before, the smaller NP 0-6-0 switch engines based at Olympia then moved the logs to the West Side log dumps. Besides handling logging trains, Northern Pacific's steam-powered switch engines moved railroad cars for various Olympia industries, such as plywood plants, sawmills, the wood-preserving plant, the Olympia Brewing Company in Tumwater, and the Port of Olympia. Northern Pacific also operated passenger trains between Everett and Portland and between Seattle and Grays Harbor, making stops at Olympia.

19

Northern Pacific passenger train at the East Olympia Station, 1950.
(Courtesy of Morris N. Knutsen Jr.)

For the purpose of improving transportation to unsettled territories, a federal grant of land was signed by Abraham Lincoln in 1864 to make way for the building by the Northern Pacific Railroad of a rail line into the West. Many years of development and financial problems followed, but eventually a railroad was completed from a location near Duluth, Minnesota, to Tacoma via the Columbia River and Portland, Oregon. In 1881, Stampede Pass was discovered in the Cascade Mountains during a survey, and a tunnel at that location was completed in 1888, resulting in a direct route to Seattle, a shorter distance to Puget Sound than the Columbia River route.

For north-south train travel between Everett and Portland, Oregon, with stops along the way, the Olympia area was served on a regular schedule by Northern Pacific at what was known as the East Olympia station, located just north of the Yelm highway near Lacey. On the occasion of the photo above, Northern Pacific's passenger train was heading south and pulling into the East Olympia station to load and unload passengers. The

steam locomotive used on this run was one of the 4–8–4 Northern Class engines operated by Northern Pacific.

The other Northern Pacific passenger service was between Seattle and Grays Harbor, with stops at Olympia and other intermediate points. The Olympia station used for the Seattle-Grays Harbor run was located at Water Street on the east shore of what is now called Capitol Lake, at the time still a tidal inlet. The rail yard area at Olympia was a busy place, with steam powered switch engines shifting freight cars there, as well as moving cars into and out of the yard.

The Grays Harbor train ran Monday through Saturday, and stopped at Olympia at 11:00 a.m. on the way to Grays Harbor and returned to Olympia at 5:00 p.m. on the trip back to Seattle. The steam engine that pulled this train is pictured on the next page while at the Olympia station. On a trip to Grays Harbor at about the time of the photo, the author recalls the conductor, as the train was pulling into Montesano, shouting "Montesano! Montesano! Gonna rain like hell!"

Northern Pacific passenger train at the Olympia Station, 1949.
(Courtesy of Morris N. Knutsen Jr.)

In the photo above, Northern Pacific steam locomotive number 2187, with the engineer leaning out of the window in traditional fashion, was pulling a passenger train and had stopped at the station on Water Street in downtown Olympia to load and unload passengers. Olympia was a regular stop on the run between Seattle and Grays Harbor. The engine had four wheels on the forward truck, six drivers, and two wheels trailing and was, therefore, of the 4–6–2 Pacific Class. At the time of the photo, the train was heading for Aberdeen and Hoquiam with other stops scheduled for towns between Olympia and Grays Harbor.

At right in the photo above is the water tank. The water spout mounted on the tank could be pivoted down by pulling on the tag line and then used to fill the boiler feed water tank, much like using a garden watering can. The engine's water tank and oil tank were located in the tender.

The bicycle in the photo was a Schwinn that belonged to my brother, Morris. The bag hanging on the handlebar was used by him as a container for newspapers when covering his delivery route on East Bay Drive in Olympia. He delivered the *Seattle Star* to a small number of subscribers and, later on, he brought *The Olympian* to more than 100 customers.

This particular model Schwinn was a good looking, top-of-the-line bike in those days and was equipped with a spring shock absorber at the front wheel. In addition to the usual rear wheel brake, this bike also featured a front wheel brake. The author's bicycle, on the other hand, was put together by the author from two second-hand, dissimilar, partially dismantled, and incomplete bikes purchased from Olympia Hardware for a total of $9.00. This bicycle served well but was not much for looks.

The last Northern Pacific steam train at the Olympia Station, 1957. (Courtesy of Morris N. Knutsen Jr.)

The last Northern Pacific steam train at the Olympia Station, 1957. (Courtesy of Morris N. Knutsen Jr.)

The last Northern Pacific steam train out of Olympia, 1957.
(Courtesy of Morris N. Knutsen Jr.)

In the photo above, the number 1776 Mikado 2-8-2, also pictured on the previous page, was about three miles west of Olympia enroute to the Grays Harbor area with a string of passenger cars on the last steam train run. The steam exhaust from the double-acting cylinders, one on each side of the locomotive, blended with the smoke that billowed up from the hot firebox. These engines were not equipped with condensers but simply sent the exhaust steam up the stack. Because of this loss of boiler water, the feed-water flow rate into the boiler was high, necessitating periodic stops to fill the water tank.

Passenger travel by rail was on the decline as airline use picked up, and with improved highways, many people were traveling by automobile. In addition, just as steam boats were eventually replaced by vessels powered by internal combustion engines, so the steam locomotives that had been around so long gave way to the diesel-powered engines for economy's sake.

Union Pacific also had a presence in Olympia and an 0-6-0 steam switch engine

was based there to take care of handling railroad cars locally. When off duty, the UP engine was parked on the south side of downtown Olympia near the railroad underpass that ran beneath Jefferson Street. The photo below shows the Union Pacific switch engine at the Port of Olympia property while undergoing repairs to a malfunctioning air compressor. The port's diesel powered locomotive crane was being used to hoist the heavy steam-powered air compressor.

The Union Pacific switch engine in Olympia, 1952.
(Courtesy of Morris N. Knutsen Jr.)

The Union Pacific freight and passenger station at Olympia, 1959. (Courtesy of Anna J. Knutsen)

Damaged Union Pacific freight car in Olympia, 1959. (Courtesy of Anna J. Knutsen).

Clearing debris from the Union Pacific wreck site on Fourth Avenue in Olympia, 1959. (Courtesy of Anna J. Knutsen)

The Union Pacific station was located on the south side of Fourth Avenue, at the corner of Adams Street, in downtown Olympia. On one occasion, in 1959, the UP buildings were rammed by runaway rail cars. The rail cars careened into and through the property, where a telegrapher was killed in the mishap.

The photo above shows the front of the Union Pacific Railroad depot after the incident. The fence at left of the building was newly constructed, as a pedestrian safety barrier, in the area where the runaway freight cars had hurtled through the facility and out onto Fourth Avenue.

The series of events that were involved in the train wreck started about two miles south of Olympia when a number of railroad cars were shunted off onto a siding and deposited there without the brakes having been properly set. The cars slowly began to move, then gradually picked up speed on the one-percent grade into Olympia. Plowing through part of the Union Pacific station, several of the cars crossed Fourth Avenue and hurtled into businesses across the street.

The two photos at upper right show cleanup work underway at the site of the wreck. The picture at top right is of a damaged Union Pacific box car that had been moved to Jefferson Street from the scene of the wreck at Fourth Avenue to permit the clearing of the disaster site. In the other photo, removal of debris was underway in the area of the train wreck. In this picture, buildings at left in the photo (on the north side of Fourth Avenue across from the UP station) were severely damaged by the runaway rail cars.

Next to the log dump near the north end of West Bay Drive, Olympia Towing Company (4, page 15) was headquartered along with its fleet of towboats. Olympia Towing was owned by members of the Willy family, and a more detailed description of this firm is found later in this book.

Hardel Plywood Company (5, page 15) was situated just to the south of Olympia Towing Company. As the name implies, Hardel was engaged in the manufacture of plywood, and the firm was owned by the Delta V. Smyth family.

Adjacent to and just south of Hardel Plywood, Reliable Welding Works (6, page 15) was in the business of steel fabrication. Reliable Welding Works built numerous small ships in support of the military effort during World War II, as well as many commercial vessels.

Also located on West Bay Drive, just to the south of Reliable Welding Works, Panama Shingle Company (7, page 15) operated as a sawmill specializing in the production of western red cedar shingles for use as roofing and siding in residential and commercial construction.

TUMWATER LUMBER MILLS CO., Inc.
Complete Line of Building Materials
TELEPHONE FLEETWOOD 7-3366
902 WEST BAY DRIVE :: OLYMPIA, WASHINGTON

One of several homes illustrated in a Tumwater Lumber Mills calendar of the 1950s. (From the author's collection)

Just south of Panama Shingle, Tumwater Lumber Mills (8, page 15) marketed manufactured homes and building products but did not actually produce lumber as the name might imply. This firm, started in the early 1920s, was operated by Amy Anderson, and the company's name was a holdover from a sawmill that Amy's brother Art, after immigrating from Sweden, had owned in Tumwater from 1919 until 1928. One of the many different manufactured homes produced over the years is shown above in a picture taken from a Tumwater Lumber Mills calendar. Hundreds of these "Ready Cut" homes were built and are still in use in the Olympia area.

Adjacent to Tumwater Lumber Mills, Olympia Harbor Lumber Company (9, page 15), pictured at right, was owned and operated by Amy Anderson's brothers Art, Ed, and Karl. The conical shaped structure at left in the photo is the burner used to dispose of mill ends and other wood scrap. These remnants were carried up on a conveyer and dumped into the fire. Mills of this type produced lumber in various dimensions by sawing logs as well as "cants," large timbers having four flat sides for resawing into smaller lumber.

Finished lumber was shipped to domestic ports and to the world from the Olympia port pier, across the channel in the background.

My father operated an Ohio steam locomotive crane for many years at Olympia Harbor Lumber beginning in 1928. When a second Ohio crane was purchased for use by the mill, my brother received tutoring from the senior Knutsen and then, in his father's footsteps, operated this second crane. Morris Sr. and Morris Jr. were running the cranes in the photo below.

Olympia Harbor Lumber Company, 1957. (Courtesy of Anna J. Knutsen)

EDWARD ANDERSON, PRESIDENT
ARTHUR ANDERSON, SECRETARY

MANUFACTURERS
OF
PACIFIC COAST
LUMBER

Olympia, Wash.

Olympia Harbor Lumber Company letterhead. (From the author's collection)

Morris N. Knutsen Sr. and the Ohio locomotive crane at Olympia Harbor Lumber Company, 1928. (Courtesy of Anna J. Knutsen)

Further mention should be made of Olympia Harbor Lumber Company's Ohio steam locomotive crane and the relationship the author's father had with it. As a young man, the author's father, Morris N. Knutsen Sr., operated this crane for Bird Lumber Company located at the river's edge in Snohomish. In 1928, the Snohomish mill burned and the crane was sold to Olympia Harbor Lumber Company. The author's father then moved to Olympia and took over operation of the crane for OHLC and remained there for many years until the mill ceased operations in the early 1960s. In the photo above, the author's father and this crane had recently begun working for Olympia Harbor Lumber Company.

The crane was powered by two single-cylinder double-acting steam engines, one at each side. The boiler was of the vertical fire tube type and the burner utilized oil as fuel. The tubes required cleaning once a week by using a water hose with nozzle to flush the soot out. Unlike modern internal combustion engine powered cranes having hydraulic controls, these steam powered cranes had massive levers to mechanically operate the clutches used for travel along the railroad tracks, for raising and lowering the boom and for hoisting and for swinging. All of these motions could be performed simultaneously by a skilled operator, and the crane might be seen moving along the track while the cab is rotating and the hoist or boom is being raised or lowered.

Pictured on the next page is the Ohio steam locomotive crane being operated by the author's brother, Morris N. Knutsen Jr., at Olympia Harbor Lumber Company while handling a load of lumber. The rigger can be seen at left center on top of the lumber pile "spotting" a load being added to the pile, or to hook onto a load to be removed from the pile. When placing a load on top of a high lumber pile, the crane operator's visibility is limited but the rigger can assist in locating the load by means of hand signals to the crane operator. To avoid trapping the hoisting cables under a load of lumber when placing it on the pile, the rigger first lays out boards to set the load on which provides a space for removing the cables.

**Steam powered crane at
Olympia Harbor Lumber Company, 1957.
(Courtesy of Anna J. Knutsen)**

The rigger can be seen on top of the pile of lumber at left in the photo above. Sometimes after a load of lumber had been placed on top of a pile, the rigger would ride the hook back down onto the ground. In the background of this photo, the Port of Olympia pier is visible through the fog.

In addition to the Ohio steam locomotive crane, a "stiff leg" crane was located at the water's edge at Olympia Harbor Lumber Company. This stiff leg crane is illustrated at right. Unlike a locomotive crane, a stiff leg crane does not travel but, instead, is fixed in place. The tall pedestal is anchored at the base and braced laterally.

The cab used for operating a stiff leg crane is mounted on the pedestal and is accessed via a ladder. A horizontal boom is hinged at the pedestal so that it can swing through a horizontal arc, and the cab rotates with the swinging boom so that the boom and hoist are visible to the operator at all times. Mounted on the underside of the boom is a hoist that travels along the boom. Power is provided by electric motors.

The stiff leg at OHLC was used for loading scows moored at the water's edge. These scows

could be towed by tug to other ports on Puget Sound or shuttled back and forth between the mill and ships loading at the pier across the channel.

Sometimes a wooden scow would contain bilge water that had seeped in through leaking seams. This water would affect stability adversely because, if the scow heeled, the bilge water would move to the side, making the tipping even worse. Bilge water was periodically removed by means of a portable gasoline-engine powered scow pump.

When performing stability calculations for a vessel, the influence of liquid in the bilge or in tanks when the ship heels must be accounted for. In ship design, the effect of liquid moving laterally as a ship heels is called "free surface effect," and is calculated mathematically. More than one ship, if only marginal positive stability is present, has capsized due to the free surface effect of liquids on board in the bilge or in tanks. Loading a scow with lumber had to be done quite carefully, using judgment to take care that the heel and trim of the scow were within limits so as to avoid an unfortunate incident.

**Stiff leg crane at Olympia Harbor
Lumber Company in the 1950s.
(Courtesy of Morris N. Knutsen Jr.)**

**Lumber spill at Olympia Harbor Lumber Company circa, 1950.
(Courtesy of Morris N. Knutsen Jr.)**

The photo above shows the chaos that resulted when lumber spilled from a scow at Olympia Harbor Lumber. Immediately after the incident happened, my brother and I assisted in the salvage effort by using the family inboard powered boat to herd the floating lumber into a corral made up of boomsticks.

By the early 1960s, times had been changing for a number of years and Olympia Harbor Lumber Company, like many mills in other towns around Puget Sound, was no longer in operation. After the mill's equipment and inventory were sold off and salvage was complete, the wooden structures were burned as shown in the photo below. Through the smoke, a portion of the Olympia downtown area and waterfront establishments can be seen. The State Capitol of Washington is at right in the background.

The burning of the remains of Olympia Harbor Lumber Company in the early 1960s.

(Courtesy of Anna J. Knutsen)

As were many other sawmills of the period, Olympia Harbor Lumber Company was powered by reciprocating steam engines. Started up in 1923, in the earlier years, the mill had a log haul i.e., a conveyor that hauled logs out of the water and into the mill for sawing into finished lumber. Later, after a fire, OHLC terminated the production of lumber from logs and became a re-saw facility. Subsequently, finished lumber was cut from large dimension cants, large flat-sided timbers that had been sawn by other, smaller mills, instead of by sawing from logs.

In 1959, Art Anderson retired from the OHLC presidency after having spent 40 years in the lumber business. In that year, Buchanan negotiated a lease to operate Olympia Harbor Lumber Company, but by the early 1960s the mill was gone, as described on the previous page. Olympia Harbor Lumber had employed between 40 and 50 people, on average, for many years, producing up to 50,000,000 board feet of finished lumber per year that was shipped to the world. The sawmill's demise gave notice that an era was ending.

Referring to the chart of Olympia's harbor on page 15, there were two boat building shops just off west Fourth Avenue near the bridge, H. A. Long Boat Shop (10) and Olympia Boat Works (11), where wooden boats ranging from dinghies to fairly large yachts and work boats were built. The two photos below show the launch of the beautiful commercial fishing boat *Centennial*, of 45 feet register length. The boat was constructed at one of these boat works, but it is not known now which of the two shops built the boat.

In the left picture below, the boat took a good roll due to the light launch weight, most of the outfitting items not having been installed yet. The floating wooden timbers were pieces of cribbing used to support the boat on the launch cradle. In the right photo, Delta V. Smyth's tug *Parthia* was preparing to cast a line aboard to tow the boat back into the builder's yard. In the background is Olympia's West Side. Northern Pacific's railroad tracks can also be seen in the background. The Fourth Avenue bridge leading from downtown Olympia to the West Side is just out of view to the left in the photos.

Henry Long also built the 46-foot wooden tug *Rufus* in 1957, the last boat Delta V. Smyth Tugs and Barges acquired before Smyth's company was sold to Foss Launch and Tug Company in 1961. About the same size as Smyth's older tug *Parthia*, *Rufus* was a new design but had a general arrangement that was quite similar to that of *Parthia*. Although not a feature of Delta Smyth's other tugs, Smyth favored having a trunk cabin over the engine room forward and the pilothouse further aft as *Parthia* had, so that the skipper could have direct access to the aft deck through the pilothouse door. *Rufus* was then built in this manner.

At the foot of State Avenue, just across the waterway from the Olympia Yacht Club, Percival Landing (12, page 15) was used by the relatively small freighters owned by Puget Sound Freight Lines to unload and load cargo. These freighters were frequent visitors to Olympia and traveled to and from several ports around Puget Sound. This will be described more fully in a later chapter.

The launching of *Centennial*, with tug *Parthia* in attendance, at Olympia, 1950. (Courtesy of Anna J. Knutsen)

Capital City Tug Company (13, page 15), an affiliate of Tacoma Tug and Barge Company, maintained an office and moorage for their tugs just north of and adjacent to Percival Landing. More information on Capital City Tug and Tacoma Tug and Barge is found in later sections.

The Union Oil Company of California fuel float and tank facility (14, page 15), adjacent to and north of Capital City Tug, supplied petroleum products to boats, as well as to customers ashore.

Continuing on north from Capital City Tug Company could be found Olympia Sand and Gravel Company (15, page 15). This firm was owned by members of the Willy family. In this photo, looking toward the south, the steam powered crane, equipped with a bucket, was being operated by my father, Morris N. Knutsen Sr. on a track laid atop a pier.

Barges loaded with sand or gravel were towed here by tug from the Pioneer Sand and Gravel pit at Steilacoom. Using the bucket, the crane unloaded the barge and transferred the materials to a storage area. The structure at far left in the photo is the hopper used for loading trucks.

The white cylindrical features at right in the background of the photo are the storage tanks for Union Oil's facility and, beyond the tanks, the Washington State Capitol dome is in view.

On the north side of Olympia Sand and Gravel, Delta V. Smyth Tugs and Barges (16, page 15) was located at Columbia Street and B. This company was in the marine towing business for many years, and the facility included a railway for hauling the tugs and a grid for scow maintenance. A later section is devoted to this firm.

Located just to the north of Delta Smyth's towing company, the petroleum company Standard Oil Company of California (17, page 15) delivered products by truck in the Olympia area and also refueled boats at the facility's moorage.

Referring again to the view of Olympia harbor on page 15, the Port of Olympia pier (18, page 15) runs in a north-south direction along the shoreline just to the right of center in the picture. The harbor channel and turning basin are dredged to accommodate ocean-going ships.

Earlier in the 1900s, as many as four ships might be moored at the Port of Olympia pier to load cargo, mainly lumber that had been produced by the Olympia and Shelton mills. However, the amount of finished lumber being delivered was decreasing in the 1950s and 1960s as more and more logs were being shipped instead. Today, finished lumber is no longer being produced in Olympia.

Olympia Sand and Gravel Company, 1961.
(Courtesy of Anna J. Knutsen)

El Cedro at the Olympia Port pier, circa 1940.
(Courtesy of Anna J. Knutsen)

In this photo, looking north at the Port of Olympia, the moderate sized freighter *El Cedro*, owned by James Griffiths and Sons, was loading lumber by means of the ship's own cargo handling gear from a scow moored alongside. *El Cedro*, 253 feet in length, 44 feet in beam, and 2512 gross tons, was powered by a 1250 horsepower steam engine and built at Ecorse, Michigan, in 1919.

At left in the background are lumber scows and sawdust scows moored at the West Side. Butler Cove is beyond the chip scows. People, such as those standing on the pier observing the cargo loading operations, could frequently be seen at the Port of Olympia in those days. Security and safety rules at the time were more relaxed than they are today, and so the port pier was an attraction for Olympia area residents. Visitors could take a stroll, while staying clear of operations, and observe the loading and unloading of ships that had called at the Port of Olympia.

As did the Griffiths steamships, Luckenbach Steamship Company operated up and down the West Coast for many years. At close to 470 feet register length and 4700 gross tons, *George Luckenbach*, illustrated in the photo on the next page, was considerably larger than *El Cedro*. Like *El Cedro*, *George Luckenbach*'s own hoisting rigging was put to work loading lumber from scows moored alongside. In the picture, Delta V. Smyth Tugs and Barges' tug *Oysterman* was juggling the lumber scows. As the ship unloaded a scow, the empty was towed back over to the mills and, when reloaded with lumber, was then brought back to the ship. Wooden scows such as this were the order of 110 feet long.

31

George Luckenbach at Port of Olympia, 1949. (From the author's collection)

At the north end of the Port of Olympia pier, The Texas Company owned and operated a facility (19, page 15) that included petroleum storage tanks. The Texaco tank farm is in the distance at left in the above photo. In a manner similar to the Union and Standard facilities to the south, the Texaco tanks were replenished by tank vessels as well as by barges brought in by tugs. Refueling of boats could be accomplished alongside the float and, in addition, petroleum products were delivered locally by tank trucks. Eventually, the Union, Standard, and Texaco petroleum facilities disappeared when, with the construction of improved highways, petroleum products began to be delivered to Olympia by truck.

Puget Sound Shipbuilding Company (20, page 15) was located just north of the Olympia Port pier on the western shore of what is known as the Port Fill (created by dumping the spoils from harbor dredging). Puget Sound Ship built many sizable wooden vessels during World War II, including four wooden steam-powered tugs for the British Admiralty. These tugs were over 150 feet in length and powered by triple expansion engines of 12, 20, 33 x 34 inch bores and stroke producing 1000 horsepower at 180 revolutions per minute. Steam was generated by hand-fired, coal burning Babcock and Wilcox boilers of the Liberty Ship type. After the war's end, with no more vessels to build, the yard ceased operations.

Associated Plywood Mills (21, page 15) was also busy at the Port Fill. The demand for the product that became known as "plywood," rela-

tively new at the time, was continuing to increase in use as a structural material. Laminated from thin Douglas fir sheets called "veneers," each layer was oriented so that the grain ran at a right angle to the grain of adjacent veneers. With the thin layers of wood glued together in this manner, the plywood sheets were dimensionally stable, had good strength properties, and were suitable for use in the construction of boats and buildings.

At the eastern edge of the Port Fill, Olympia Wood Preserving Company (22, page 15) was known locally as the "pole yard" or the "creosote plant." Olympia Wood Preserving pressure-treated wood products such as pilings and telephone poles, to delay potential damage from rot and decay.

In addition to Associated Plywood (21, page 15) in Olympia, Washington Veneer Company (23, page 15) and Olympia Veneer Company (27, page 15) were also in the business of producing plywood. Washington Veneer actually operated both a plywood plant and a sawmill (also denoted as 23, page 15). On the next page, reproduced from the cover of the November 1940 *West Coast Lumberman* magazine, is an aerial view of the Port Fill with the location of the Washington Veneer Company plants superimposed.

Graystone (24, page 15) was a company similar to Olympia Sand and Gravel Company, supplying sand, gravel, concrete, and other building materials. Graystone, with the company's steam locomotive crane at work, can be seen just to the right of the Washington Veneer Company stack in the photo shown on the next page.

WEST COAST LUMBERMAN

NOVEMBER
1940
▼

Graystone

Washington
Veneer
Plywood
plant

Washington
Veneer
sawmill

▲

Washington Veneer
Company's plant at
Olympia, Washing-
ton. This is a fine ex-
ample of tree utiliza-
tion. The operation
embraces not only a
plywood plant, but
a remanufacturing
plant and a sawmill.
The company also
operates a large cen-
tral power plant
wh'ch furnishes pow-
er for the various
units.

◀

25c • 30c in Canada

Yet another sawmill, the Springer Mill (25, page 15), was operating in Olympia during the time period covered here. People who lived in the area were well acquainted with the industries there, and a comment might be heard such as "So and so? Oh, he's workin' over 't Springer's."

Olympia Shingle Company (26, page 15), located at the south end of East Bay in Olympia, produced cedar shingles for use as roofing or siding. Plants, such as Olympia Shingle, were known as "shingle mills" if making sawn shingles or "shake mills" if producing split shakes.

Besides H. A. Long Boat Shop and Olympia Boat Works, Joe Ritner (28, page 15) operated as a boat builder for many years at 607 East Bay Drive, a location toward downtown from the author's boyhood home. Joe's boatshop and haulout rails were built on pilings at the water's edge, and the house he lived in was across the street from his shop. The boats that Joe constructed were of wood and of a variety of sizes and designs similar to those built by Henry Long and Olympia Boat Works. Beautiful half models, hand-carved under the guidance of the sculptor's eye, hung on the walls of the shop and were used to establish the shape of hulls under construction. While some boats were constructed from drawings, others were built by taking off dimensions directly from half models in lieu of using a lines drawing.

Log raft storage areas (29, page 15) were dispersed at several locations in Olympia's harbor. These rafts were moored to pilings in relatively shallow water near the shore where they would not interfere with navigation. Some of these log rafts were accessible by tug only when there was sufficient water depth during higher stages of tide. In fact, at some locations, portions of these rafts would be residing on the exposed mud flats at low tide. At an early stage of a flood tide or late in an ebb, it was not unusual for a tug's keel to drag in the mud. Working with the logs during a late stage of ebb, with the water depth dropping, a tug might wind up grounded until the next flood.

A barge storage area was located off Priest Point at Ellis Cove (30, page 15) where scows could be moored to await the tugs that were scheduled to deliver them to their destinations.

North of Olympia were other companies whose business interacted with marine activities.

Northwest of Olympia in the town of Shelton, at the end of Hammersley Inlet (also known locally as Big Skookum), Simpson Logging Company (1, page 16) operated a sawmill and conducted extensive logging operations. The logs were brought out of the woods and dumped into the water. Assembled into rafts, the logs awaited being cut into lumber at the Simpson mill or transfer by towboat to other sawmills around Puget Sound.

Located near the Simpson Logging mill, Rainier Pulp and Paper Company (2, page 16) produced pulp from wood chips for use in making paper. The pulp was not only used domestically but was also marketed to Japan. During the Great Depression, Rainier, with the research assistance of Dupont, developed a pulp suitable for the manufacture of what was called "rayon." This new type of pulp was given the name "Rayonier," combining the names rayon and Rainier. In 1937, the Rainier plant at Shelton was consolidated with the Rainier plants in Hoquiam and Port Angeles to form Rayonier Incorporated, the new name being taken from the pulp called "Rayonier."

Shelton Towing Company (3, page 16) was based on the southern shore of Hammersley Inlet. Shelton Towing was primarily engaged in handling logs for the Rainier and Simpson companies. The firm, owned by Frank Wolf and described in a later chapter, operated three tugs.

The large wood products firm, Weyerhaeuser (1, page 17), operated a log dump and rafting area in Henderson Inlet (locally known as South Bay). This operation is described later in the book.

South along the beach from Johnson Point, John Lister (2, page 17) built boats. He and his wife, Wilma, lived in a house with a wonderful view across the water toward Anderson Island. A real do-it-your-selfer, John built the facility himself. In all, about 800 wooden boats were built by John. Of these, over 400 were of a 16-foot design that proved to be popular with sports fishermen. These boats were of round bottom design with cedar planking and powered with small air-cooled inboard engines, such as those produced by Briggs and Stratton or Wisconsin. The sport fishing boats were housed at the site and launched or hauled out using the marine railway. In addition to his boatbuilding skills, John was talented with the banjo, violin, guitar, and mandolin.

Over at the eastern edge of the Nisqually Flats, the E. I. du Pont de Nemours and Company explosives handling facility was known locally as the "powder plant" (3, page 17), and more is presented about this in a later chapter. A loading pier extended from the beach out over the water. The company owned a small wooden freighter named *Dupont* for shipping explosives to other ports. On occasion, as a teenager, I moored a small boat under the powder plant pier and fished for perch that were grazing on the mussels that had found a home on the pilings.

North of du Pont near the town of Steilacoom, Pioneer Sand and Gravel Company (4, page 17) operated a mining pit for the extraction of sand and gravel. These products were hauled to various ports around Puget Sound by the firm's own fleet of tugs and barges, as well as by towboats and barges belonging to other companies. This firm is described in detail later in the book.

As noted before, the southern Puget Sound companies listed here are representative of the types of industries that existed in other areas of Puget Sound in the earlier days, also. A few of these companies are still in business, but most of them are gone. In retrospect, it seems hard to believe now that so much industry and marine transportation, each supportive of the other and perhaps taken for granted at the time, existed on the shore and in the harbor of small cities such as Olympia, Shelton, and surrounding areas, as well as at other locations around Puget Sound.

At the sawmill, *Oysterman* makes ready to tow a loaded lumber scow out.

A DECKHAND'S RECOLLECTIONS OF LIFE ABOARD THE EARLIER TUGS

When George Losey, Captain of Delta V. Smyth Tugs and Barges' tug *Nile*, called that day a long time ago to say that they were short one crewmember and offered me the job, the skipper advised bringing along a change of clothes. With all of the wisdom of a teenager, I either declined or forgot to bring the change of clothes on board. This trip would be no more than a couple of days or so towing a log raft from Olympia to Tacoma and return. In making up the tow in Olympia, however, this new deckhand, carrying a pike pole out on the log raft, fell waist-deep into the water. The first lesson learned was that, when down in the water between two logs, a pike pole laid across the logs can be a good aid for hauling oneself back up out of the cold water. The second lesson was taught by the discomfort endured while standing the remainder of the watch in wet clothes. Aboard *Nile*, I acquired the nickname "Kiddo," and other lessons were learned along the way, too.

So there are old and vivid memories, like photographic snapshots, residing in my mind like data stored in a computer's hard drive.

A heavily built wooden tug constructed at Bellingham in 1917, *Nile*, pictured here while enroute with a wooden scow from Olympia to Steilacoom to pick up a load of sand and gravel, was fairly sizable at 75 feet register length, which would make the overall length about 80 feet. Origi-

nally, *Nile* had been designed by Naval Architect H. C. Hanson as a steam powered cannery tender for Pacific American Fisheries (PAF). The design of *Nile* is described in more detail later in the book. As George Losey once said, "This boat's so tough if we ever hit a boomstick we'd probably break the stick in two."

The upper deckhouse enclosed the raised wheelhouse forward and, just aft, the "Texas" that housed the skipper's stateroom. A doorway provided access between the wheelhouse and the stateroom. The wheelhouse did not have inside access from other spaces in the deckhouse, but instead, a sloping ladder out in the weather at the forward end of the main deckhouse provided a route from the main deck up to the bridge deck.

As was typical of towboats at the time, the only access to any compartment in the main deckhouse was from outside. Forward in the main deckhouse was the galley and dinette, the cook stove being fired with diesel oil. Abaft the galley were small spaces for lockers and a head. Most of the aft half of the main deckhouse, however, was taken up by the large engine room. There were no sleeping accommodations in the main deckhouse, but a sloping ladder in an enclosed scuttle on the main deck forward provided access down into the fo'c'sle where the mate, two deckhands, and cook were berthed.

Nile with an empty gravel scow in Balch Passage, 1949. (From the author's collection)

The reason *Nile*'s engine room was large was because the direct reversing diesel engine that powered the tug was big. *Nile* was powered by a six-cylinder, 200-horsepower, Fairbanks-Morse, two-stroke cycle engine turning at not much over 300 revolutions per minute maximum. This engine was sometimes derisively referred to as a "Fairbanks Remorse" or, as John Lister at his boat shop near Johnson Point used to exclaim regarding this type of engine, "That !@#?&@#*! two-cycle!" The engine was started by introducing compressed air at 100 or more pounds per square inch from the air receiver tank into the combustion chambers, thus turning the engine over.

When the tug was required to back down, the engine was stopped and started in the reverse mode. The engine ahead and astern starting, as well as the engine speed, was controlled from the wheelhouse. If a lot of maneuvering was done in a short time period, the air pressure could be reduced to a dangerously low level that might be insufficient to start the engine. A main-engine driven air pump supplied air to the receiver when under way. In addition, there was one small diesel-engine driven electrical generator set in the engine room that also supplied compressed air to the air receiver.

The towing winch was not as sophisticated as a modern winch. A brake could be loosened to pay out the stranded steel wire cable while George, the captain, ran the boat ahead at slow speed. Mounted on the frame was a six-cylinder Chrysler gasoline engine to supply the power for the winch when shortening up on the tow line.

Unfortunately, one of the shortcomings of this winch, when shortening up on the towline, was the fact that it did not have a level wind, a device that travels back and forth laterally so that the incoming cable would spool neatly onto the winch drum. It was up to the deckhand to try to push and pull the incoming cable laterally back and forth as each layer was filling in on the spool in an effort to form an orderly spiral winding and prevent a pile up of cable on the drum. This substitution of one average size deckhand for a level wind was not very productive. If ten men and a boy were available to move that taut tow line sideways against the tension in the cable while the tug was pulling ahead, it might have worked well enough. Worse yet, invariably sprinkled along the length of the cable were broken strands of wire poking out which were not kind to the hands unless gloves made of unobtainium were worn.

The anchor windlass, operating on compressed air, was forward on the main deck. When not in use, the anchor was stowed on deck, and when it was necessary to hang off the hook, the anchor chain was flaked out back and forth, fore and aft along the main deck. Using the davit, the anchor was lifted from the deck, swung over the side, and then let go into the water, the anchor then dragging the long length of chain after it through a bulwark closed chock.

When the anchor was dropped into the water, well, talk about noise when that long length of chain went clattering along the deck and interrupted sleep for those off watch in their berths below deck! And as the old saying goes—never step into the bight of the line. The same applied to the deckhand on watch for, to avoid being caught and injured by the rapidly moving chain when the anchor and chain went overboard, the rule was to stay back! To weigh anchor, the chain was hauled in by the windlass, and the anchor was picked up by the davit.

Typical of most tugs in those days, *Nile* had been built with a fantail stern, and as a result, the vertical height in the lazarette aft was limited. The rudder stock, therefore, penetrated up through the main deck so that the quadrant was just above the deck. A wooden grating in place over the quadrant was used for stowing manila lines. The steering wheel utilized a sprocket and a roller chain that led down through the forward end of the main deckhouse where the galley and mess were located. The ends of the roller chain were connected to stranded wire cables that were then directed aft through pipes laid on the main deck port and starboard and attached to the rudder quadrant located more than 50 feet away. Most modern towboats are equipped with compressed air or hydraulic steering assist. Since *Nile*'s roller chain and cable system was all mechanical, without any power assist, it took some effort to turn the steering wheel. In tight situations, when maneuvers had to be accomplished as rapidly as possible, it took some work at the wheel for George, the captain, to avoid getting into a hazardous situation.

Navigation equipment consisted of a compass plus charts for the areas normally operating in. There was no radar, no loran, no global positioning system, no knotmeter, no depth finder, and not even a radio. To determine the distance off of the beach in a pea soup fog, the skipper blew the air whistle and then judged the time required for the echo to return the sound off the bank. To determine depth of water, the deckhand out on the foredeck dropped a lead line into the water, and the depth readings were shouted up to the wheelhouse to the skipper or mate, who was leaning out of an open window. A recess at the bottom of the lead weight contained tallow into which grains of bottom sediment might be imbedded, thus giving a clue as to bottom composition, hence location per notes on the navigation chart.

The oil-fired iron galley range utilized the same diesel fuel that the main propulsion engine did. This range was left burning continuously day and night, and a pot of coffee was on at all times. The galley range was also the only heat source aboard *Nile*, except for the heat radiated by the big propulsion engine. In chilly weather, the warm, cozy galley was the first choice as a place to spend any idle moments.

If, on a summer night, time passed slowly while standing a wheel watch during the dark hours following midnight, while the tug was moving at low speed with a log raft out behind, a crewman was offered the compensation of the Aurora Borealis. In those days there were fewer people in the Puget Sound area and, therefore, fewer shoreside lights, which allowed the night sky to be seen clearly. Viewed from the darkened wheelhouse, dimly illuminated only by a low wattage compass light to avoid the degradation of vision through the windows to the outside, the Northern Lights were an awesome sight.

Nile was an "inside" boat, meaning a tug that operated in the relatively sheltered waters of Puget Sound rather than out in the open sea. Because a tow was usually of no longer duration than a week or so, less time than many of the ocean tows, watches were on the standard inside boat schedule of six hours on and six hours off, each watch starting at six or twelve around the clock. An "outside" boat's schedule for crew members was four hours on and eight off when at sea, which re-

quired more people in the crew. Some of the small Puget Sound tugs were "day" boats engaged in juggling logs and scows locally in harbors and so did not require on and off watches. These working schedules are still used today.

Nile's crew consisted of captain, mate, two deckhands, and a cook. Seniority took precedence, and so Captain Losey and deckhand Robin stood the six in the morning and six in the evening watches. The mate, whose identity varied from time to time, and I, the junior deckhand, stood the less desirable watches that started at noon and midnight. A crewman going off watch awakened the replacement crewman.

Meals were prepared by the cook and served at six in the morning, twelve noon and six in the evening. Crew members going on watch would take their meals just before these times, and crew menbers going off watch, just after these times. The eats were substantial and appetizing. Because of the meal schedule, Gene, the cook, did not stand two watches per day but, instead, arose early in the morning and was back into his berth in the evening. When towing logs, the speed being not much over a knot or so, the cook enjoyed securely placing a fishing rod at the stern, and so, occasionally, fresh troll-caught salmon embellished the dinner menu.

Sleeping conditions in the fo'c'sle were spartan, and the wooden bulkheads and overheads in *Nile* were not insulated. Engine-caused vibration was always present and the sound of the big Fairbanks diesel engine, just abaft the fuel tanks and only a few feet away from the berths, was loud and insistent but eventually could be gotten used to. In fact, at the end of a long tow, having lived with the Fairbanks aboard the tug, the quiet ambience back home could actually take a bit of time to grow accustomed to.

As was standard practice, the seams between the thick wooden deck planks of the main deck contained strands of caulking over which hot tar had been payed. Unfortunately, with swelling and shrinking of the planks due to changing weather conditions, the seams would eventually begin to leak here and there. Because of this, during a rain, for crew members off watch and berthed in the fo'c'sle, sleep had to be gotten as best possible while enduring a wet berth.

Except for good solid meals, crew comforts were primitive by today's standards, but in those days, these kinds of conditions were somewhat to be expected aboard workboats. When decking aboard one Bristol Bay, Alaska, power scow, I found the head to consist of a bucket of sea water, the contents to be thrown overboard after use. Typical of most of the boats at the time, there was no shower on board *Nile* and so it could be supposed that a week-long towing job without a shower would be intolerable for some.

Knowing the current patterns in Puget Sound is very important when slowly towing a big, cumbersome log raft, since bucking the tide could cause the tug and tow simply to maintain position with no forward movement over the ground or, even worse, move backward. However, as in a river, the current sweeping around a point of land causes an eddy at the downstream side of the point as the water proceeds to fill that area. Hence, when bucking the tide, good headway can be gotten by moving in under the point, taking advantage of any back eddies. Steering in along the beach like that is referred to as "beachcombing." With a favorable tidal current aiding *Nile*, George used to exclaim "We're really walking the dog!"

Since a tug on a long tow operates 24 hours a day, navigation lights were required on the tow at night. For a scow, an oil lamp was placed on the deck at each corner. If a scow load of sand or gravel was under tow, a steel staff was set into the pile of sand or gravel near each corner of the barge, and a lamp was then hung from a hook near the top of each staff. When towing a log raft, this staff was driven into a log near each corner to provide for lights, a lamp then being hung on each staff's hook. These oil lamps were simply left burning night and day.

The drawing at the bottom of the page illustrates towing arrangements for log rafts. On longer tows, the tug's towline would normally be centered on the log raft, as in the upper two drawings. In a harbor, a small tug would normally utilize a hook line attached to the boom chain ring at one corner of the raft as depicted in the lower drawing. The towline for a triple string raft, not shown, would be rigged with a bridle as for the single string raft, the two additional strings being chained at the sides of the center raft.

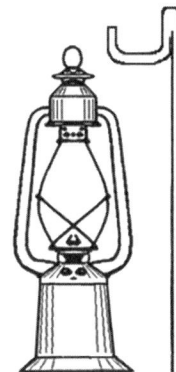

N.KNUTSEN

Lantern and staff.

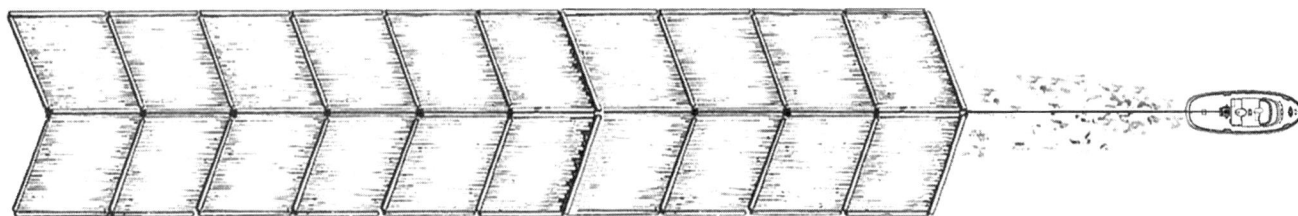

DOUBLE STRING LOG RAFT

SINGLE STRING LOG RAFT WITH THE TOWLINE BRIDLE
ATTACHED TO BOOM CHAIN RINGS AT TWO CORNERS

SINGLE STRING LOG RAFT WITH THE TOWLINE
ATTACHED TO A BOOM CHAIN RING AT A CORNER

N.KNUTSEN

Log raft towing arrangements.

Towing a log raft through Deception Pass was tricky and could only be done at or near high or low slack water. With the current running at eight knots or more through the pass at mid-tide, a tug with logs would not be able to buck the current. On the other hand, running the pass with the current would be far too dangerous. If the timing for slack water was off when traveling westbound with logs, the tug and tow would hole up in Cornet Bay just east of the pass and wait for the slack. Since Deception Pass is so narrow, one of Dunlap Towing Company's towboats out of La Conner was frequently used to act as a tail boat, the tug making fast to the aft end of the log raft, thus helping to steer the raft through the narrow pass.

Nile also assisted cargo ships calling at the Port of Olympia. When *Nile* had moved a large vessel in close to the pier, personnel on the pier cast a heaving line to the ship's crew, who attached the heaving line to a heavy mooring line that could be hauled in and placed around a bollard on the pier. The weight on the end of a heaving line is called a "monkey fist," so named because of the appearance of the rope work that is used as a covering for the spherical metal weight.

"Cork boots" were worn when working out on a log raft in order to maintain footing and not slip, especially when walking on boomsticks. Boomsticks are logs that have had the bark removed, and the relatively smooth surface can become notoriously slippery when wet. These items of footwear were leather boots with laces but, in those days, were frequently called "shoes" by many who worked aboard the boats. The term "cork" is a Pacific Northwest pronunciation of the word "caulk." Cork boots, or shoes, have hobnails on the soles and heels to provide footing on the logs. To avoid marring the deck, wearing corks aboard *Nile* was not allowed, so a crewman would change into and out of his corks while sitting on the bulwark with feet outboard on the guard.

In connection with cork boots, it should be mentioned that the old hands in the Pacific Northwest also refer to the process of sealing the planking seams in wooden boats as "corking" the seams. This is done by tapping strands of yarn into the seam with a caulking iron and mallet and then applying seam compound. As a child, and be-

fore even knowing how to spell caulking, I heard boat builders talking about "corking" the seams in a boat, and in fact, I didn't think much about it one way or the other; that was simply the language of boat building.

A riveted iron or steel ship has lapped seams, the lower edge of one hull plate overlapping the upper edge of the plate below to permit riveting the plates together. The lower edge of the outer plate is then upset by driving a chisel like tool against the plate edge which forces the lapped plate tightly against the inner plate, thus sealing the joint against water leakage. Many years ago while attending a Naval Architecture class at the University of Michigan, I was ordered by Prof. Henry Adams ("Hank" when he was out of earshot) to the blackboard to give an explanation of the caulking technique as it applied to a riveted ship. Not knowing it was a mispronunciation in the East, I just naturally used the phrase "cork the seam" as always. Prof. Adams blew his cork, and startled everyone in class when he hollered out, "It's caulk, not cork!" Prof. Adams has passed on by now, but much was learned from him about ships. A few years ago, I had occasion to phone the Caulkers Union in Seattle; the call was answered with the response "Corkers Union."

Pike poles are essential tools aboard a logging tug for use at the beginning and end of a log tow, just as they were aboard a tug like *Nile*. A pike pole has a long shaft with a steel fitting on one end that has a point in line with the shaft and a point at a right angle to the shaft. Pike poles are obtainable in lengths ranging from eight feet to more than sixteen feet, the shorter to mid-range lengths commonly being found aboard tugs while the longer lengths are frequently used for making up log rafts at the booming grounds.

Pike pole handles, or shafts, were only of wood in the earlier days but today are available in both wood and hollow aluminum. A pike pole with a hollow aluminum handle will float if dropped into the water. A pike pole having a wooden handle will also float, with the point down, if the handle is long enough to provide sufficient buoyancy.

N. KNUTSEN

Pike pole.

A pike pole is an aid to the user for maintaining balance when walking on a floating log, in a manner similar to a tight rope walker, but the pike pole has other more important uses including pushing or pulling when moving floating logs. The pointed prong that projects at a right angle to the axis of the pole can be used as a hook for pulling, as well as for retrieving the end of a partially submerged boom chain. Also, by sticking the point that is in line with the shaft into a piling or log, the pike pole can be used for pulling, as long as the force used is not so great that the point would pull out of the piling or log.

A boom chain is a length of steel chain several feet long with a large ring at one end and a toggle, or bar, at the other end. Boom chains are used to tie boomsticks together at the corners of each section of the log raft, a section being square-shaped with a boomstick forming each of the four sides. A raft, then, was made up of many sections. A boomstick has a hole bored through near each end. The toggle end of the chain is swiveled endways and passed down through the hole in one boomstick, brought back up through the hole in the other stick, and then the toggle is passed through the ring and swiveled sideways so that it does not pass back through the ring, thus securing the boomsticks by tying them together.

I got some fast-paced experience in decking aboard a small, busy log-handling tug at the Weyerhaeuser log dump in Henderson Inlet when the crew was shorthanded. This tug was *R. A. McDonald*, a wooden day boat 41 feet in length built at Everett in 1928. While cork boots were not permitted to be worn on the deck of *Nile*, so as to avoid damage to the planking, it was acceptable aboard *R. A. McDonald* because the tug had wooden expendable strips, or cleats, fastened on top of the deck planking to take the wear and tear. However, corks were not permitted in the engine room, where no provisions had been made to prevent damage to the wooden ladder and floorboards from the hobnails.

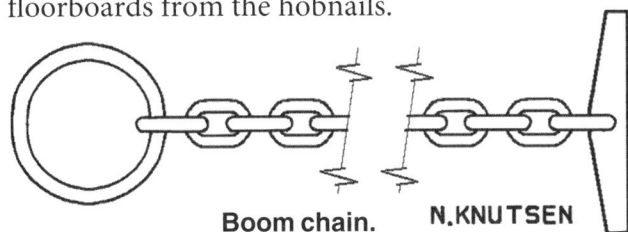

Boom chain. N.KNUTSEN

R. A. McDonald was powered by a 75 horsepower, three-cylinder, slow-speed, Atlas Imperial diesel engine that was started by injecting air under pressure directly into a cylinder combustion chamber. However, unlike the larger engine in *Nile*, the Atlas was not directly connected to the propeller but instead operated through a clutch and reverse gear. When starting the engine, first thing in the morning and then after lunch, the engine had so much torque that when the air was shot into a cylinder causing the big engine to rotate, the tug would react by rolling several degrees in the opposite direction.

As a typical small tug, *R. A. McDonald* did not have a towing winch but instead had a towing bitt. So in moving a log raft from the booming area to the storage area, a manila hook line, having a large galvanized steel hook on one end, was used. For towing, the hook was attached to a boom chain ring at one corner of the raft, and the free end of the tow line was wrapped several times on the towing bitt. Half hitches were never used; in an emergency it might take too much time to release the towline from the bitt in such a situation. As an option, the hook end of the towline was sometimes wrapped once around the head stick (the transverse boomstick at the forward end of the raft) with the hook brought back and placed over the towline itself to secure the attachment.

At the Weyerhaeuser log dump in Henderson Inlet, the logs were brought in by truck and rail car. The entire load of logs was lifted off the bunks, and with the boom swung out over the water, the logs were turned loose and dropped into the water with a big splash and a lot of noise. These logs, floating inside of a large corral formed by boomsticks, were sorted and assembled into a raft, the raft then being pulled by *R. A. McDonald* out of the booming area and over to the log storage area where they were moored.

At the log raft storage, two people, known as "scalers," in a small outboard motor powered boat measured the log diameters and, from that, determined and recorded the number of board feet in the raft. It is important to know the number of board feet in a log raft because the logs are priced by the board foot. The log rafts then awaited movement by a towboat to a sawmill somewhere on Puget Sound.

Newly assembled log rafts were towed from the booming area and moored in a storage area. With a new raft in tow, the tug was maneuvered in alongside one of the rafts already moored in the storage area, and the deckhand, carrying a boom chain in one hand and a pike pole, bucket of white paint, and brush in the other, jumped off onto the moored raft while the tug was still moving ahead with the tow. Walking to the head end of the moored raft, the deckhand passed the chain through the boom chain ring at the corner and then watched as the new raft moved alongside. At the proper moment, the deckhand slipped the chain through the boom chain ring at the forward corner of the moving raft and secured it.

While the deckhand was painting an identification number on the end of a log, the skipper, aboard the tug, turned loose of the tow, moved the tug to the tail end of the towed raft, and pushed that end in next to the moored raft. By that time, the deckhand had finished painting the number and had hurried along the length of the moored raft to secure the tail end of the new raft with a boom chain. A fresh string of boomsticks was then towed back to the area near the beach where the rafting process was continuing. It is interesting that one can, without sinking, walk across a raft of small logs, none of which would support one's weight very well, if done rapidly enough without pausing. Perhaps this would be akin to running on water, as one might see in a cartoon.

Hemlock logs tend to soak up water at a faster rate than some other species of wood and can eventually sink in the water. To delay this sinkage, several logs are wrapped together with steel cables or straps to form each bundle, thereby providing more reserve buoyancy. The raft, known as a "bundle raft," is then made up of many of these log bundles. A bundle raft can contain considerably more board feet than can a raft that is made up of individual logs.

The mooring lines and towlines used at the time were "Manila," made from the natural fiber Manila hemp. Manila lines have very little stretch. I have been at work on the aft deck of a tug when the Manila towline parted while pulling on a log raft. The portion of the broken line that was attached to the towing bitt simply dropped to the deck. Some synthetic lines, on the other hand, would, because of stretch, have whipped through the air like a huge rubber band, resulting in severe injuries to anyone in its path.

The unexpected can happen at any time aboard a towboat. One summer day, American Tug Boat Company's *Irene* was heading out of Henderson Inlet with a Weyerhaeuser bundle raft in tow, and a section of the raft came apart when the end of a boomstick sheared out at the eye. Some time was spent by *R. A. McDonald* and crew in rounding up the stray bundles of hemlock logs and herding them back into the raft. Repairs were made to the raft, and *Irene* was on the way.

R. A. McDonald in Henderson Inlet.

SOME NOTES ON THE EARLIER TUGS

In the early to mid portion of the last century, the industries that flourished in the Puget Sound area required extensive services provided by marine transportation. Tugs, owned by a variety of towing companies, as well as towboats that were employed by industries for use in their own operations, were home-ported at Shelton, Olympia, Tacoma, Seattle, Eagle Harbor, Port Gamble, Everett, La Conner, Anacortes, Bellingham, and Port Angeles. Mills and plants were sufficiently busy and in need of towing services that even at the small city of Olympia, for example, three towing companies, whose combined fleets totaled 15 or more tugs, operated from their headquarters there. At times during this era, a total of more than 200 towboats were operating from various Puget Sound ports.

There have always been three choices when a marine transportation company requires an additional vessel that can pitch in and help out on the firm's workload: build a new boat, lease an existing boat, or purchase an existing boat. For economic reasons, many existing boats of various types were purchased which, at times, required major rework to make them ready for the new owner's intended service.

Many boats newly introduced to towing service had originally been in operation as steamers engaged in the carriage of cargo and passengers. Eventually, as more highways were built, freight hauling by truck and passenger travel by automobile replaced the services offered by the steam boats. Many of these steamers, if in acceptable condition, were converted to towing.

The typical steamboat hull form was similar to that of a tug, with a sheer line that was high at the bow and low at the stern and, therefore, adaptable for towing. However, these cargo and passenger vessels featured large superstructures and deckhouses that did not suit the arrangements required for towing service. In many cases, these steamers needed extensive rebuilding to modify them for use as towboats, and the superstructures and deckhouses were partially or entirely removed before reconstruction was undertaken. Some of these vessels that had been modified into towboats, then, featured a combination of old and new structure in their deckouses. Typically, a new or modified deckhouse was sized and arranged to provide large open spaces on deck for handling lines and also to permit the installation of a tow bitt or winch on the aft deck. Following the introduction of internal combustion engines in commercial service in the 1920s, the power plant of a passenger or cargo steamer might either be retained for use in towing service or replaced with an internal combustion engine.

The tug *Ajax*, shown on the next page, had started life as a cannery tender but was later employed in towing service. Unlike the passenger/cargo steamers, *Ajax* only needed a minimum amount of modification before entering into towing service because the general arrangement of the vessel as a cannery tender was also suitable for towing. Many other cannery tenders changed hands and were adapted to working in the towing business, also.

In the early part of the 1900s, few Puget Sound towboats could have been found that had the same appearance as any other tug. Perhaps that is why these earlier tugs seemed to take on a human quality; no two people are identical in appearance or capability either. Featuring a distinctive appearance, a tug seen from afar could be recognized and identified long before the distance had closed sufficiently that the name on the hull or name board could be read.

In the late 1940s, surplus government vessels that were no longer needed for the war effort were offered for sale. These vessels had been built in a variety of classes, each class having an intended purpose. Within each class were groups of boats that had the same appearance. As a result, many identical ex-government tugs that found their way into commercial towing service differed only in the company colors of the various owners. Even so, for some time after World War II, the preponderance of towboats still consisted of the earlier vessels, all varying in size, lines, and shapes, as well as beauty or not as judged by the beholder.

Ajax in Elliott Bay, 1950. (From the author's collection)

Ajax, 73 feet in length, was constructed of wood in 1917 by the Elliott Bay Yacht and Launch Company at Seattle for use as a cannery tender by the Apex Fish Company of Anacortes. *Ajax* is pictured above as adapted to towing service. At left in the photo, the wooden steam passenger vessel *Virginia V*, described later in the book, can be seen beyond *Ajax*'s bow. *Ajax* was originally designed with a brailing boom attached to the forward mast, as shown in the drawing on the next page. At the time of this photo, however, the boom had been relocated and fitted to the aft mast.

Ajax was originally outfitted with a 110-horsepower oil engine of the semi-diesel type, a design that was beginning to gain favor for reasons of economy in operation at a time when most vessels in a similar line of work were still powered by steam or gasoline engines. An oil engine also had the added advantage of safety compared with a gas engine, since oil is not as volatile as gasoline.

The semi-diesel engines utilized a glow plug or hot surface in the combustion chamber to assist in igniting the oil/air mixture (full-diesel engines had not yet been developed). The engine as installed in *Ajax* was manufactured by the Atlas

Gas Engine Company of Oakland, California. The engine was built with four cylinders, each cylinder having a bore and stroke of 9 inches by 12 inches, and provided a speed of 10 knots for the boat, a respectable speed indeed. Fuel consumption on the trial trip was reported as being a modest 5 1/4 gallons per hour.

The H. W. McCurdy *Marine History of the Pacific Northwest* describes a race, at Anacortes in 1918, between two Apex Fish-owned cannery tenders, *Ajax* and *Superior*. On a four mile course, the 110-horsepower semi-diesel engine powered *Ajax* sneaked out a win over the 200 horsepower, 80-foot gas-engine-powered *Superior*.

It might be expected that the longer length, higher horsepower *Superior* would have had an advantage over the shorter, lower horsepower *Ajax*, but other factors, such as differences in loading, trim, and hull form, play a part in speed, also. Thus, the significance of the race result was inconclusive, but the event did serve to publicize the fact that awareness of an engine fueled by oil, as a potential replacement for the gasoline engine, was growing in the consciousness of commercial boat operators.

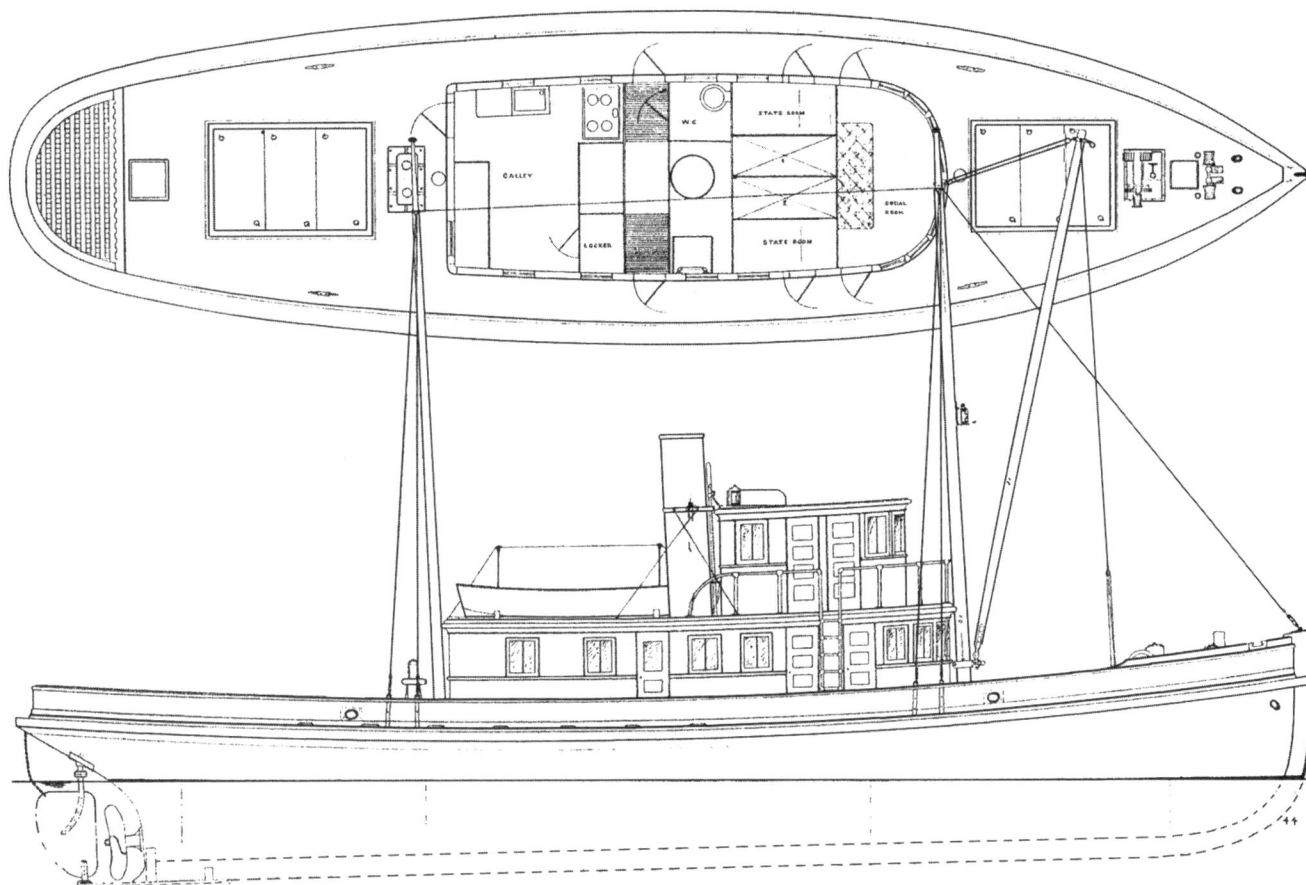

Ajax profile and arrangement, 1917. (From *Pacific Motor Boat* October, 1917)

The 1917 fish packer *Ajax* was designed by J. H. Martinolich, and the outboard profile and arrangement drawing is shown above. At the time when the design of *Ajax* was being worked out, John Martinolich had been operating the Puget Sound Dry Dock Company at Dockton, on Quartermaster Harbor, for 12 years. As noted previously, however, Ajax was built by Elliott Bay Yacht and Launch Company in Seattle rather than by Puget Sound Dry Dock.

Ajax was designed with a breadth of 17 1/2 feet, which resulted in a length-to-beam ratio of well over 4, certainly not a beamy vessel but typical of the practice at that time. An approximate keel draft aft, as shown on the drawing, was a modest 6 feet. The drawing, however, may have been done as a representation of the vessel in the unloaded condition, not an uncommon practice when delineating designs of boats intended for use in the fishing industry. If so, the draft would have been considerably greater when the packer was loaded with fish. It can be seen in the photos on the previous page and next page that, in later

years as a tug, *Ajax* trimmed aft and sat deeper in the water compared with the boat at the waterline as shown in this drawing.

The cannery tender was designed with a hold forward and a hold abaft the house. Cargo handling was taken care of by means of the mast and boom forward, the rigging being worked by an electric winch designed and built by Nilsen and Hanna of Seattle. In later years, as a tug, the boom was mounted to the aft mast as shown in the photo on the previous page.

As was the custom at the time, the accommodation spaces in the deckhouse were entered from the weather deck, the only exception being the head on the port side, which had a door that opened from the upper engine room grating platform deck in the fidley. The galley, located aft, was large. An interesting space, located forward in the deckhouse, was labeled "social room" on the drawing and was available as a lounge. A transom seat in this space was usable as a berth, thus adding to the sleeping accommodations that were available in the two staterooms.

45

Ajax at Port Angeles, 1963. (From the author's collection)

By the time the photo above of *Ajax* was taken, the rigging had been altered by modifying the forward mast and removing the ratlines. The ratlines, as shown in the previous photo and used for access to the upper part of the masts, were not commonly installed aboard tugs. In addition to these changes, the rectangular windows had been replaced with round portlights at the sides of the main deckhouse and an open array radar had been installed. At the time of this photo, *Ajax* was in towing service for Peninsula Towing Company operating out of Port Angeles.

It was not unusual for the boats owned by towing firms to change hands periodically according to business conditions, so ownership of the tugs at any given time is uncertain. In fact, not only were tugs purchased and sold periodically, but so were the companies that operated them. Some firms of medium size, such as Gilkey Brothers Towing Company at Anacortes, maintained several tugs in the towing business. Like Peninsula Towing, however, there were numerous small towing companies owned by men such as G. S. Atwood at Seattle, Boyer Halvorsen at Bainbridge Island, the Peck brothers at Everett, Captain A.

G. Rouse at Seattle, Otis Shively at Seattle, Robert Shrewsbury at Seattle, Pat Stoppleman at Seattle, and Frank Wolf at Shelton, some of whom operated as few as one or two tugs.

Those who started their own marine towing firms had various backgrounds, but most of them had spent time working on the water prior to owning their companies. Originally, while working for others, many of these men had risen from deckhand to captain aboard the tugs. Others had been captains aboard steamers that carried passengers and freight, and in some cases, they also owned the steamboats. In fact, many of these steamers began a new career when they were later converted for use in commercial towing.

As time went on, business ceased for most of these smaller towing firms, or the activities were absorbed into larger companies, except that Halvorsen Towing Company and Bob Shrewsbury's Western Towboat Company grew into large operations with modern tugs operating on Puget Sound, as well as in Alaska waters and on the open ocean. Some of the towboats operated by these firms are shown here, as well as elsewhere in the book.

46

Sound, n.d. (With permission of Anacortes Museum)

Wyadda were acquired by Gilky Brothers Towing Company. *Intrepid* was later operated by American Tug Boat Company, Delta V. Smyth Tugs and Barges, and Bellingham Tug and Barge Company. *Klatawa* was eventually owned by Olympia Towing Company.

Shown at left is the 57-foot Gilkey steam tug *Sound*. In 1926, the towboat was repowered with a 270-horsepower Washington-Estep diesel engine. The manufacturer's name included "Estep" when the company's chief engineer, A. C. Estep, improved on the semi-diesel engine design, thus enabling Washington Iron Works to produce full-diesel engines. After Foss Launch and Tug acquired the vessel in 1940, the deckhouse was rebuilt and the Washington-Estep diesel was removed in favor of a 200 Enterprise.

Gilkey Brothers Towing Company was started at Anacortes in 1918 as a partnership consisting of Charles, Mark, and Walter Gilkey. In 1923, the other three Gilkey brothers, David, Frank, and William, joined the firm. In the beginning, the company was a single-boat operation with the purchase of the 41-foot tug *Governor*, powered by a 50-horsepower gas engine.

As time went on, other vessels such as *Bahada*, *Hioma*, *Hyak*, *Intrepid*, *Klatawa*, *Sea King*, *Sound* (later *Carl Foss*), *Vigilant* (later *Anna Foss*), and

C. B. Smith, owned by G. S. Atwood and pictured below while heading north off Hyde Point, was a 53-foot, 165 horsepower, wooden tug built at Everett in 1902. Through the mist, Ketron Island can be seen in the background.

C. B. Smith off Hyde Point, circa 1947. (From the author's collection)

47

Georgeanne H in Eagle Harbor, 1963. (From the author's collection)

In the photo above, Halvorsen Towing Company's tug *Georgeanne H* was outbound in Eagle Harbor on Bainbridge Island. This wooden tug was 61 feet in length and was one of two built at the penitentiary on McNeil Island in 1943. The tug, painted white, had a yachtlike appearance.

The two wooden tugs shown below belonged to the Peck Brothers Tow Boat Company. The Peck family had originally lived at Glendale, on Whidbey Island, where steamers stopped for firewood and supplies. The 37-foot *Glendale*, named after that community, was built at Mukilteo in 1908, and the 37-foot *Western* was built at Seattle in 1890. The extensive mill activity that existed along the Everett shoreline is evident in the background of the photo.

Glendale and *Western* at Everett, n.d. (With permission of Everett Public Library, Northwest Room)

Katy at Ballard, circa 1947. (From the author's collection)

Katy, an 80-foot wooden tug, was built as a steamer at San Francisco in 1868, only three years after the Civil War ended. As a newly built vessel, *Katy* was operated in the United States Coast and Geodetic Survey fleet. Later on, with a diesel engine having replaced the steam plant, *Katy* was used in towing service for many years by Shively Tow Boat Company out of Seattle. Eventually, the old tug was tiring after years of hard work, and not wanting to part with his boat, Otis Shively continued to coax more life out of *Katy*. Finally, in early 1952, *Katy*, 84 years old, could no longer keep up with the workload, and so, after metal items had been salvaged, the boat was burned on the mudflats near Marysville.

The wooden tug *Vamoose*, owned by Pat Stoppleman, is pictured below on a towing assignment at the Maritime Administration facility at Gull Harbor just north of Olympia. *Vamoose* was 37 feet long and built at South Bend in 1912.

Vamoose at the Maritime Administration facility in Budd Inlet, 1949. (From the author's collection)

Nitinat Chief in Hammersley Inlet, 1965. (Courtesy of Elizabeth Wolf)

Traditionally, the Puget Sound area, British Columbia, and Alaska have had a close relationship and much in common, especially regarding the wood products industries and marine transportation. In the photo above, the British Columbia tug *Nitinat Chief* was in Hammersley Inlet with a bundle raft of logs. *Nitinat Chief,* powered by a 260-horsepower Washington diesel engine, was 72 feet long and built of wood at Vancouver, British Columbia, in 1941.

Comments have previously been made about the potential for breaking a towline, as happened at least once while I was decking aboard the towboats. Such an event can occur when the towline contains broken strands or when the towline meets with excessive stress while the tug and tow are rolling, pitching and yawing in rough seas. As an example of the devastation that can occur when things go wrong, shown in the photo below is a large United Transportation petroleum barge that grounded and was being pounded by the surf on the beach at Moclips on the Washington coast after the tug's towline parted.

At right in the photo, the barge's towing vessel, *Sea Witch,* was standing by while pitching violently in the huge swells out beyond the surf line. The steel tug *Sea Witch* and sister *Sea Giant,* each powered by a 2000-horsepower Enterprise diesel engine, were 115 feet long and built in 1957 by Pacific Coast Engineering of Alameda, California, for the Shipowners and Merchants Towboat Company of San Francisco.

Sea Witch standing by a barge on the beach at Moclips, 1964. (From the author's collection)

Foss No. 19, foreground, *Bee* and *P & T Pioneer*, right, at the Ballard Locks, 1963.
(From the author's collection)

In this interesting picture at the Ballard Locks, three tugs, outbound with their tows, required the combined space of both large lock chambers. Foss Launch and Tug's Company's *Foss No. 19*, in the foreground, was alongside an empty steel sand and gravel barge. Washington Tug and Barge Company's *Bee*, behind *Foss No. 19*, had an empty wooden sand and gravel scow in tow. Behind *Bee*, Pope and Talbot Timber Company's *P & T Pioneer*, with logs on the towline, waited while the water in the lock was lowered.

The 72-foot *Foss No. 19* was built of wood at San Francisco in 1895 as the U. S. government steam powered fisheries patrol vessel *Wigwam*. Later, during employment with Alaska Packers Association, the vessel's steam plant was removed and replaced with a Fairbanks-Morse engine. *Wigwam* was acquired by Foss Launch and Tug Company in the 1920s and renamed *Foss No. 19*. By the time of the above photo, *Foss No. 19* had

undergone extensive renovation, and propulsion was provided by a 200-horsepower Enterprise diesel engine. *Bee*, 58 feet in length, was built of wood at Everett in 1901 and the 60-foot *P & T Pioneer* was built of wood at Seattle in 1951. These two tugs are described more fully later in the book.

Crew quarters were spartan and, in some cases, barely adequate aboard most of the earlier Puget Sound tugs. There was no insulation against heat, cold, and engine noise and, during a rain, sleep might have to be gotten in a damp berth located under a leaky deck. But, in those days, life for most people was quite simple, and perhaps folks were more willing to put up with such circumstances than might be the case today. Generally, though, working on the water was a pretty good way of life. As George Losey, skipper of the tug *Nile*, once said, when he started getting a little fidgety at home between tows, it was time to get back out on the salt water.

51

Of all the towboats that were surplused by the U.S. government and put into commercial use after World War II, perhaps the tugs of the Mikimiki LT Class were the most classic and pleasing of line. And they were good tugs, designed by Leigh H. Coolidge and of wooden construction, mostly using Douglas fir. The U.S. Army Transportation Corps tugs followed closely the design of a Young Brothers, Ltd. tug, built of wood in 1929 and also designed by Coolidge, named *Mikimiki* that operated out of Honolulu, Hawaii. The two designs were similar in appearance and about the same size.

A number of surplused Mikimiki tugs were in commercial operation on Puget Sound after World War II. Having a register length of

117 feet and overall length of about 126 feet, the tugs that entered commercial service were primarily used for towing barges in the open ocean, as well as between Puget Sound and Alaska. In addition, the tugs were sometimes engaged in towing log rafts.

The Mikimiki tug in the drawing below featured twin diesel engines driving twin screws for propulsion. The sheer followed a sweeping, curved line, high in the bow to minimize the boarding of seas and low in the stern for towing. Many of the Mikimikis were built on the West Coast where experienced shipwrights and suitable timber were readily available.

These tugs were built in both single and twin screw versions, with heavy duty diesel engines for power. Early in World War II the production of propulsion engines had not caught up with the number of hulls being launched by the shipyards, hence, the earlier built boats were powered by a single engine.

Red Stack Mikimiki tug *Sea Breeze*, of San Francisco, California, at the Ballard Locks in the early 1960s. (From the author's collection)

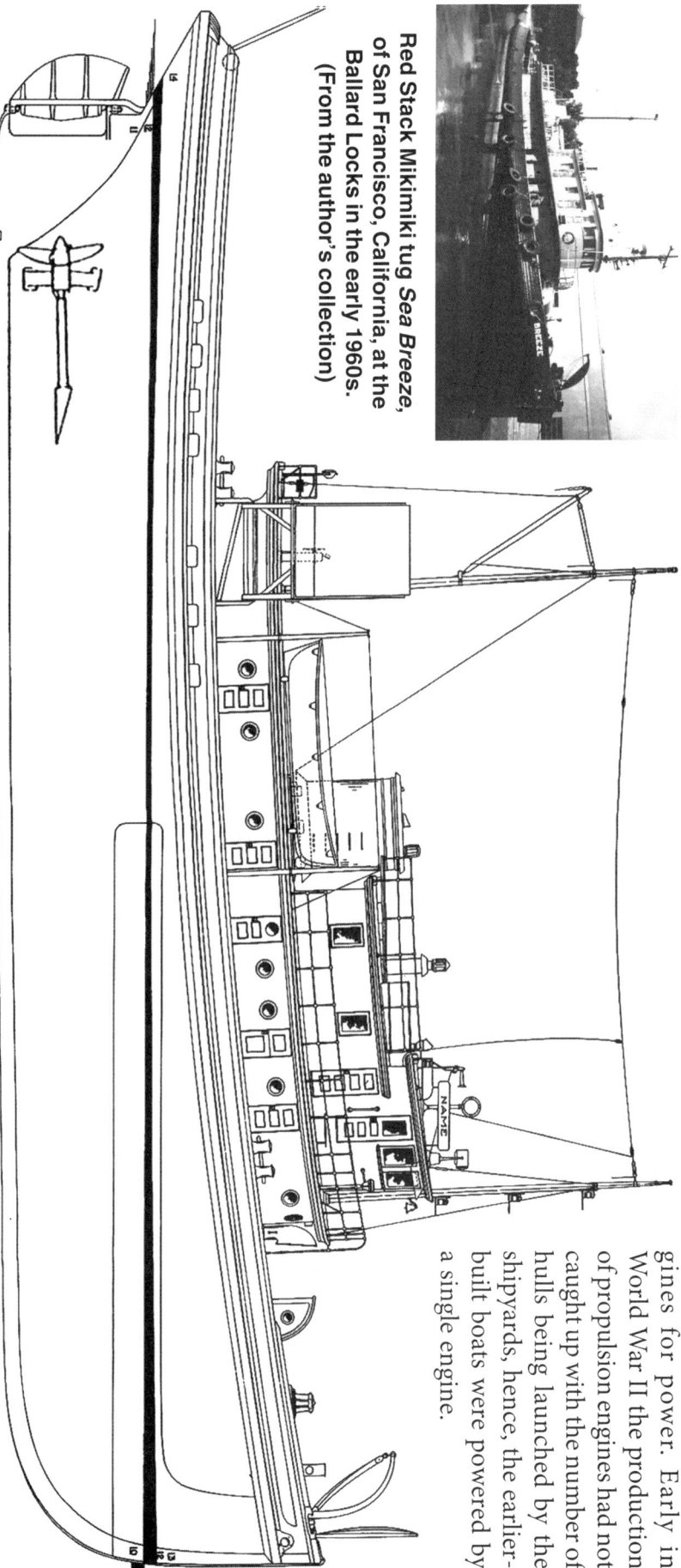

Twin screw Mikimiki type tug outboard profile, 1940s. (From the author's collection)

52

Illustrated here are arrangements for the main deck, boat deck, and pilothouse top for a single-screw Miki. In this drawing, gun tubs are included on top of the pilothouse but, following the war, these were removed for commercial towing service. The accommodations are extensive because, while at sea on long tows, a sufficient number of crew members in a Mikimiki was required for standing three watches during each 24 hour day. A considerable amount of space in the Mikimiki main deckhouse was occupied by the upper engine room.

All spaces in the Mikimiki main deckhouse were accessed from outside, typical of the tugs of those times. The beam of these tugs was not generous enough to allow space for inside passageways. However, space was provided for an inside stairway between the main deck and the upper house. Berthing was also provided forward and below in the fo'c'sle, as illustrated in the drawing on the next page.

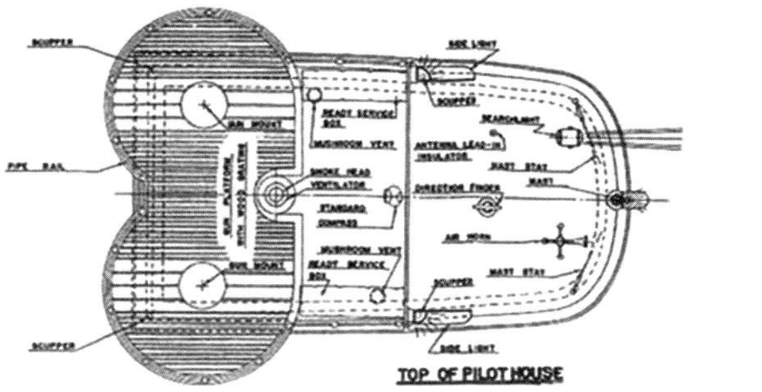

TOP OF PILOTHOUSE

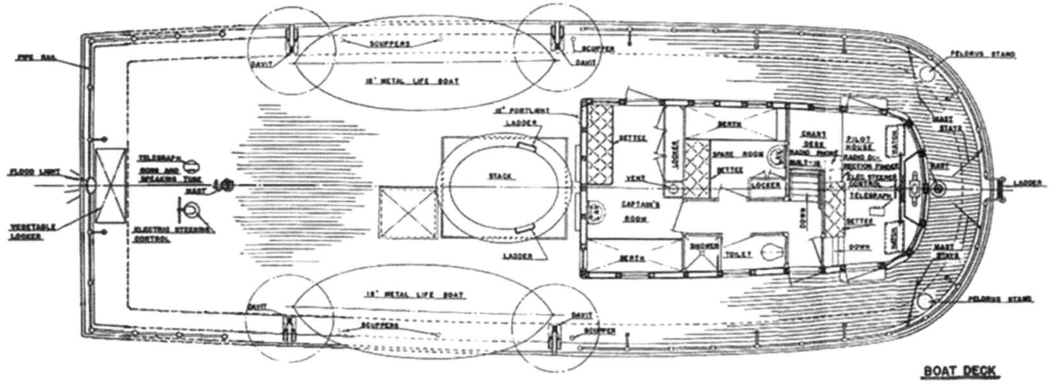

BOAT DECK

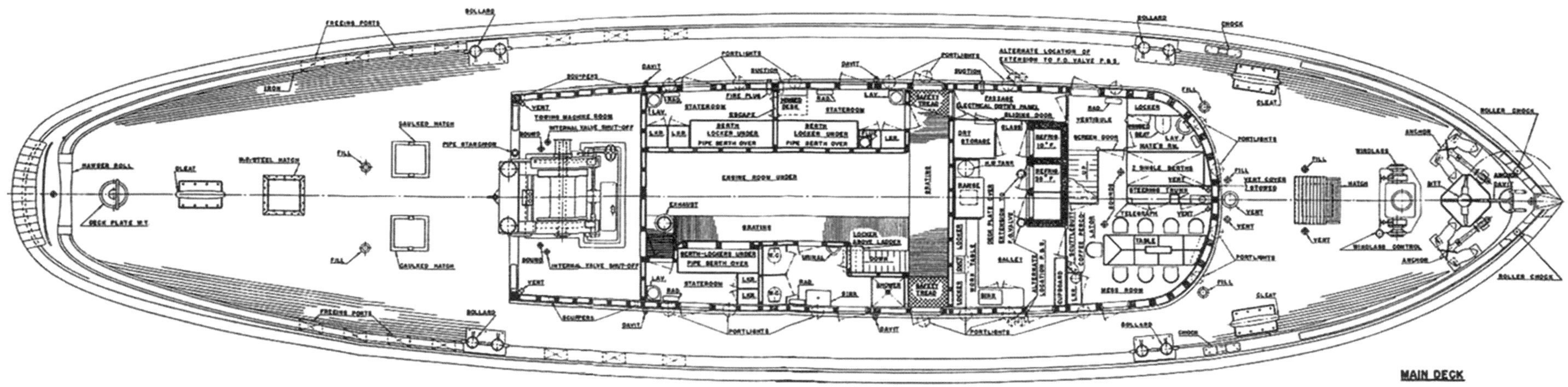

MAIN DECK

Single screw Mikimiki type tug main deck, boat deck, and pilothouse top arrangements, 1940s.
(Courtesy of U.S. Army Transportation Museum)

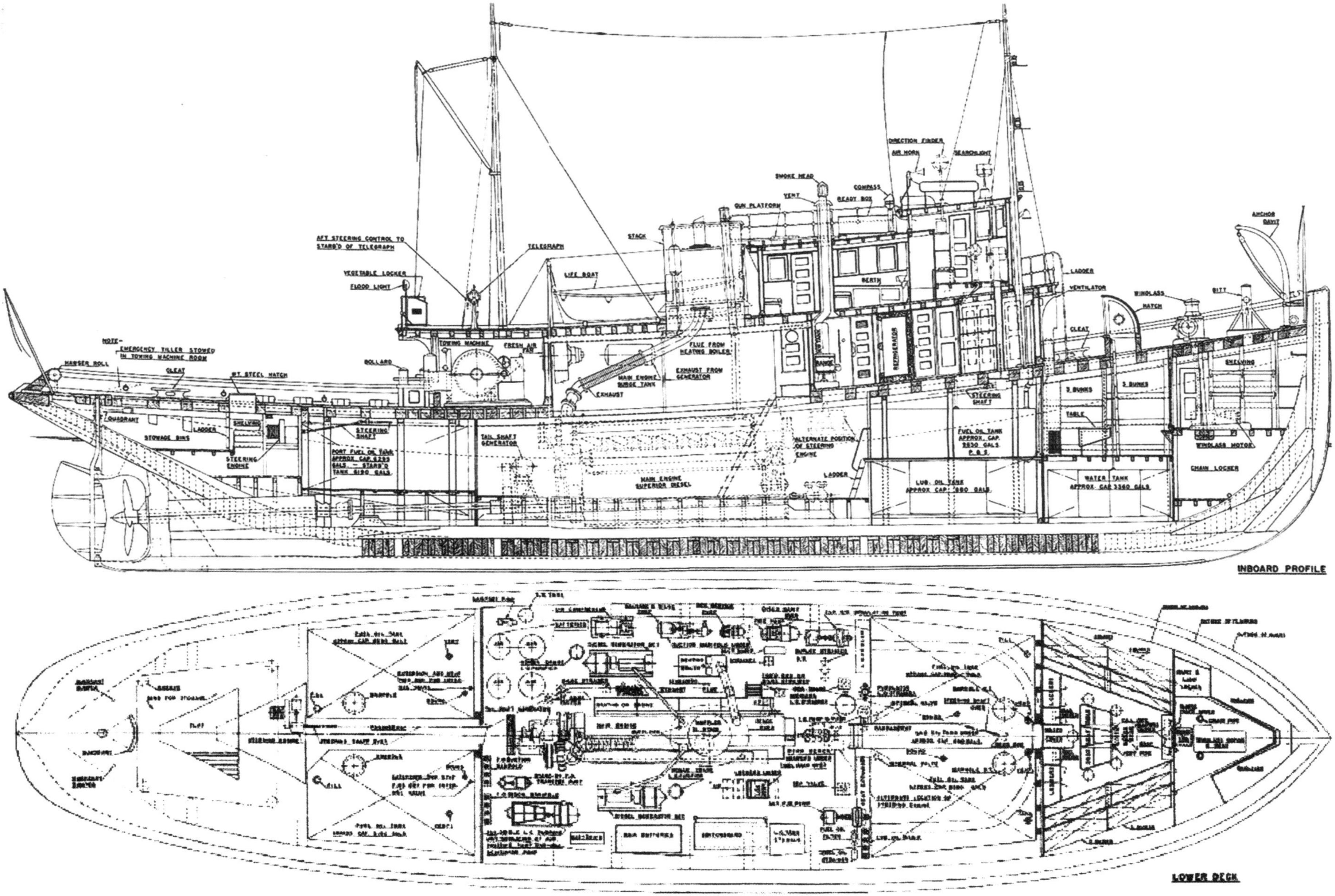

Single screw Mikimiki type tug inboard profile and lower deck arrangement, 1940s.
(Courtesy of U.S. Army Transportation Museum)

54

Most of the earlier Puget Sound vessels were built of wood. Since the 1800s, wood was the material of choice for West Coast boatbuilding because of the availability of Douglas fir, western red cedar, and in Oregon, Port Orford cedar. These cedars are quite rot-resistant. Douglas fir is moderately rot-resistant and long lasting if joints are tight and sealed with compound. In addition to these West Coast woods, white oak is a strong, rot resistant wood suitable for both sawn and steam-bent frames, as well as other framing members. For the YTB illustrated on the next page, white oak was even used for the hull planking.

Many vessels were built almost entirely out of old growth Douglas fir that was readily available. Old growth Douglas fir trees were slow growing, as evidenced by the narrow growth rings to be seen on the end of a sawn log, and the fine wood grain contributed to the excellent strength properties. Because of the large size of these trees, pieces of long length and great width could be gotten for framing and planking timbers.

Below is a midship section drawing of a single-engine Mikimiki type wooden tug, the view oriented so that the viewer is looking aft through the hull. The drawing, as well as other illustrations in this chapter that are credited to the Society of Naval Architects and Marine Engineers, is from the paper "Effect of Deadrise on Loadline Rules" presented before the Society by naval architect H. C. Hanson in the 1960s.

The Mikimiki tugs utilized transverse framing on 23-inch centers. The longitudinally arranged planking could then lie across and be fastened to these frames. Although steam-bent frames were used in smaller vessels, heavily built tugs of most sizes utilized sawn frames as shown here. It can be seen on the drawing that planking, laid fore and aft and thicker than the outer planking, was fastened to the inside of the transverse frames. These inner strakes, called "ceiling," contributed a great deal to the longitudinal strength and stiffness of the hull.

Wooden boat construction would be expensive at today's labor rates due to the time required to cut pieces of wood into such complex shapes and to assemble them with closely fitted joints. In fact, wood suitable for boat building is no longer even readily available in sufficient quantity to support construction of larger vessels such as tugs.

The engine shown in this Mikimiki midship section drawing was an Enterprise direct-reversing, slow-speed diesel that was fastened down to wooden girders of very large size. The earlier Enterprise engines, as well as Superior engines, were built with exposed rocker arm assemblies but, later, utilized valve covers on top of the cylinder heads as shown in this drawing.

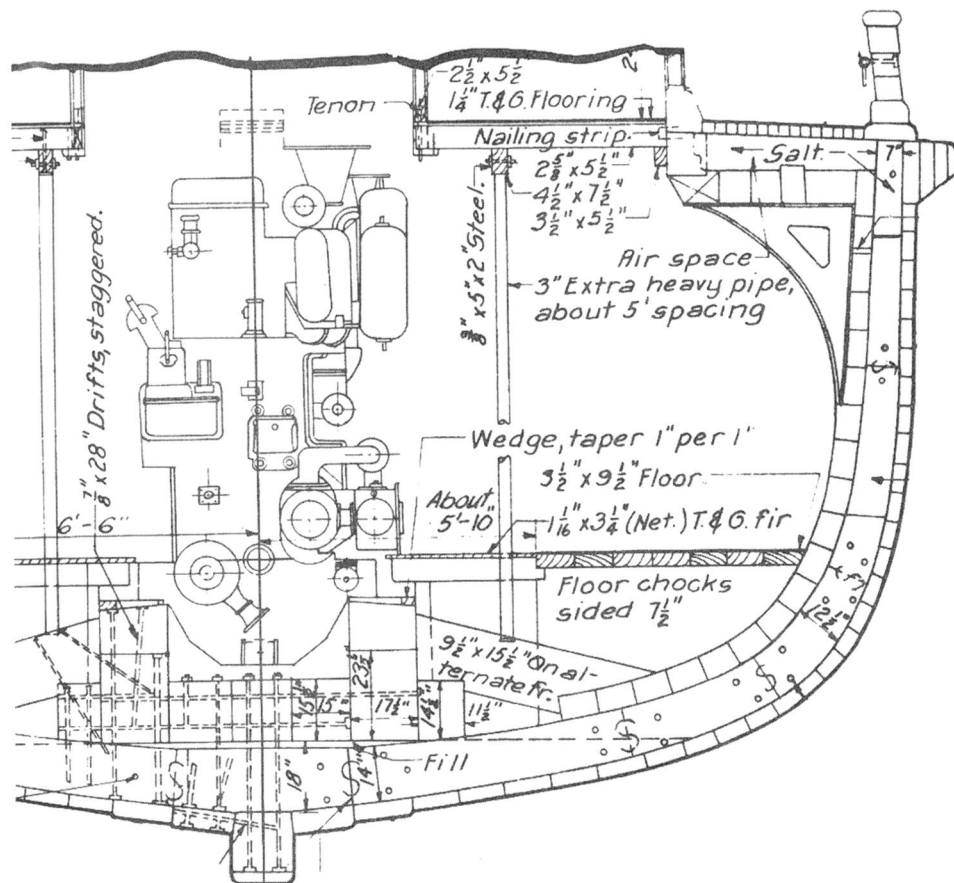

Single screw Mikimiki type tug midship section, 1940s. (With permission of the Society of Naval Architects and Marine Engineers)

55

Dry rot in wood requires at least moderately warm air and, despite the "dry" in the name, a certain amount of moisture to grow. It is important to note that seawater causes little or no rot. Fresh water, as from rain, causes most of the decay whereas the salt in seawater tends to inhibit the introduction of rot. It is important to prevent rainwater from being admitted into a wooden vessel so as to avoid the formation of decay fungus, and if workmanship and maintenance are good, then a wooden ship will last a very long time. Note in the drawing on the previous page that salt was specified to be placed in certain areas of a Mikimiki Class tug's hull as a preservative. Adequate ventilation is also important in a wooden hull to delay fungus growth.

If joints in the hull timbers are made accurately and tight, and if a compound is applied to the faying surfaces of a joint, the wooden hull will serve well. For sealing and preserving wood, red lead, white lead, and petroleum based compounds, as well as zinc, copper, chromium, and arsenic based formulations, were commonly used in the old days. Most of these products are considered to be hazardous materials today.

Wooden construction may have unique problems but so does steel. Instead of the potential rot that can occur in wooden ships, steel vessels are subject to rust. For new construction, a steel hull is sandblasted and then coated with a primer be-

fore painting. As in wooden construction, good ventilation inside the hull and deckhouse is very important. The compartment at the aft end of the hull, called the "lazarette," is a prime candidate for rust formation due to lack of proper ventilation. Air circulation by forced air has even been used for ventilation. Unlike wood, steel tends to "sweat" with moisture condensing from the air in a compartment onto relatively cool surfaces, thus hastening the rusting process.

Fiberglass has not seen extensive use in the construction of tugs although *Suzi*, a small tug owned by Dunlap Towing Company and described later in the book, was built of fiberglass. Like steel, fiberglass tends to sweat also, and in addition, this material does not react well to ultraviolet light from the sun. Fiberglass continues to age over time, which tends to cause it eventually to become somewhat brittle.

Another class of tugs surplused after the end of World War II was the YTB group built in large numbers for the war effort. This picture of a YTB running light is from the treatise by H. C. Hanson referenced on the previous page.

As did the Mikimiki Class of tugs, quite a few of the sturdy YTB towboats entered commercial service on Puget Sound after World War II. No longer needed by the U. S. Government, these tugs were obtained by towing companies at a price far less than replacement cost.

YTB Class tug running light, 1940s.
(With permission of the Society of Naval Architects and Marine Engineers)

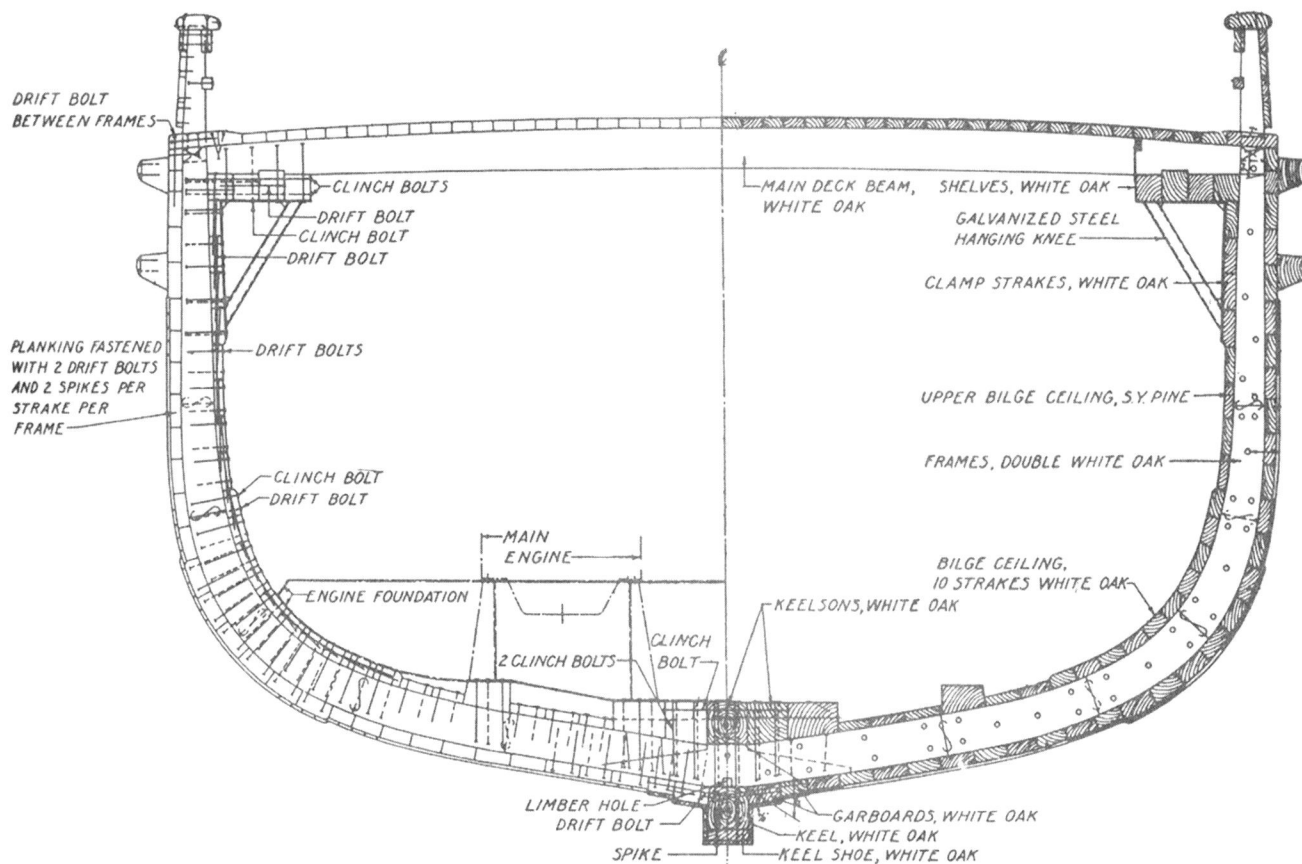

YTB Class tug midship section, 1940s.
(With permission of the Society of Naval Architects and Marine Engineers)

The heavy scantlings making up a tug hull are illustrated by this midship section of a Navy YTB Class tug, of 110-foot overall length. Numerous YTBs were built from this design and, as mentioned previously, many found their way into commercial service after being surplused by the U.S. Government following World War II.

As in the Mikimiki tugs, the YTB hull had transverse sawn frames, usual construction for heavily built hulls; the YTB's frames, though, were of white oak rather than Douglas fir and spaced 24 inches. The hull planking was of 3 1/2 inch thick white oak, while the deck planks were 3 inches thick, just a bit over the 2 3/4 inch thick deck planking of the Mikimiki. Deck planks are sawn quite narrow in width; the Mikimiki deck planks, for example, were only 2 3/4 inch wide. If wide planks were used, the change in width would be too great because of shrinkage due to drying in the sun alternating with swelling due to the presence of rain or seawater. As a result, this repeated shrinking and swelling could cause the seams eventually to open up and admit water.

The large, heavy duty diesel engines used in many of these boats were impressive. Unlike the open-frame steam and early semi-diesel reciprocating engines, these later full-diesel engines had enclosed crankcases so that the crankshaft and connecting rods could not be seen. However, most of the diesel engines did not have valve covers on top of the cylinder heads and so the intake and exhaust valve rocker arms were visible. The intake and exhaust valve rocker arms, aligned along the top of the engine, could be seen oscillating in sequence about the axis of the rocker arm shaft while the engine was turning at a speed of perhaps 300 revolutions per minute, all marvelous to see and hear, and in keeping with the slower pace of those earlier times.

There were numerous manufacturers of this type of heavy duty, slow-turning diesel engine, both foreign and domestic. Typical heavy-duty diesel engines of the four-stroke-cycle type are represented on the following pages as taken from the 1947 catalog of Seattle's Washington Iron Works manufacturing company.

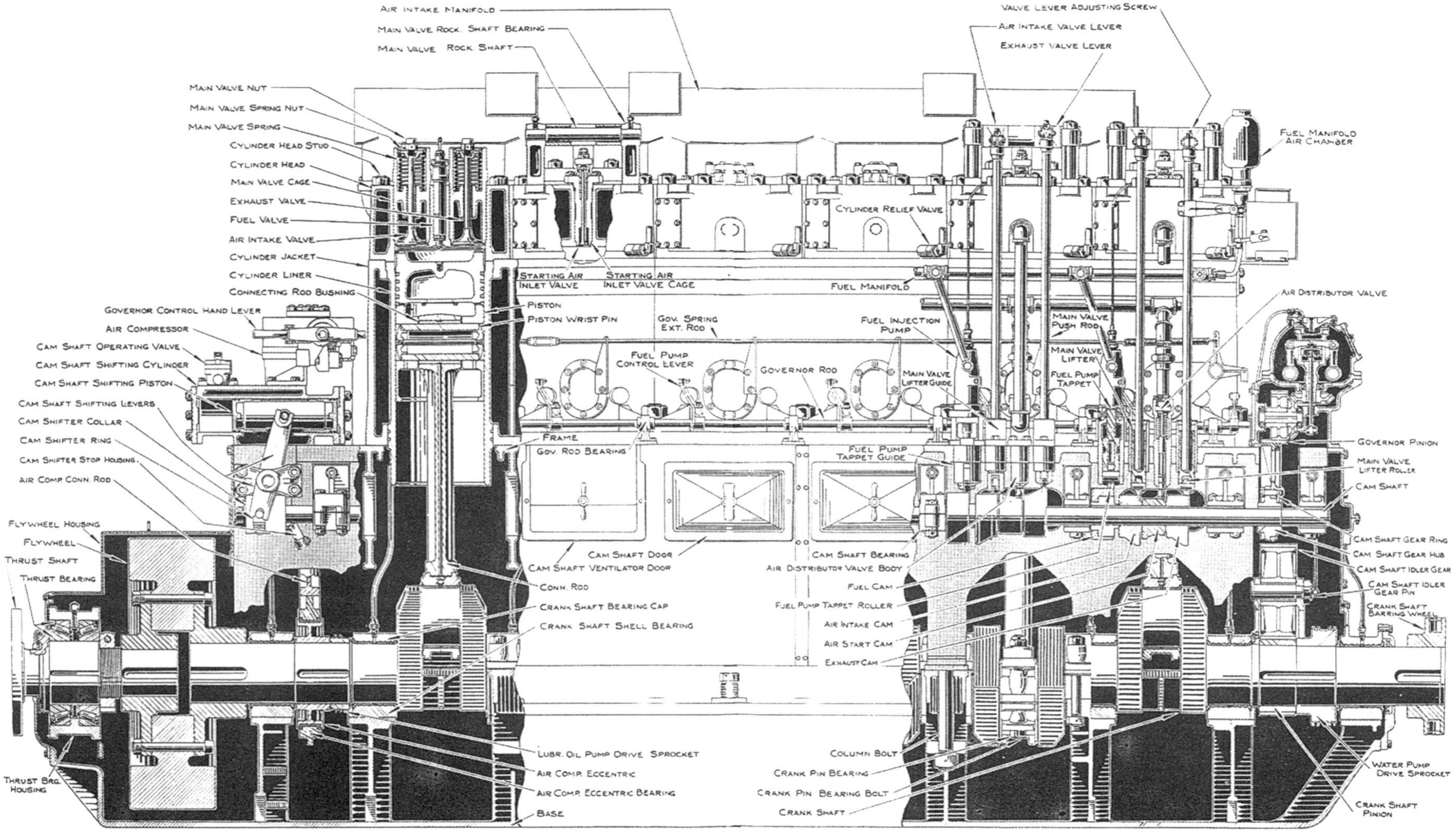

SECTION---DIRECT REVERSING WASHINGTON DIESEL ENGINE

WASHINGTON IRON WORKS

58

Operating side of Six Cylinder 375 H.P. Direct Reversing Marine Engine. Generator mounted above thrust bearing for ships service

Operating side of Four Cylinder Marine Engine equipped with electro-pneumatic control on reverse gear

Operating side of Eight Cylinder 500 H.P. Direct Reversing Marine Engine

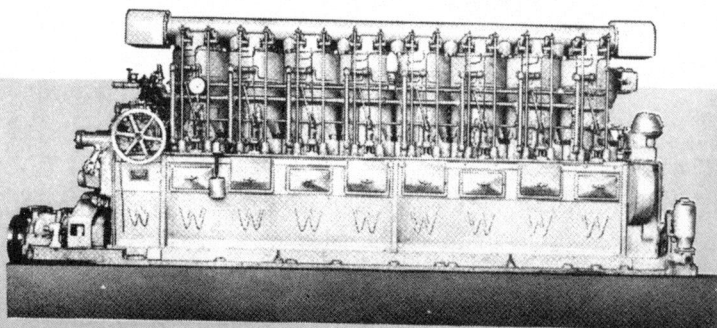

WASHINGTON DIESEL ENGINES

MODEL NUMBER	B. H. P.*	NO. CYLS.	BORE AND STROKE	R. P. M.	WEIGHT DRY MARINE ENGINE	WEIGHT DRY STATIONARY LESS FLYWHEEL
3-125	90	3	9" x 12½"	400	13,500	8,600
4-125	120	4	9" x 12½"	400	14,700	10,300
5-125	150	5	9" x 12½"	400	15,900	13,000
6-125	180-200	6	9" x 12½"	400-450	16,500	13,600
8-125	240-270	8	9" x 12½"	400-450	20,500	18,100
3-13	120	3	10¼" x 13½"	360	15,800	10,450
4-13	160	4	10¼" x 13½"	360	18,500	13,000
6-13	240-265	6	10¼" x 13½"	360-400	23,000	18,000
8-13	320-350	8	10¼" x 13½"	360-400	26,500	25,000
4-15	200	4	11½" x 15"	327	25,500	20,700
6-15	300-330	6	11½" x 15"	327-360	31,500	27,000
8-15	400-440	8	11½" x 15"	327-360	40,000	36,000
6-160	375-400	6	12¾" x 16"	327-360	42,000	38,000
8-160	500-550	8	12¾" x 16"	327-360	53,000	49,000
6-18	450-500	6	14½" x 18"	277-300	62,500	55,000
8-18	600-665	8	14½" x 18"	277-300	80,000	73,000
6-20	600-640	6	16" x 20"	257-277	80,000	71,000
8-20	800-850	8	16" x 20"	257-277	103,000	94,000

* Ratings shown above are for standard engines. Ratings for supercharged engines are available upon request to factory.

WASHINGTON IRON WORKS

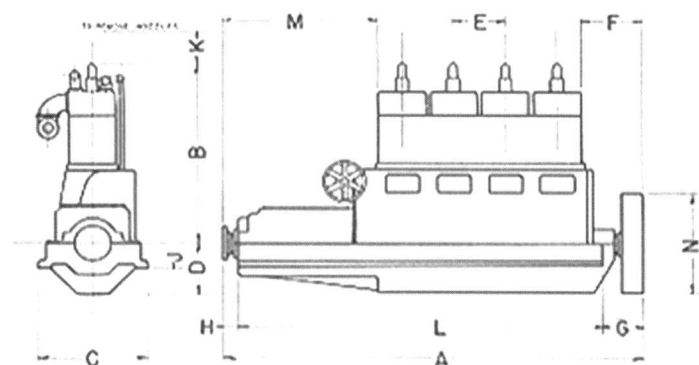

R E V E R S E
G E A R
E N G I N E S

MODEL	A	B	C	D	E	F	G	H	J	K	L	M	N
3C125	10' 7⅞"	5' 6"	3' 1½"	16½"	14½"	2' 3"	11½"	4"	4"	3"	9' 4⅜"	4' 6"	42½"
4C125	11' 10⅜"	5' 6"	3' 1½"	16½"	14½"	2' 3"	11½"	4"	4"	3"	10' 6⅞"	4' 6"	42½"
3C13	11' 4⅜"	5' 10¼"	3' 4"	18"	16½"	2' 4"	12"	4"	5"	3"	10' 0⅜"	4' 7"	42½"
4C13	13' 1½"	5' 10¼"	3' 4"	18"	16½"	2' 4"	12"	4¼"	5"	3"	11' 9¼"	5' 0"	42½"
4C15	14' 1"	6' 6¼"	3' 10"	21"	18½"	2' 6¾"	13"	4½"	5"	4"	12' 7½"	5' 0"	46"

DIRECT REVERSING ENGINES WITH SAILING CLUTCH
(SEE DRAWING ON PAGE 15)

MODEL	A	B	C	D	E	F	G	H	J	K	L	M
5R125C	12' 9¼"	5' 6"	3' 1½"	16½"	14½"	2' 3"	11½"	4½"	4"	3"	11' 5¼"	4' 2"
6R125C	13' 11¾"	5' 6"	3' 1½"	16½"	14½"	2' 3"	11½"	4½"	4"	3"	12' 7¾"	4' 2"
8R125C	16' 4¾"	5' 6"	3' 1½"	16½"	14½"	2' 3"	11½"	4½"	4"	3"	15' 0¾"	4' 2"
5R13C	12' 4¼	5' 10¾"	3' 4"	18¼"	16½"	2' 4"	12"	4½"	4"	3"	10' 11¾"	4' 2½"
6R13C	15' 1¼"	5' 10¾"	3' 4"	18¼"	16½"	2' 4"	12"	4½"	4"	3"	13' 8¾"	4' 2½"
8R13C	18' 4¾"	5' 10¾"	3' 4"	18¼"	16½"	2' 4"	12"	4½"	4"	3"	17' 0¼"	4' 9"
6R15C	17' 6"	6' 6¼"	3' 10"	21"	18½"	2' 5"	12"	5¾"	5"	4"	16' 0¼"	5' 6"
8R15C	21' 1¼"	6' 6¼"	3' 10"	21"	18½"	2' 5"	12"	8¼"	5"	4"	19' 5"	6' 0"
6R160C	18' 11¼"	7' 1"	4' 2"	21½"	20¼"	2' 6"	8¾"	8¼"	5"	4"	17' 6¼"	6' 0"
8R160C	22' 3¾"	7' 1"	4' 2"	21½"	20¼"	2' 6"	8¾"	8¼"	5"	4"	20' 10¾"	6' 0"

GENERAL DIMENSIONS

WASHINGTON IRON WORKS

D I R E C T
R E V E R S I N G
E N G I N E S

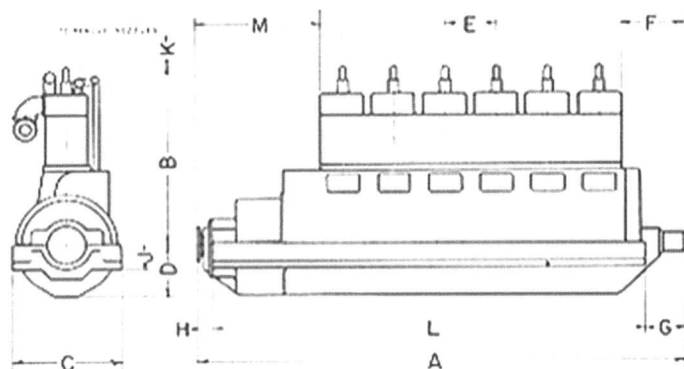

MODEL	A	B	C	D	E	F	G	H	J	K	L	M
5R125	11' 8½"	5' 6"	3' 1½"	16½"	14½"	2' 3"	11½"	4½"	4"	3"	10' 4½"	3' 1½"
6R125	12' 11"	5' 6"	3' 1½"	16½"	14½"	2' 3"	11½"	4½"	4"	3"	11' 7"	3' 1½"
8R125	15' 4"	5' 6"	3' 1½"	16½"	14½"	2' 3"	11½"	4½"	4"	3"	14' 0"	3' 1½"
5R13	12' 8¾"	5' 10¾	3' 4"	18¼"	16½"	2' 4"	12"	4½"	5"	3"	11' 4¾"	3' 3¼"
6R13	14' 1¼"	5' 10¾"	3' 4"	18¼"	16½"	2' 4"	12"	4½"	5"	3"	12' 9¼"	3' 3¼"
8R13	17' 2"	5' 10¾"	3' 4"	18¼"	16½"	2' 4"	12"	6¼"	5"	3"	15' 8¼"	3' 7"
6R15	16' 0"	6' 6¼"	3' 10"	21"	18½"	2' 5"	12"	5¾"	5"	4"	14' 6¼"	4' 0"
8R15	19' 7¼"	6' 6¼"	3' 10"	21"	18½"	2' 5"	12"	8¼"	5"	4"	17' 11"	4' 6"
6R160	17' 5¼"	7' 1"	4' 2"	21½"	20¼"	2' 6"	8¾"	8¼"	5"	4"	16' 0¼"	4' 6"
8R160	20' 9¾"	7' 1"	4' 2"	21½"	20¼"	2' 6"	8¾"	8¼"	5"	4"	19'4¾"	4' 6"
6R18	20' 5¼"	7' 10½"	4' 8"	2' 2"	23½"	2' 11"	12½"	8¼"	6"	4¼"	18' 8½"	5' 4"
8R18	24' 4¼"	7' 10½"	4' 8"	2' 2"	23½"	2' 11"	12½"	8¼"	6"	4¼"	22' 7½"	5' 4"
6R20	22' 6¾"	9' 2"	5' 0"	2' 3"	2' 3¾"	2' 9"	13"	9½"	6"	5"	20' 8¼"	5' 5"
8R20	26' 2¼"	9' 2"	5' 0"	2' 3"	2' 3¾"	2' 9"	13"	9½"	6"	5"	24' 5¾"	5' 5"

The illustrations on the previous pages of the four-stroke-cycle diesel engines that were built to order by Washington Iron Works are representative of this type of heavy-duty diesel engine. These engines were also referred to as "four stroke," or "four cycle" as described by the old hands. Other American manufacturers included Atlas-Imperial, Cooper Bessemer, Enterprise, Nordberg, Superior, and Union.

Diesel engines receive fuel, injected into the combustion chamber under high pressure, just before top dead center at the end of each compression stroke. The fuel and compressed air then burn in the combustion chamber, driving the piston down during the firing, or expansion, stroke. In a four-cycle engine, this power cycle occurs at every other revolution. Alternating with the firing strokes are the exhaust strokes, during which the piston expels the exhaust gases in the course of the piston's upward movement. The heavy rotating flywheel carries the engine revolutions on through the non-firing, or exhaust, revolutions.

Fairbanks-Morse was the most well-known builder of heavy-duty, slow-speed diesel engines utilizing the two-stroke-cycle, frequently referred to as "two stroke" or "two cycle." In a two-cycle engine, fuel is injected at each revolution of the engine, thereby producing a power stroke at each revolution. Exhaust scavenging occurs during the upward stroke of this same engine revolution.

The huge dimensions, as given for the engines in the Washington Iron Works catalog, illustrate why the engine rooms in the earlier tugs were so large, despite the fact that most of the slow-speed engines at the time produced only a few hundred horsepower. In addition to the main engine, space was needed for auxiliary machinery, also.

The 90-horsepower, three-cylinder engine had a 9-inch bore and a 12 1/2-inch stroke, was about 10 feet long, and weighed over 13,000 pounds. This engine was quite similar to, but a bit more powerful than, the three-cylinder Atlas engines used by Delta V. Smyth Tugs and Barges' *Oysterman* and Weyerhaeuser Timber Company's *R. A. McDonald*. The largest Washington engine, utilizing eight cylinders to produce over 800 horsepower, had a bore and stroke of 16 inches by 20 inches, was about 26 feet, long and weighed 103,000 pounds. This engine was quite similar to, but of somewhat more power than, the eight-cylinder Washington engine installed in Foss Launch and Tug Company's *Arthur Foss*.

Because of the low speed of the larger diesel engines, reduction gears were usually not needed. The three-and four-cylinder engines, however, did operate with a clutch and reverse gear. The larger engines with six or more cylinders were directly connected to the propeller so that the propeller rotated in the same direction as the engine at all times. When the direct connected engine was in forward motion, reverse was accomplished by stopping the engine and changing its rotation, and vice versa when going from reverse to forward. The change in direction of the engine's rotation was accomplished by a sliding camshaft, having two sets of lobes, and moved longitudinally by air pressure. Ahead or reverse rotation depended upon which of the two sets of lobes was positioned at the lower end of the valve pushrods. Air at high pressure was then injected directly into the cylinders to rotate the engine for starting.

The early tugs had an engineer in the crew for each watch. When maneuvering, the pilothouse communicated with the engine room via a jingle and gong system so that the engineer, who was below next to the engine, could respond to the audible signals and change speed and rotation of the engine locally. Gradually, the jingle and gong system gave way to wheelhouse controls so that the engine could be operated without need for an engineer to be stationed in the engine room.

A tug, underway several thousand hours per year, must be able to operate for long lengths of time without failure, and the large, slow-speed engines, turning at only 250 to 450 revolutions per minute, could do that. For a towing company, downtime is expensive; a tug is not making money while idle at the moorage. Modern engines, both two-and four-cycle, are manufactured today by various companies, but these engines are smaller in dimensions, higher in speed, and produce more horsepower per pound of weight. The life span is less than for the earlier slow-speed engines, but the life-cycle cost of the newer engines is still favorable. As time went on, the new smaller and lighter-weight engines were being placed into service, and most of the old engines went away along with those who manufactured them.

Boom boats at Anacortes, 1963. (From the author's collection)

No overview of tugs would be complete without a look at the boom boat, the Mighty Mouse of the industry. Also called pond boats, bulldozers, or just plain dozers, they are to be found in large numbers at log ponds and booming areas all around Puget Sound. Starting in the 1950s, the various designs for these little tugs were firming up into more or less a common pattern that evolved through experience.

These mighty mites ride herd on logs when making up rafts and working around the sawmill. In action, these little tugs are dynamic when going through the movements of rapid turning, fast forward, fast reverse, rolling, and pitching while pushing logs around. As small as 16 feet in length or less and having a beam of one half the boat length, these boats are real pumpkin seeds. Some of the earlier dozers were built without a shelter but, for operator comfort during the Pacific Northwest winter weather, a small pilothouse became standard. Many of the boats, including those shown in the above picture, are equipped with a tow bitt and are, therefore, capable of towing as well as pushing logs. The pilothouse aft bulkhead is simply left open so that the operator, who is

both skipper and deckhand, has quick access to the aft deck when towing logs.

The relatively deep draft of three feet or more permits swinging a propeller of two feet or larger in diameter. A dozer could have 100 horsepower driving the propeller through a 3:1 or 4:1 reduction gear, which provides a lot of thrust for handling logs. A shroud or basket is frequently installed around the propeller, or "wheel," as it is commonly called, to protect the blades of the propeller in case a log finds its way under the stern.

While some of these boats have been built of wood, most are heavily constructed of welded steel, with the hull plating commonly being 1/2 inch thick laid over substantial frames. The boats take a real beating and, as a consequence, the hull plating may suffer denting over time. On the other hand, the seams of a planked wooden hull could start to open up from this rough treatment so steel is the usual material of choice for the hull. Steel also became more economical than wood for construction because the material cost is lower than that of boatbuilding quality wood, and using welding and flame cutting, the fabrication cost is less than it is for wood.

SHELTON TOWING COMPANY
Shelton

There was a lot of towboat activity in southern Puget Sound during the earlier days. Over Shelton way, Foss tugs towed barges in and out of Shelton and handled log rafts that were stored in Mud Bay and at Kamilche in Little Skookum Inlet. The Simpson mill's own fleet of small tugs and boom boats attended to that company's log pond. Shelton Towing Company boats juggled scows for the Simpson mill and made sure a plentiful supply of logs was floating in the log pond for sorting and use by the Rayonier pulp plant.

Shelton Towing Company owned three tugs: *Hemlock*, *Spruce*, and *Skookum Logger*. Shelton Towing was started in 1945 by local Shelton resident Frank Wolf, and company colors were black hull with buff and white deckhouse. Earlier, Albert "Bert" Hurst, the father of Frank's wife, Elizabeth, more familiarly known as "Betty" to her friends, had owned two work boats, *Morning Star* and *Dumor T*, in the Shelton area. Frank Wolf operated *Dumor T* (the name derived from the phrase "do more things") for a time before acquiring other boats for his Shelton Towing.

The company's operations were headquartered at the residence of Frank and Betty, located on the southern shore of Hammersley Inlet. Moorage was in place for the tugs at their residence, and much of the maintenance could also be done there. Routine underwater hull maintenance that would periodically be required was done with the boats high and dry on the beach between tides.

All three of the company towboats were powered by Caterpillar diesel engines: *Hemlock* with 44 horsepower, *Spruce* with 77 horsepower, and *Skookum Logger* having 170 horsepower. *Hemlock* was a small boat that provided assistance as needed when handling tows in limited space. *Spruce* was skippered by Randolph "Randy" Estvold, also a Shelton resident, while *Skookum Logger* was under the charge of Frank Wolf.

As an aid when pushing logs and boomsticks, each tug was outfitted with what is called a "comb" or "hob," a steel bar with teeth on it, attached in a vertical position on the stem at the waterline. Log handling tugs are frequently equipped with this serrated bar so that when nudging against logs or boomsticks the fitting's teeth can bite into the bark or wood and prevent the boat's bow from slipping and moving sideways.

The good-looking, 33-foot long *Spruce*, pictured below, was built of wood to Frank Wolf's specifications by Tregoning at Seattle in 1948.

Spruce, n.d. (Courtesy of Elizabeth Wolf)

Please Remit to

SIMPSON LOGGING COMPANY

Simpson
QUALITY SINCE 1895

1010 WHITE BUILDING • SEATTLE 1, WASHINGTON

SHIPPED FROM **Mill # 1, Shelton, Wash.**

INV. NO. **1-4698**

ORDER NO.
CUST'R ORDER NO.

INVOICE TO **Shelton Towing Co.**
Rt 3, Box 292
Shelton, Wash.

Date **Oct 14, 1952**
Car No.
Routing

SHIPPED TO

PRICES F. O. B.

Rate
Terms: Cash

SALESMAN: Eby

Interest at legal rates charged after maturity

Ticket No 15842	B & Btr Clear, VG Fir S4S			
2x4-R/L		1200'	140.00	168.00
2x5-R/L		2150'	140.00	301.00
3x12-2/24	B & Btr. Clear, Fir S4S	144'	140.00	20.16
4x6-22/14		616'	140.00	86.24
4x6-5/20		200'	140.00	28.00
4x8-2/24		128'	140.00	17.92
4x12-4/18		288'	140.00	40.32
5x12-4/20		400'	140.00	56.00
5x14-1/16		93'	140.00	13.02
9x11-1/36		297'	175.00	51.98
10x14-1/36		420'	175.00	73.50
10x16-1/24		320'	175.00	56.00
12x14-1/12		168'	175.00	29.40
6x12-1/12 1/18 1/20 1/24 1/26		600'	175.00	105.00
Ticket No 15843	B & Btr Clear Fir S4S			
8x12-1/12		96'	175.00	16.80
10x14-2/28		653'	175.00	114.28
2x4-R/L	#1 (25%#2) HorM Fir	503'	76.00	38.23
2x6-10/14	#1 (25%#2) Fir S4S	140'	75.00	10.50
2x12-R/L	#1 (25%#2) Fir S4S	1200'	75.00	90.00
		9616'		1316.35
	3% Sales Tax			39.49
				1355.84

We interpret these prices not to be over our
maxima under C.P.R.-128 of 3-18-52.

Any transportation tax collected by the carrier is in addition to the amount shown on the Invoice, and is for the account of the consignee.
Grades, Terms and conditions of sale in accordance with Association Rules governing item shipped unless otherwise stated.
Claims must be filed within 5 days after delivery date, supported with affidavit if for shortage. Our receipt from Transportation Company in good
order constitutes Delivery. Any claim for damage, breakage or loss in transit must be made against Transportation Company.
Seller agrees that this material has been produced in compliance with the "Fair Labor Standard Act of 1938."

MANUFACTURERS OF PLYWOOD, DOORS, LUMBER AND INSULATING BOARD PRODUCTS

Invoice for Douglas fir used in the construction of *Skookum Logger*, 1952.
(Courtesy of Elizabeth Wolf)

Skookum Logger was completed by Sagstad Shipyard at Seattle in 1953, and the design was by Ira Libby of that yard while construction was led by Howard Sagstad. In designing the boat, Ira relied primarily upon a model that he had built, and therefore, few drawings were necessary for fabrication and assembly by these professional boat builders. *Skookum Logger* was 39 feet long, about 6 feet longer than Shelton Towing's *Spruce* that had been built five years earlier by Tregoning. At about 13 1/2 feet in breadth, *Skookum Logger* was a beamy little towboat.

Skookum Logger under construction at Sagstad Shipyard, 1953. (Courtesy of Elizabeth Wolf)

Skookum Logger, Frank Wolf at the wheel, with a log tow in Hammersley Inlet, 1953.
(Courtesy of Elizabeth Wolf)

Referring to the invoice, shown previously, for lumber shipped from Simpson's Mill Number 1 at Shelton, almost 10,000 board feet of quality Douglas fir were used in the construction of *Skookum Logger*, in addition to other species of wood required for the boat. As ordered from the mill, the price for the Douglas fir used in the construction of *Skookum Logger* averaged about 14 cents per board foot in 1952; for comparable quality lumber, the mill price at the present time would be many, many times the 1952 price. In addition, the Washington state sales tax was 3 percent at that time over 50 years ago, compared to a tax today of about three times that rate.

The cost would vary with the dimensions of the purchased lumber, the price being higher for wide boards. A lumber supplier might have a limited quantity of clear Douglas fir in stock for only the smaller dimensions, and therefore, an order might have to be placed with a mill which, in fact, is what Frank Wolf did. For *Skookum Logger*, a considerable amount of wood in sizes up to 16 inches in width was required.

These large sizes, particularly for vertical grain lumber, would have been cut from great trees that no longer exist in the numbers that could be found in the forests of many decades ago. Today, therefore, a search would have to be made for a source,

and the larger size of Douglas fir lumber, if available, would command a very high price.

As shown in the photo below, *Skookum Logger* and *Spruce* were careened on the southern shore of Hammersley Inlet while undergoing some bottom maintenance between tides. At high tide, once more afloat, the tugs were ready to go back to work. The Wolf residence at this waterside spot, on a point of land with a small inlet alongside, is at left in the picture.

Frank Wolf passed on in 1962. Betty Wolf's brother, John Hurst, an experienced boatman, then skippered *Skookum Logger* for two years until the tug was sold to a new owner in Alaska. John eventually took over as captain aboard Manke Lumber Company's tug *Danielle*, at the time brand new out of the Nichols yard on Whidbey Island. Randy Estvold, whose background also contained a wealth of experience on the water for Foss Launch and Tug Company, including a good many years as captain aboard *Foss No. 16*, purchased Shelton Towing Company and *Spruce*. In the process, Randy replaced the tug's four-cylinder Caterpillar diesel with a six-cylinder Cat, which more than doubled the horsepower to 180. With the repowered *Spruce*, Randy continued on with towing assignments for Rayonier and Simpson Logging as he had been doing for a number of years.

Skookum Logger, left, and *Spruce*, right, on the beach for hull maintenance, n.d.
(Courtesy of Elizabeth Wolf)

CAPITAL CITY TUG COMPANY
Olympia

The location of Capital City Tug Company was at the foot of Thurston Avenue in Olympia, and perched on pilings there, the diminutive building in the photo at right was commonly referred to as "Pete's shack." Pete, who I knew but not his last name, worked as a watchman at Capital City Tug, and this was his home. A wooden walkway in front of Pete's shack provided access to the gangway that led down to the company's tug moorage. Some years later, this building, by then vacant, became the office for the ChrisCraft yacht sales agency.

Capital City Tug Company was founded by Captain Volney Young, and the firm usually operated four tugs in Olympia. *Malamute*, *Mizpah*, and *Virgo Young* were mostly assigned to harbor work at Olympia while *Edward A. Young*, the largest

**Pete's shack at Olympia, 1961.
(Courtesy of Anna J. Knutsen)**

tug, was used for towing jobs to other ports around Puget Sound. The company colors for the boats were black hull, buff and white deckhouse, and buff exhaust stack. *Edward A. Young*, pictured below, was 59 feet long and built of wood at Tacoma in 1926.

Edward A. Young.

69

Capital City Tug was eventually acquired by Tacoma Tug and Barge Company, and after the change in ownership, some of the boats had a large white letter T against a black triangular shaped background on the stack signifying Tacoma Tug and Barge Company, described later in the book. The tugs were used primarily for the towing of logs, boomsticks, and barges.

The 50-foot wooden towboat *Mizpah*, shown at the Capital City Tug moorage in the photo at right, was completed as a small freight and passenger steamer at Olympia in 1905 to the order of Captain Young. Captain Young operated the boat on a run between Olympia and Kamilche, with stops at Hunter Point and Oyster Bay, as well as anywhere else along the route when hailed by someone who had been transported out from the beach in a rowboat.

Originally, *Mizpah* carried freight on the main deck and passengers in an upper deckhouse. *Mizpah* burned to the waterline in 1915. The steamer was then converted for use as a tug, as was done for many other freight and passenger steamboats. The tug's deckhouse as shown here had been shortened from the original house to provide additional deck space aft for towing work.

Mizpah at the Capital City Tug Company moorage in Olympia, 1939.
(From the author's collection)

At the time of the photo, *Mizpah* was powered with a Fairbanks-Morse diesel engine of 140 horsepower. Olympia residents with a practiced ear would know, even at night, that *Mizpah* was working in the harbor by recognizing the familiar sound of the engine exhaust with its rhythmic "plunk–plunk–plunk–plunk …"

In the background of this photo, a dredge, with its bucket raised, can be seen. The Delta V. Smyth Tugs and Barges moorage was located on the far side of the dredge. Beyond the Smyth moorage, the Washington Veneer Company sawmill conveyor, overhanging the water, is visible. The conveyor was used to load sawdust, used as hog fuel, into scows.

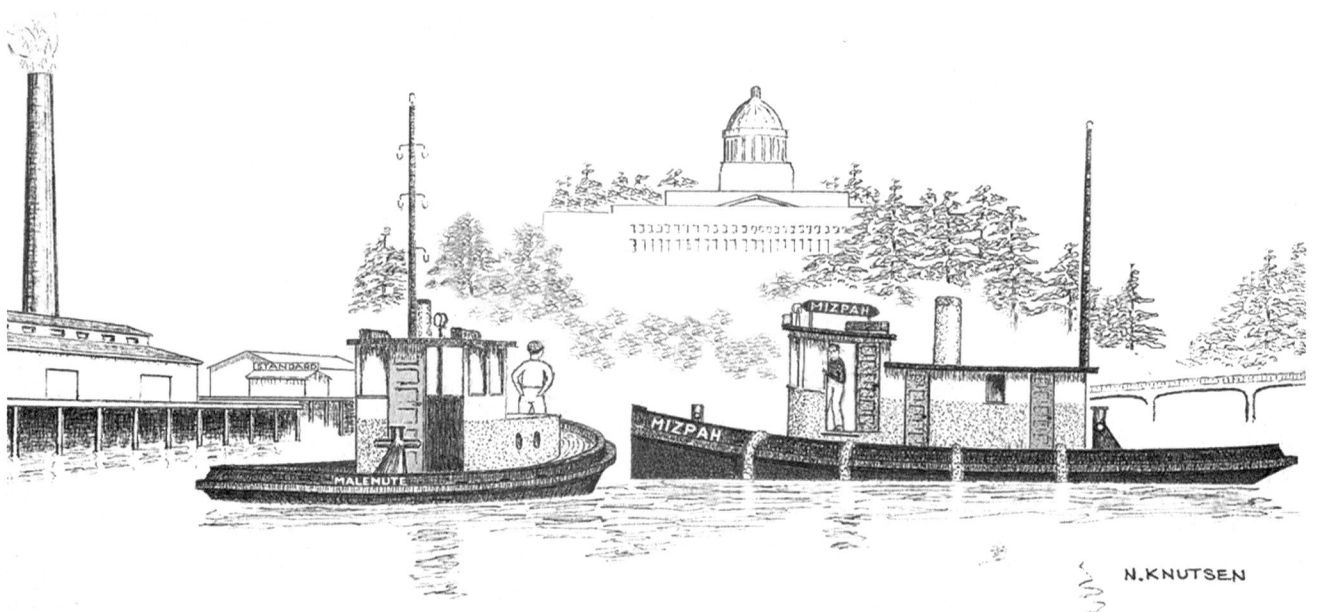

Malamute and Mizpah at Olympia.

Virgo Young was a busy tug working around Olympia's harbor. A 44-foot wooden boat, *Virgo Young* was built as *Brown's Bay* at Winslow in 1912. The hull was built with a raised deck forward, which maximized the interior space in this modest sized tug.

When handling lines in a busy situation, caution by the deckhand would have to have been exercised when negotiating the high step in the deck. Access to the engine room was through the doorway at the aft end of the trunk cabin, a typical arrangement. In later years, *Virgo Young* was powered with a 165-horsepower General Motors 6-71 diesel engine.

In the photo above, *Virgo Young* was between towing assignments at Capital City Tug Company's Olympia moorage. Tacoma Tug and Barge Company's logo can be seen on the side of the exhaust stack, which indicates the affiliation between the two companies. Note the Olympia Sand and Gravel Company sign in the background, just above the tug's pilothouse.

In the photo below, *Virgo Young* was heading south, without a tow, along Olympia's West Side

Virgo Young at the Capital City Tug Company moorage, 1939.
(From the author's collection)

on a quiet, foggy September day. The fenders hanging on the side were woven from recycled Manila lines that had been worn and frayed from previous use as mooring and towing lines, a commonly used method of cushioning against bumps and bruises that a tug is constantly subjected to.

What some call "portholes" are visible on the side of the hull forward. In the marine business, the more appropriate term used for these fittings would be "portlights." Portlights may be of the opening type or fixed, depending upon whether or not they are to be used for air ventilation, in addition to admitting light. To avoid admitting sea water, the portlights located on the sides of *Virgo Young*'s hull forward would have been fixed lights.

Reliable Welding Works, at the time of the photo operating as a shipyard, is at right in the background of this photo. Three months after this photo was taken, the Japanese bombed Pearl Harbor, and the United States was drawn into World War II, a conflict that had already involved many other countries. For quite a few years, Reliable Welding Works was busy building steel boats during and after the war.

Virgo Young running light at Olympia, 1941.
(From the author's collection)

DELTA V. SMYTH TUGS AND BARGES COMPANY
Olympia

Left to right, *Oysterman*, *Sand Man*, and *Audrey* at the Delta V. Smyth Tugs and Barges moorage in Olympia, 1948. (From the author's collection)

The headquarters of Delta V. Smyth Tugs and Barges was located a couple of blocks north of Capital City Tug Company at Columbia and B in Olympia. This photo, a view looking toward the east, shows the company facilities and, left to right, the tugs *Oysterman*, *Sand Man*, and *Audrey*. Company colors for the tugs were black hull, buff and white deckhouse, and buff stack, quite similar to the colors for Capital City Tug Company's boats. A grid, out of sight behind *Oysterman* in the photo, was used for hauling and performing maintenance work on scows. The office and the gangway access to the moorage is in view behind *Sand Man*. The workshop, warehouse, and marine railway used for hauling the boats out of the water for maintenance is just to the right of *Audrey*.

The various industrial firms and businesses, such as Standard Oil company, whose tanks can be seen in the background at left, that were in the vicinity of Smyth's facility are all gone now. Many years after this photo was taken, these companies, as well as the Smyth tug moorage, were replaced by the Farmers Market, Percival Landing park and boardwalk, a hotel, apartment residences, offices, shops, restaurants, and yacht moorages.

Delta V. Smyth was associated with commercial boats for about 50 years. Oyster growing was, and still is, an important industry in the inlets around the Olympia area, and Delta Smyth worked for the Brenner Oyster Company in the early part of the last century. Brenner ordered a new wooden tender to be built for working at the oyster beds, and so the 39-foot register length *Oysterman* was launched at Tacoma in 1913.

Later, Smyth purchased *Oysterman* from Brenner, and after adding a low bulwark and making a few other changes, he began using the boat for towing purposes. Over the years, Smyth owned many different tugs, the number and type of boats varying according to need. *Oysterman*, though, stayed with Smyth on a continuous basis after the towboat was originally acquired by his towing company. *Oysterman* was sometimes referred to as the "cute tug" by Olympia kids and, in truth, the little towboat did bear a resemblance to a tug that might be found in a child's storybook.

A gravel scow on the grid at Delta V. Smyth Tugs and Barges in Olympia.

The grid that was mentioned on the previous page, used for scow maintenance that needed to be performed out of the water, consisted of pilings driven into the mud over which large wooden cross-timbers were fastened, thus forming a horizontal support. At high tide, a scow that had been scheduled for upkeep was moved by one of the tugs to a position over the grid. As the tide ebbed, the scow settled onto the grid, and the beach gradually became exposed.

With the beach partially exposed, the workers in rubber boots then waded into the mud beneath the scow and scraped seaweed and barnacles from the bottom. As the water receded further with the outgoing tide, the crew members continued to work their way toward the water's edge while cleaning the bottom of the scow. Next, a fire was built on a large piece of sheet metal, and two people walked while carrying this fire under the scow to warm and dry the bottom.

Antifouling paint was then applied to the bottom of the scow, the crew members working their way back up the muddy beach as the tide was coming in. The antifouling coating normally applied was, and still is, a paint containing tiny copper particles in suspension, which impedes the growth of sea life. This process was all completed during the tide change in a time span of several hours. At or near high tide, one of the tugs moved in and towed the scow, once again afloat, over to the storage area near Ellis Cove or took it to an assigned location for loading with cargo.

Over time, in salt water, the immersed surface of a vessel will acquire a growth of sea life even though the underwater surface has been coated with antifouling paint. This growth consists mostly of barnacles and seaweed and for best speed through the water, the bottom of a vessel must be cleaned periodically.

Due to "resistance," a floating object naturally shows some reluctance to being moved through the water. Total resistance is mostly made up of wave-making resistance and friction resistance. The growth of sea life produces a roughness on the underwater surface of a vessel's hull, which causes a dramatic increase in the friction portion of resistance. This added friction resistance, in turn, increases the effort needed to move a vessel through the water, hence, the need for periodic cleaning of the underwater portion of a hull. In particular, the total resistance of a barge, which has a flat bottom and is towed at a moderate speed, is mostly made up of friction resistance, which is increased by a layer of sea life on the bottom.

Delta Smyth's marine railway and scow grid were the only such facilities south of Tacoma that could handle the weight of a towing company's tugs and barges. Joe Ritner's boat shop on East Bay Drive in Olympia utilized a marine railway, but the capacity was insufficient for hauling these kinds of heavy loads. The McNeil Island federal penitentiary was in possession of a high-capacity marine railway, but it was used strictly for hauling their own floating equipment.

Sand Man, Oysterman, and Audrey, left to right, at the Delta V. Smyth moorage in Olympia, 1939. (From the author's collection)

Sand Man, one of the most well known tugs operating in southern Puget Sound and shown at left in the photo above, was a 49-foot wooden tug built at Tacoma in 1910. *Sand Man* was originally powered with a heavy-duty 50-horsepower Frisco Standard gasoline engine and, later, was repowered with a 100-horsepower Fairbanks-Morse diesel engine. Still later, after many more years, a higher speed 100-horsepower Caterpillar diesel engine was installed in *Sand Man*.

The unique towing winch can be seen in the photo above. This winch was powered by a Stanley Steamer steam automobile engine converted to run on compressed air.

Most of Smyth's tugs did not use a towing winch but, instead, were outfitted with a large bitt secured to the aft deck. A tug with a winch utilizes wire rope wound onto the drum as a towline, and this wire can be let out to lengthen the towline or reeled in to shorten or retrieve the line. A tug utilizing a bitt works with Manila or synthetic rope as a towline, the line being wrapped onto the bitt. A tug outfitted with a bitt is sometimes referred to as a "hawser tug."

In the photo below, Delta Smyth's tug *Sand Man* was alongside a loaded wooden gravel scow off Devil's Head and heading for Johnson Point on the way to Olympia after having loaded at the Pioneer Sand and Gravel pit located near Steilacoom. The one-way distance by water between Olympia and Steilacoom is approximately 25 miles, and at the location shown in the picture, Sand Man was nearly halfway home.

Sand Man with a loaded gravel scow off Devil's Head, 1947. (From the author's collection)

The elapsed time for a round trip between Olympia and Steilacoom with a scow could be around twelve hours, more or less, depending upon the tide, tug's installed horsepower, and length of time needed to load at the pit. The duration of the trip could be somewhat unpredictable if other tugs and barges were already out ahead at the pit. A queue consisting of tugs and barges waiting to take on sand and gravel might have formed at the pit, and the extra time spent while waiting for others to load would delay the return to Olympia.

In the photo below, Delta Smyth's tug *Sand Man* was hauled out on the marine railway at the company's moorage in Olympia. Evident in the photo, *Sand Man*'s hull was designed with a greater hull depth than many towboats of comparable size.

The pair of horizontal lines visible on the hull and straddling the water line mark the upper and lower edges of sheathing, installed on most wooden towboats to protect the planking from abrasion. The material used for sheathing was iron bark, a very dense and hard wood. *Sandman*'s deckhouse doors, except for the pilothouse doors, were built in two halves, upper and lower, known as Dutch doors, a common feature aboard towboats. Opening the upper portion of the door provides ventilation and additional natural light, while the lower portion, when left closed, prevents water from splashing into the deckhouse.

Routine maintenance consisted of cleaning and repainting the bottom and topsides of the hull, painting the deckhouse, tightening or repacking the shaft log gland as needed, tightening or repacking the rudder stock stuffing box, and checking, repairing, or replacing the through-hull fittings and valves. Not needed so often would be work such as recaulking deck and hull seams, refastening hull planks to the framing, repairing or replacing canvas covering on the deckhouse top, and installing new bearings for the propeller shaft and rudder stock. Mechanical maintenance of a main engine and auxiliary equipment could either be performed on the railway or done while the boat was afloat.

The marine railway consisted of two heavy, sloping timbers supported by pilings. A pair of railroad tracks was attached to the upper surface of these two timbers, and a steel-wheeled platform or cradle could travel on these rails into and out of the water. Out of sight behind the building at right was a winch that moved the cradle by means of a wire rope. Because of differences in size and hull shape, each boat to be hauled required a different wood blocking arrangement on the cradle to fit the particular hull.

Sand Man hauled out on Delta Smyth's marine railway, 1948. (From the author's collection)

The buildings shown in the photo on the previous page housed space for warehousing material and equipment and also provided workshop space. Clem Keegan was the port engineer for Delta V. Smyth Tugs and Barges and had, for a time, been a captain aboard Smyth's tugs. The title port engineer was commonly used as a designation for someone like Clem who was responsible for rebuilding and maintaining the tugs and other floating equipment in the fleet. Clem lived a few miles north of Olympia at Gull Harbor.

Audrey was purchased by Delta Smyth in 1939, and the boat was partially dismantled and in a state of disrepair at that time, as shown in a photo later in this chapter. The 64-foot wooden vessel was built at Tacoma in 1909 as a passenger and freight steamer for use on the Wollochet Bay route. Following the purchase of *Audrey*, Smyth refurbished the boat with a new deckhouse and new outfitting items, as shown in the photo below. The tug's propulsion was furnished by a 200-horsepower Fairbanks-Morse diesel engine.

The new house was shaped and built with a pleasing rake as shown in the photo below, and the deck outfit was all arranged for towing service. The generous hull freeboard, no doubt, created a bit of an inconvenience for deckhands when it was necessary to move between the relatively high deck and a low-on-the water log raft.

In this photo, hanging beneath the aft overhang of the main deckhouse roof are the oil lamps, which were available for placement at the four corners of barges and log rafts to serve as navigation lights for operation at night, as described in the chapter "A Deckhand's Recollections of Life aboard the Earlier Tugs." An anchor handling windlass is visible on the fore deck. *Audrey* was well equipped for towing, and the outfit included a winch installed on the aft deck, rather than a bitt, for use with a wire rope towline.

At right in the background of this picture, just above the towing winch, a hopper used for loading dump trucks is just visible at Olympia Sand and Gravel Company.

Audrey at the Delta V. Smyth moorage in Olympia, 1941. (From the author's collection)

Many of the earlier towboats did not have the more modern, sophisticated towing winches, such as those manufactured by Markey in Seattle or Almon Johnson in New York. These items of machinery were quite expensive, and not all of the tug companies had sufficient funds to purchase new towing winches. Hence, a variety of towing winches sometimes found their way aboard tugs to do the job of handling the towline. Some winches were built by the towing companies themselves using parts and assemblies from equipment that had been used in other applications, such as logging. Winches were also built from scratch by a towing company if the capability was there to do that.

Like *Nile*'s towing winch, as described earlier in these pages, *Audrey*'s winch was not equipped with such advances as a level wind that would have given the wire rope towline the direction needed for spooling onto the winch drum in a neat and orderly manner when being hauled in. If not fed through a level wind, the cable tends to pile up on a winch drum in a random manner when being taken in. But *Audrey*'s towing winch did have a quaint appearance with its decorative curved and scalloped steel frame. Mounted on the port side of the towing winch was a spool-shaped feature known as a "gypsy," which, driven through a clutch by the same shaft that the towline drum was mounted on, could be used for warping lines.

Oysterman, pictured at right, was operated as a day boat by a crew consisting of the skipper and a deckhand. In service on short tows, the little tug did not require much in the way of amenities for the crew. However, a stove was installed in *Oysterman*'s pilothouse which provided warmth during the cold months,

and the stove could also be used to brew coffee or heat simple meals. Most of the small day boats, though, such as Weyerhaeuser's logging tug *R. A. McDonald*, did not have heating for the interior of the deckhouse, except for whatever warmth flowed from the engine room.

Tugs can take quite a beating at times, hence, bumpers are usually installed at the bow and stern, as well as along the sides. The fender wrapped around *Oysterman*'s horseshoe stern was made from used automobile and truck tires. This heavy fender was made of rectangular pieces that had been cut from tires and then laced together by steel rods threaded through the pieces of rubber. The entire assembly was then attached to the hull. A similar bumper at the forward end of the hull, covering most of the stem, was installed, also.

Oysterman utilized Manila side fenders braided from used and worn Manila mooring and towing lines, but many tugs used, and still use, automobile tires. Very large tugs could put discarded truck, tractor, or aircraft tires to work for this purpose.

Oysterman at the log storage.

In addition to replaceable bow, stern, and side fenders, wood sheathing was frequently installed to protect against the wear and tear that the hull side planking would have otherwise endured when the boat was moving alongside logs and floats. This sheathing, of strong and dense iron bark as previously scribed for *Sandman*, was attached to the sides of the hull. The sheathing installation was made to cover an area that extended from just above the waterline to just below the waterline.

The sheathing strakes on the side of the hull were bedded in against and fastened to the hull planking but were arranged parallel to the waterline rather than following the curve of the hull planks. The tough wood that was employed for sheathing had a long life even though it was obliged to do its job under harsh conditions.

In the photo below, *Oysterman* was hauled out for maintenance on the marine railway at Delta V. Smyth Tugs and Barges in Olympia. In preparation for receiving a tug to be hauled, the cradle was rolled down the track to a location such that the submergence depth in the water was sufficient that the boat, having several feet of draft, could move in over the cradle. The cradle was then hauled back up the incline by means of a wire rope and engine-powered winch.

The upright timbers braced to the cradle were tall enough that they projected up above the surface of the water when the cradle was submerged. These acted as guides for use when piloting the boat into position over the submerged cradle and, braced strongly enough, could also be used to keep the boat from tipping over sidewise until blocking, as needed, could be placed under the hull.

The small to medium sizes of towboats could be handled by this marine railway, but a much larger, heavier tug, such as *Nile*, would have been beyond the size and load capacity of the cradle. In addition, hauling a towboat such as *Nile* would have sorely taxed the capability of the winch to pull the heavy weight up the incline.

Oysterman on Delta Smyth's marine railway at Olympia, 1942. (From the author's collection)

A view of the interior of *Oysterman*'s wheelhouse is shown in the photo at right. Forward and reverse gears were operated by turning the handwheel, at right in the photo. Just beyond the handwheel was a stove for providing welcome warmth in the pilothouse when the weather was cool and damp. For many years, *Oysterman*'s engine was a three-cylinder heavy duty Atlas Imperial diesel engine of 50 horsepower.

In the photo below, *Oysterman* and *Ketchikan* were between towing jobs and tied up at the float. The bow of *Audrey*, recently purchased by Delta Smyth, is at left in the photo. *Ketchikan* was a 52-foot wooden tug built at Ballard in 1906. In the photo,

Interior of *Oysterman*'s wheelhouse, 1939.
(From the author's collection)

Ketchikan was displaying a newly constructed deckhouse. Smyth operated the tug for several years until he sold the boat in the 1940s.

***Audrey*'s bow, left, *Oysterman*, center, and *Ketchikan*, right, at Delta Smyth's moorage in Olympia, 1939.**
(From the author's collection)

Ketchikan and *Oysterman* at Delta Smyth's moorage in Olympia, 1939. (From the author's collection)

In the photo above, *Ketchikan* was at the Delta V. Smyth Tugs and Barges moorage between assignments. *Oysterman* is at right, and the office is at left in the background.

In the photo, the wooden icebox on the port side at the aft end of *Ketchikan*'s deckhouse is a reminder of a time when mechanical refrigeration was in use by only a few. About 15 years before this photo was taken, the first self-contained refrigerators appeared on the market, but they commanded a price that most people could not afford. As a result of increased production during the World War II years, though, the price of refrigerators gradually declined to a more affordable level, and by 1945, many homeowners had discarded their iceboxes and were enjoying the luxury of self-contained refrigeration.

At the time of the photo above, Puget Sound towboats did not have the benefit of refrigeration but, instead, utilized a wooden icebox for keeping meat, eggs, and vegetables cool. Even in later years, after refrigerator/freezers were in widespread use in homes, most of the Puget Sound tugs still utilized wooden iceboxes. Many of the towboats were

arranged with a low-height trunk over the engine room, and aboard those tugs, the icebox was usually attached to the top of this trunk cabin at the edge within easy reach for the cook. *Ketchikan*'s deckhouse, however, was of standing-room height; hence, the icebox was placed out on deck at a low level for accessibility.

Delta Smyth's tug *Alice*, pictured on the next page, had a long working history. *Alice* was built of wood as a passenger steamer at Tacoma in 1897 to the order of Captain William Bradford. The new steamer was named after Captain Bradford's wife, and the vessel began operating on a run out of Tacoma as a replacement for his earlier, smaller steamer, *Susie*.

Beginning in 1900, the vessel passed through a series of Alaska ownerships as a passenger and freight steamer working for the fish canneries there, remaining in that line of work for more than 20 years. While in Alaska, the deckhouse and arrangements received a makeover, resulting in a tug that was more adapted to handling barges than the original passenger and freight carrying configuration had been suited for.

The 65-foot-long *Alice* was acquired by Delta Smyth in 1925. At the time of the purchase, the deckhouse was a two-level house, consisting of a pilothouse atop the main deckhouse. This deckhouse was not the towboat's first, but rather, it had been constructed by an Alaska owner as a replacement for the original house.

Alice with a lumber scow in tow.

In 1930, Smyth undertook a major rebuild of *Alice* and gave the towboat a third deckhouse by modifying the two-level deckhouse into a single-level house with the wheelhouse raised somewhat higher than the aft portion, as shown in the illustration above. Smyth also increased the fuel capacity and repowered the towboat with a 135-horsepower Washington Iron Works diesel engine as a replacement for the old original steam plant.

Delta Smyth operated *Alice* until 1941 when, along with Smyth's steam powered tug *Olympian*, ownership passed to Foss Launch and Tug Company. *Alice* was then renamed *Simon Foss*, and *Olympian* was given the name *Adeline Foss*.

In 1964, Foss retired *Simon Foss* from service, and ownership passed to Gordon Newell, an author of Pacific Northwest history books. Gordon had the boat brought to his waterfront home near Dickenson Point north of Olympia, and there the tug was placed on the beach for use as an office and archive. Later, ten years after being purchased by Gordon Newell, *Alice* was reborn as an operating tug when Miles Hargitt, a towboat operator in Anacortes, acquired and prepared the boat for a return to towing service.

The 47-foot *Parthia*, pictured at left, was built of wood at Winslow on Bainbridge Island in 1906. The tug, with an 80-horsepower Cummins diesel in the engine room, was employed by Delta V. Smyth Tugs and Barges for many years towing scows and log rafts in Olympia's harbor. Later, after a long tenure with Smyth, this engine was replaced with a 165-horsepower GM 6-71 diesel engine.

In this illustration, the author's boyhood home located on East Bay Drive is depicted at upper left. In those days, *Parthia* was known by some Olympia children as the "stuck-up tug" because of the boat's rakish appearance.

Parthia in East Bay at Olympia.
At left in the background is the author's boyhood home.

Parthia running light in Olympia's harbor, 1939. (From the author's collection)

In the photo above, *Parthia* was heading south and running light in Olympia's harbor. In the background of the photo, Olympia Harbor Lumber Company is to the left of *Parthia*, and Panama Shingle Company is to the right.

Olympia Harbor Lumber Company, previously described, was representative of typical lumber mills of the time. A few additional comments on this mill can be made. Just to the left of *Parthia*'s bow, the log haul, a sloping conveyer used for hauling the logs from the water and into the mill, can be seen. The mill caught fire some time after the photo was taken, and back in operation following repairs, the company no longer used the log haul but, instead, cut finished lumber from large, squared-off timbers called "cants" rather than from logs. The burner, used for disposing of scrap wood, is just above *Parthia*'s wheelhouse. The stiffleg crane, used for loading lumber onto scows, is just to the left of the burner.

There is uncertainty now as to whether or not the steam-powered Olympia Harbor Lumber Company was in operation at the time of the photo, as evidenced by the lack of smoke emanating from the tall stack and the absence of steam exhausting from the engines. Panama Shingle Company, also steam-powered, was obviously in full operation, as indicated by the large quantity of smoke and steam at the mill.

From the beginning of settlement on Puget Sound, the demand for lumber was great. In the early to mid 1800s, sawmills were built in the Pacific Northwest next to fast-flowing rivers and used huge water wheels to power the saw. To move a log through the saw, the carriage feed also used water power, but some mills employed oxen or horses to pull the carriage. At that time, the equipment used to cut lumber was somewhat primitive, resulting in planks that varied considerably in thickness from end to end.

The water-power era was closely followed by the establishment of the first steam-powered sawmills. By the late 1800s, steam power had pretty well supplanted water power in the sawmills. These steam-powered mills utilized large, heavily built machinery that, with regular lubrication and proper attention to the boiler and firebox, seemingly could keep on running forever. Accuracy of the cutting operation improved, and in the late 1880s, the first planer was put into operation to supply lumber that had a smooth surface finish. There were big trees in those days, and planks up to four feet wde could be gotten out by some mills. Steam continued to be a prime source of power for sawmills into the mid 1950s and beyond.

By that time, though, the decline in demand for finished lumber cut by Puget Sound mills was setting in as more logs were being shipped out than was finished lumber. Into the 1960s, Puget Sound sawmills such as those pictured above started to fold up shop, cease operations, and disappear, one by one. A sawmill was a busy place during a working shift, but during the lunch break and the period between shifts, calm and quiet settled in over the mill. The sound of the steam whistles, which emanated from the mills and proclaimed the start of a shift, beginning and end of the lunch break, and the conclusion of a shift, could be heard like clockwork anywhere in a town that possessed a sawmill.

Parthia entering Delta Smyth's moorage at Olympia, 1939. (From the author's collection)

In the photo above, *Parthia* had finished a towing job and was entering the moorage at Delta V. Smyth Tugs and Barges in Olympia. The Standard Oil facility is just at right of center in the background, and a small tank ship can be seen unloading there. This little ship was *Petroleum II*, a 111-foot tanker built at Alameda, California, in 1911. The tanker shuttled between the tank farm at Point Wells and Olympia for many years carrying cargoes of oil products. The author has childhood memories of lying in bed at night listening to the "whoomp ... chunk, chunk, chunk, chunk, chunk" exhaust from *Petroleum II*'s 250-horsepower Union gas engine as the tanker rounded Dofflemyer Point on her way into Budd Inlet.

Atlanta, with stern visible at right in the picture above, was built as a 90-foot, 200 horsepower passenger steamer on Lake Washington in 1908, according to McCurdy's *Marine History of the Pacific Northwest* of 1966. Quoting the same reference, in 1938, "The *Atlanta* was purchased by Russell G. Gibson for $510, and resold to Delta V. Smyth of Olympia, her 9 1/2, 22 x 16 compound engine going into Smyth's tug *Olympian*."

In the photo below, *Patty Mae*, with the old deckhouse still in place prior to the rework done by Delta Smyth, was heading north in Olympia's harbor. This 49-foot wooden tug was built at Poulsbo in 1930. The Port of Olympia pier and a Navy heavy-lift crane are in the background.

Patty Mae at Olympia, 1942. (From the author's collection)

Patty Mae on Delta Smyth's marine railway at Olympia in the late 1940s.
(From the author's collection)

As shown in the photo above, a raised deck had been added to the mid-length of *Patty Mae's* hull, and a new deckhouse had been constructed, too. At the time of the photo, the rudder had been unshipped from *Patty Mae's* hull, and the loose rudder was supported by a line at the stern of the boat. The bottom of a rudder stock rides in a bearing set into the metal shoe at the bottom of the skeg, and at the top of the rudder stock, a bolt flange connects to the upper stock in the hull.

The rudder had been unshipped, and the propeller had been removed to permit withdrawal of the shaft for repair or replacement. Since the rudder is in line with the propeller shaft, it is necessary to remove the rudder to provide clearance for removal of the shaft. The aft end of a propeller shaft is tapered and has a slot called a keyway. To reinstall the wheel, a key is inserted into the keyway on the shaft, and the prop is placed onto the shaft taper and key, then drawn up tightly by a threaded nut. The temporary covering, visible in the photo, on the shaft taper was to protect the exposed threads from damage.

In the photo at left, *Patty Mae* with her new deckhouse had just left Seattle's West Waterway and was heading out of Elliott Bay with a barge alongside.

Patty Mae in Elliott Bay, 1949. (From the author's collection)

Audrey, Oysterman, Mukilteo, and **Ketchikan,** left to right,
at the Delta V. Smyth Tugs and Barges moorage in Olympia, 1939.
(From the author's collection)

In the photo above, *Mukilteo* and *Ketchikan* were between towing jobs and tied up at Delta V. Smyth's moorage in Olympia, while *Oysterman* was temporarily idle and undergoing mechanical repairs. *Audrey*, in a state of disrepair, is at left in the photo. Other towboats owned by Smyth at the time of the photo, *Alice*, *Olympian* (ex-*Flosie*), *Parthia*, and *Sand Man*, were out on the job.

The smoke pipe extending up through the top of *Oysterman's* deckhouse was the uptake for the heating stove installed in the aft starboard corner of the wheelhouse. In the photo, Jim Maxin, *Oysterman's* long time skipper, was bending over on *Oysterman's* aft deck while working on the repair of mechanical components. The gentleman seated on the float and wearing a white longshoreman's cap is unidentified.

At the time of the photo, *Audrey* had recently been purchased by Delta Smyth and had not yet undergone the refit that was described previously.

As can be seen, *Audrey* was in a deteriorated state at the time of purchase.

The-50 foot-long *Mukilteo* was built of wood at Mukilteo in 1907. Many years later, the towboat was purchased and then operated for several years by Delta Smyth. *Mukilteo* had a raised deck along the mid-length of the hull upon which the deckhouse was placed. The new deckhouse and raised deck that was constructed later for *Patty Mae*, pictured on the previous page, followed quite closely the form of the house and raised deck that was built for *Mukilteo*.

Another boat owned by Delta V. Smyth, the 75-foot long wooden tug *Nile* of 1917, was described in the earlier chapter "A Deckhand's Recollections of Life aboard the Earlier Tugs." *Nile* was purchased by Smyth following the towboat's government service during World War II. Design drawings for *Nile* as shown on the next two pages are the only ones known still to exist.

Shown here are design drawings by Harold C. Hanson, Seattle naval architect, for the tug *Nile* when built as a steam-powered cannery tender for Pacific American Fisheries, located at Fairhaven, in 1917. These drawings may have been done as H. C. Hanson's first design commission. The steam machinery occupied a huge amount of space in the hull and deckhouse.

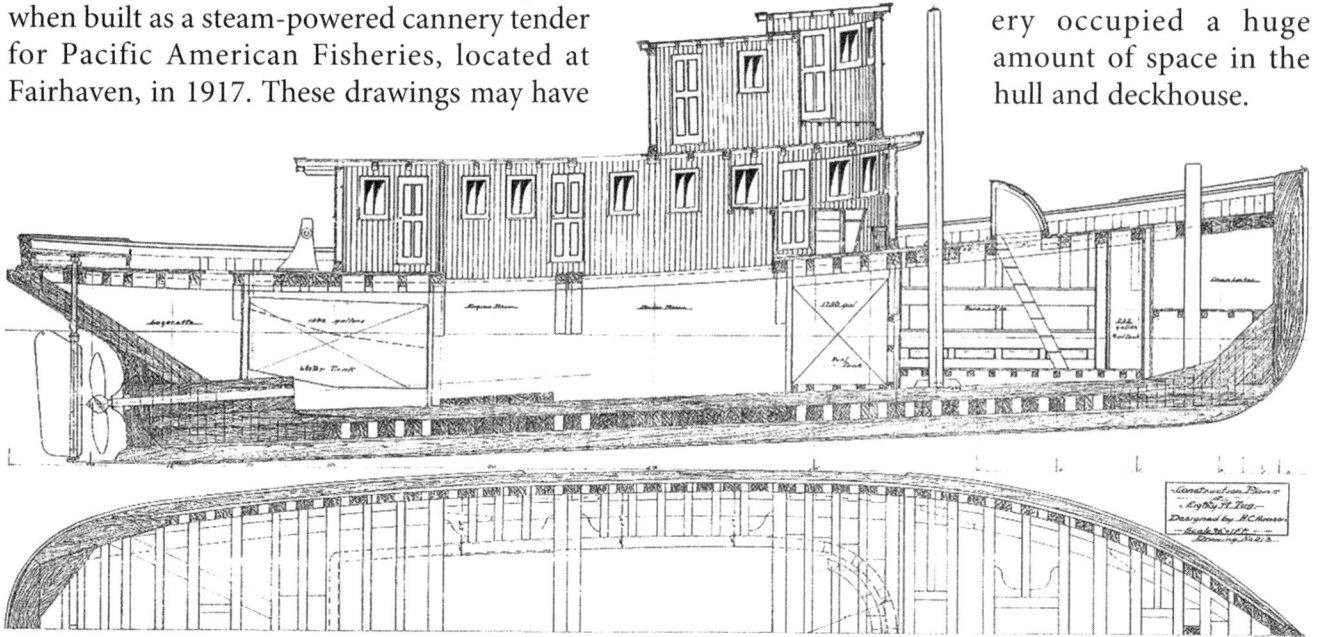

Nile construction plan, 1917. (With permission of Whatcom Museum of History and Art, H. C. Hanson Collection drawing 213)

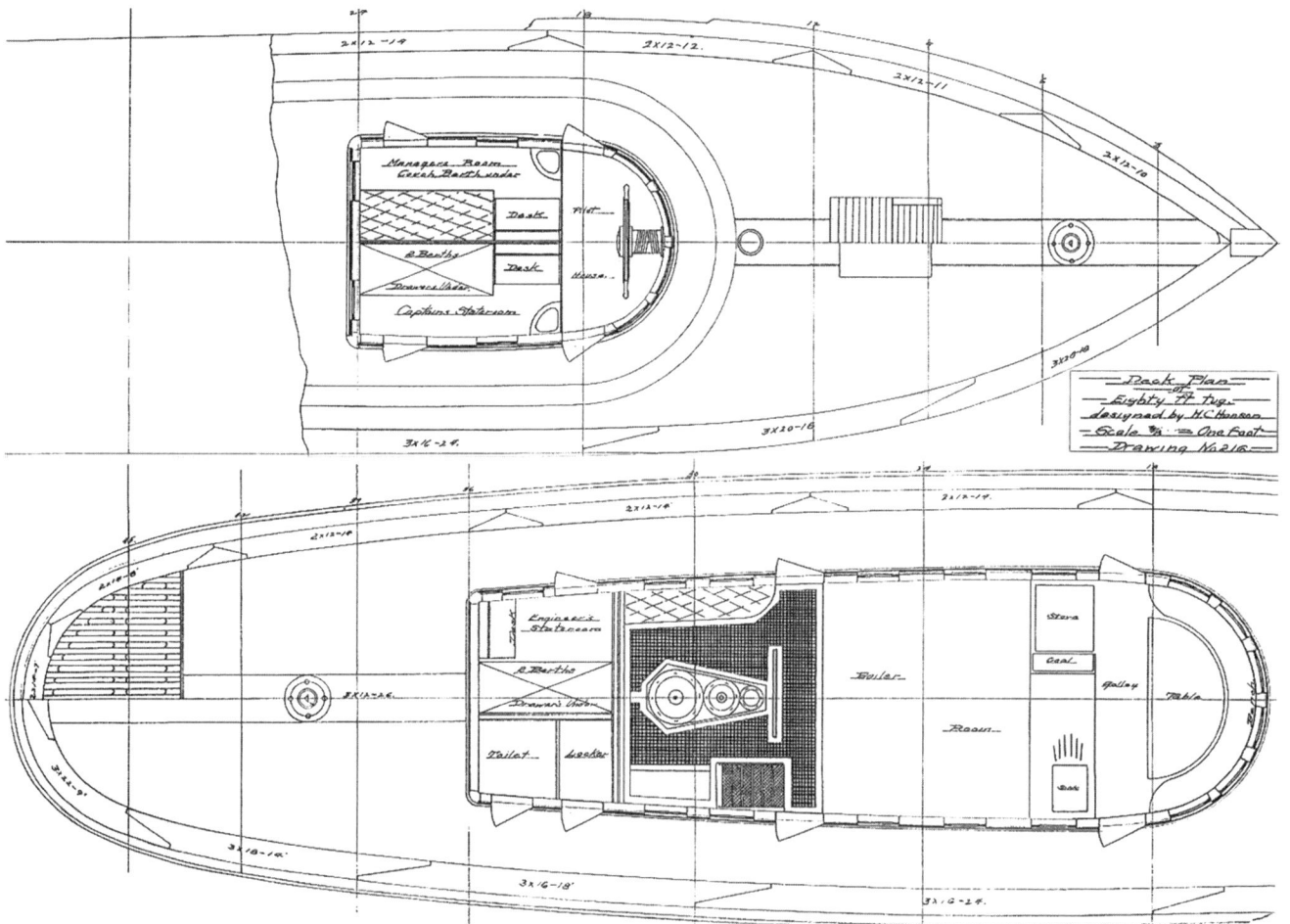

Nile deck plan, 1917. (With permission of Whatcom Museum of History and Art, H. C. Hanson Collection drawing 216)

Pacific American Fisheries salmon can label (half size), n.d.
(With permission of Whatcom Museum of History and Art)

Nile, 1949.
(From the author's collection)

For reasons unknown, the lines drawing shown below was noted as being "copied Feb 1923." Originally, *Nile* was powered by a triple-expansion steam engine, as indicated in the deck plan on the previous page. Later, the towboat was repowered with a Fairbanks-Morse diesel engine. At some point, the original rectangular windows at the forward end of the main deckhouse were changed to portlights. Other changes were also made over the years, including modifications to the arrangements in the deckhouse.

Pacific American Fisheries frequently branded their salmon cans with unusual names such as "Auk," "Jack Horner," "Minnehaha," and "Uwanta." Another interesting brand name for PAF canned North Pacific salmon was "Nile." The Nile brand label pictured at the top of the page even features an illustration of camels and pyramids, which might lead someone into believing that the salmon had originated in an exotic desert land.

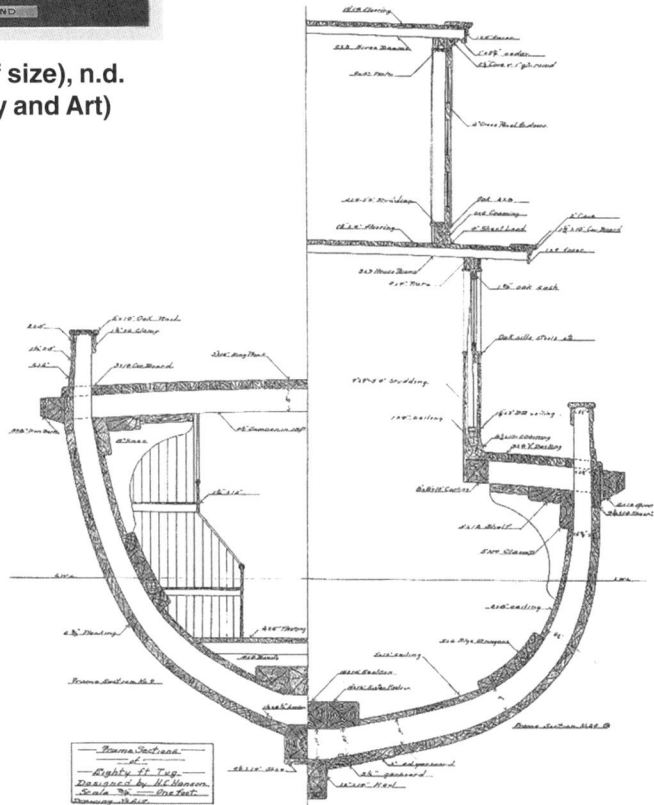

Nile frame sections, 1917. (With permission of Whatcom Museum of History and Art, H. C. Hanson Collection drawing 214)

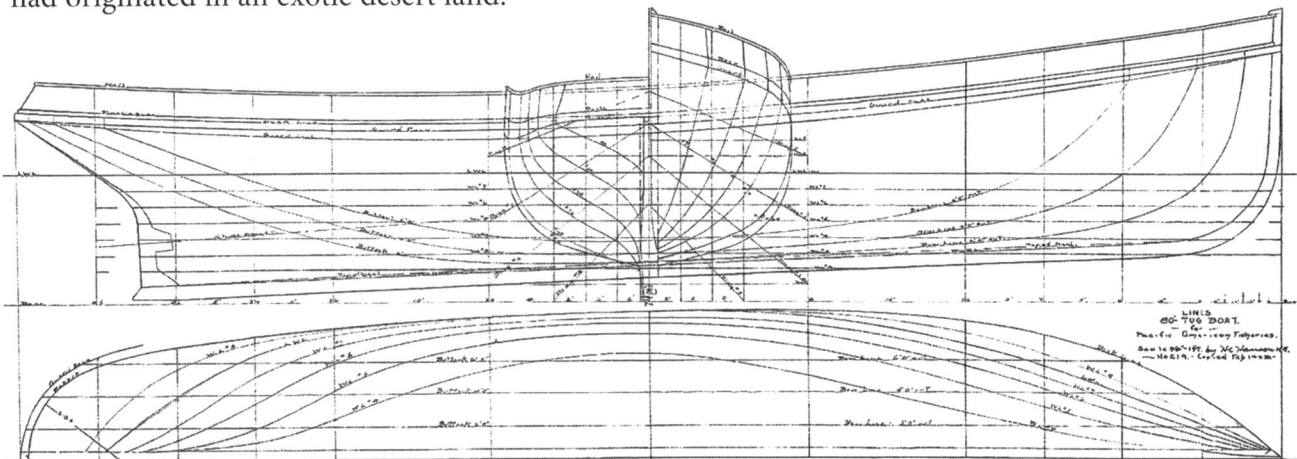

Nile lines, 1923. (With permission of Whatcom Museum of History and Art, H. C. Hanson Collection, drawing 219)

Lumberman, built of wood at Seattle in 1899, was originally powered by steam. Pacific Towboat in Seattle was the first owner, and the deckhouse at that time was a single-level structure with the pilothouse raised only slightly. Delta V. Smyth purchased the tug in 1924 for towing jobs out of Olympia. Later on, the boat was repowered with a 220-horsepower, six-cylinder, direct reversing Atlas diesel engine, and a new house was arranged so that the pilothouse was mounted on top of the main deckhouse.

The original deckhouse was installed in a position somewhat aft that allowed for access to the crew accommodations forward below the main deck. The replacement deckhouse was installed in the same location as the original house. Delta Smyth operated *Lumberman* until the tug was sold to Otis Shively in 1938, who operated the tug for a time before ownership passed to Samson Tug and Barge of Sitka, Alaska.

Lumberman had a quaint and pleasing appearance. The towboat was considerably smaller than most tugs that feature a two-level deckhouse. The register dimensions were 57-foot length, 17 foot beam, and 6 1/2-foot depth. Per admeasurement rules, the 57-foot length measured from the forward end of the planking to the rudder stock would have resulted in an overall length of something a bit more than 60 feet. The register beam, measured to the outside of the planking, would have been the same as the overall beam. Per the rules, the 6 1/2 foot register depth was measured at midship "from the underside of the main deck to the bottom of the hold" so that the actual outside depth of the hull would have been greater.

It cannot be said that the drawing below is an exact depiction of *Lumberman*; the drawing was made by the author from limited pictorial and dimensional data, as well as recollections from viewing the tug some years ago.

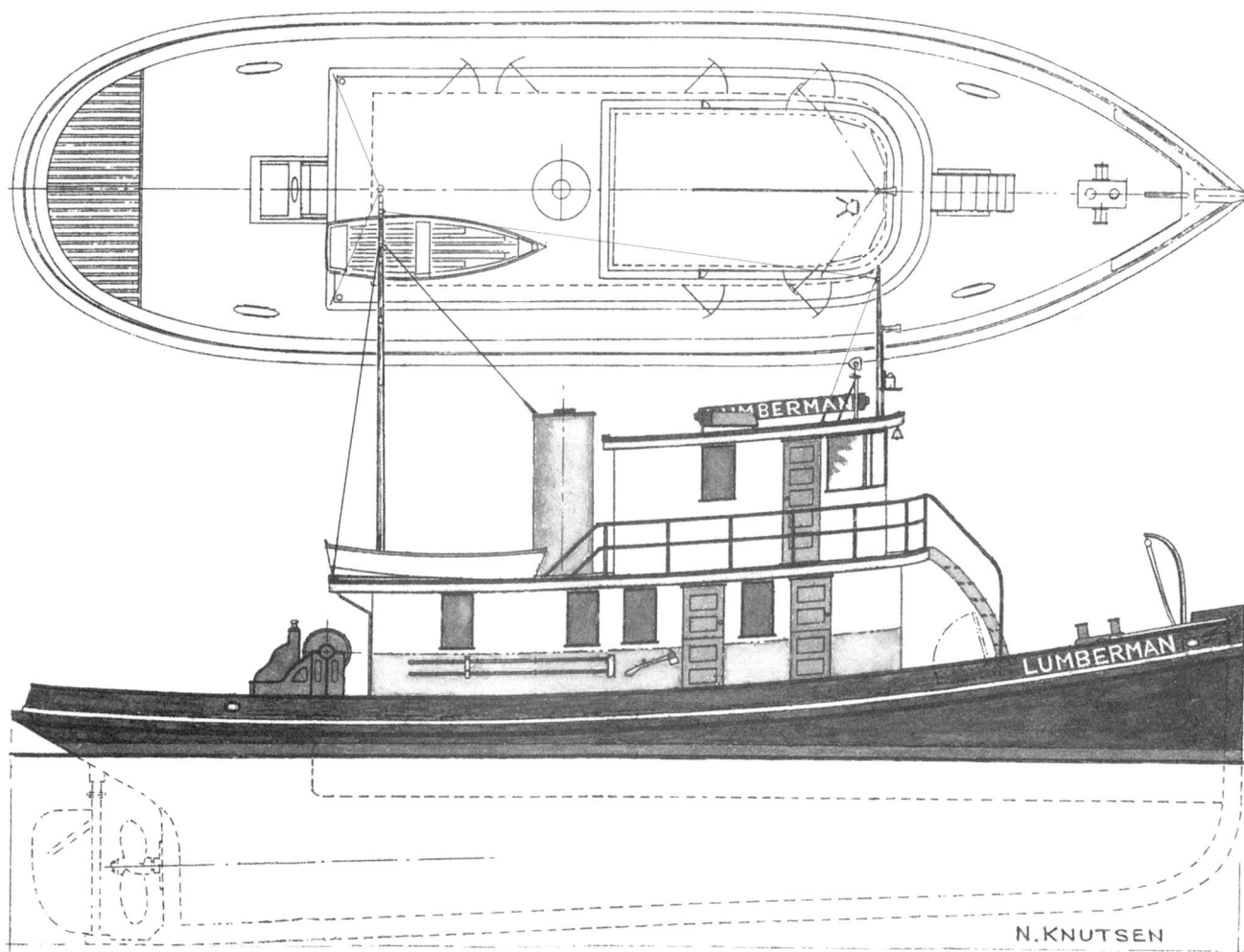

Lumberman.

Lumberman.
(Model constructed by the author)

Hoonah in Elliott Bay, 1951. (From the author's collection)

Pictured above, *Hoonah* was a 66-foot wooden cannery tender built at Bellingham in 1919 for Pacific American Fisheries. Delta Smyth purchased *Hoonah* after this photo was taken and operated the boat in towing service until Foss Launch and Tug Company bought Delta V. Smyth Tugs and Barges in 1961. Following three years of towing for Foss, *Hoonah* was sold, but a short time later, in foul weather, the tug stranded on the jetty at Grays Harbor without loss of life.

Hoonah and ***Rufus*** assisting the Liberty Class freighter ***Anne Quinn*** at Olympia, 1964.
(From the author's collection)

A couple of years prior to the time of these photos, Foss Launch and Tug Company had purchased Delta V. Smyth Tugs and Barges, as mentioned on the previous page. In these photos, *Hoonah* and *Rufus* were now decked out with Foss green and white.

In the upper left photo, *Hoonah* was heading out through the harbor at Olympia to meet and assist the cargo ship *Anne Quinn*, inbound through the shipping channel. The draft marks showing at right in the photo are on the bow of *Texaco California*, tied up at the north end of the port pier to offload oil at the Texaco tank farm.

In the upper right photo, *Hoonah* had arrived alongside *Anne Quinn*, approaching the Olympia port pier. *Texaco California* is at right in the photo. The crane at the port pier, used at the time for loading and unloading cargo, was commonly called a "whirly" and operated on a pair of widely separated rails supported on the pier.

In the lower left picture, *Anne Quinn* was backing down to stop forward motion in preparation for being turned 180 degrees in the large ba-

sin that had been dredged many years ago for the purpose of turning ships. *Hoonah* was beginning to push against *Anne Quinn*'s bow to swing the ship. The Washington State Capitol is silhouetted at left in the background.

The procedure for rotating a ship was to use two tugs, one tug pushing or pulling on the bow and the other tug working in the opposite direction at the ship's stern. *Rufus* had joined in, and in the lower right photo, with *Anne Quinn*'s bow now pointed north toward the channel, *Hoonah* and *Rufus* were nudging the freighter in toward the pier. The shore crew then tossed heaving lines, with monkey fists attached, to the crew aboard the ship. These heaving lines were then used by the crew on the pier to haul in the large diameter mooring lines.

Hoonah was powered by a 210-horsepower diesel engine manufactured by Hendy in San Francisco, an engine not commonly found in marine service. *Rufus*, with a 300-horsepower supercharged Cummins diesel engine, could supply a lot of push, especially for a small tug.

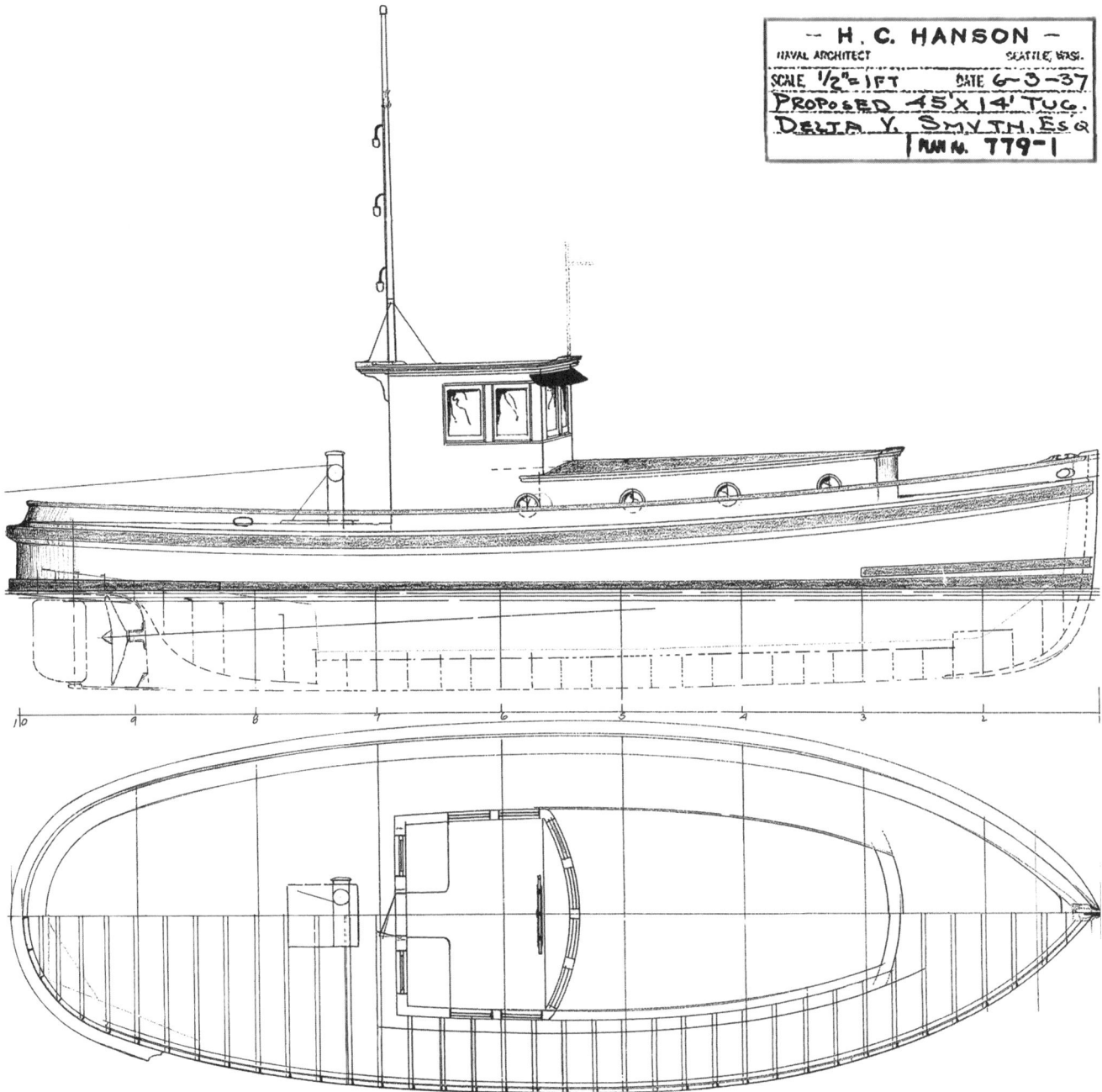

Proposed tug for Delta V. Smyth Tugs and Barges, 1937.
(With permission of Whatcom Museum of History and Art, H. C. Hanson Collection design 779)

Illustrated above is a towboat suitable for harbor work, of overall length 45 feet, as proposed by H. C. Hanson, naval architect, for Delta V. Smyth Tugs and Barges in 1937. So far as the author knows, this tug, intended to be constructed of steel, was never built precisely as drawn. However, *Rufus*, built by Henry Long at Olympia in 1957 and pictured on the previous page, was similar in appearance to this 1937 design but was constructed of wood. Other differences appear to be more minor. Perhaps this 1937 design was dusted off and used as a reference for planning the construction of *Rufus*.

When Foss Launch and Tug Company purchased Delta V. Smyth Tugs and Barges in 1961, *Audrey*, *Hoonah*, *Oysterman*, *Parthia*, and *Rufus* were the only boats still working for Smyth. All were eventually sold except for *Oysterman*. After the engine and metal components had been removed from *Oysterman*, the little towboat was burned in Commencement Bay as part of the 1963 Independence Day celebration.

OLYMPIA TOWING COMPANY
Olympia

Lenore at Olympia Towing Company's moorage, 1941.
(From the author's collection)

Olympia Towing Company was located on Olympia's West Side near the Northern Pacific Railroad log dump at the north end of West Bay Drive. This company was owned and operated by members of the Willy family. Boat colors that represented Olympia Towing were black hull and red and white deckhouse.

In the photo above, taken very late in the afternoon, the little tug *Lenore* was tied up at the Olympia Towing moorage between towing jobs. *Lenore*, built of wood, was the smallest tug in Olympia Towing's fleet, having a length of little more than 30 feet. *Lenore* was a day boat so sleeping accommodations were not required. The towboat was used in the harbor primarily for working with logs, a steady job in the logging and lumbering town that Olympia was at the time.

Lenore did not have bulwarks around the perimeter of the deck, which no doubt made it somewhat easier for the crew when stepping over the side onto a log raft or stepping back up onto the deck when reboarding. Bulwarks are not a necessity aboard a tug, but on the other hand, without the barrier that bulwarks would provide, care has to be taken that lines stay on deck to avoid their slipping over the side and becoming entangled in the wheel.

In the photo below, Olympia Towing's *Virginia*, a 41-foot wooden tug built at Seattle in 1929, was running light on a foggy day in Budd Inlet. The towboat's propulsion plant was a Waukesha diesel engine, and the tug was always very busy working in the harbor, mainly handling log rafts.

At the time these pictures were taken, Olympia Towing Company also owned three other towboats, *Klatawa*, *Leonine*, and *Nemah*, all larger than *Virginia* and better suited to more extended towing jobs. *Crosmor*, a tug that joined the fleet somewhat later, was the largest in service with Olympia Towing. With more spacious accommodations than the other boats, *Crosmor* was especially capable of handling tows of longer duration between ports on Puget Sound.

Virginia running light in Budd Inlet, 1942.
(From the author's collection)

Nemah running light at Olympia, 1941. (From the author's collection)

In the above photo, Olympia Towing Company's tug *Nemah* was running light in Olympia's harbor. A 50-foot wooden boat, *Nemah* was built at Hoquiam in 1925. Propulsion power was provided by a heavy-duty, slow-speed diesel engine of 120 horsepower. The anchor handling system was similar to *Nile*'s, consisting of a davit and rigging mounted at the bow. The trunk cabin forward of the wheelhouse housed the crew accommodations. Moored log rafts are in the background at Olympia's West Side.

In the photo below, *Nemah* was joined by *Virginia* at the Union Oil float in Olympia. There was a large number of old towboats, built in the late 1800s or around the turn of the century, operating on Puget Sound at the time of these photos. Many of these boats were originally built for use as towboats, while numerous vessels of a different design were constructed for other purposes but were later converted to tugs. In 1941 when this photo was taken, though, *Virginia* and *Nemah* were relatively new out of the shipyard.

Virginia and *Nemah* at the Union Oil float in Olympia, 1941. (From the author's collection)

Leonine at the Union Oil float in Olympia, 1939. (From the author's collection)

Olympia Towing Company's tug *Leonine* was built of wood at Anacortes in 1915 and, at a length of 50 feet, was the same size as *Nemah*. As pictured above, *Leonine* was tied to the float at the Union Oil Company facility in Olympia. Union Oil eventually disbanded the operation there, and the float became known as the City Float, a moorage available to transient boats. In the background of the photo, just to the right of *Leonine*, the little tanker *Petroleum II* is visible while unloading at the Standard Oil facility.

Unfortunately, some years after this photo, *Leonine* hit on hard times and sank, as pictured on the next page. It was reported at the time that *Leonine* had a tow and while the tug was swinging during a maneuver, the towline became stretched out over the side athwartship. This caused the tug to roll sufficiently that the deck edge went under, causing flooding into the hull. This is referred to as being "in irons," a situation from which there may not be a chance to recover.

Sailboats can get up in irons in a different way if, when sailing on a tack upwind and then coming about so that the boat does not swing suffi-

ciently to turn to the opposite tack, the boat becomes caught directly upwind and the sails cannot fill with air. In this case, the sailboat simply stops forward motion until the heading is changed a bit and there is normally no danger. The term "in irons" is different for a towboat; a tug described as being in irons is caught with the towline athwartship. In such a situation, the sideways pull of the towline can exert a large heeling force on the tug, and recovery before the deck edge goes under may be very difficult or impossible.

As the years went on, partially to minimize the danger a tug faces when in irons, modern towboats were being designed and built with greater beam so as to make the tug "stiffer" by increasing stability. The weight distribution of components going into a tug were being accounted for to ensure that the center of gravity of the vessel was low enough for safety. U.S. Coast Guard oversight was beginning to be implemented, and for the newer large tugs, a freeboard load line painted on both sides of the hull was eventually required to ensure that the deck at side was at a sufficient height above the water to minimize risk of loss.

Leonine sunk at Olympia's West Side, 1949. (From the author's collection)

In the photo above, after the mishap described on the previous page, *Leonine* was mostly submerged on the beach near Olympia Towing Company's moorage on Olympia's West Side. In the background are Northern Pacific's log dump railroad tracks built on pilings and extending out over the water. Olympia Towing's 50-foot tug *Klatawa* is at left in the background of the photo.

Klatawa, built of wood at Shaw Island in 1912, was with the Olympia Towing fleet for many years. Before Olympia Towing ownership, *Klatawa* was also operated for a time by Gilkey Towing at Anacortes. The tug, pictured below at Anacortes, was no longer in the employ of Olympia Towing Company and looking a bit worse for wear at the time of the photo.

Klatawa at Anacortes, 1963. (From the author's collection)

Crosmor in Budd Inlet, 1949. (From the author's collection)

In this photo, Olympia Towing Company's tug *Crosmor* was enroute north in Budd Inlet while pulling on a log raft. *Crosmor*, built of wood at Seattle in 1928, was a well proportioned 66-foot, 180-horsepower tug with pleasing lines. The largest boat in Olympia Towing's fleet, *Crosmor* had space for adequate crew accommodations and so was suited to towing jobs of greater distance and longer duration than some of the smaller tugs. Just as many other Puget Sound tugs changed ownership according to work load and business conditions, *Crosmor* later passed into the hands of Dunlap Towing Company of La Conner.

In low-speed work, such as towing logs or handling ships, a large, slow-turning propeller is ideal. At such a low speed, the conditions approximate those that result in what is known as "bollard pull," that is, the towline force produced by a tug at zero forward speed.

This force at zero hull speed can be measured by testing. A newly built tug, or one that has been repowered, is sometimes given a bollard pull test in which the towline is fastened to a pier and the tug remains in place while pulling on the towline at the maximum revolutions per minute that the engine is rated for. A dynamometer, installed in the towline, can measure the tension force in the line. The resulting force on the towline would likely be at least 25 pounds per horsepower for a well-designed tug.

Although *Crosmor* was not so equipped, a device known as a Kort Nozzle, which is a circular steel shroud or ring surrounding the propeller blade tips, can be installed to increase the pulling ability. For use in a Kort Nozzle, the propeller blade tips appear to be squared off but are actually trimmed to a radius that clears the inside of the circular shroud by only a fraction of an inch, thus greatly decreasing "tip losses" that occur due to water flow around and over the propeller tips.

Some Kort Nozzles have been installed so that they can rotate about a vertical axis for steering, eliminating the need for a rudder. The 2400-horsepower *Shelley Foss*, 90 feet in overall length and built of steel by Albina Engine and Machine Works at Portland, Oregon, in 1970, features twin steerable Kort Nozzles. *Shelley Foss* is still in service, frequently performing ship-handling duties that require a lot of propeller thrust at almost zero hull speed.

Johnny Jr. at Olympia Sand and Gravel Company in Olympia, 1961.
(Courtesy of Anna J. Knutsen)

Olympia Towing Company's *Johnny Jr.* was 38 feet long and built of wood in 1939 for use by the U.S. government during construction of Grand Coulee dam on the Columbia River in eastern Washington. In this photo, *Johnny Jr.* had brought a scow load of sand from the Pioneer pit at Steilacoom to Oympia Sand and Gravel Company, which was located on Columbia Street in Olympia. Both Olympia Towing Company and Olympia Sand and Gravel Company were owned by members of the Willy family.

In this picture, only moments after the loaded barge had been secured, the steam-powered locomotive crane, sending out great quantities of smoke and steam, had already begun unloading sand from the scow by means of a bucket and was depositing the materials in the storage areas. At the time of the photo, my father had only recently begun running this crane after his previous em-

ployer, Olympia Lumber Company, had cease operations. Further descriptions have already been given elsewhere in this book about the Ohio steam locomotive crane that he operated for many years at Olympia Harbor Lumber Company.

At left in the background, just above the barge's cargo of sand, the Delta V. Smyth Tugs and Barges wooden towboat *Rufus*, built by Henry Long at Olympia in 1957, can be seen hauled out on Smyth's marine railway. At about the time this photo was taken, Foss Launch and Tug Company had begun the process of purchasing Smyth's towing company; therefore, it is not known whether or not, on the occasion of the photo, *Rufus* was still owned by Smyth or if the boat had been taken over by Foss. Further in the background at left is the stack at the wood products company owned by Georgia Pacific. This company formerly was Washington Veneer Company.

Nespelem and *Wellpinit* under construction on the bank of the Spokane River, 1939.
(With permission of the University of Washington, Special Collections, negative UW21892)

Johnny Jr. was originally given the name *Nespelem* and was one of two identical boats built to work on the construction of Grand Coulee dam. The other tug was named *Wellpinit*. In the photo above, these two boats are shown while in final stages of construction on the shore of the Spokane River. Since they were twins, it is not known which of the two vessels pictured above was *Nespelem*. The tugs were assigned to various jobs during the building of the dam, including moving an unpowered barge-like ferry that was used for transporting personnel to various job sites.

Nespelem was acquired by Olympia Towing Company in the mid 1950s, was subsequently modified to suit the company's intended usage, and was renamed *Johnny Jr.* After Olympia Towing Company bought the vessel, the aft bulwark was reduced in height to permit the crew to step on and off the boat more readily. In addition, the tug was repowered with a 150-horsepower Cummins diesel engine. *Johnny Jr.* was reported as being quite efficient and able to put a good pull on a towline, especially considering the tug's own relatively small size. In fact, *Johnny Jr.* was reportedly able to out-pull *Virginia*, a tug that had worked many years for Olympia Towing.

One of the reasons for *Johnny Jr.*'s effective towing ability was the installation of a larger propeller. To accommodate this larger wheel, the existing shaft log bore in the keel was plugged, and a new hole was then bored on a centerline that was about six inches lower at the aft end of the skeg. The design and rework were accomplished at Marine Construction and Design Company in Seattle. The new shaft location then provided sufficient space for the installation of a propeller that was considerably larger than the previous one. As previously stated, a large diameter propeller contributes greatly to towing ability, especially when the speed is very low.

98

OLSON TUG BOAT COMPANY
Tacoma

Magnolia, **Paddy Craig**, and **Madrona**, left to right,
at the Olson Tug Boat Company moorage in Tacoma, 1949.
(From the author's collection)

Olson Tug Boat Company was established by Ole Olson as Magnolia Tug Boat Company in 1898. Not only one of the oldest towing companies in the Puget Sound area, the firm was long-lasting, too, remaining in business until the assets of the company were purchased by Halvorsen Towing of Bainbridge Island in 1965.

This photo, looking to the southeast, shows the Olson Tug Boat Company moorage in the Milwaukee Waterway at Tacoma. Tied up at the moorage were the tugs *Magnolia*, left, *Paddy Craig*, moored on the far side of the scow at center, and *Madrona*, right. Olson's colors were all white with black and red trim.

The Olson Tug Boat Company office is at extreme right in the background of this picture. Access to the moorage from the shore was via the wooden walkway and gangway just beyond *Madrona*. The old Eleventh Street Bridge is in the background and, after many years of service, now shows a great deal of wear and tear.

All three boats pictured here were built of wood at Tacoma. *Magnolia* was a 42-foot tug built in 1943. The smallest of the three, *Paddy Craig*, was only 33 feet long and was built in 1928. *Madrona* was larger than the other two at a length of 54 feet and was built in 1923. *Madrona*'s lines and deckhouse style bore resemblance to Delta V. Smyth's Olympia tug *Sand Man*, but *Madrona* was longer than *Sand Man* by about five feet.

The two smaller tugs, *Magnolia* and *Paddy Craig*, mainly worked at towing jobs in Commencement Bay. *Madrona*, being considerably larger with more extensive crew accommodations, would frequently be seen on towing assignments at other locations around Puget Sound.

Tacoma Tug and Barge Company's *Favorite*, left, and Olson Tug Boat Company's *Magnolia*, right, nudging the newly launched and uncompleted tuna clipper *Mary E. Petrich* into the pier at the yard of the builder Western Boat Building Company, 1949. (With permission of Tacoma Public Library, Northwest Room)

In the 1949 photo above, Tacoma Tug and Barge Company's *Favorite*, left and also pictured in the next chapter, and Olson Tug Boat Company's *Magnolia*, right, were teamed up to gently move the new tuna clipper *Mary E. Petrich* into the pier following the fishing vessel's launch at Western Boat Building Company in Tacoma. This tuna boat was a good sized burden for the 55-horsepower *Favorite* and the 65-horsepower *Magnolia* to manage.

Mary E. Petrich had a register length of 150 feet and was powered by a 1600-horsepower, ten-cylinder Fairbanks-Morse opposed piston diesel engine. As can be seen in the photo, construction of *Mary E. Petrich* had not yet been completed. The most obvious components not yet installed are the pilothouse (shown lashed down at the aft end of the vessel) and mast, boom, and rigging, but these and many other items of outfit are usually not placed until after a new vessel has been launched. The main engine may be installed either before or after launch, but in either case, final shimming of the engine to align with the propeller shaft is not done until after the vessel is in the water because the hull may change shape slightly when buoyancy replaces the building stocks that had supported the hull on dry land.

One important reason for launching an uncompleted ship is that if contracts are in hand to begin construction of other vessels then it is desirable that work commence on the next hull as soon as possible. Launching of a ship frees up the building ways to permit assembly to begin on the next vessel.

Paddy Craig in Commencement Bay, 1947. (From the author's collection)

Two pictures of *Paddy Craig* and *Madrona*, taken while the towboats were out on the job, are shown here. The harbor tug *Paddy Craig* was equipped with a towing bitt for use with Manila line, while the longer ranging *Madrona* was outfitted with a winch for use with wire rope.

Madrona off McNeil Island, 1949. (From the author's collection)

The 76-foot wooden tug *Manzanita*, pictured at right, was built at Seattle in 1899. Under a succession of names, including *North Star* and *Queen City*, the tug was operated for many years off the Washington and Oregon coasts.

After Olson Tug Boat Company acquired the towboat, refurbishment work was undertaken in 1954 to provide the boat with upgrades. Following completion of the work, *Manzanita* emerged with a virtually new appearance and increased performance.

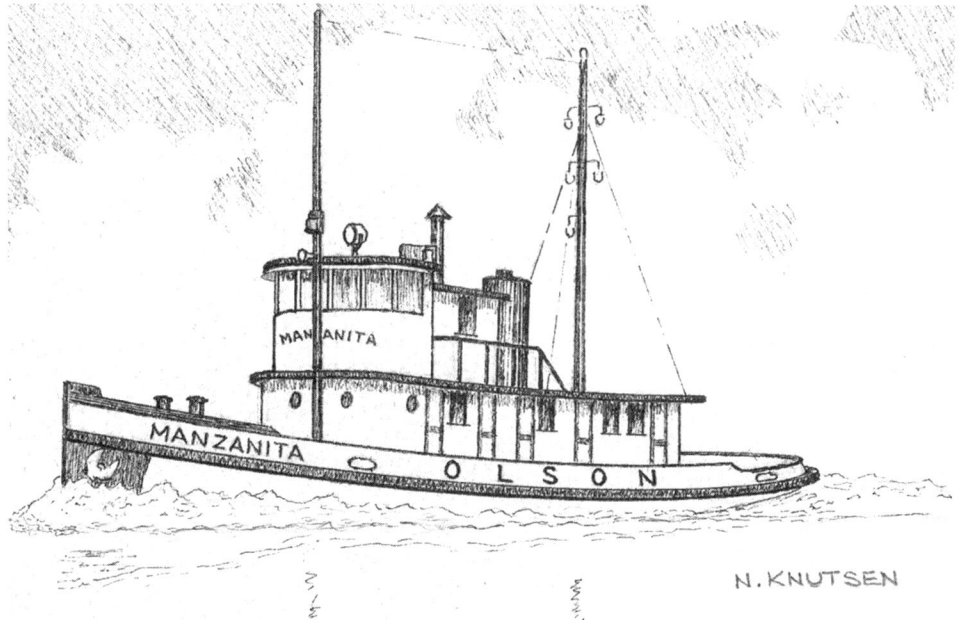

Manzanita.

Included in the rework was the replacement of the old engine with an interesting power plant, a General Motors 6-110 Tandem-Twin diesel engine setup driving a single propeller. This new propulsion arrangement consisted of two six-cylinder engines coupled together to a single shaft, sending over 400 horsepower through a five-to-one reduction gear to the five-foot-diameter, three blade propeller. Fuel tankage was increased to 5000 gallons, and with beefed up power and extended range, *Manzanita* was put to work in Alaska and British Columbia waters, in addition to towing barges and logs on Puget Sound.

In the illustration below, the 80-foot tug *Capt. O. G. Olson*, named after the founder of the owning company, is shown pulling on a log raft with a shortened tow line. *Capt. O. G. Olson* was built of wood at Tacoma in 1927 and was powered by a 240 horsepower diesel engine. The towboat was built to the order of Magnolia Tug Boat Company, which, as mentioned above, was later renamed Olson Tug Boat Company. During World War II *Capt. O. G. Olson* (as *ST-66*) was involved, along with a number of other Puget Sound tugs, in barge operations between Puget Sound and Alaska for the Alaska Barge Line, a unit of the Army Transportation Service.

Capt. O. G. Olson shortened up on a log raft.

TACOMA TUG AND BARGE COMPANY
Tacoma

Perhaps the oldest marine towing firm on Puget Sound, Tacoma Tug and Barge Company was founded about 1884 by Robert McCullough, an immigrant from Ireland. In later years, the company continued operations under the guidance of Robert's sons. Tacoma Tug and Barge colors were black hull with buff and white deckhouse, the same as those of Capital City Tug Company. The company's facility was located in the Hylebos Waterway just upstream from the Eleventh Street Bridge in Tacoma.

The picture below shows the Tacoma Tug and Barge moorage and some of the towboats. Not long after this photo was taken, Tacoma Tug and Barge Company was sold to Puget Sound Tug and Barge Company. In the photo are *Edward A. Young* in the left background, little *Favorite* just astern of *Edward A. Young*, *Fairfield* in the center, and *Falcon* (with the stack removed) moored to *Fairfield*'s starboard side. As described in a previous chapter, *Edward A. Young*, in fact, was in operation for Capital City Tug Company out of Olympia, but at the time of the photo, the boat had been acquired, along with other Capital City Tug assets, by Tacoma Tug and Barge Company.

Tacoma Tug and Barge Company moorage at Tacoma, 1949. (From the author's collection)

Tacoma was a shipbuilding town in the earlier days, and all of the tugs pictured on the previous page were constructed of wood there. As mentioned before in the book, *Edward A. Young* was 59 feet long and built in 1926. *Favorite*, built in 1937, was the smallest of the Tacoma Tug and Barge fleet at 32 feet in length. *Fairfield* was 61 feet long and was built in 1898, while *Falcon* was 60 feet long and built in 1902. In addition to these boats, Tacoma Tug and Barge Company owned *Betty Earles*, *Fearless*, and *Fawn*, all pictured on the following pages.

Tacoma Tug and Barge's founder, Robert McCullough, worked at various jobs after arriving in the United States from Ireland until he moved to western Washington, where he landed a job as engineer aboard the steam tug *Favorite*. Later, in settlement of back wages that hadn't been paid, McCullough was given the towboat. *Favorite* then became the beginning of a growing fleet of tugs with names that started with "F," the exceptions being *Betty Earles* and boats of Capital City Tug Company.

Following ownership of the firm by Puget Sound Tug and Barge from 1950 to 1958, a group of ex-Tacoma Tug and Barge employees purchased the assets and retained the name Tacoma Tug and Barge Company. A few years later, the firm again changed hands and operated for a time as Tahoma Tug and Barge. However, the "F" fleet, like many other early towboat firms, is gone now.

In this 1949 photo, *Favorite* was tending the newly launched purse seiner *Sea Rose*. The 70-foot *Sea Rose* was designed and built of wood by Kazulin-Cole, located on the shore of the Hylebos Waterway in Tacoma.

Favorite assisting *Sea Rose* following launch of the purse seiner by Kazulin-Cole at Tacoma, 1949.
(With permission of Tacoma Public Library, Northwest Room)

Betty Earles, pictured at right and below, was built by Johnson Brothers and Blanchard at Seattle in 1913 for use on Lake Crescent, nestled in the Olympic Mountains. Of wooden construction, the 60-foot boat was hauled in sections to the shore of the lake, assembled, launched, and then operated as a transport for guests at the Sol Duc Hot Springs Resort. The original engine installed in *Betty Earles* was a three-cylinder, 80-horsepower Frisco Standard. The boat was named for the little daughter of Michael Earles, the owner.

Eventually, *Betty Earles* left service on Lake Crescent and was hauled back to Puget Sound and converted for towing service. Tacoma Tug and Barge purchased *Betty Earles* in 1924.

In these pictures, *Betty Earles* was outbound and had just entered the large lock at Ballard. The fire monitor on top of the pilothouse could be used for washing the decks of sand and gravel scows, as well as for fighting fires. In tow was an empty wooden gravel scow, the destination probably being the Pioneer gravel pit at Steilacoom to load sand and gravel. A current flows slowly through the lock, which tends to carry a tug and barge

**Betty Earles at the Ballard Locks, 1947.
(From the author's collection)**

with it. When outbound downstream, the stern of a towed scow is tied off to a bitt located on the concrete wall. To accomplish this, the tug backs to the forward end of the scow and the deckhand climbs up onto the scow's deck, using a ladder if necessary. The deckhand then moves to the aft end of the scow to handle the line.

When inbound against the slowly moving current, a mooring line can be passed from the tug's bow to a bitt on the lock wall, to tie the tug off, and the stern of the scow can also be tied down.

As an option, when inbound and heading upstream, the aft end of the tow is often tied off to a bitt on the lock wall, and the tug, with the engine running slowly, pulls ahead on the tow. Because of the tie line at the aft end of the tow, the tug and tow, alongside the lock wall, then simply remain stationary in the current while still having the ability to maintain control.

In the photo at left, with the water level in the lock having been dropped to a height nearly equal to the level of the water in Puget Sound, the gates were opened and *Betty Earles* was exiting with the gravel scow in tow. Because the water in the lock is still a bit higher than the water in Puget Sound when the gate is opened, a fairly fast current flows out temporarily until the water levels equalize.

**Betty Earles exiting the Ballard Locks, 1947.
(From the author's collection)**

In the photos on the previous page, *Betty Earles* was using a bridle that was shackled to the end of the towline, as is the usual practice when towing a barge in the open water of Puget Sound. The towline bridle, combined with the towline, forms a Y-shaped configuration, and the two lines that make up the bridle are attached to the two forward corners of the scow by slipping the spliced eyes over the bitts.

The bridle aids in steering the scow when the tug changes course; if the tug turns to starboard, for example, the bridle line attached to the port bitt on the scow becomes taut and picks up the towing load while the other bridle part tends to go slack, thus swinging the tow in the direction the tug is going. Another advantage of using a bridle is that, when the tug is backing against the tow, which in turn causes the towline and bridle to go slack, the two parts of the bridle hang down in the water on either side of the tug rather than over the stern. In that position, it is unlikely that the bridle cables would be sucked in under the stern by the reversed rotation of the propeller when backing, thus reducing the risk of fouling the rudder or wheel. When transiting the lock, the towline is shortened in the close quarters of the lock chamber but would normally be let out to a longer length when in open water.

Illustrated below is the Lee and Brinton design for *Betty Earles*, used by Sol Duc Hot Springs Resort as a passenger boat on Lake Crescent. The main purpose of the vessel was to meet hotel guests who had arrived at the east end of the lake by buses, or "stages" as they were known as in those days. *Betty Earles* then transported them to the Sol Duc Hot Springs Hotel at Fairholm, which was located at the west end of the lake.

It is interesting that the arrangements laid out for *Betty Earles* provided for the separation of men and women passengers, the men in the cabin forward and the women in the larger space aft. Perhaps, however, it was considered proper for men and women to fraternize in the awning-covered seating area on the weather deck aft. The transformation of *Betty Earles* was representative of numerous conversions that were undertaken in the earlier days to convert freight and passenger vessels to towing service.

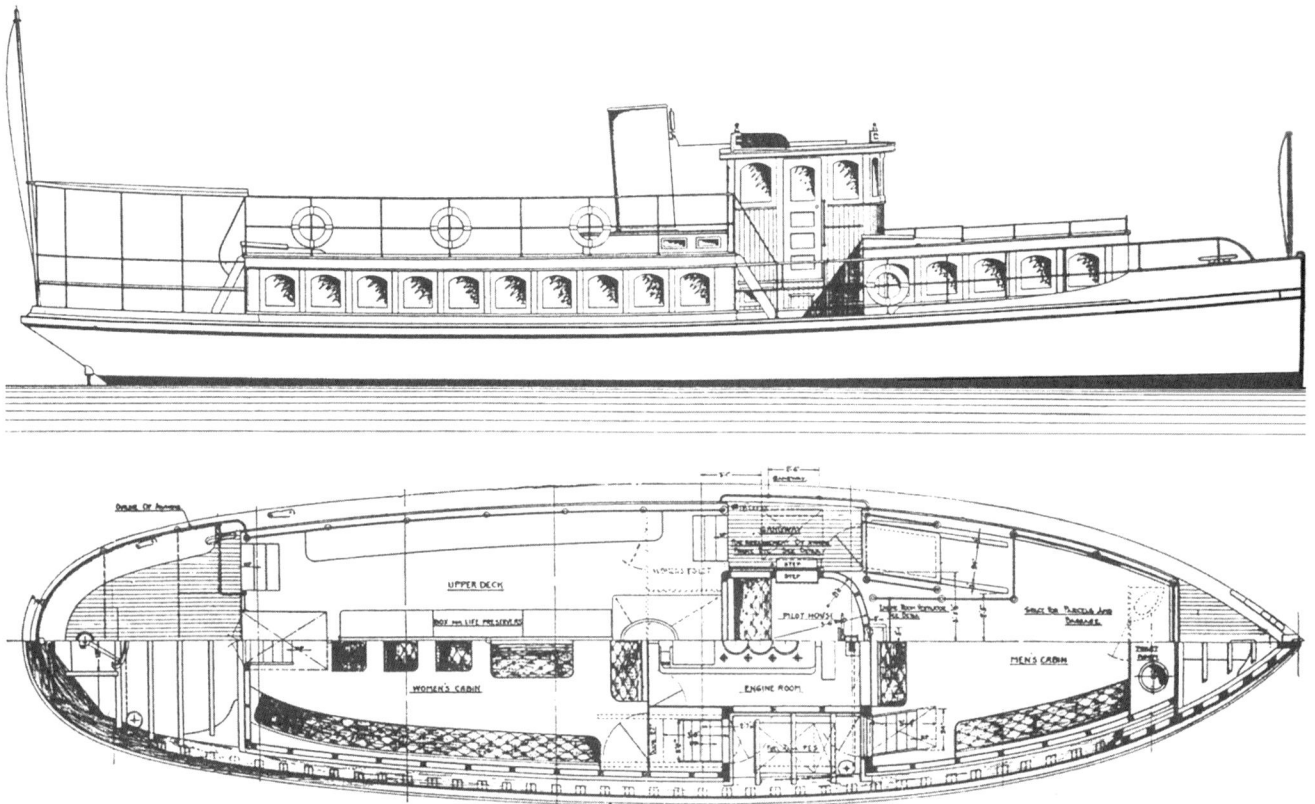

Betty Earles **outboard profile and arrangement as originally designed for passenger service in 1913.**
(From *Pacific Motor Boat*, August 1913)

Tacoma Tug and Barge Company's 57-foot tug *Fearless* was built of wood at Tacoma in 1926. In this photo, *Fearless* was heading south off Devil's Head with the tank barge *Lighter No. 7* in tow. *Lighter No. 7* is pictured on the next page while under tow by *Fearless* on this same trip.

As was sometimes done aboard a tug while underway, the deckhouse paint was being removed by the deckhand in preparation for repainting during any idle time available while enroute. In those days, removing paint was accomplished by the risky method of heating and softening the paint with a gasoline-fueled blowtorch and scraping, taking care, of course, to avoid setting the boat on fire. From the looks of *Fearless* in this picture, much of the paint had been removed from the port side of the deckhouse and pilothouse.

A busy time aboard a tug occurs at the beginning of a trip when the tow is turned loose from its mooring and the tow line is made fast to it. Then, at the destination, the tow line is shortened, and the tow is made fast at the designated location. While enroute, though, life is sometimes routine for crew members while standing their regular watches. However, if an unforeseen event occurs, such as the tow line breaking or a log raft under tow starts coming apart, for example, then the crew may be very busy indeed.

If all is proceeding in good shape aboard a towboat while underway, some types of maintenance can be performed by a deckhand when on watch, work that would otherwise have to be done in port. Chores done while on a tow reduce the amount of time the tug might be laid up and out of service while maintenance is performed. A tug typically is at work for several thousand hours per year, and it is important that the towboat continue working hard and producing revenue.

Fearless off Devil's Head, 1947. (From the author's collection)

Lighter No. 7 off Devil's Head, 1947. (From the author's collection)

Tide Water Associated Oil Company's 106-foot tank barge *Lighter No. 7* is pictured above. In this photo, *Lighter No. 7* was under tow by *Fearless* off Devil's Head at the time the photo on the previous page of *Fearless* was taken. *Lighter No. 7* was built of steel at Oakland, California, in 1924. Although the barge's deck was nearly awash, in fact, the small amount of freeboard was not unusual for fully loaded oil barges in operation on Puget Sound at the time.

Tacoma Tug and Barge's 41-foot wooden towboat *Fawn*, pictured below, was built at Burton in 1910. *Fawn* worked in the harbor at Tacoma and, like other tugs in the company's fleet, was outfitted with a towing bitt and Manila line rather than a winch and wire rope.

Fawn in Commencement Bay, 1947. (From the author's collection)

PIONEER TOWING COMPANY AND PIONEER SAND AND GRAVEL COMPANY
Seattle and Steilacoom

An affiliate of Pioneer Sand and Gravel Company, Pioneer Towing Company was primarily engaged in towing barges loaded with sand and gravel to Seattle from the Pioneer pit at Steilacoom. Company colors were black hull and red and white deckhouse for some boats, blue and white house for others.

Mining of the huge deposit of sand and gravel at Steilacoom has been going on for 100 years and still continues today, although Pioneer Towing Company is no longer in operation. These products have been delivered to locations spread out all the way from Olympia to Bellingham. A bulk commodity, such as sand and gravel, is ideally suited to delivery by water transportation. This type of cargo requires a vehicle with large capacity and weight-carrying ability, and speed is secondary; hence the stream of tugs and barges traveling to and from the pit.

Mooring buoys just offshore from the Steilacoom gravel pit permit a tug and tow to make fast and hold while waiting for any boats out ahead. On occasion, if the buoys are already in use, a tug might have to drop the anchor instead of mooring to a buoy. Emerging from the queue, the tug then shifts the scow to the pier where the loading crew attaches cables that move the barge beneath the tipple so as to spread the load of sand and gravel over the length of the scow.

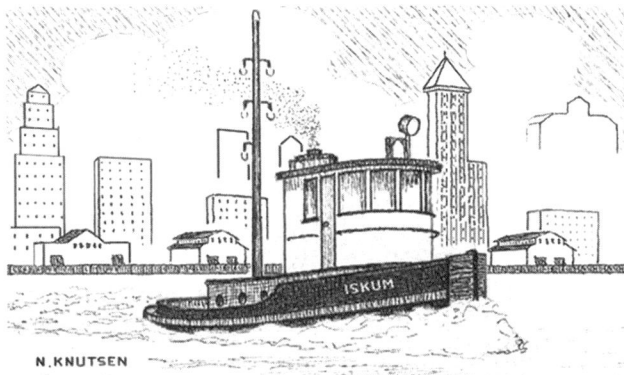

Iskum in Elliott Bay.

Ashore, long lengths of belt are set up to convey the sand and gravel from the dragline at the back of the pit and on through the sorting and washing operations. A belt moves the material to the tipple, where it spills onto the barge. A scale weighs and tallies the material being passed along by the belt and a final wash is applied to the material before it reaches the tipple.

About 10,000 tons of material can be loaded into barges during two work shifts. Some material inevitably spills into the water during loading, and therefore, a small suction dredge is used periodically by the shore crew to remove sand and gravel from the bottom to maintain adequate water depth at the pier.

With the loading operation finished, the tug moves back in and attaches the towline to the barge in preparation for getting under way. The current at The Narrows can reach a velocity of five or more knots so, if the tide stage is unfavorable, a north-bound tug with a loaded scow might remain at the pit and moor to a buoy, if available, to await the change of tide before departing.

There would be little point in bucking a flood tide in The Narrows since minimal or no progress would be made with a loaded scow or two behind, unless the tug had a lot of horsepower. In fact, if a north-bound tug and tow were to enter The Narrows before mid-stage of a flood tide, the current may, in short order, build to a point where forward progress changes to losing ground by actually moving backward.

As mentioned earlier in the book, however, beachcombing in under a point of land could make use of a back eddy where the current is reduced. With favorable conditions and sufficient horsepower, though, a tug and loaded barge could be off Shilshole ready to move in to the Ballard Locks in about six hours out from the Steilacoom pit.

Iskum, pictured at left and operated by Pioneer Towing Company, was a 51-foot long towboat built of wood at Winslow in 1912.

Service, left, and Anne W, right, at Steilacoom, 1948. (From the author's collection)

In the photo above, *Service* was just leaving the Pioneer Sand and Gravel pit at Steilacoom with a loaded scow while *Anne W* was moving in with an empty scow to be loaded. The protuberances at left in the photo are the conveyors and tipples that drop sand and gravel onto a barge's deck during loading. *Anne W's* unusual towing arrangement, with the towline fed through fittings at the top of the deckhouse, can be seen.

Anne W's deckhand had climbed up onto the forward end of the gravel scow, ready to handle mooring lines at the loading facility. The deckhand, silhouetted against the background in this foggy morning picture, can barely be perceived while he was sitting on the wooden bitt at the forward end of the barge.

In the photo below, *Service* had departed the Pioneer pit at Steilacoom and was heading north toward The Narrows with a loaded gravel scow. *Service* was a 48-foot long wooden tug, built at Seattle in 1917. *Service* was constructed with a raised deck for about two thirds of the length, which stepped down aft to be closer to the water for handling lines.

**Service, with a gravel scow on the towline, heading north toward The Narrows, 1949.
(From the author's collection)**

Anne W at the Ballard Locks, 1948. (From the author's collection)

In the photo above, *Anne W* was exiting the east end of the large lock at Ballard and pulling hard on two loaded gravel scows up from the Pioneer Sand and Gravel pit at Steilacoom. *Anne W* was built at Portland in 1913 as a 100-foot-long, wooden, steam-powered vessel for use on the Columbia River. In the late 1920s, *Anne W* was repowered with a direct reversing, six-cylinder Atlas diesel engine that put out 275 horsepower at about 275 revolutions per minute.

After spending some time working in Alaska, the towboat began operations for Pioneer Towing Company on a line haul run towing sand and gravel barges between Steilacoom and the Pioneer Sand and Gravel facility in Seattle. That run was made for many years, and as some said, *Anne W* wore a groove in the water.

With a draft of not much more than five feet, *Anne W* had been designed to operate in the shallows of the Columbia River. Shallow draft boats are interesting from a design point of view. With a length of 100 feet, *Anne W* was doing the job that a boat having much less length but a deeper draft could do if there was sufficient water depth for the smaller boat. However, since *Anne W* was originally designed specifically for shallow water operation, with a resulting draft limitation, the only way this type of vessel could gain enough buoyancy in the water to support the weight, particularly when carrying heavy steam machinery plus fuel and boiler feedwater as originally designed, was to provide a good deal of length or beam, or both. For *Anne W*, typical of river boats, a lot of length was put into the hull to ensure sufficient buoyancy.

The towing arrangements aboard *Anne W* are of interest. A conventional towing bitt or winch was not installed on the aft deck. The winch was located below deck and the line ran up vertically from the winch, out the top of the deckhouse, and then over a sheave system to the aft deck.

The drawing on the next page, showing a section looking to port through a "tunnel stern" towboat hull, is generic and is not intended to depict *Anne W* necessarily; it illustrates, though, how a tunnel stern can accommodate a large propeller in a shallow draft hull. In designing a tunnel, the bottom lines of the hull are swept up in the tunnel to a height that can accommodate a large propeller. The diameter of the propeller may be nearly equal to the draft of the boat. The top of the propeller is at or close to the waterline in the drawing, and in some designs, the upper blade tips may actually be above the waterline. The amount of foam in the picture of *Anne W* is indicative of a propeller that is not deep in the water.

111

Further comment concerning the drawing of a tunnel stern, shown at right, should be made. Although the top of the tunnel at the location of the propeller is at or near the waterline, it drops back down at the stern to a point below the surface of the water.

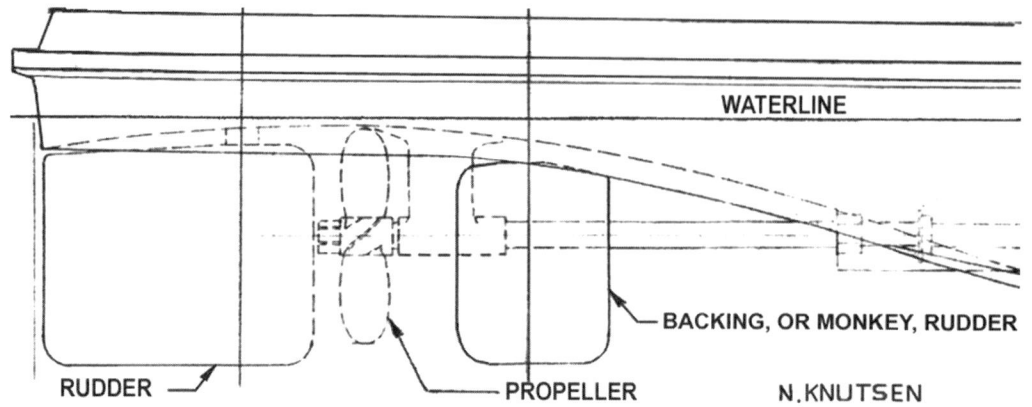

Aft end of tunnel stern hull looking to port.

With the aft end of the tunnel below the water surface, the amount of air drawn into the tunnel is minimized when backing down with the propeller in reverse rotation. If air is drawn into the tunnel, the propeller will be rotating in aerated water and backing thrust is less than it would be from a wheel operating in solid water. The top of the propeller and tunnel can actually be above the waterline and still function since the tunnel fills with water during operation. The efficiency of a propeller in a tunnel is less than that of an open water propeller, though. In the drawing, the rudder forward of the wheel is known as a backing rudder or monkey rudder.

Below, differing from the tunnel stern type of hull, a typical tug hull form of the 1940s is reproduced from a towing tank model test report published by the Society of Naval Architects and Marine Engineers. The resistance data for this particular hull indicated good propulsion characteristics, even though the hull was quite beamy.

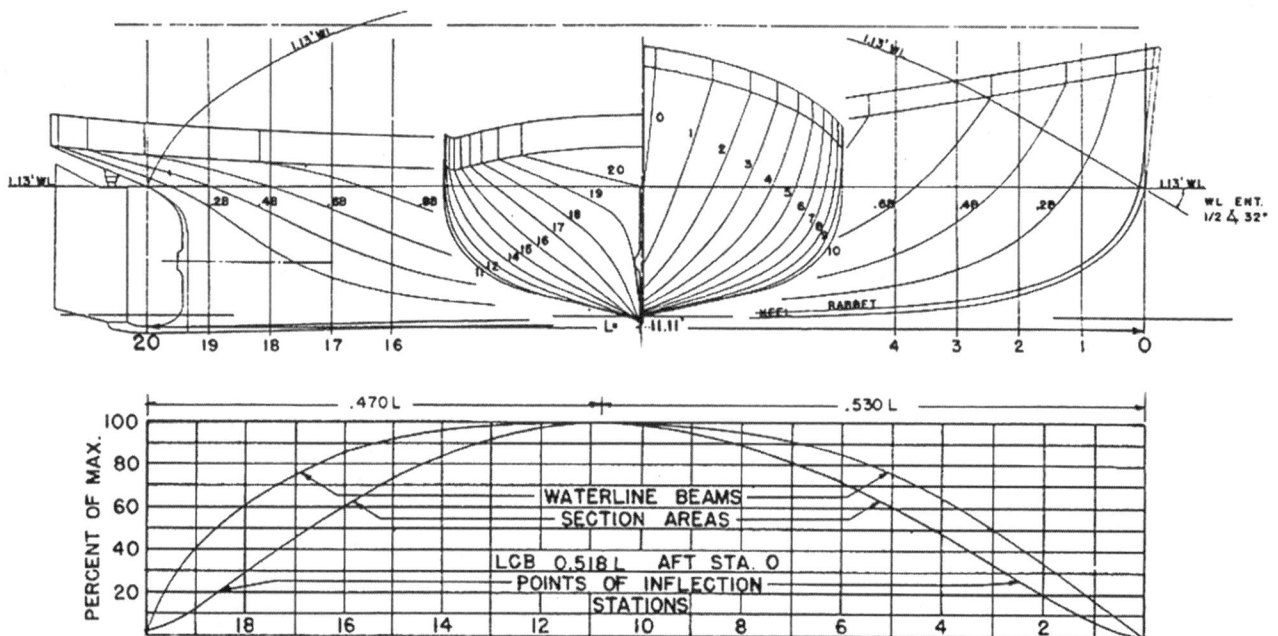

Conventional tug hull form.
(With permission of the Society of Naval Architects and Marine Engineers)

Commando **in the large lock at Ballard, 1963. (From the author's collection)**

In the photo above, Pioneer Towing Company's tug *Commando* is shown in the large lock at Ballard. This boat was 55 feet long and built of wood at Decatur in 1911.

Another photo of *Commando* is shown below and was taken during the tug races held at Seattle in 1950. To promote long engine life and increase time between repairs, engines installed in working vessels frequently feature a governor. An engine governor functions so that, when the boat is running with a heavy load on the towline at a relatively slow speed through the water, the amount of fuel injected into the cylinders is limited; as a result, the horsepower developed is restricted so that the engine is not overloaded beyond the manufacturer's continuous rating.

On the other hand, when running free without a tow, the engine is not as heavily loaded because, at a higher hull speed through the water, the propeller rotates with less effort. Because of this, when running light, the governor limits the speed of the engine so that it does not exceed the revolutions per minute as recommended by the manufacturer.

Judging by the appearance of *Commando*'s black exhaust smoke and huge wake, it can be assumed that to get all speed possible the engine governor was temporarily disconnected while the tug was running the race. At this speed, the towboat's stern had settled down and the aft deck may have been awash.

Commando **in the Seattle tug race of 1950.
(From the author's collection)**

113

Invader in Salmon Bay at Seattle, 1949. (From the author's collection)

In the photo above, Pioneer Towing Company's wooden tug *Invader* had just exited the large lock at Ballard on the way into Salmon Bay with a gravel scow from the Steilacoom pit. *Invader* was 61 feet long and built at Mare Island, California, in 1919.

The 66-foot, 900 horsepower tug *Marauder* was built of wood as the cannery tender *Chomly* at Dockton in 1915. A couple of months after this photo was taken, *Marauder*, with two barges in tow and bound for Steilacoom, caught fire and was beached at West Point as a total loss.

Marauder outbound from the small lock at Ballard, 1964. (From the author's collection)

114

CARY–DAVIS TUG AND BARGE CO. AND PUGET SOUND TUG AND BARGE CO.
Seattle

Cary-Davis Tug and Barge Company, initially consisting of the steam tug *Chehalis*, was started in 1913 by George Cary and Lindley Davis. In 1929, Pacific Tow Boat Company, Gilkey Brothers, and Drummond Lighterage joined Cary-Davis to form a new corporation called Puget Sound Tug and Barge Company.

Puget Sound Tug and Barge was created as an operating firm to maintain a lower overhead, and any floating equipment belonging to one company remained under ownership of that company.

Humaconna at Bay City, Michigan, circa 1970.
(From a serigraph by T. L. Dickinson)

In addition to acting as the operating company for the four towing companies, Puget Sound Tug and Barge also owned a fleet of tugs consisting of *Active*, *Commissioner*, *Neptune*, *Starling*, and *Tyee*, as well as other vessels as time went on. The paint scheme for the boats consisted of black hull and buff and white deckhouse.

The big steam tug *Humaconna*, illustrated above from a serigraph by T. L. Dickinson, was built for the United States Shipping Board at Superior, Wisconsin, in 1919. As depicted here, circa 1970, *Humaconna* had returned to the fresh water of the Great Lakes and was laid up at Bay City, Michigan, at the southern end of Lake Huron.

The vessel's length was 142 feet and propulsion power was supplied by a coal fired steam plant producing 1250 horsepower, giving the tug a reported top speed of 16 knots. *Humaconna* was originally engaged in wrecking and salvage work in the North Sea, Mediterranean, and in the waters off Bermuda and the Azores, as well as in

towing activities along the Atlantic coast. In 1921, Cary-Davis Tug and Barge Company purchased the tug for towing huge log rafts, assembled by Benson Lumber Company, from Astoria, Oregon, to San Diego, California.

Each Benson raft contained several million board feet of logs, and during assembly, the logs were lashed together to enable the raft to withstand the ocean swells that were encountered during coastwise towing. Even so, more than one raft broke up in heavy seas, leaving thousands of logs strewn along the Pacific Coast beaches. *Humaconna* was also engaged in ship-rescue work, in addition to a variety of other deep-sea towing assignments. In 1923, the tug's boiler was converted to oil firing by the Todd yard in Seattle.

In addition to employment with Cary-Davis, the tug had been operated by Merrill and Ring Lumber Company in the Pacific Northwest and was also in the service of handling car barges for Western Pacific Railway on San Francisco Bay during *Humaconna*'s career on the West Coast.

Commissioner, foreground, and *Douglas* at Seattle, 1948. (From the author's collection)

In the photo above, Puget Sound Tug and Barge Company's *Commissioner* and Cary-Davis Tug and Barge's *Douglas* were at their pier 59 moorage in Seattle.

The 108-foot, 600 horsepower *Commissioner* was built of wood at Brunswick, Georgia, in 1918. *Commissioner*'s massive lifting gear is an indicator of the vessel's previous work in marine salvage for Merritt, Chapman and Scott.

Douglas was 94 feet long and built of wood at Rocky River, Ohio, in 1919. At the time of the photo, *Douglas* was powered by a 300-horsepower Atlas diesel engine. The straight sheer, rather than a curved sheer, that was built into the hull of *Douglas* was originally intended to facilitate cargo handling on deck.

Pictured below are the Carey-Davis tug *Delwood* and Puget Sound's tug *Starling*. Both towboats were 57 feet long and built of wood at Seattle, *Delwood* in 1928 and *Starling* in 1913. As shown, *Starling*'s deckhouse had been modified from the original.

Delwood, left, and *Starling* in the ship canal at Seattle.

Monarch at Seattle, 1948. (From the author's collection)

In this photo, Cary-Davis Tug and Barge Company's Mikimiki type tug *Monarch* was tied up at the pier in Seattle between towing assignments. The 117-foot *Monarch* was built of wood at Quincy, Massachusetts, in 1944 and the installed horsepower was 1200.

The single davit forward, tied down with stays on the foredeck to prevent it from swinging in a seaway, was used for anchor handling. The brass bell can be seen mounted on the forward mast. The trumpet-shaped feature above the forward end of the pilothouse was the air horn. The ring mounted on a stanchion at the top of the wheelhouse was a radio direction finder for homing in

on a radio signal in order to determine position, and the searchlight is just to port of that. The white stanchion at the port railing near the pilothouse door very likely served as a support for a pelorus, which could be used for taking bearings on shoreside features or other ships when needed. Because of the absence of a radar, the radio direction finder and pelorus would have been important pieces of equipment for navigation.

The Cary-Davis tug *Hercules* is pictured on the next page moored at the end of the home pier. Identical to *Monarch*, with 1200 horsepower and twin screws, *Hercules* was built at Morgan City, Louisiana, in 1943.

In the photo at right of the Cary-Davis Mikimiki *Hercules*, the whistle call of a long and a short for Puget Sound Tug and Barge tug assistance is painted on the building. The big Manila fender on *Hercules'* bow is called a "pudding."

Another view, below, at the Cary-Davis/Puget Sound pier in Seattle shows the Puget Sound Tug and Barge towboat *Tyee*, ex-San Francisco, California, tug *Crowley*

Hercules at Seattle, 1949. (From the author's collection)

No. 28, passing the time between towing jobs. *Tyee* was 80 feet long, powered with a 400-horsepower Union and built at Alameda, California, in 1927. *Hercules* is at right in the photo.

On the next page is pictured the Cary-Davis towboat *Equator*. *Equator* was originally an 82-foot long schooner built of wood at Benicia, California, in 1888. *Equator* is well known as the little ship that novelist and poet Robert Lewis Stevenson used for his voyage from San Francisco, California, to Sidney, Australia, and Samoa in 1889 and 1890. While in the South Seas, Stevenson's experiences while visiting the islands and the time spent aboard *Equator* provided inspiration for his writings.

Prior to this voyage, while employed as a tender to canneries and the whaling fleet, *Equator* had been equipped with a 9, 18 x 18 compound steam engine operating at 125 pounds per square inch. The schooner was also fitted out with upper and lower deckhouses while still keeping her two masts and a portion of the sails. The large deckhouses drastically altered the vessel to a rather ungainly and top-heavy form, at least in appearance. The deckhouse was later modified to the arrangement shown in the photo.

Following service as a tender to the Arctic whaling fleet, *Equator* was bought by the newly formed Cary-Davis Tug and Barge Company in 1915. Cary-Davis repowered *Equator* with a 200-horsepower semi-diesel engine in 1922 which, in turn, was replaced with a 250-horsepower full-diesel engine in 1941.

Equator was retired and partially dismantled at Seattle in 1956, and upon completion of salvage work, the towboat's hull was deposited without ceremony as part of a jetty in Port Gardner at Everett.

Tyee at Seattle, 1949. (From the author's collection)

Equator in Salmon Bay at Seattle, circa 1950. (From the author's collection)

Wando is pictured at right as illustrated in a Standard Oil Company of California advertisement of 1957. This 115-foot vessel, originally steam, was built of steel by the Charleston Navy Yard at Charleston, South Carolina, in 1916 and then served for many years with the U.S. Navy.

Per McCurdy's 1966 *Marine History of the Pacific Northwest*, *Wando* was purchased by Puget Sound Tug and Barge Company sometime during the period 1950-1951. After acquiring the vessel, Puget Sound Tug and Barge overhauled the tug and replaced the steam machinery with diesel power.

Mention was made in the Standard Oil of California advertisement of *Wando*'s voyage to Baltimore to pick up a large ferry. In 1953, the state of Maryland put five ferries up for sale. The state of Washington was looking for additional ferries to augment the fleet that was then operating on Puget Sound and placed bids on the two largest ferries that were made available by the state of Maryland. The bids were successful, and following the 1953 hurricane season, *Wando*, along with *Monarch*, proceeded to Baltimore, Maryland, and brought the ferries 6000 miles to Seattle. For operation on Puget Sound, the ferries were named *Olympic* and *Rhododendron*.

Wando, 1957. (From a
Standard Oil Company of California advertisement)

119

The 1916 tug *Wando* outboard profile as drawn in support of
the conversion from steam to diesel power in 1948. (With permission of
Whatcom Museum of History and Art, H. C. Hanson Collection design 1026)

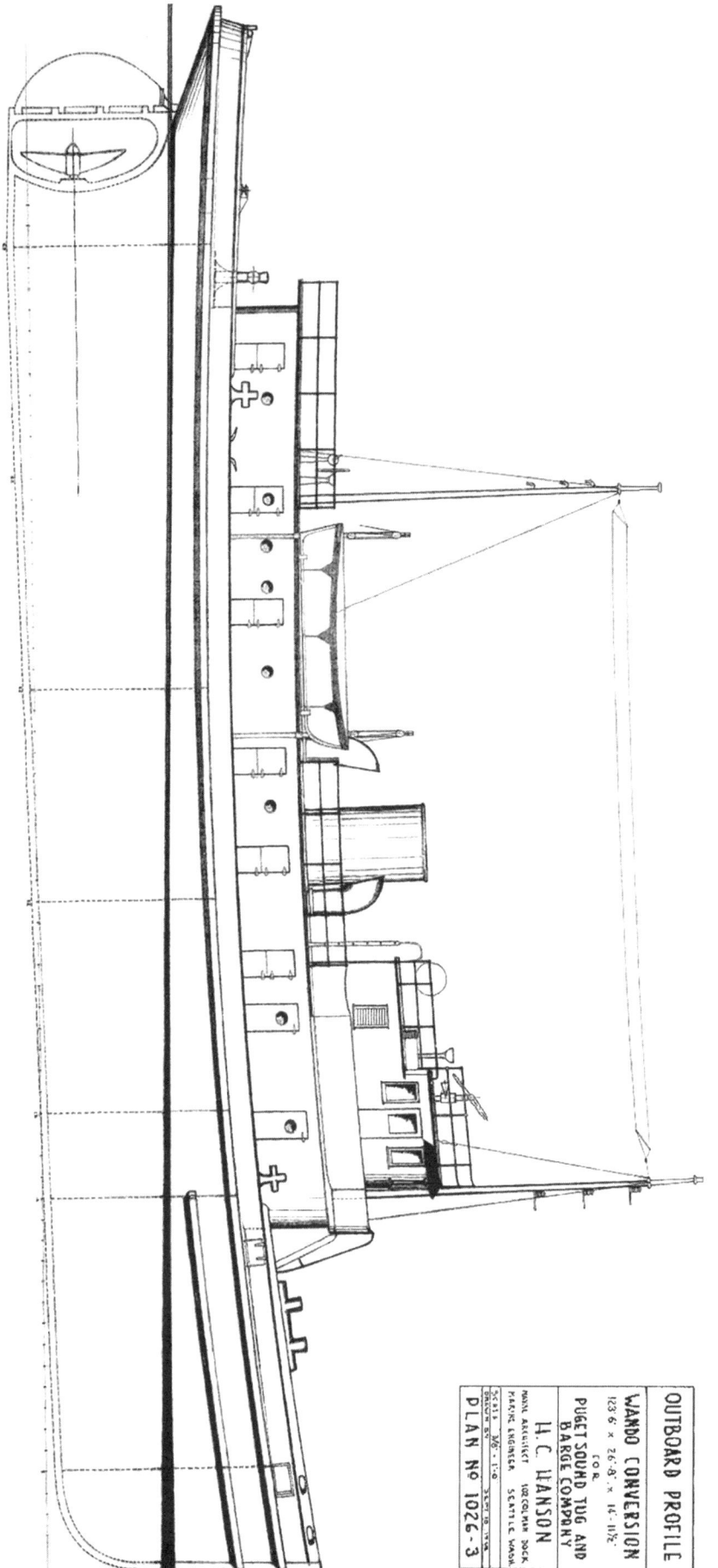

The above outboard profile drawing and other drawings on succeeding pages were done by Naval Architect H. C. Hanson in support of the major refit to convert *Wando* from steam to diesel. As noted on the previous page, according to *Marine History of the Pacific Northwest*, *Wando* was purchased by Puget Sound Tug and Barge Company sometime during 1950-1951. However, the outboard profile drawing shown on this page carries the date "Sept. 18, 1948" in the title block, apparently at variance with a 1950 or 1951 purchase. It is known that the huge amount of work involved in renovating

Wando was done over a fairly long period of time, and that *Wando* was operational as a diesel tug by fall of 1951. It would seem, then, that the purchase date for *Wando* would more likely have been around 1948 rather than 1950 or 1951.

The outboard profile drawing shows that *Wando* was built with a rudder post utilizing pintle and gudgeon rudder hinges, which offers a clue for approximate dating of a vessel. After World War I, this type of rudder attachment was gradually being replaced by a stock fixed to the rudder and projecting down through the hull bottom.

OUTBOARD PROFILE
WANDO CONVERSION
123'6" x 26'-8" x 14'-11½"
FOR
PUGET SOUND TUG AND BARGE COMPANY
H. C. HANSON
NAVAL ARCHITECT   MARINE ENGINEER   1020 COLMAN DOCK
SEATTLE WASH.
PLAN Nº 1026-3

INBOARD PROFILE

WANDO CONVERSION
123'-6" x 26'-6" x 14'-11½"

for

PUGET SOUND TUG
AND BARGE CO.

H. C. HANSON
NAVAL ARCHITECT   102 COLMAN DOCK
MARINE ENGINEER   SEATTLE 4 WASH

DRAWN   DATE

Scale 3/8"=1'0

PLAN NO. 1026-1

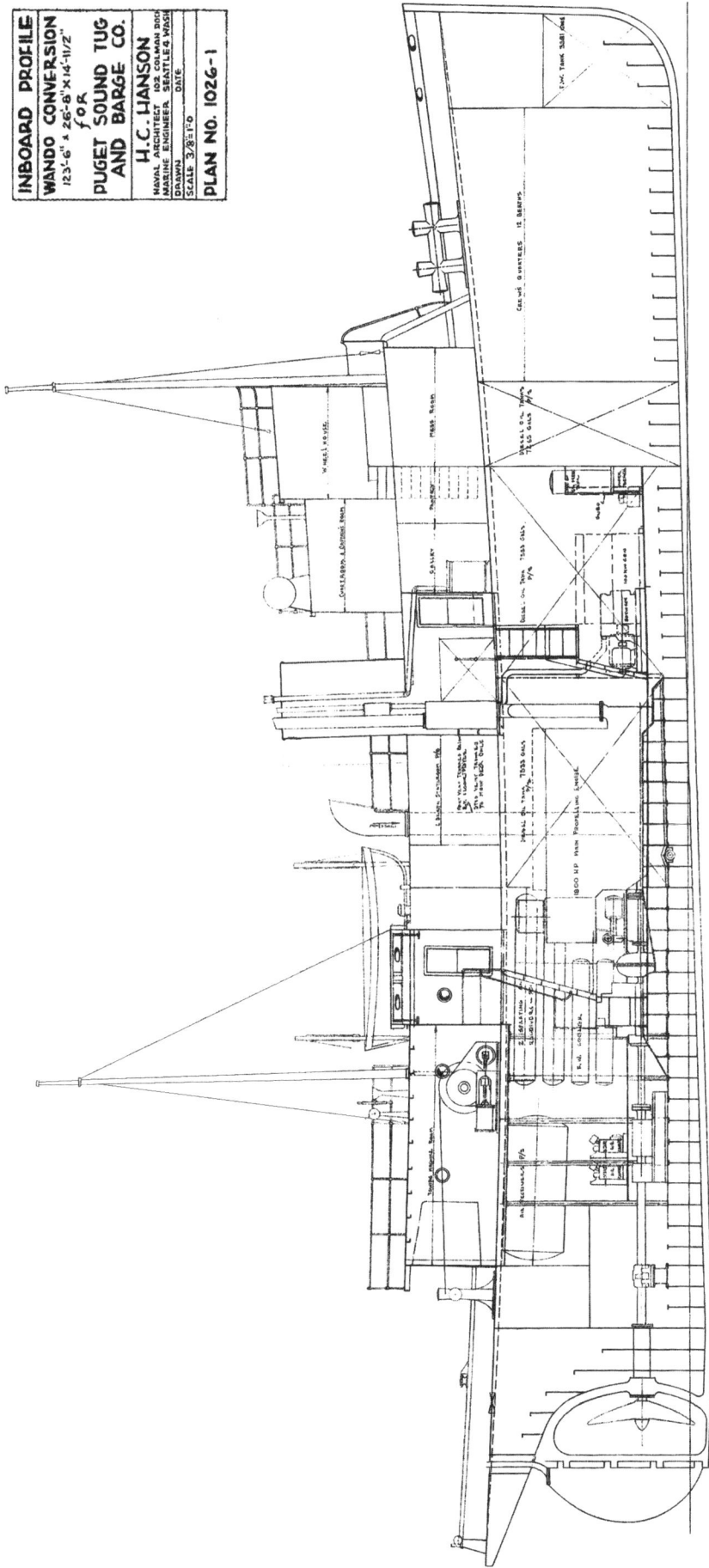

The 1916 tug *Wando* inboard profile as drawn in support of the conversion from steam to diesel power in 1948. (With permission of Whatcom Museum of History and Art, H. C. Hanson Collection design 1026)

For a tug the size of *Wando*, it is an enormous task to make an upgrade that results in, essentially, a new vessel. A large share of the conversion work for the tug was done by Puget Sound Tug and Barge company's own employees, and the refit of the tug moved along at a measured pace as time and personnel were available. A good deal of effort was needed just to remove and dispose of the steam propulsion and auxiliary machinery, and there was much additional work required before the refurbishment could begin, as well. New berthing accommodations were provided for up to 18 in the crew.

To permit a long range without refueling during extended time at sea, tanks were provided for about 45,000 gallons of diesel oil. Tank capacity for potable water and lube oil, as well as spaces for galley, mess, provisions, and spares, were of a size commensurate with long periods away from home port. The design drawings make clear, though, that there was no access between spaces inside the deckhouse, typical for earlier tugs. Access between spaces was only via weather deck routes, but *Wando*'s 25-foot beam was simply insufficient to make room for internal passageways.

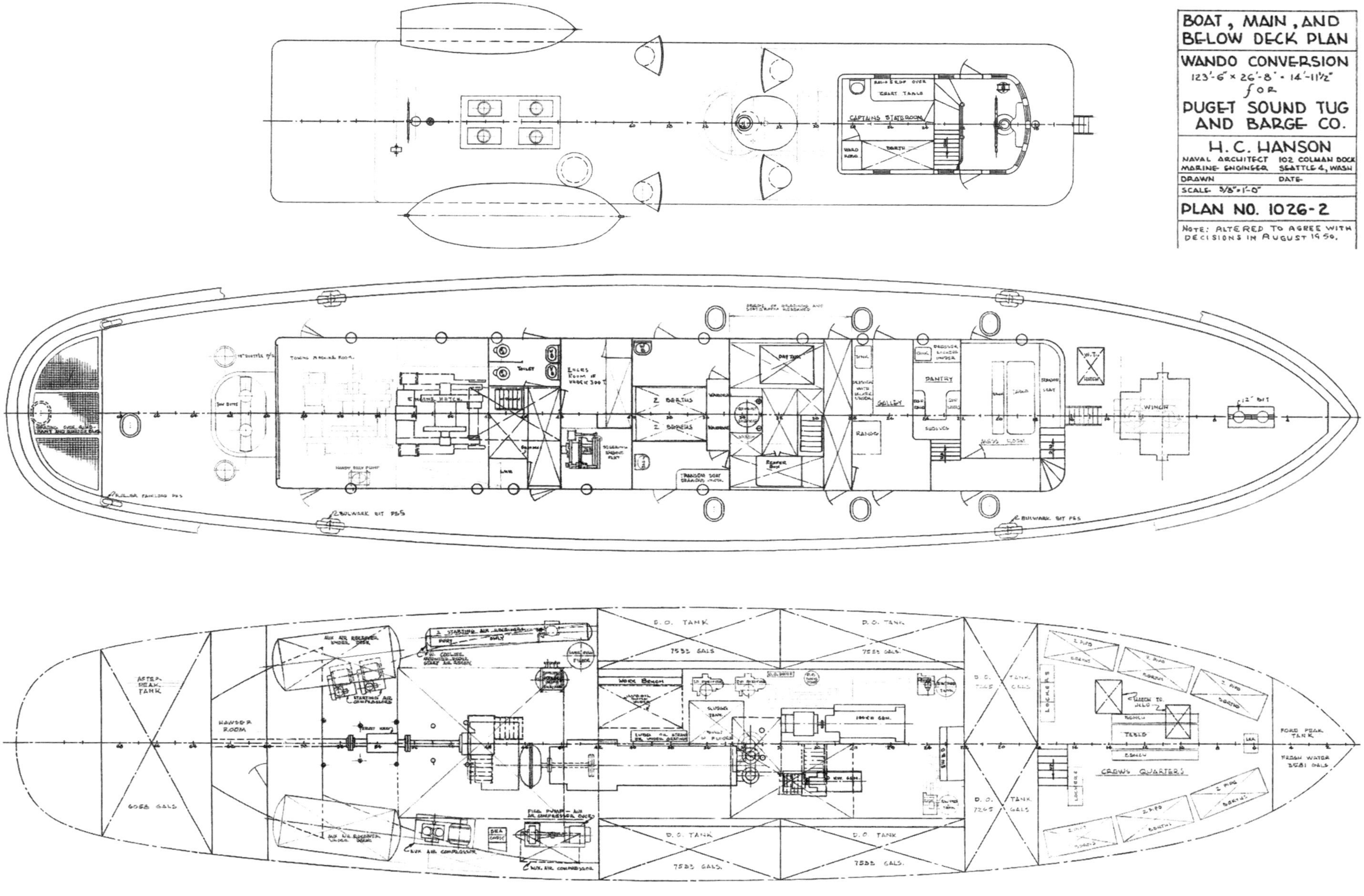
BOAT, MAIN, AND BELOW DECK PLAN
WANDO CONVERSION
123'-6" × 26'-8" • 14'-11½"
for
PUGET SOUND TUG AND BARGE CO.
H. C. HANSON
NAVAL ARCHITECT 102 COLMAN DOCK
MARINE ENGINEER SEATTLE 4, WASH
DRAWN DATE
SCALE 3/8"=1'-0"
PLAN NO. 1026-2
NOTE: ALTERED TO AGREE WITH DECISIONS IN AUGUST 1950.
CAPTAINS STATEROOM
PANTRY
GALLEY
WINCH
D. O. TANK
7533 GALS.
WORK BENCH
CREWS QUARTERS
HAWSER ROOM
AFTER PEAK TANK
6068 GALS
FORE PEAK TANK
LOCKERS

The 1916 tug *Wando* boat deck, main deck and below deck arrangements as drawn in support of the conversion from steam to diesel power in 1948. (With permission of Whatcom Museum of History and Art, H. C. Hanson Collection design 1026)

When viewing the *Wando* conversion design drawings, it may be noticed that there are faint lines, here and there, that appear to describe certain features, for example, the towing winch as evident in the main deck arrangement plan on the previous page. A duplicate of the towing winch, drawn with heavier lines, is at a more forward location. The ghost lines are, no doubt, remainders of lines that had not been completely erased after changing the location of the winch.

The location of some features in the drawings may not agree from view to view; for example, there are six doors shown on the starboard side in the main deck arrangement plan and eight doors on the starboard side in the outboard profile. Change is a part of the design/build process and, occasionally, some details are incorporated in the hardware that are not reflected in the drawings. It appears that as-built drawings were not needed so revisions were not made on the drawings.

As a replacement for the steam-propulsion plant, an 1800-horsepower, 10-cylinder, two-cycle, opposed-piston Fairbanks-Morse diesel engine that had been surplused from a World War II landing craft was installed. This engine drove an 8 1/2 foot-diameter propeller supplied by Coolidge Propeller Company of Seattle, giving *Wando* a speed of more than 14 knots when running light. Power was transmitted to the propeller through a 2 1/2 to 1 reduction gear. Electrical power was supplied by two GM diesel generators, one producing 100 kilowatts and the other 30 kW.

Referring to the below-deck arrangement plan on the previous page, it will be noticed that the propulsion engine was set about two feet off centerline to starboard and power was delivered transversely, rather than vertically as is usually done, through the reduction gear to the propeller shaft. Setting the main engine off center has not been a common practice with most engines, but perhaps there was a space problem with the tall FM opposed piston engine.

The Fairbanks-Morse opposed-piston engine was mainly developed for use in railroad locomotives. However, it also saw use in some of the military vessels, including submarines, during World War II.

In the illustrations at left, the difference between the Fairbanks-Morse opposed-piston engine and a more conventional engine, in this case an Enterprise, can be seen. The design of the FM engine is unusual because it does not have a cylinder head. Two opposed pistons in each cylinder, forming a common combustion chamber between, move in opposite directions to rotate upper and lower crankshafts that are connected through gears to a common output shaft.

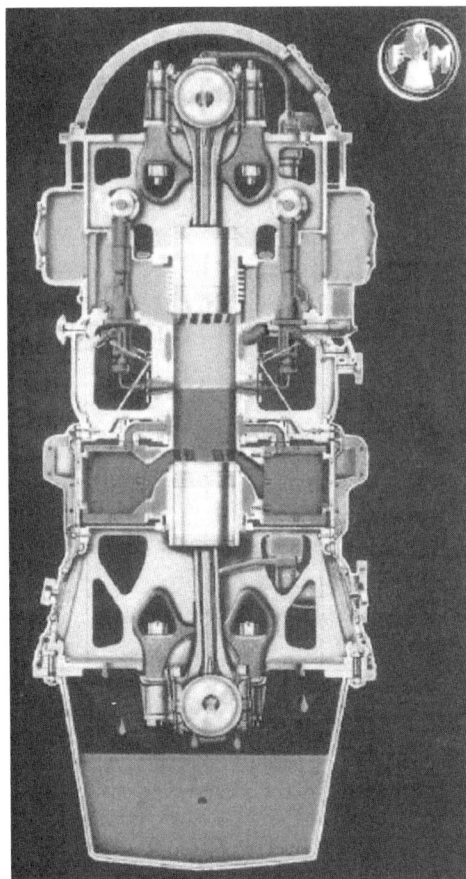

Section through Fairbanks-Morse two-cycle opposed piston diesel engine. (From Fairbanks-Morse Company literature, 1940s)

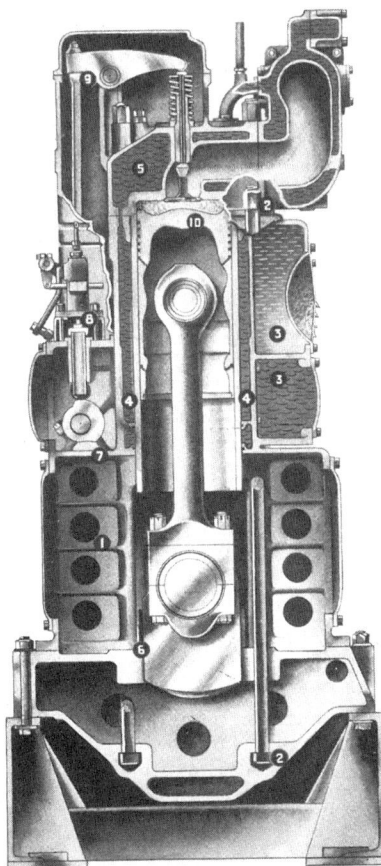

Section through Enterprise four-cycle diesel engine. (From Enterprise Engine and Foundry Company literature, 1940s)

The first *Neptune* with two deck barges in tow, n.d. (Courtesy of Randolph Estvold)

In the photo above, the first in a series of three tugs named *Neptune* operated by Puget Sound Tug and Barge was towing a pair of deck barges on Puget Sound. The 109-foot long *Neptune* was built of steel as the U.S. Public Health Service quarantine vessel *R. M. Woodward* at Baltimore, Maryland, in 1904 and was based on San Francisco Bay for the purpose of boarding incoming ships.

The vessel was purchased by Puget Sound Tug and Barge in 1937 and then underwent an extensive renovation and upgrade in accommodations and outfitting. Included in the refit was the installation of a Fairbanks-Morse 1050-horsepower diesel engine, which gave the tug a 13-knot speed. *Neptune* was employed in towing a Milwaukee Railroad car barge between Seattle and Bellingham. In addition, the tug was also engaged in bringing to Puget Sound the San Francisco Bay ferries that had been purchased for Captain Peabody's Black Ball system. The tug also towed a Benson log raft from Astoria, Oregon, to San Diego, California, and worked at a number of other assignments. Foss Launch and Tug Company acquired *Neptune* in 1946 and renamed the tug *Wedell Foss*, pictured elsewhere in the book.

One of the Cary-Davis fleet, *Dolly C*, pictured below, was a 66-foot wooden tug built at Dockton in 1922. The tug was originally fitted with a 150-horsepower diesel engine built by Werkspoor in Europe. *Dolly C* was renovated in 1950, and as part of the upgrade, the tug received a 500-horsepower diesel engine. A few years after this photo was taken, *Dolly C* sank in Admiralty Inlet while bound for Bellingham with an oil barge in tow.

Dolly C in The Narrows, 1949. (From the author's collection)

Left to right, *WSA-18*, the second *Neptune*, and *Dolly C* at the Reserve Fleet in Budd Inlet, 1947. (From the author's collection)

In the photo above, the second *Neptune* operated by Puget Sound Tug and Barge was partnered with *Dolly C* while attending to a hospital ship at the Reserve Fleet in Budd Inlet. The 142-foot *Neptune* was built of steel as the steam tug *Barryton* at Elizabeth, New Jersey, in 1919 for service with the U.S. government. In 1941, ownership passed to Moran Towing and Transportation Company in New York, the tug's name then being changed to *Thomas E. Moran*. While a member of the Moran fleet, the tug's steam plant was removed and replaced with a diesel engine of 1400 horsepower.

At the time of the photo, *Neptune* was registered to Harbor Tug and Barge of San Francisco, California, but was in operation for Puget Sound Tug and Barge. *Neptune* was probably the largest tug to operate on Puget Sound since the earlier era of the giant steam powered tugs, such as *Humaconna*, and was also notable for the vessel's huge red and black funnel. At left, next to the bow of the hospital ship, the U.S. Maritime Administration's tug *WSA-18* is silhouetted.

A couple of years after this photo was taken *Neptune* was gone, done in by a mishap. During a storm in November 1949, *Neptune* was dispatched to help the ocean-going steamship *Herald of the Morning*, disabled off the mouth of the Columbia River. Accompanied in the rough seas by the San Francisco tug *Sea Fox*, *Neptune* worked in close to *Herald of the Morning*, but with both ship and

tug rolling and pitching in the heavy seas, *Neptune* was stove in by the big freighter. *Neptune* sank rapidly, but the crewmen, except for one soul who died in the cold water, were rescued by the U.S. Coast Guard cutter *Balsam*.

In 1956, a new 100-foot *Neptune*, powered by a 1280-horsepower Fairbanks-Morse opposed piston diesel engine, was built of steel by Gunderson Brothers Engineering at Portland, Oregon, to a design by Philip F. Spaulding and Associates, Seattle naval nrchitects.

In 1946, the National Defense Reserve Fleet was established to moor government-owned ships that were no longer needed in the World War II effort. The system consisted of fleets at eight locations in the United States, including the anchorage just north of Olympia. The combined fleets totaled more than 2000 ships, of which nearly 200 were moored in the Olympia Reserve Fleet.

The ships were mothballed and protected so that, if the occasion arose, they could be placed back into government service. For that purpose, the locations selected were near large shipyards having the capability to perform reactivation work if needed. Over the years, though, many of these ships were sold into commercial service. Others were sold for scrap, the majority to ship breakers in foreign countries where scrap prices were relatively high. By the middle of 1972, the waters of Gull Harbor in Budd Inlet that had been host to the Olympia Reserve Fleet were empty of ships.

Goliah at Seattle, 1948. (From the author's collection)

In this photo, Cary-Davis Tug and Barge Company's *Goliah* was between tows at the Cary-Davis/Puget Sound pier in Seattle. *Monarch*'s bow can be seen at the end of the pier.

The 112-foot *Goliah* was built at Philadelphia in 1883. Though it is not certain, it is likely that *Goliah* was built of steel, a relatively new alloy at the time that was displacing the use of durable, but lower strength, low-carbon wrought iron. The vessel's structure was riveted, the standard method of assembly at the time of construction, only eighteen years after the end of the Civil War. Forward, low on the sunlit side of the hull, a lapped rivet joint can be seen on the plating. For lifeboat handling, the davits aboard *Goliah,* as shown in the photo, are called radial davits and rotate about a vertical axis. *Monarch* and *Hercules* were outfitted with quadrantal davits that simply swing outboard for launching the boat.

Goliah was powered with a huge 600-horsepower MacIntosh and Seymour slow-speed diesel engine installed by Cary-Davis. With sleek, slim hull lines, the tug was fast when running light and was reported as having attained over 14 knots on trials with the new engine. The sound of the exhaust was rhythmic and very quiet.

Goliah at the Reserve Fleet in Budd Inlet, 1949. (From the author's collection)

Above is a port-side profile view of *Goliah* at the Reserve Fleet in Budd Inlet. *Goliah* was an old-time looking tug with long, low and slim lines.

In the photo below are, left to right, *Active*, belonging to Puget Sound Tug and Barge, *Goliah* and the U.S. Maritime Administration's *WSA-18*, a tug assigned to work with the Olympia fleet of mothballed ships at Gull Harbor. *Active* and *Goliah* were alongside the Liberty Class ship that they had just brought to the layup area and were finishing up on their work there. When not working with ship assist, *WSA-18* tied up at the Maritime Administration facility pier there on the shore at Gull Harbor.

Active, left, *Goliah*, center, and *WSA-18*, right, at the Reserve Fleet in Budd Inlet, 1949.
(From the author's collection)

Goliah entering Dana Passage, 1949. (From the author's collection)

Active entering Dana Passage, 1949. (From the author's collection)

In these two photos, *Goliah* and *Active* had finished with the delivery of a Liberty Ship for layup up in the Budd Inlet Reserve Fleet of ships, as described on the previous page, and were about seven miles out of Olympia and just entering the southwest entrance to Dana Passage enroute north back to Seattle.

At right in the background of the top photo is Brisco Point, upon which a light marks the south-ern end of Hartstene Island. Off to the right, out of sight beyond this point, is the entrance to Hammersley Inlet which leads west to Shelton.

Goliah has been previously described, but *Active* was 100 feet long and built of steel as a steam tug by Union Iron Works at San Francisco in 1888 for Spreckels. With sweeping lines, *Active*'s ap-pearance had those qualities that make for a clas-sic-looking towboat.

128

Active was requisitioned by the U. S. government in 1898 and later, after completing that service, the towboat was purchased by Cary-Davis Tug and Barge and renamed *Lively*. In 1934 the steam plant was removed and a six-cylinder, 550-horsepower MacIntosh and Seymour diesel engine was installed. Shown here is a design drawing by Naval Architect H. C. Hanson for the conversion of *Lively* from steam to diesel.

Installed in the engine room were two large air receivers not only to provide the compressed starting air for the MacIntosh and Seymour but also to power the windlass and towing winch. Accommodation for the deck crew was in the fo'c'sle forward, and berthing for the engine room crew was located below deck just abaft the engine room, with access through a hatch. This location for the engine crew seems a bit uninviting, but such was life in the earlier days aboard a working vessel.

Following several years of operation for Cary-Davis, *Lively* passed to Puget Sound Tug and Barge and the name was changed back to the original name, *Active*, that had been given at launch. In that employment, *Active* put in many years of ocean-towing as well as work on Puget Sound.

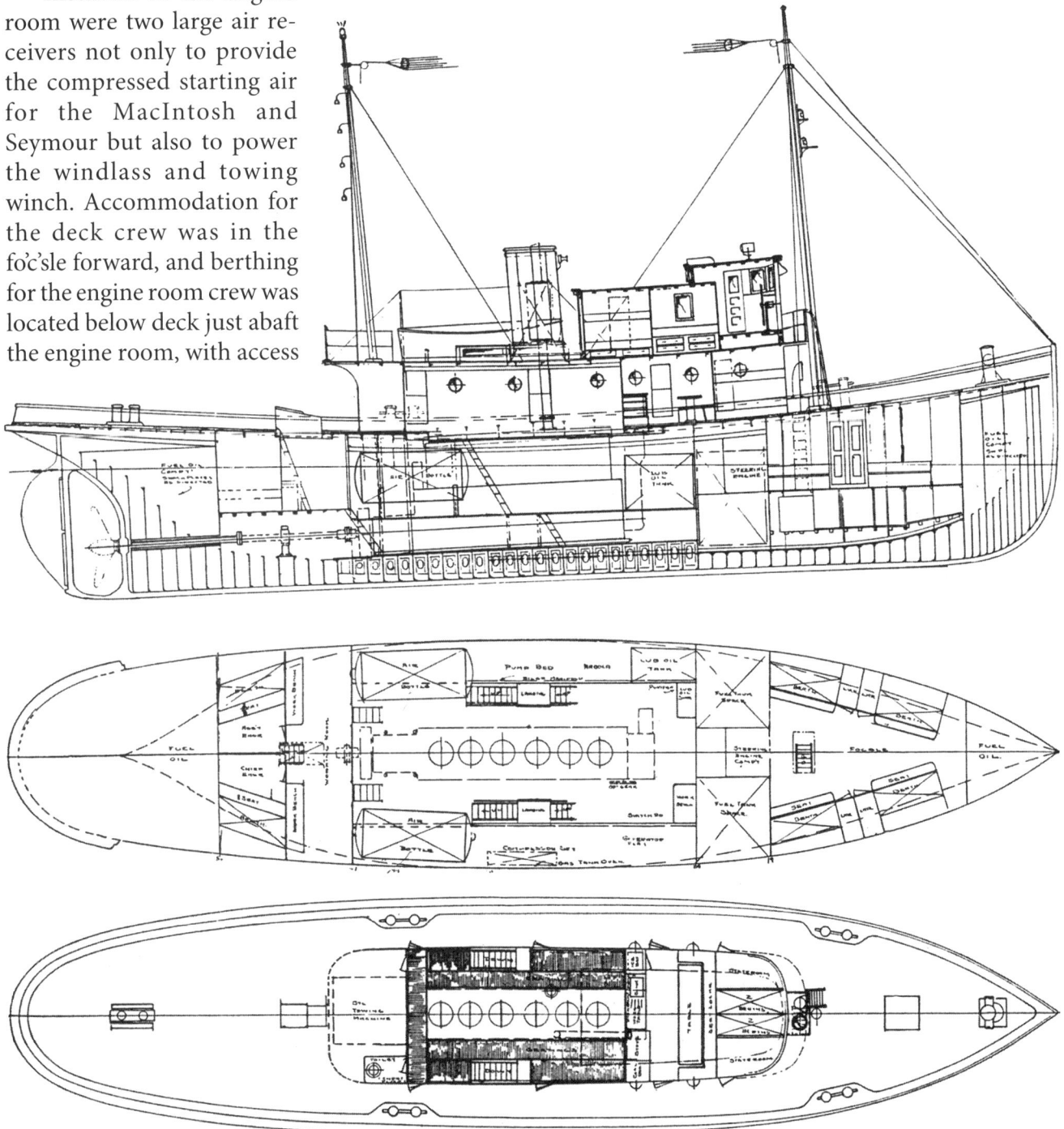

Lively inboard profile and arrangement, 1934. (From **Pacific Motor Boat**, June 1934)

WASHINGTON TUG AND BARGE CO.
Seattle

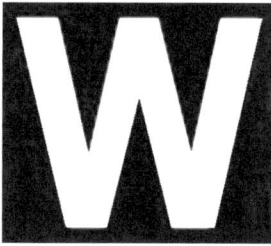

W Washington Tug and Barge Company was started in 1909 by Captain Harry Crosby and L. S. Wood with the 93-foot steamer *Lydia Thompson*, built at Port Angeles in 1893. Company colors were black hull and red and white deckhouse, while the stack was black with a large white W on both sides.

The wooden tug *Bee*, in the photo below, was operated by Washington Tug and Barge for many years. At the time of the photo, however, the tug had recently been acquired by Robert Shrewsbury for use by his Western Towboat Company. As a result, Washington Tug's red was then changed to Western's buff on the lower portion of the deckhouse. *Bee*, 58 feet long, was built of wood at Everett in 1901. The tug went through a series of Superior heavy-duty diesel engines of increasing power while in the employ of WT&B, but at the time of the photo below, the towboat had been re-engined with a Caterpillar turbocharged diesel. In this photo, *Bee* was in the big lock towing an empty wooden deck scow outbound to take on a load of sand and gravel, probably at the Pioneer Sand and Gravel Company pit at Steilacoom.

Employing a very short tow line while transiting the locks, the tug has backed the stern against the forward end of the barge and was in reverse to stop the forward motion of the scow, as evidenced by the wheel wash at the stern. By this time, the deckhand would have climbed onto the deck of the scow in preparation for passing a line to the lock attendant on the lock wall who would then tie the stern of the barge off to a bitt.

After leaving the channel at Shilshole for open water, with the deckhand back aboard, the towline would have been let out to a much longer length. The longer towline would then act as a spring to absorb shocks introduced by the relative motions of the tug and barge in rougher water, and for best speed, the longer distance between tug and tow would minimize the impingement of prop wash against the scow.

Bee at the Ballard Locks, 1963. (From the author's collection)

Reliance, shown in the photo at right while in Elliott Bay, was a good-looking 79-foot wooden tug constructed at the Cook and Lake yard in Ballard in 1912 as *Forest T. Crosby*. As built, the tug was powered by a triple expansion steam engine of dimensions 11, 15, 25 x 16 utilizing steam supplied by a Scotch boiler.

Reliance in Elliott Bay, 1950. (From the author's collection)

In 1936, the steam plant was removed, and a 300-horsepower Washington diesel engine was installed. Many years later, the Washington was removed and replaced by a 500-horsepower Caterpillar diesel engine.

In the photo below, Washington Tug and Barge Company's *Triumph* was standing by while the tug's tow, *W.T.B. Co. No. 62* barge carrying petroleum products in ex-railroad car tanks, was being unloaded at the Union Oil Company tank farm in Olympia. Built of wood at Parkersburg, Oregon, in 1889, *Triumph* operated as a bar tug engaged in towing sailing ships across the rough water entrances at Oregon harbors such as Coos Bay. In 1931, the steam engine and boiler were removed in favor of a 300-horsepower diesel engine.

At right in the lower photo, just beyond *Triumph*'s stern, is the Olympia Yacht Club, looking much different from how it looks today. At the time of the photo, the yacht club consisted mostly of moorages that were open to the weather, with only a few yachts housed in wooden boat houses as shown here providing shelter from the elements. Today, the yacht club moorage is mostly composed of metal boat houses to protect the power boats from the weather. From a practical standpoint, sailboats, of course, cannot utilize this type of shelter because of the tall rigging.

Triumph at Olympia, 1948. (From the author's collection)

Sally S at Shelton, 1965. (Courtesy of Elizabeth Wolf)

In this picture, Washington Tug and Barge Company's *Sally S* was standing by at Shelton while the tug's tow, an oil barge, was unloading. The 70-foot *Sally S*, from the boards of Naval Architect Ted Geary, was built of wood at Port Blakely in 1927 as a cannery tender for operation by Sunny Point Packing Company. Designed originally with a 180-horsepower Eastern Standard engine, the tug was later upgraded with the installation of a 325-horsepower Caterpillar diesel engine. At the time of the photo, the tug had recently been traded to Washington Tug and Barge by Robert H. Shrewsbury's Western Tow Boat Company in exchange for Washington Tug and Barge Company's *Triumph*.

The outboard profile and arrangement drawing for *Sally S* is shown on the next page. The appearance and general arrangement were typical of many cannery tenders of the time and of this size, but the accommodations were more generous than those found aboard many of the early work boats. Six berths were provided down forward in the fo'c'sle, entered from the foredeck,

and four berths were installed in the deckhouse. In addition, just abaft the pilothouse, the captain was provided with a stateroom outfitted with a single berth.

The galley and dinette were forward in the deckhouse, and it is interesting to see that the galley range was fired with coal, rather than with diesel oil as used aboard most of the earlier cannery tenders and towboats. Coal was readily available in a small container alongside the stove, and additional coal was stored in a bin below deck at the aft end of the fo'c'sle. While the forward portion of the deckhouse was situated at the main deck level, the sole in the aft two thirds of the house where the crew accommodations were located was raised above the deck. This was done to clear the top of the large Standard engine.

Exterior deck outfit aboard *Sally S* included a towing bitt aft and an anchor windlass and a davit forward. In addition, a necessity for and typical of most cannery tenders, a mast, stayed with stranded wire rope, and a swinging boom were installed on the foredeck.

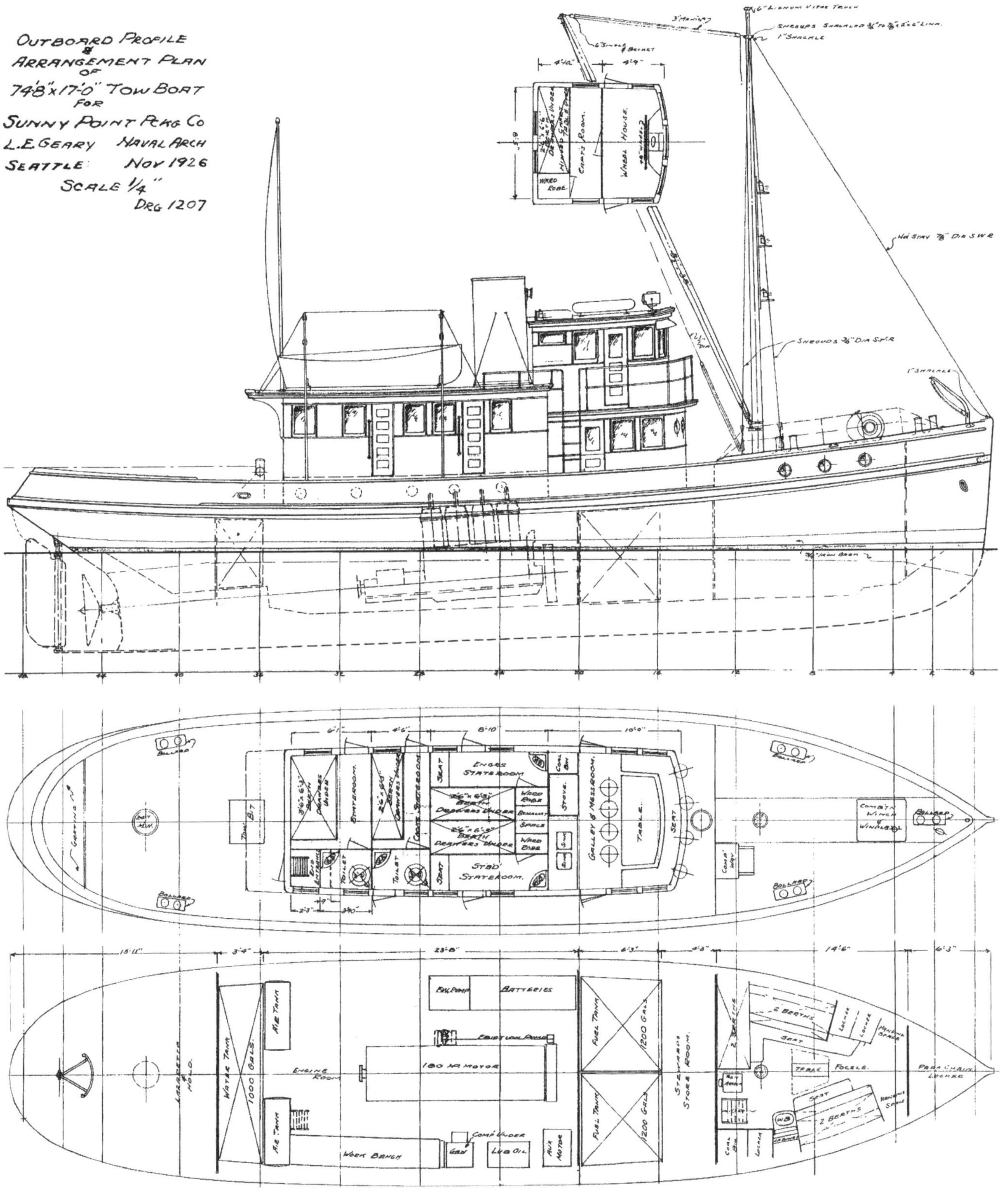

Sally S outboard profile and arrangement, 1926.
(With permission of Puget Sound Maritime Historical Society, Ship Plans Collection)

Other towboats operated for a time by Washington Tug and Barge were the twins *Hornet* and *Wasp*, ownership of *Hornet* then passing to Puget Sound Bridge and Dredging Company and pictured later in the book as *Alfred*. In the 1950s, the firm also acquired the 96 foot wooden, 450-horsepower *Tartar*, a tug that had been surplused by the U.S. Army after World War II.

FOSS LAUNCH AND TUG COMPANY
Tacoma, Seattle, and Port Angeles

Many stories have been told about the start of Foss Launch and Tug Company by Andrew and Thea Foss in the late 1800s and the success that followed. Certainly during the period covered by this narrative, the green and white Foss colors were worn by the largest flotilla of towboats and other equipment, including barges, derricks, cranes, and dredges, on the West Coast and, no doubt, one of the largest in the world.

For the express purpose of taking care of this fleet, Foss, very early, established a shipyard at Tacoma and, eventually, a drydock and yard at the Seattle headquarters. In later years, in addition to maintaining existing floating equipment, Foss shipwrights built new tugs to augment the fleet.

The picture below shows the Foss moorage at Nickerson Street on the south shore of the ship canal in Seattle. It can be seen that, considering the large number of tugs that made up the Foss fleet, there were very few of the company's boats at the moorage on the day of the photo since, typically, most would have been be out on the job.

It is probable that not even the founders of Foss Launch and Tug, immigrants from Norway Andrew and Thea Foss, could have envisioned that the company would grow to such a large size, especially considering that the firm started in such a tiny way with the purchase by Thea, around 1890, of a rowboat. Andrew had taken a job aboard a towboat belonging to Tacoma Tug and Barge Company, and this was followed later by employment in a shipyard. His brothers, Iver and Peter, arrived in the Pacific Northwest from Norway and went to work in a sawmill. Pooling their talents, the brothers salvaged a steam engine and boiler from a derelict vessel, built a new boat to utilize the machinery, named the boat *Blue Star*, and found a buyer for the little steamer.

Meanwhile, after applying new paint to the small rowboat that she had initially bought, Thea then sold the boat for a sum that was more than she had paid for it. Additional small rowing boats were purchased by Thea and, after some freshening up was applied to the boats, were then sold at a profit also.

While Andrew was busy with his endeavors, including building houses, Thea continued to buy and sell boats and expand her fleet of rowboats that were for hire. Along the way the slogan "Always Ready" was born.

The Foss Launch and Tug Company mooorage at Seattle, 1949. (From the author's collection)

As Thea's fleet of small boats expanded, Andrew began to recognize that Thea was making more money than he was, and as a result, he joined in the business of buying and renting boats. With Iver and Peter, Andrew also began building launches for hire. Launches powered by the distillate "naphtha," heated in the boat's boiler and fed as a pressurized vapor to the engine in a cycle similar to that of a steam plant but avoiding the steamboat inspection laws, were put into operation. Later, launches propelled by gasoline engines were acquired. These boats entered service for carrying passengers and for the recreational pleasure of renters, as well as for towing jobs.

Three sons, Arthur, Henry and Wedell, were born to Andrew and Thea and, as the boys grew a bit older, they participated in the business to the extent that their schooling permitted. Having grown up around the water and by now skilled in the operation of the company's launches, these young fellows carried the mail, delivered supplies to ships in the harbor, and even provided rescue service for boats that were in distress.

Eventually it became apparent that boats with more capability should be put to work on the towing jobs. Andrew undertook the design and construction of *Fossberg*, huskier and more powerful than the launches and, thus, better suited to the rigors of handling barges and log rafts. With *Fossberg* and the addition of other boats, plus years of inventiveness, hard work, and good management by the Foss family, the firm that Thea Foss had started with the purchase of a rowboat was on its way to becoming a legend.

In the upper photo shown here, by Marvin D. Boland, about half of the boats that made up the Foss fleet at the time were posed at the Foss headquarters located on Dock Street in Tacoma. Left to right are *Andrew Foss*, *Foss No. 21*, *Foss No. 18* (mostly hidden, but also pictured in the lower photo), *Foss No. 16*, *Peter Foss*, *Justine Foss*, *Foss No. 17*, *Grace Foss*, *Henrietta Foss*, *Rustler*, *Foss No. 12*, *Diamond B*, *Peggy Foss*, and a small work boat. Later, the facility on Dock Street burned and the headquarters were moved to the shore of the Middle Waterway in Tacoma.

Above, thirteen of the Foss towboat fleet posed for a portrait by Boland at Tacoma in 1931 and, right, a portion of a Boland photo of the Foss tugs taken from a different angle on the same occasion as the photo above. *Foss No. 18*, third from left and mostly hidden in the photo above, is shown more clearly in the photo at right. At the time, *Foss No. 18*, as well as some of the other boats, bore little resemblance to the appearance as later modified. (With permission of Tacoma Public Library, Northwest Room)

Most of the towboats in the photo on the previous page are also pictured later in the chapter. As time went by, several of the pictured tugs changed in appearance, though, mainly because of modifications made to the deckhouses.

In the photo, *Peter Foss* was a nearly new towboat only one year old since being launched at the Foss yard at Tacoma. Later, in 1942, fire broke out aboard *Peter Foss*, which nearly destroyed the tug. The reconstruction of the boat included a new and different deckhouse, and in the process, a rounded form was used for the forward end of the new house, as pictured later in the chapter, instead of the flat shape as shown in the picture on the previous page.

Justine Foss, built by the shipwrights at the Foss yard in Tacoma, was also only a year old at the time of the photo. *Henrietta Foss*, though, was the most recent addition to the Foss fleet at the time the picture was taken.

Peggy Foss, one of the smallest towboats in the Foss fleet, was only 32 feet long and built of wood at Seattle in 1912. *Peggy Foss* was powered by a Hall-Scott gas engine of 75 horsepower and was employed as a harbor boat for towing logs and boomsticks.

The photo below shows the old 123-foot, 750 horsepower steam tug *Kenai*, built of steel at San Francisco in 1904 as the fort tender *General Mifflin* for service with the U.S. Army. *General Mifflin* then put in many years of service tending the needs of U.S. Army installations on Puget Sound. Alaska Steamship Company acquired the steamer in the early 1930s and renamed the vessel *Kenai*. After an extensive rebuild to convert the former fort tender to a configuration more suitable for carrying freight and passengers, Alaska Steam put the vessel to work as a mail, passenger, and freight carrier on a run to supply several ports in Alaska.

Pacific Tow Boat Company of Everett, later a Foss-owned firm, purchased *Kenai* in 1944 and made the vessel ready for towing assignments. In this employment, *Kenai* towed logs from Alaska to Puget Sound and was used for ship handling on Puget Sound.

After several years working for Pacific Tow Boat and Foss, the steamer finally surrendered to age and the costs of operating a steam powered towboat. At the time of the photo below, taken at the Foss moorage in Seattle, *Kenai* had recently been removed from service and laid up. In the photo, *Kenai* was painted in Pacific Tow Boat Company's colors of black hull and buff and white deckhouse. Later, *Kenai* was sent to the boneyard and cut up for scrap.

At left, far in the background of this photo, the steam tug *Adeline Foss*, ex-*Olympian*, ex-*Flosie*, formerly in the service of Delta V. Smyth Tugs and Barges at Olympia, is visible while in retirement. Like *Kenai*, *Adeline Foss* was destined shortly for the boneyard.

Kenai at the Foss moorage in Seattle, 1949. (From the author's collection)

Wedell Foss in the East Waterway at Seattle, 1949. (From the author's collection)

Wedell Foss, pictured above and ex-*Neptune* of Puget Sound Tug and Barge Company, was a 109-foot steel tug built at Baltimore, Maryland, in 1904. A 1050-horsepower Fairbanks-Morse diesel engine powered the towboat to frequent wins in the tug races held for many years just off the Alaskan Way waterfront at Seattle.

Grace Foss, shown below handling logs at the Seattle Cedar Mill in Ballard, was a wooden 55-foot tug built at Astoria, Oregon, in 1911. The towboat's relatively shallow hull (register hull depth of three feet) seriously limited the weight of engine and fuel that could be carried while still maintaining an acceptable amount of freeboard.

Grace Foss in Salmon Bay at Ballard, 1949. (From the author's collection)

Over time, as business grew for Foss Launch and Tug Company, other smaller towing firms were purchased by the company. One such towing company bought by Foss was Rouse Towing Company, operated by Captain A. G. Rouse of Seattle. In 1920, members of the Foss family began buying stock in Rouse Towing Company. Eventually, the rest of the Rouse stock was purchased and Rouse Towing became a subsidiary of Foss Launch and Tug Company.

Four of the towboats that had been operated by Captain Rouse, *Peggy*, *Rival*, *Rouse*, and *Winona*, were renamed as Foss tugs. *Peggy*'s name was changed by simply adding the surname *Foss* while *Rival* became the first of two boats to carry the name *Roland Foss*. *Rouse* and *Winona* are pictured on these pages, along with photos of the two tugs after being modified by Foss and renamed *Wallace Foss* and *Hazel Foss*, respectively.

The 58-foot-long *Rouse*, pictured below, was built of wood at Tacoma in 1899 as *Oscar B*. Originally powered by a compound steam engine, the tug later received a semi-diesel engine and, still later while under Foss ownership, a 110-horsepower Western Enterprise full-diesel engine.

In 1945, the boat's name was changed to *Wallace Foss*. In 1949, *Wallace Foss* underwent an extensive rebuild including, as can be seen in the photo on the next page, a new and different deckhouse. With the pilothouse installed on top of the main deckhouse, visibility was improved, and additional space was then available in the main deckhouse for a new galley and improved accommodations for the crew. A 225-horsepower Buda diesel engine was installed, also. About ten years later, the Buda was replaced with a 230-horsepower Caterpillar diesel engine, and a Caterpillar diesel generator set was installed, as well.

Rouse at Seattle, 1936.
(With permission of the University of Washington, Special Collections, negative UW21891)

Wallace Foss, foreground, and *Hildur Foss*, behind, at the Foss moorage in Seattle, 1949.
(From the author's collection)

Hildur Foss, moored just beyond *Wallace Foss*, was a 63-foot wooden tug built by the Jensen Yard at Friday Harbor in 1907. The tug was originally constructed as a cannery tender named *Venture* and was powered by a 175-horsepower steam engine. Along the way during a series of ownerships, the steam plant was replaced by a 150-horsepower Eastern Standard engine. *Venture* was then acquired by Foss Launch and Tug Company and renamed *Hildur Foss*. At the time of the photo, *Hildur Foss* was worn out and in the process of being decommissioned after more than 40 years of towing service. A few months after the photo was taken, the tug was scrapped and scuttled in Commencement Bay.

Winona, pictured on the next page, a 60-foot wooden tug built at Tacoma in 1907, was originally powered by a 50-horsepower gasoline engine, which was later replaced with an 80-horsepower gas engine during a series of ownership changes. Eventually passing into the hands of Rouse Towing Company, the tug was then included in the purchase by Foss of Rouse Towing, and subsequently, the boat was repowered with a 120-horsepower Western Enterprise heavy-duty diesel engine. After a sinking incident, the tug was salvaged and the deckhouse was rebuilt in a configuration that was somewhat different from the original. In the process, the 120-horsepower Western Enterprise was removed and installed in the tug *Rouse* that had also been acquired by Foss. *Winona* then received a 110-horsepower diesel engine built by the same manufacturer which was, nearly ten years later, replaced with a 165-horsepower Buda diesel engine.

Under Foss ownership, *Winona* eventually received the name *Hazel Foss* and is pictured along with *Winona* on the next page. It is interesting that a towing winch was not installed aboard *Hazel Foss* during the rebuild by Foss, but instead, the towing bitt was left in place, as can be seen in the photo. Referring to the photos of the tugs in the chapter that describes Tacoma Tug and Barge Company, it can be seen that even their larger boats were equipped with bitts rather than winches, also.

Without doubt, the absence of a towing winch must have placed an unwelcome burden upon the deckhand when called upon to wrestle a few hundred feet of large circumference Manila towline aboard. Lacking a winch, it might be expected that *Hazel Foss* handled barges alongside, rather than astern on a towline, whenever possible. A towing bitt is satisfactory aboard a harbor tug working with a short towline, but a winch is much preferred aboard a towboat on a longer haul.

139

Winona at Seattle, 1936.
(With permission of the University of Washington, Special Collections, negative UW21890)

The photo above shows *Winona*, formerly in the employ of Rouse Towing Company, at Seattle. In the photo below, *Hazel Foss* (ex-*Winona*), together with an oil barge in the tug's charge, was tied temporarily to the moorage floats at Delta V. Smyth Tugs and Barges in Olympia.

Hazel Foss at Olympia, 1949. (From the author's collection)

Patricia Foss, late 1930s. (Courtesy of Randolph Estvold)

The 80-foot *Patricia Foss*, pictured above, was built of wood as *Arcata* at Oakland, California, in 1903. The vessel was originally steam-powered and for many years was employed as a cutter for the United States Revenue Service. Foss bought the vessel in 1936, removed the aft portion of the original long main deckhouse, and rigged the boat for towing. As pictured, *Patricia Foss* was early in her career with Foss as evidenced by the short length of the pilothouse as originally built; the pilothouse was later lengthened. At the time of the photo, also, the tug was likely powered by the open crankcase Sumner engine installed by Foss to replace the original steam plant. The Sumner was later replaced with a 350-horsepower Atlas.

The 67-foot wooden tug *Catherine Foss*, in the picture below, was westbound exiting the large lock at Ballard with a string of boomsticks in tow. *Catherine Foss* was built at Seattle in 1899 as the steam-powered *Kathadin*. Powered later on with a 350-horsepower heavy-duty Union diesel engine, *Catherine Foss* was a storybook tug, good looking and complete with old fashion jingle-and-gong engine-room signals.

Catherine Foss exiting the Ballard Locks, 1949. (From the author's collection)

The 68-foot *Gary Foss*, originally named *Trojan*, was a wooden towboat designed by H. C. Hanson and built at Winslow in 1935 to handle barges for Alaska Juneau Gold Mining Company's operations in Alaska. Alaska Juneau's barges were of a self-dumping design and hauled tailings from the mining operation at Juneau into open water for disposal. *Trojan* proved to be a seaworthy tug for this all-weather operation.

In 1956, *Trojan* was purchased by Foss Launch and Tug Company, renamed *Gary Foss,* and placed in towing service on Puget Sound. *Gary Foss* was originally powered by a 250-horsepower Atlas diesel engine, but this engine was later removed and replaced with a Caterpillar diesel engine of 765 horsepower.

Trojan became the second *Gary Foss* in the employ of Foss. The first *Gary Foss* was the ex-ST166, a towboat built by Reliable Welding Works at Olympia for the U. S. Army in 1943. Following service for Foss, the first *Gary Foss* was sold and went through ownership changes as *Pacific Rocket* and *Bronco*. Dunlap Towing Company eventually purchased the boat, did a rebuild, and changed the name to *Swinomish*. This tug, with a deckhouse as modified by Dunlap, is pictured later in the book.

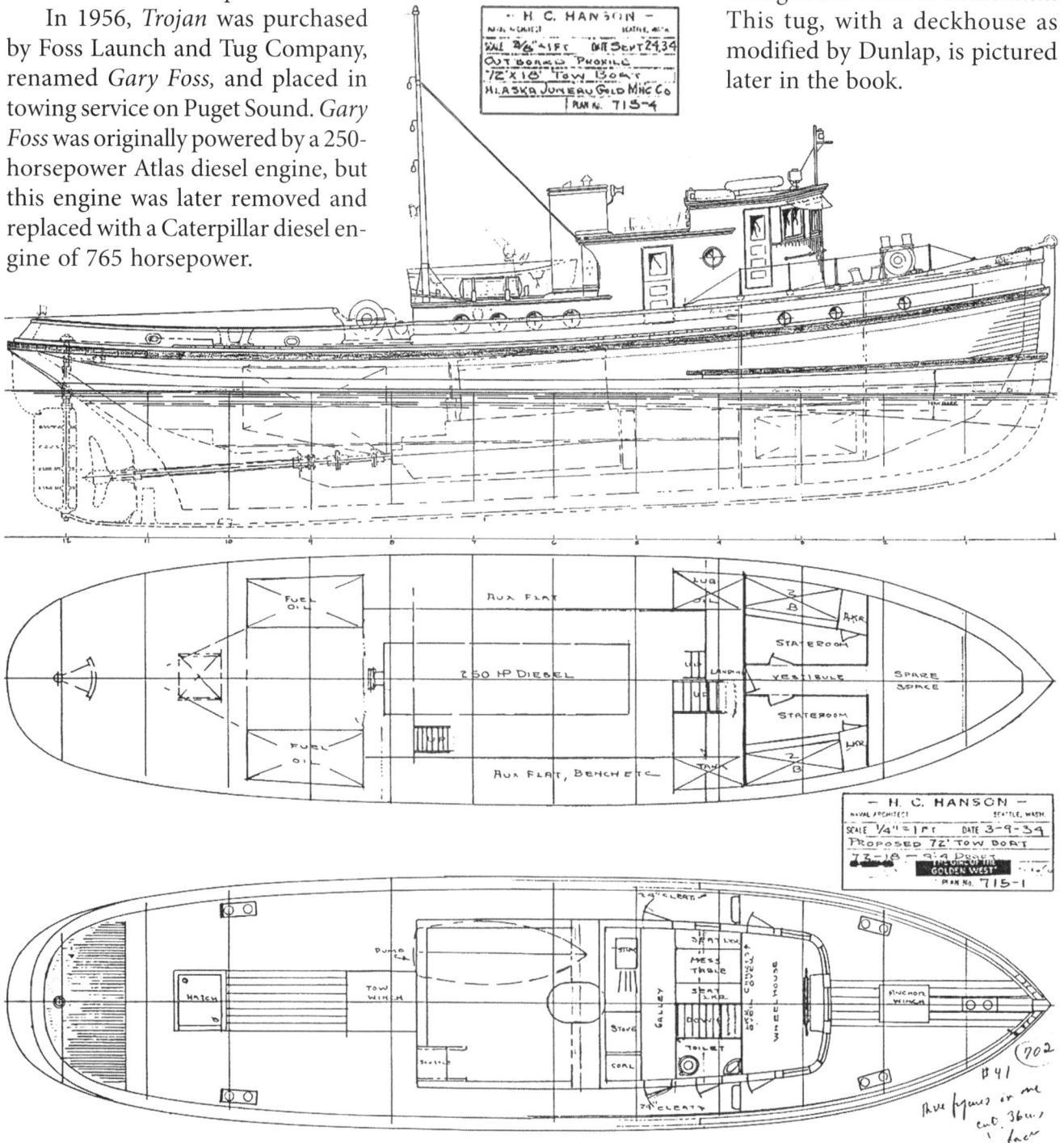

Trojan outboard profile and arrangement, 1934.
(With permission of Whatcom Museum of History and Art, H. C. Hanson Collection design 715)

142

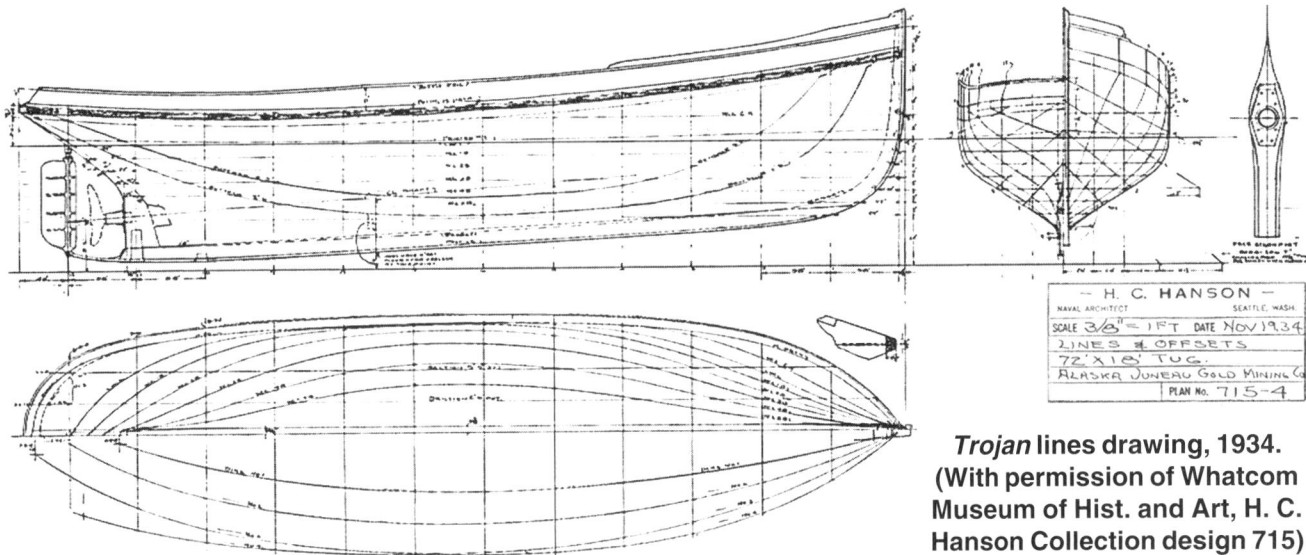

Trojan lines drawing, 1934. (With permission of Whatcom Museum of Hist. and Art, H. C. Hanson Collection design 715)

It will be noticed that the plan view main deck arrangement drawing for the Alaska Juneau Gold Mining tug on the previous page indicates a door on the starboard side that was intended for access to the head. The boat was actually built without this door, in conformance with the outboard profile, and inside access to the head was then provided at the transverse passageway. In addition, the title block for the arrangement drawings indicates that the client was the Girl of the Golden West Mining Company. These arrangements were worked out in the spring of 1934 as a proposed design. By the fall of 1934, a go-ahead had been given, and the profile drawing was completed, but the name of the client company had been altered to Alaska Juneau Gold Mining Company.

The body plan for *Trojan* in the lines drawing above indicates extreme deadrise, or transverse slope of the hull bottom. The bilge is quite hard, i.e., laid out with a small radius, quite different from the barrel shape of the design for *Nile* as shown earlier in the book. The harder bilge would tend to decrease rolling in a seaway, and by the time *Trojan* was designed, Hanson had concluded that a lot of deadrise together with a small bilge radius would contribute greatly to the longitudinal strength and stiffness of a wooden hull. If a tug designed with a significant amount of deadrise grounds in shallow water, though, there is danger that when the tug heels over as the tide goes out then flooding could occur over the deck edge, unless the sills at the base of the doors are of sufficient height.

The 58-foot long *Myrtle Foss*, pictured below while pulling a log raft through the Narrows, was built of wood at Seattle in 1909 as a cannery tender for Ainsworth and Dunn. The original name of the boat was *Kingfisher*. *Kingfisher* was used in the fisheries on Puget Sound and, later, used in the Alaska fishing industry.

About 20 years after launch, ownership of *Kingfisher* passed to Wagner Towing Company of Seattle for use in handling log rafts and other duties. In 1937, Foss bought Wagner Towing, and *Kingfisher* was renovated and renamed *Myrtle Foss*. The old Fairbanks-Morse engine was replaced with a 200-horsepower Atlas diesel engine that had been removed from Pacific Tow Boat Company's *Chicamauga*. A new house, having horizontal lines rather than a form that followed the sloping curve of the hull sheer, was built. This design no doubt provided good headroom in the spaces below.

Myrtle Foss, mid 1940s. (From the author's collection)

143

Craig Foss with ***Foss 142*** deck barge at the Ballard Locks in the early 1960s.
(From the author's collection)

In the photo above, *Craig Foss* was entering the east end of the large lock at Ballard with a barge load of construction materials. The tug was 88 feet long, powered by a 600-horsepower Atlas direct-reversing diesel engine and built of steel at New Orleans, Louisiana, in 1943. In a mishap, *Craig Foss* sank in deep Alaska waters in 1965.

The original *Lorna Foss* is pictured below while towing a gravel scow through the Narrows. The 63-foot wooden tug was built as a steamer at Hoquiam in 1903, and was later repowered with a 200-horsepower Superior diesel engine. After selling *Lorna Foss* in the 1950s, Foss transferred the name to the newly purchased tug *Palomar*.

The first *Lorna Foss* in the Narrows, 1949. (From the author's collection)

144

The second *Lorna Foss* with *Foss 101* in tow off Kingston, 1964. (From the author's collection)

The second *Lorna Foss*, with a length of 79 feet and powered by a 320-horsepower Atlas diesel engine, was built of wood at San Diego in 1926. In the photo above, the second *Lorna Foss* was heading north off Kingston with *Foss 101* oil barge on the towline. The tug, originally *Palomar*, was owned by Star and Crescent and later by Bellingham Tug and Barge but was renamed after passing into Foss ownership.

In the photo below, *Foss No. 18* was on the job as tail boat while moving a section for the new Lake Washington Evergreen Point Floating Bridge. *Phillips Foss*, pictured later in the book, was pulling at the head end. The 69-foot *Foss No. 18* was built of wood at Alameda, California, in 1892. "The Eighteen" had beautiful lines and, with a 450-horsepower Enterprise direct-reversing diesel in the engine room, she was fast, too.

Foss No. 18 at the Ballard Locks, 1963. (From the author's collection)

Foss No. 18, pictured on the previous page, began life in 1892 as the steam-powered cannery tender *Alice*. Following work in Alaska, the boat was purchased by Pacific American Fisheries for similar service, and in 1905, ownership passed to Crosby Tow Boat Company, which later merged with Chesley Tow Boat Company.

Foss purchased *Alice* in 1919 and replaced the steam plant with a 250-horsepower Sumner semi-diesel. In 1940, the Sumner was replaced with the Enterprise diesel engine previously mentioned, and in addition, the original two-level deckhouse was removed and a new house was built, as shown in the photo on the previous page.

The 112-foot steam vessel *Wallowa*, later *Arthur Foss*, was built of wood at Portland, Oregon, in 1889. Heavily built, the hull planking and ceiling were four-inch-thick Douglas fir, and the sheathing laid on the outside of the hull was one inch-thick iron bark. The power plant installed, driving an eight-foot-diameter wheel, was a double compound steam engine of 122 horsepower built by Union Iron Works in 1887. This machinery had been salvaged from the California tug *Donald*, brought north to the Columbia River in 1877 to work for Oregon Railway and Navigation Company before being retired in 1889.

With the machinery from the tug *Donald* as power, *Wallowa* then worked as a Columbia River bar tug for the Oregon Railway and Navigation Company. After nine years with this company, *Wallowa* was purchased by White Star Line and put to work towing between Puget Sound and Alaska during the Gold Rush. This employment was followed by several years' service for Pacific Clipper Line on Puget Sound-Alaska runs.

In 1903, *Wallowa* found employment with Puget Sound Mill and Timber Company of Port Townsend for 25 years, towing logs on Puget Sound and along the coast. During this time, the power plant that had been salvaged from the tug *Donald* was removed and replaced with a new compound engine. *Wallowa*'s next employer was Merrill and Ring Logging Company, who assigned the towboat to log towing from their Pysht River storage on the Strait of Juan de Fuca.

***Wallowa* as the movie tug *Narcissus*, 1933. (With permission of Tacoma Public Library, Northwest Room)**

146

In 1929, *Wallowa* was purchased by Foss Launch and Tug and continued to tow logs. In 1933, Metro-Golden-Mayer leased *Wallowa* from Foss to represent the fictional tug *Narcissus* in the film *Tugboat Annie*. *Wallowa* was never actually a municipal garbage tug as the photo of the tug on the previous page might lead one to believe; as seen in that photo, *Wallowa* was in screen makeup for the movie role. Marie Dressler played Annie Brennan, captain of *Narcissus*, and Wallace Beery undertook the role of Annie's competitive rival, Captain Bullwinkle. Much of *Tugboat Annie* was filmed in the Puget Sound area, and the movie had its premier in Tacoma.

Tugboat Annie was written by Norman Reilly Raine, and the story first appeared in serial form beginning in the *Saturday Evening Post* of July 31, 1931. In preparation for writing the fictional account of Annie, Bullwinkle, and Annie's tug *Narcissus*, Norman Reilly Raine spent a good deal of time in the Puget Sound area researching the towboats and getting to know the people who were involved in the towing business.

Following *Wallowa's* brief career in motion pictures, a complete overhaul was begun. In the process, the deckhouse was removed and replaced with a new house. In addition, the steam machinery was removed, and an eight cylinder, 700-horsepower Washington Iron Works diesel engine was installed. Renamed *Arthur Foss*, the tug went back into service as one of the most powerful diesel towboats on the West Coast, towing lumber barges from Puget Sound to California ports.

In early 1941, *Arthur Foss* began work under charter to contractors engaged in construction jobs for U.S. government projects in the Pacific Islands. On December 7, 1941, the Japanese attacked Pearl Harbor, thus drawing the United States fully into World War II. On December 23, 1941, the Japanese took possession of Wake Island after a battle with the overwhelmed and much smaller force of U.S. Marines. *Arthur Foss* and *Justine Foss*, pictured later in this chapter, were on the job at Wake Island when the Japanese attacked. *Arthur Foss* got underway and safely left Wake Island with only hours to spare, but *Justine Foss* and crew, captured by the Japanese, did not fare as well.

Safely arriving in Hawaii from Wake Island, *Arthur Foss* continued service for a few more years with contractors working on U.S. government construction projects there. After returning to Tacoma and undergoing needed maintenance and repairs, the tug acquired the new name *Theodore Foss*, and the name *Arthur Foss* was handed to an ex-U.S. Army steam tug that Foss purchased and converted for service in the fleet.

As *Theodore Foss*, the towboat was then put back to work towing logs on the Strait of Juan de Fuca. In 1970, *Theodore Foss* was retired and donated to the S.O.S. Society, the name derived from "save our ships" and later changed to Northwest Seaport. In the process, the tug's name was restored to *Arthur Foss*, and the long-lived, hardworking towboat, pictured below, is still a member of the Northwest Seaport fleet.

***Arthur Foss* at Olympia, 1992. (From the author's collection)**

Andrew Foss, 1935.
(With permission of University of Washington, Special Collections, negative UW21888)

The 97-foot *Andrew Foss,* shown above, was built of wood at Seattle in 1905 as a steam-powered U.S. Army tender for the defense forts then in place on the West Coast. Purchased by Foss in 1923, the vessel was modified into a tug, and a 600-horsepower, steam triple-expansion engine was installed. After a fire aboard in 1928, the boat was upgraded with the installation of a 450-horsepower Western Enterprise diesel engine. While towing a barge off southeast Alaska in 1951, *Andrew Foss* met an untimely end when the tug collided with the Alaska Freight Lines Mikimiki tug *Macloufay*. With the hull stove in, *Andrew Foss* sank in deep water with the loss of one life.

Wanderer, pictured on the next page, was 128 feet long and built of wood by Hall Brothers in 1890 for Port Blakely Mill Company. This powerful tug was equipped with a coal-fired boiler and an 800-horsepower steam engine. In those days, schooners and square-rigged ships arrived off Cape Flattery to haul lumber to hungry markets at ports located all over the world. Port Blakely mill teamed up with three other sawmills to provide efficient tug service for towing these sailing ships from the open ocean off Cape Flattery through the Strait

of Juan de Fuca and on in to the Puget Sound mills where they could be loaded with lumber.

Unlike powered vessels, square riggers under sail needed a lot of sea room and their maneuverability, subject to the vagaries of the winds, was not predictable enough to safely navigate the confined waters of Puget Sound. In fact, if the winds were unfavorable, a sailing vessel might remain off the cape for days or weeks, unable even to enter the Strait of Juan de Fuca. As a result, tug assistance was essential.

Joining *Wanderer* in providing ship assistance were tugs supplied by three other mills: *Richard Holyoke* by Washington Mill Company, *Tacoma* by Tacoma Mill Company, and *Tyee* by Pope and Talbot. These four towboats were large and powerful to handle the sometimes heavy seas off the cape, and the consortium thus formed in the early 1890's was named Puget Sound Tugboat Company.

Eventually, the fleet of four tugs grew in number to nine or more, but later in the first decade of the 1900s, the economy slumped. Because of the recession and the gradual appearance of steam-powered, propeller-driven vessels, the sailing ships and tugs such as *Wanderer* were out of a job.

148

Wanderer in Salmon Bay at Seattle, 1937.
(With permission of University of Washington, Special Collections, negative UW21889)

In 1916, Merrill and Ring Lumber Company bought *Wanderer* for towing log rafts from their operations on the Olympic Peninsula to Port Angeles and ports on Puget Sound. In 1936, Foss Launch and Tug purchased the 46-year-old *Wanderer*, and in later years, the tug towed Milwaukee Railroad car barges between Seattle, Port Townsend and Bellingham, as did the railroad's own tug *Milwaukee*. Finally, in the late 1940s, *Wanderer* was finished, and after machinery and metal items had been salvaged, the tug was beached in the bone-yard at Nisqually Reach.

Wanderer departing Seattle with a Milwaukee Railroad car barge on the towline.

Donna Foss at the Ballard Locks, 1948.
(From the author's collection)

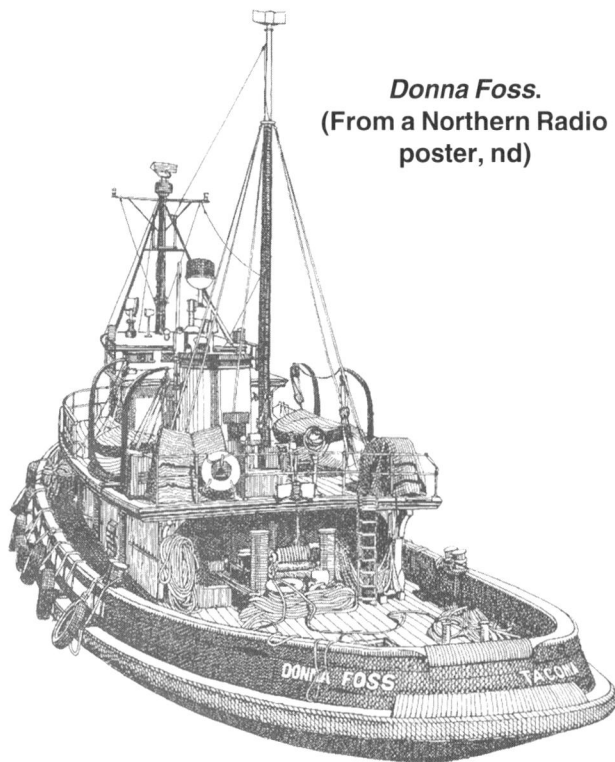

Donna Foss.
(From a Northern Radio
poster, nd)

months before the photo was taken.

While in service for Foss, *Donna Foss* was assigned to a variety of towing jobs on Puget Sound and in areas of the Pacific Ocean ranging from Alaska to Panama and west to Hawaii. The tug was finally retired from Foss service in 1970 and sold to Philippine interests.

Barbara Foss, pictured below, began life as the Hood Canal logging tug *Wego*. From the boards of Seattle naval architects Lee and Brinton, as shown on the following pages, the 53-foot register length towboat was built of wood at Seattle in 1925 for Pleasant Harbor Towing Company, that firm being part owner of Snow Creek Logging Company. The name *Wego* was derived from Webb and Gould, the owners of Pleasant Harbor Towing. Installed power was a three cylinder 110-horsepower Washington-Estep diesel engine. The three-cylinder engines were not direct-reversible but, instead, supplied power through a clutch and reverse gear.

In 1929, Foss Launch and Tug purchased the towboat and placed the name *Barbara Foss* on the bow. The trunk housing over the engine room was partially removed, and to provide more interior space, the deckhouse was extended aft in the manner shown in the photo. In addition, the exhaust uptake was moved aft, and the rigging was changed, including removal of the boom. *Barbara Foss*'s career ended in 1942 when the towboat burned and sank near Marrowstone Island.

In the photo at the top of the page, *Donna Foss*, one of several U.S. Army Transportation Corps Mikimiki type tugs acquired by Foss after World War II, was outbound from Salmon Bay and entering the big lock at Ballard. The 117-foot *Donna Foss*, with a 1500-horsepower Enterprise diesel engine, was built of Pacific Northwest wood at the Lake Washington town of Kennydale in 1944 and had entered Foss service only

Barbara Foss with Foss 57 work barge in tow, 1930s.
(Courtesy of Randolph Estvold)

150

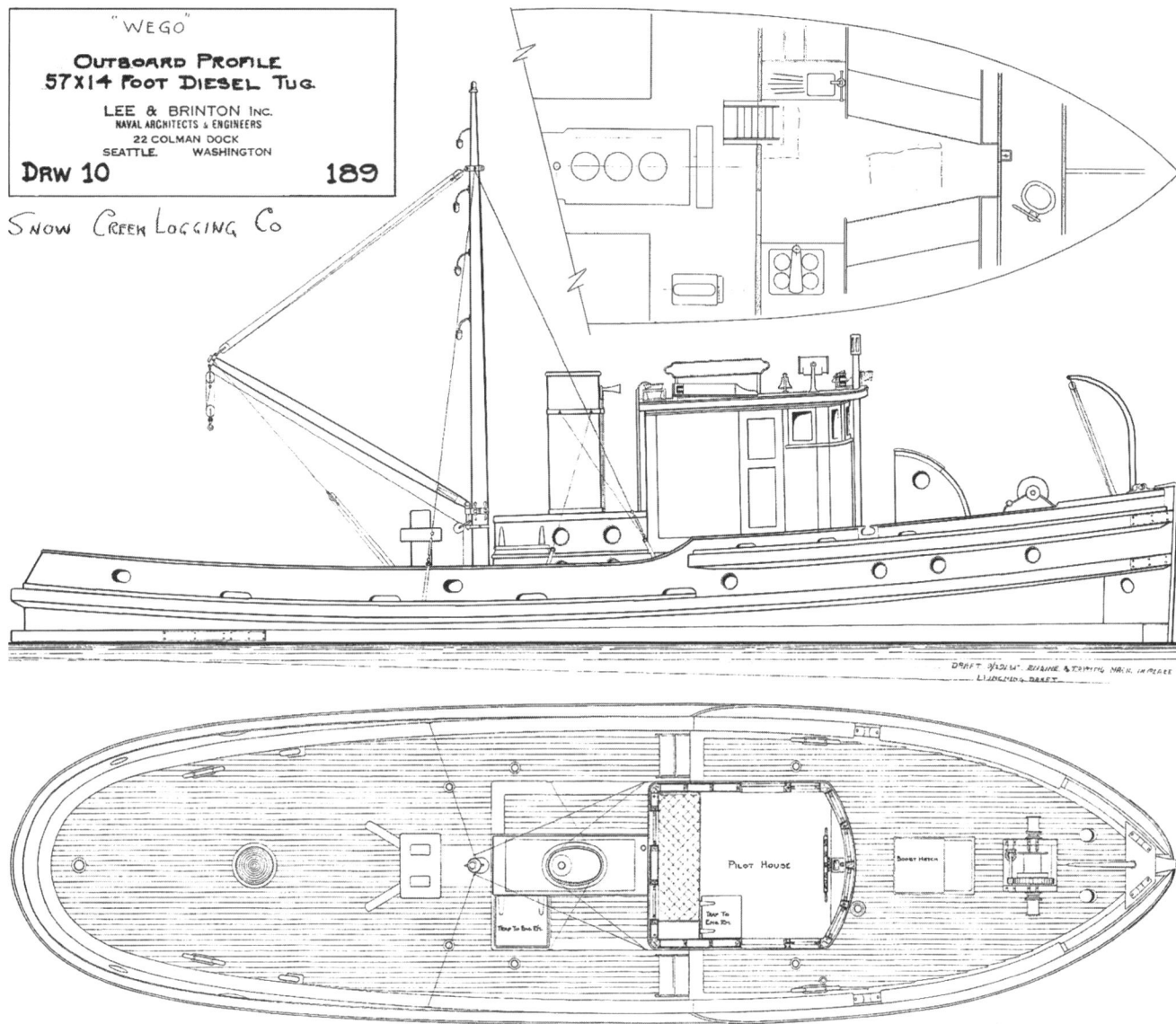

Wego outboard profile and arrangement, 1925.
(With permission of Puget Sound Maritime Historical Society, Ship Plans Collection)

Wego's pleasingly clean appearance is evident in the outboard profile shown above. Accommodations aboard *Wego* were modest with two berths, a stove, a sink with small counter, and a head below the raised deck forward, plus a settee in the pilothouse. A small mess table appears to be partially sketched in between the berths. Simple hand pumps supplied fresh water for the sink and sea water for the toilet.

In this drawing, a note under the bow reads "draft 9/29/25 engine & towing mach. in place launching draft," although a towing bitt is shown on the drawing rather than a winch. Apparently, draft readings were taken at launch, and the water line was then marked on the drawing.

It is also noteworthy that the hull was designed with identical drafts forward and aft, as shown in the scantling drawing on the next page, a departure from the usual practice of applying "keel drag." When designed with keel drag, the aft end of the keel is deeper in the water than the forward end, which provides additional room for swinging a propeller and also enhances directional stability when the boat is moving ahead. Too much keel drag, however, can make maneuvering difficult when going astern. If excessive keel drag is present directional stability may be degraded when going astern; in this situation, a boat that turns off course may continue to swing in that direction in spite of attempts to correct with rudder application.

There are two conflicting lengths, 57 feet and 54 feet, noted on these drawings. If these were intended to describe overall length, a frequent practice in design, then the 57-foot length conforms well with the 53-foot register length that was recorded by the admeasurer for documentation purposes. In addition, arrangements for accessing spaces below deck do not match on the various drawings.

There are three parties involved in the design and construction of a vessel: the owner, the designer, and the builder. As design and construction progress, much discussion amongst these participants usually takes place, and as a result, it can be expected that various design features would evolve and be modified. Apparently, changes were made that were not reflected consistently in all of the *Wego* drawings.

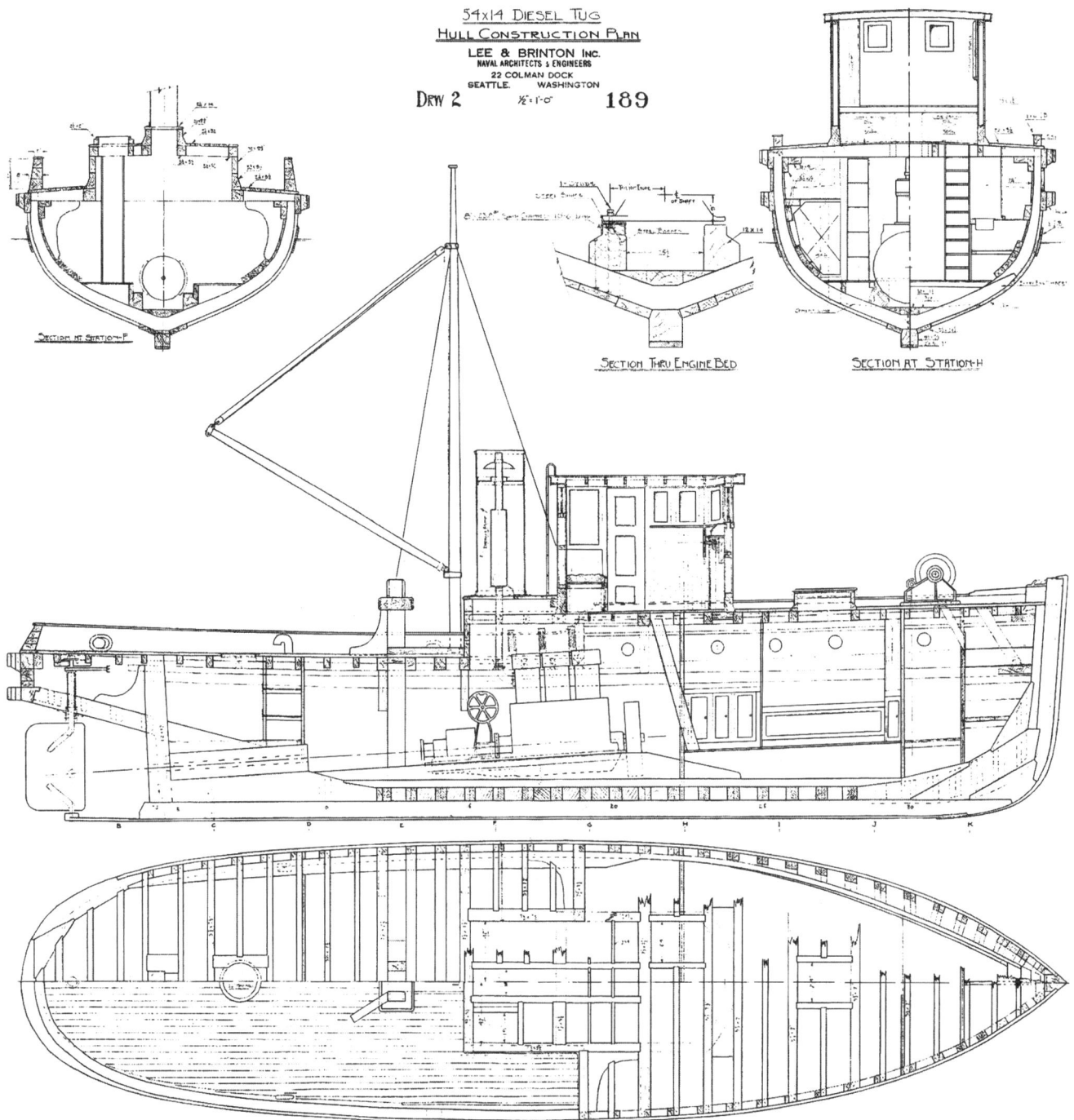

Wego construction details, 1925.
(With permission of Puget Sound Maritime Historical Society, Ship Plans Collection)

The midship section drawing, shown below, illustrates the scantlings specified for building *Wego*. The tug was heavily built; the beam knees were big and stout, and the planking used in the construction of *Wego*'s hull was 2 3/4 inches net thickness. This planking thickness can be compared, for example, with the lighter 1 3/4 inch planking applied to the hull of Delta Smyth's 49-foot towboat *Sand Man*, which was only a few feet shorter in length than *Wego*. In contrast to the wooden engine bed that was detailed in the drawing on the previous page, the midship section drawing shows a steel engine foundation. As reported in *Foss: Ninety Years of Towboating* by Michael Skalley and James A. Cole, the steel engine beds were chosen for *Wego*.

The amount of deadrise given *Wego*'s hull by Lee and Brinton is generous but a bit less than the deadrise designed by H. C. Hanson in 1934 for *Trojan,* later *Gary Foss* and illustrated on previous pages. *Wego*'s bilges are considerably softer than those of *Trojan*, also.

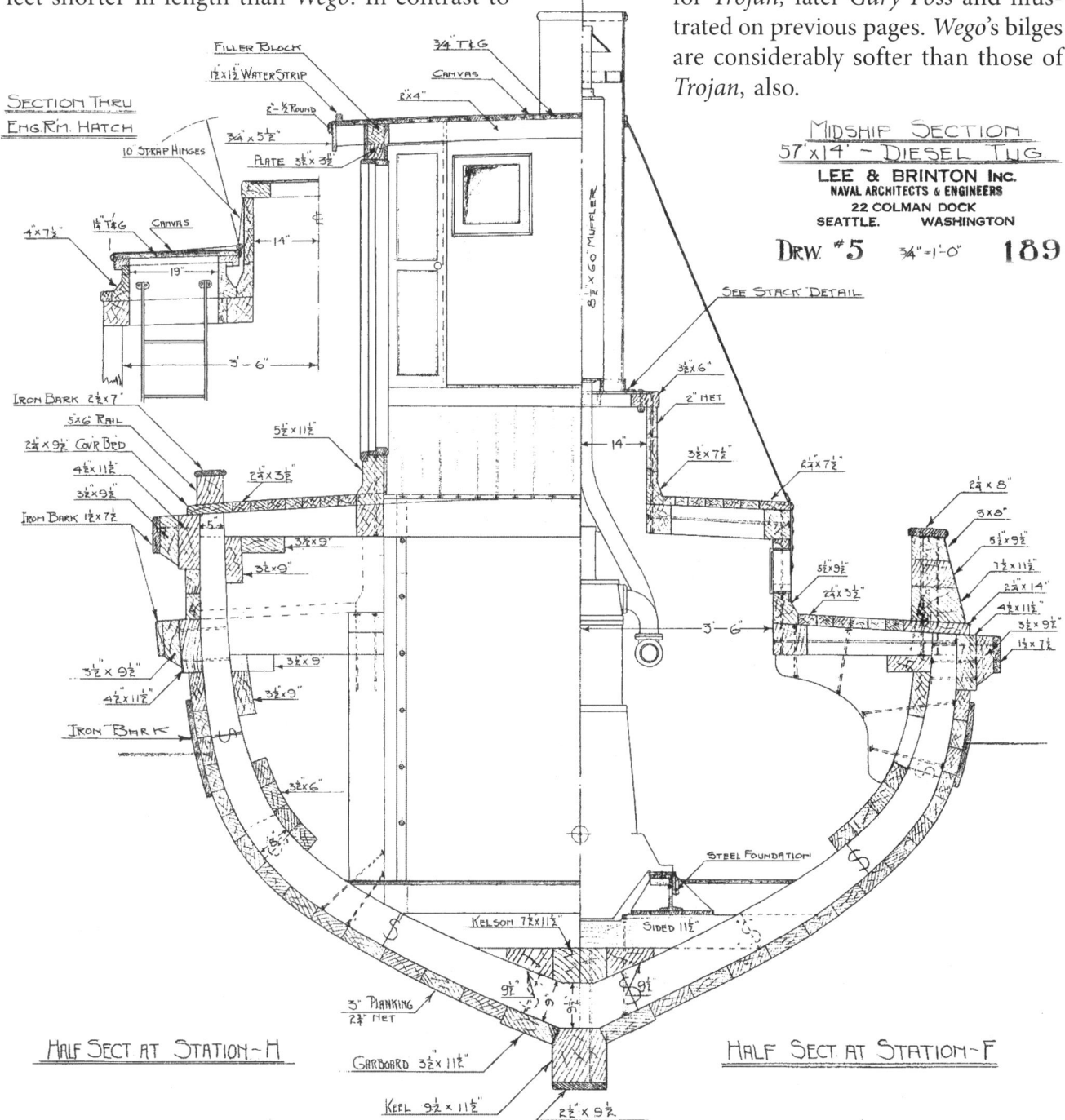

SECTION THRU ENG. RM. HATCH

MIDSHIP SECTION
57' x 14' - DIESEL TUG.
LEE & BRINTON INC.
NAVAL ARCHITECTS & ENGINEERS
22 COLMAN DOCK
SEATTLE. WASHINGTON
DRW. #5   3/4" = 1'-0"   189

HALF SECT. AT STATION - H

HALF SECT. AT STATION - F

Wego midship section, 1925.
(With permission of Puget Sound Maritime Historical Society, Ship Plans Collection)

Martha Foss was built of wood as the 88-foot-steam-powered cannery tender *Dolphin* at Astoria, Oregon, in 1886. After Foss Launch and Tug Company purchased the vessel in 1926, a thorough renovation was undertaken.

To suit operations as a cannery tender, *Dolphin*'s deckhouse had been located in the aft portion of the boat, which provided space for a hold forward in the hull. Such an arrangement is not ideal for a tug that needs more deck space aft for towing than would a cannery tender. During the subsequent conversion to towing service by Foss, a new deckhouse was built, and an Ingersoll-Rand diesel engine of 240 horsepower was installed. This rework provided increased deck space aft, and the boat was rigged for towing, the outfit including an air operated towing winch.

Work for *Martha Foss* included many runs towing gravel and oil barges on Puget sound. Trips between Puget Sound and Alaska with an oil barge were also undertaken when weather permitted. In addition, working out of Port Angeles, the tug handled Olympic Peninsula logs in the Strait of Juan de Fuca and also brought log rafts from British Columbia to Puget Sound.

Martha Foss.

After 20 years of Foss employment in the waters of Puget Sound, the Strait of Juan de Fuca, British Columbia, and Alaska, *Martha Foss* met an untimely end in the Strait of Juan de Fuca when the vessel was rammed and sunk by the steamer *Iroquois* while the vessels were navigating in a heavy fog. Unfortunately, one crewman aboard *Martha Foss* was killed when the bow of *Iroquois* sliced into the tug's hull.

The 97-foot wooden tug *Erik Foss*, pictured below, was built as *Gleaner* at Bandon, Oregon, in 1908. Foss purchased *Erik Foss* in 1953 following a series of other ownerships in which the tug had been employed in towing logs and barges along the West Coast, working with the whaling fleet and service on Puget Sound with the U.S. Army during World War II. By then, the original 400-horsepower steam plant had been replaced by a 900-horsepower General Motors diesel engine.

Working for Foss, *Erik Foss* undertook assignments that included ship-assist work at Puget Sound ports, as well as log and barge towing on the waters of Puget Sound, British Columbia, and Alaska. In addition, long term employment for the tug was towing a Milwaukee Railroad car barge on a regular run between Seattle and Port Townsend.

Erik Foss, n.d. (With permission of Puget Sound Maritime Historical Society, negative 5312)

Foss Launch and Tug Company moorage at Tacoma, 1949.
(From the author's collection)

In this view, five tugs of the Foss fleet were tied up at the Tacoma facility on the Middle Waterway where the Foss Tacoma headquarters had been moved to following a fire at the old site located just north of the City Waterway.

In the photo are *Foss No. 21*, center, *Foss No. 11*, at left of *Foss No. 21*, *Joe Foss*, bottom left of center, *Lela Foss*, bottom right of center, and *Peter Foss* with the forward end of the pilothouse in view at bottom far right. These towboats were tied up at the moorage between towing jobs or for receiving some needed maintenance.

By far the largest boat in the photo, *Foss No. 21* was 80 feet long and built of wood at Tacoma in 1900 as the 400-horsepower steam tug *Fearless* for Tacoma Tug and Barge Company. *Fearless* was engaged in towing logs and lumber barges and also assisted sailing vessels in from the sea and on through the Strait of Juan de Fuca and into Puget Sound ports.

After 25 years as a member of the Tacoma Tug and Barge fleet, *Fearless* was purchased by Foss Launch and Tug Company in 1925, and the name was changed to *Foss No. 21*. A renovation was undertaken that included construction of improved accommodations and the installation of a 240-horsepower Ingersoll-Rand diesel engine as a replacement for the steam machinery. In addition, the engine room auxiliary machinery was upgraded, and the deck outfit was reworked to include a towing winch.

Handling barges and log rafts occupied the tug's life for many years while in Foss employ. The size of *Foss No. 21*, as well as the completeness of outfit and accommodations, permitted the tug to operate continuously for extended periods of time. The mast and boom aboard *Foss No. 21* were used for hoisting the heavy gear needed when towing rough-water log rafts in the Strait of Juan de Fuca and off the Washington coast.

At about the time of the photo, *Foss No. 21* was repowered with a 400-horsepower Superior diesel engine as a replacement for the 240-horsepower Ingersoll-Rand that Foss had installed after purchasing the tug. In 1966, *Foss No. 21* was finally retired from 40 years of Foss service.

Foss No. 11 with a minesweeper newly launched by the Tacoma Boat Building yard in Tacoma, 1955.
(With permission of Tacoma Public Library, Northwest Room)

Foss No. 11, pictured on the previous page and in the photo above, was 52 feet long and built of wood at the Foss shipyard in Tacoma in 1927. In this photo, *Foss No. 11* had charge of a new and unfinished minesweeper just launched from the yard of Tacoma Boatbuilding Company.

Occasioned by the ongoing war in Korea, beginning in 1951, contracts were awarded by the U.S. government to a number of Puget Sound shipyards for the construction of wooden non-magnetic minesweepers of several sizes. Contracts for several vessels were awarded to Tacoma Boat, the minesweeper pictured here being of the 144-foot class.

Originally, as a new boat, *Foss No. 11* was put to work handling towing jobs in Tacoma's harbor and elsewhere on Puget Sound. Although the towboat's size was modest in relation to the changeable weather conditions and the exposure to the openness of the ocean along the Washington coast, *Foss No. 11*, in the early days of the

tug's career, did a considerable amount of work handling barges in the Hoh River area. This assignment was in support of the construction of a stretch of Highway 101. Further from home, during World War II the tug was chartered out to work on construction projects in the Pacific islands.

At the time of the photo on the previous page, *Foss No. 11* was laid up for refurbishing, which included the installation of a Buda diesel engine as a replacement for the worn out Waukesha engine. The tug then returned to towing work in Tacoma's harbor, rounding out a career with Foss that lasted for well over 40 years.

Joe Foss, a 43-foot tug built of wood at the Foss yard in Tacoma in 1942, is also in the photo on the previous page. Used for harbor work in Commencement Bay, *Joe Foss* was powered by a 165-horsepower General Motors 6-71 diesel engine. The tug was kept busy handling barges, shifting log rafts, and seeing that the log ships that had called at Tacoma were supplied with logs.

156

Pictured below is diminutive *Lela Foss*, with *Peter Foss* just behind, at the Foss moorage in Tacoma. With a length of 32 feet, of wood construction, and powered by a 140 horsepower Cummins diesel engine, *Lela Foss* was new in 1942 out of the Foss Tacoma yard.

Log storages are always located in water of little depth out of the way of vessel traffic to avoid creating a navigation hazard. Having a shallow draft and a tunnel stern, *Lela Foss* was put to work handling logs at these shallow water storages in Tacoma's harbor.

Unfortunately, as Randolph Estvold, who skippered the boat for a time, has related, the little tug's freeboard aft was so low that when backing there was a tendency for seawater to climb up over the stern and slosh along the aft deck. To prevent this annoyance, care had to be exercised when going astern to avoid using too much power.

In an effort to relieve this situation, not long after this photo was taken, the decision was made to reduce the horsepower in *Lela Foss* by install-ing a smaller power plant, a 110-horsepower General Motors diesel engine. In the 1920s and the 1930s, the engine in a tug the size of *Lela Foss* would probably have been less than 50 horsepower and a problem such as that which showed up for *Lela Foss* might never have occurred. At the increased pace of life in the later years when *Lela Foss* was operating, though, more horsepower was being used to get the job done.

Low freeboard aft for a log handling tug is favorable for a crew member when stepping back and forth between the logs and the towboat's deck. In addition, a tunnel stern is advantageous for minimizing a tug's draft when work has to be done in shallow water. The propeller tunnel reduces the buoyancy aft, though, and this loss of buoyancy must be accounted for when deciding on a suitable amount of draft and trim. In addition, an acceptable and safe amount of freeboard must be given to this, or any other, type of boat. All of these factors must be accounted for, but frequently, compromises are necessary.

Lela Foss, with *Peter Foss* behind, at the Foss Tacoma moorage, 1949. (From the author's collection)

In the photo below, *Peter Foss* had just started going ahead with the engine to catch up with and put a line aboard a new tuna clipper speeding down the ways at Puget Sound Boat Building Company in Tacoma. *Peter Foss*, built of wood at the Foss Tacoma shipyard in 1930, was 62 feet long with a 375-horsepower Enterprise diesel, later replaced by a 600 Enterprise, in the engine room.

It was previously noted in this chapter that, on one occasion, *Peter Foss* suffered extensive damage when the tug caught fire. The tug's deckhouse as shown here, built five years before this photo was taken, was a replacement for the original house. The original deckhouse was built with a squared-off surface at the forward end of the wheelhouse; the rounded forward end of the replacement house can be seen in this photo. In addition, the deckhouse as originally built con-sisted of a full-height pilothouse and a low trunk over the engine room. The newer deckhouse was built in three tiers, as shown in this photo, with the wheelhouse raised above the deck to provide headroom for accommodations below, a short full-height house just aft, and a low trunk over the engine room, typical of many Foss boats.

If not reined in, ships launched end-wise, as in this photo, can travel a good distance through the water after leaving the building ways. Hence, in restricted waterways, the tug in attendance must move in quickly, as *Peter Foss* is doing in this photo, to get a line aboard and stop the travel of the launched vessel before it collides with the op-posite shore. In fact, in this photo the tuna boat has not yet traveled down the ways far enough to pick up the buoyancy needed to float freely but, instead, is still supported on the ways.

Peter Foss in attendance during the launch of a tuna clipper at the Puget Sound Boat Building yard in Tacoma, 1947. (With permission of Tacoma Public Library, Northwest Room)

Although the bow-first launch of the tuna boat on the previous page is not unusual, most vessels are launched stern-first. Which orientation is used depends on the vessel's hull form, freeboard, and other factors. The speed down the greased ways is fairly fast, and some vessels that are of relatively slow speed when afloat and in operation under their own power never achieve the speed that had been experienced at launch.

In narrow channels, such as those found on the Mississippi and Ohio Rivers, side launchings are standard practice, the launched vessel literally being thrown sidewise by momentum out onto the water in a spectacular fashion. At the finish of a side launch, because the vessel leaves the ways ends in a sidewise attitude, there is very little travel through the water toward the opposite bank, even though the speed down the ways is quite high.

The 57-foot, 200-horsepower Atlas-powered *Justine Foss* was built of wood at the Foss shipyard in Tacoma in 1930 and is pictured below.

This versatile tug, one of many different boats of various sizes built by the Foss yard shipwrights for use by the parent firm Foss Launch and Tug Company, not only towed log rafts and barges on the relatively sheltered waters of Puget Sound but also engaged in similar work in the Strait of Juan de Fuca and the open ocean along the Washington, Oregon, and California coasts, as well as in Alaskan waters.

Later, while a long way from home, the career of *Justine Foss* and the crew was cut short in late December of 1941 by hostilities in the Pacific. While the towboat was handling barges in support of a construction job undertaken by a consortium of American companies on U.S. government contract at Wake Island, the tug and crew were seized by Japan after that country's takeover of Wake Island. Forced to continue work on the construction project for the Japanese occupiers, some of the crew members were finally executed, and *Justine Foss* was scuttled.

Justine Foss, 1935. (With permission of Tacoma Public Library, Northwest Room)

In the photo below, it was a sunny launch day in 1931 for the new 49-foot wooden tug *Henrietta Foss* at the Foss shipyard in Tacoma. On board for the occasion were the shipwrights who built the new towboat, as well as other Foss employees. As shown here, *Henrietta Foss* had been moved down the slope to the end of the ways where the rising tide would simply float the new tug off, rather than being launched in the more dynamic fashion of being turned loose at the head of the greased ways to slide freely at high speed out into the water.

As is evident in this photo, the tug's angle of declivity on the launch cradle is fairly large; hence, it is probable that the boat was oriented with the bow, which has more freeboard than the stern, toward the water to avoid flooding the deck before the hull pivoted and rose as the buoyancy increased with the incoming tide, as might have happened if the launch had taken place with the stern toward the water.

Most vessels are launched stern first, partly to facilitate the tradition of breaking a bottle of champagne on the bow, which would take place at the head of the ways. If technical considerations are unfavorable for a stern-first launch, though, then a bow-first launch can be done, as was arranged for the tuna clipper being attended to at launch by *Peter Foss* as described earlier in the chapter. The tuna boats were designed with low freeboard aft, and it certainly made sense to avoid flooding the deck with water. Unlike the static launch of *Henrietta Foss*, the tuna boat slid freely down the ways and generated a wave that the bow could handle much better than the stern with its much lower freeboard.

The pilothouse of *Henrietta Foss* was built with esthetically pleasing arched windows all around which provided good visibility. The hull was designed with a stern that sat down into the water, rather than the typical fantail stern given to tugs of earlier times. Equipped with a 160-horsepower, heavy-duty Washington diesel engine when built, the boat was later repowered with a lighter weight, higher speed Cummins diesel engine rated at 140 horsepower. Still later, *Henrietta Foss* was given a third diesel engine, a 165-horsepower General Motors 6-71. *Henrietta Foss* is pictured at the top of the next page while wrestling with a barge load of scrap in the City Waterway at Tacoma.

Launch of *Henrietta Foss* at the Foss yard in Tacoma, 1931.
(With permission of Tacoma Public Library, Northwest Room)

With her pleasing finish work, *Henrietta Foss*, pictured at right, could very well be considered as the jewel of the Foss fleet. With her versatile capabilities, *Henrietta Foss* could frequently be seen in Commencement Bay and various areas of the southern sound, handling log rafts, boomsticks, and scows loaded with lumber, hog fuel, or as shown in this photo, scrap.

Henrietta Foss in the City Waterway at Tacoma, 1948. (From the author's collection)

In the photo below, *Carl Foss*, a frequent visitor to Olympia, was handling logs near Olympia's West Side. The towboat was originally built as a wooden steam cannery tender for Coast Fish Company at Anacortes in 1912 and later employed as the Gilkey Brothers towboat *Sound*, pictured earlier in the book. Foss purchased and undertook an extensive renovation of the 57-foot Gilkey tug in 1941 and replaced the old name with *Carl Foss*. The two-level deckhouse was removed, and a new house was built as shown in the photo. The captain's stateroom was located at the main deck level just abaft the pilothouse, and the galley and other accommodations were placed forward below the wheelhouse and raised deck. A 200-horsepower, direct-reversing Enterprise diesel was installed for propulsion, and the tug was ready for work again, primarily towing barges and logs on Puget Sound with an occasional run to the Strait of Juan de Fuca, British Columbia, and Alaska.

Carl Foss at Olympia, 1947. (From the author's collection)

In the photo at right, *Elmer Foss* was in Commencement Bay while heading into Tacoma with a log raft far behind on the towline. *Elmer Foss*, originally the freight and passenger steamer *Maj. Evan Thomas* in service for the U.S. Quartermaster Corps, was 100 feet long and built of wood at Ballard in 1904. By the time this photo was taken, the tug's old steam plant had been removed and replaced with a 350-horsepower diesel engine.

Elmer Foss in Commencement Bay, 1947. (From the author's collection)

At the time of the photo, Foss had recently purchased the Everett firm Pacific Tow Boat Company. Also, at about that time, Foss purchased the tug *Retriever*, then in operation for Puget Sound Tug and Barge Company, and renamed the vessel *Elmer Foss*. However, *Elmer Foss* was not repainted with Foss green and white, but instead, the PST&B black hull and buff and white deckhouse were retained. *Elmer Foss* was later put to work in the operations of Pacific Tow Boat, whose house colors were similar to those of Puget Sound Tug and Barge, and renamed *Sea Ranger*.

The 48-foot *Foss No. 17*, in the photo below, was built of wood at Ballard in 1903 as the steam tug *Harold C*. Later, for a few years in the early 1920s, the towboat was operated under the original name by Delta V. Smyth at Olympia. Purchased, rebuilt and renamed by Foss in 1926, *Foss No. 17* was given a 120-horsepower Fairbanks-Morse diesel engine. At the time of the photo, the tug had been repowered with a 140-horsepower Cummins diesel engine. *Foss No. 17* was mainly engaged in towing activities in Commencement Bay. In addition, the tow boat, equipped with a monitor on top of the pilot house, played an important roll in quelling waterfront fires.

Foss No. 17 at the Foss Tacoma moorage, 1948. (From the author's collection)

Foss No. 12 at the Foss moorage in Tacoma, 1948. (From the author's collection)

The 43-foot harbor tug *Foss No. 12*, pictured above, was built of wood for Foss at Gig Harbor in 1914 and, at the time of the photo, was powered by a 140-horsepower Cummins diesel engine. On July 4, 1967, *Foss No. 12*, after a long career, was burned in Commencement Bay as part of a celebration, the same fate as Delta Smyth's *Oysterman* had suffered a few years earlier after being purchased by Foss.

The big tug *Agnes Foss*, shown below, was built for service as a 142 foot long Army mine layer, hence the long open working deck forward. *Agnes Foss* was constructed of steel at Philadelphia, Pennsylvania, in 1904. After Foss Launch and Tug purchased the vessel, a refurbishment, including the installation of twin Enterprise 750-horsepower diesel engines, was undertaken for conversion to towing service just as World War II was approaching. Following wartime employment for the U.S. Navy, *Agnes Foss* was put back to work by Foss in a variety of ocean towing assignments, and the tug continued in that career for many years.

Agnes Foss in the Middle Waterway at Tacoma, 1949. (From the author's collection)

Foss No. 16 with a log tow in Dana Passage, 1948. (From the author's Collection)

In the photo above, *Foss No. 16*, with a 200-horse-power Enterprise direct-reversing diesel engine, was heading south in Dana Passage with a log raft on the towline. *Foss No. 16* was 63 feet long and built of wood at Tacoma in 1907.

In the photo at right, *Anna Foss* (ex-Gilkey Brothers *Vigilant*) was alongside an oil barge in her charge at the Texaco facility located at the north end of the Olympia port pier. *Anna Foss* was a wooden tug 69 feet long and built at Tacoma in 1907, the same year that *Foss No. 16* was built. Both *Anna Foss* and *Foss No. 16* were built as steam tugs and later were repowered with diesel engines. At the time of the photo, *Anna Foss* was equipped with a 300-horsepower Enterprise diesel engine.

In the two photos on the next page, *Iver Foss* was leaving the Foss moorage in Tacoma. In the upper photo on the next page, *Henrietta Foss*,

Anna Foss at Olympia, 1942. (From the author's collection)

right, and *Foss 21* and *Mathilda Foss,* far left, are described elsewhere in this chapter. The 90-foot *Margaret Foss*, also in the upper photo at near left, was powered by a 450-horsepower Fairbanks-Morse and was originally a U.S. Army World War II tug built of wood at Stockton, California, in 1944. Washington Tug and Barge Company's tug *Tartar* was similar to *Margaret Foss*.

In the upper photo, the young woman at right is my wife, Sharon. In the lower picture, the Foss dredge *Foss 301* is in view while moored at the far shore of the Middle Waterway.

Iver Foss departing the Foss moorage at Tacoma, 1963.
(From the author's collection)

Iver Foss passing by *Foss 301* dredge, in background, at Tacoma, 1963.
(From the author's collection)

Iver Foss, ex-*Angeles*, was a 65-foot wooden tug built at Port Angeles in 1925 for Angeles Gravel and Supply Company. *Angeles* was from the boards of L. H. Coolidge, naval architect.

In 1926, Foss acquired the assets of Angeles Gravel, including the towboat, which was originally powered by a six-cylinder Sumner semi-diesel engine of 200 horsepower at 265 revolutions per minute. Later, the Sumner was replaced by a 275-horsepower Atlas diesel engine, and much later, the Atlas was replaced by a 400 Enterprise.

The towboat, renamed *Iver Foss* after being acquired by Foss Launch and Tug Company, continued as before to tow barges, as well as log rafts that were specifically built to withstand the ocean swells along the Washington coast and in the Strait of Juan de Fuca. Later, the tug was put to work in various areas of Puget Sound towing barges and flat rafts.

In 1965, *Iver Foss* embarked on an unusual towing job. The Seattle Marine Aquarium had been on the lookout for an orca to be added to the aquarium sea life. A killer whale had been captured at the northern end of Vancouver Island, and Foss volunteered *Iver Foss* for the job of towing the orca, at the time residing in a floating pen at Port Hardy, British Colum-

bia, to Seattle for delivery to the aquarium. The penned orca, named "Namu," was delivered safely by *Iver Foss* to Seattle after a successful voyage of about two weeks. The master aboard *Iver Foss* on this trip was George Losey, and the trip with Namu in tow was without mishap.

George Losey had been skipper aboard the Delta V. Smyth Tugs and Barges towboat *Nile*, operating out of Olympia, in the late 1940s when I was decking aboard that tug. A few years after that, however, George went to work as a captain for Foss, his last command being *Brynn Foss*. In 1973, George passed on.

Although the 200 horsepower installed in *Angeles* was a moderate amount, the height of the Sumner semi-diesel engine above the engine bed was an enormous eight feet. The tug was designed with a deep hull, but this engine height needed even more in the way of headroom; hence, the deckhouse sole abaft the pilothouse was built nearly a foot and a half above the main deck.

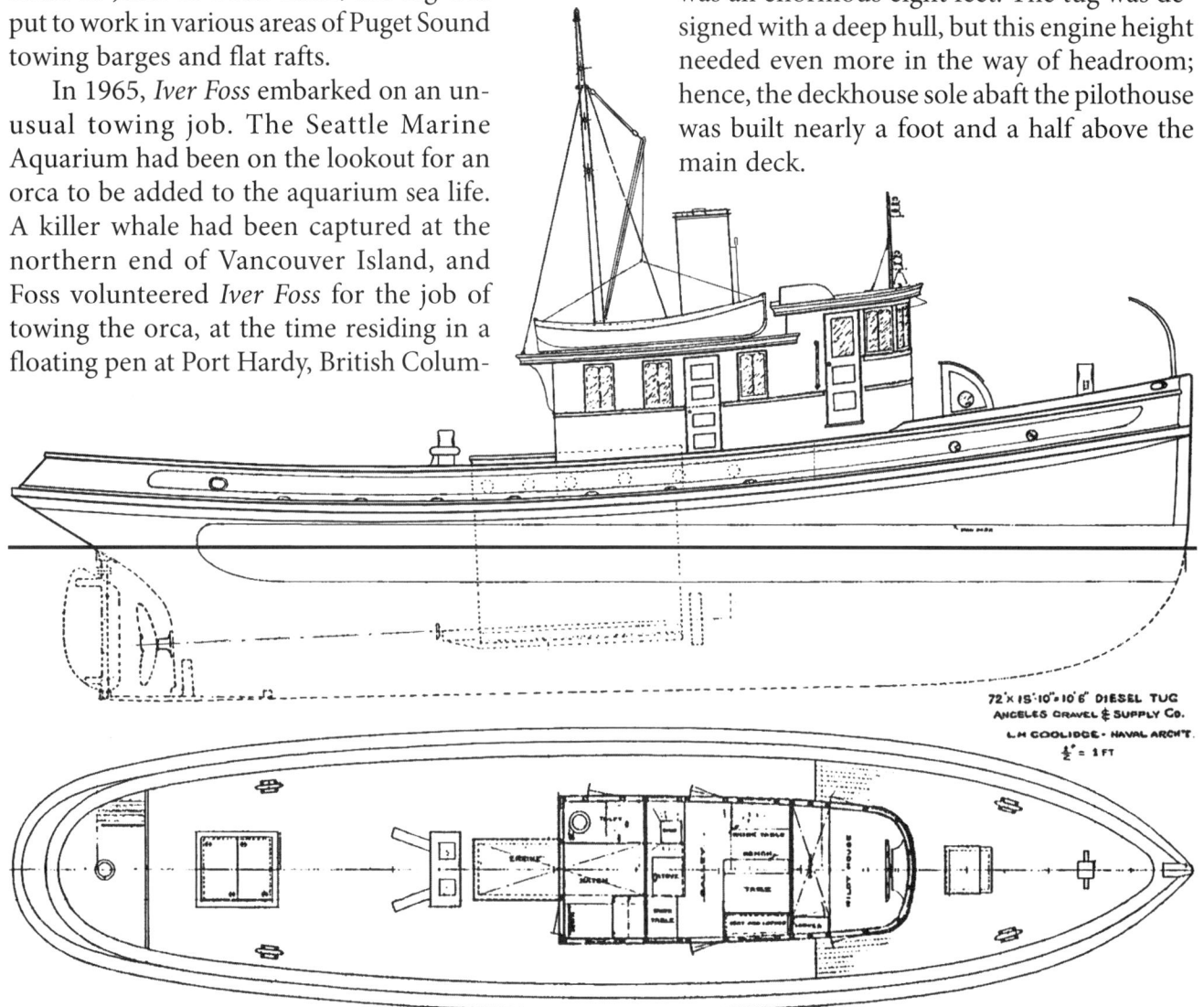

Angeles outboard profile and arrangement, 1925.
(With permission of Puget Sound Maritime Historical Society, Ship Plans Collection)

Provision for sufficient headroom to accommodate the early direct-reversing engines was a common design problem in those days, and frequently, the deckhouse was raised a bit above the deck to allow sufficient space. The height of later engines was considerably less than the Sumner engine. For example, the 400 Enterprise eventually installed in *Iver Foss* was about a foot and a half lower in height than the lesser horsepower 200 Sumner.

The house was rebuilt by Foss, and the lower height of the later engine permitted reducing the height of the deckhouse also so that the sole was located at or near the main deck level. The deckhouse was also extended aft over the engine hatch area, which provided more interior space. The pilothouse remained in the original position. Changes also included the installation of a towing winch to replace the original wooden bitt.

Early design drawings such as those for *Nile, Trojan,* and *Angeles* illustrate a generous amount of freeboard given to the hulls. Later, however, modifications were often made and outfitting, fuel, and fresh water capacity were frequently increased by owners. These changes re-sulted in more weight being carried; hence, in later years the tugs typically operated with less freeboard than had been originally designed for.

***Iver Foss* preparing to put a towline on a hog fuel scow at Ellis Cove in Olympia, 1947. (From the author's collection)**

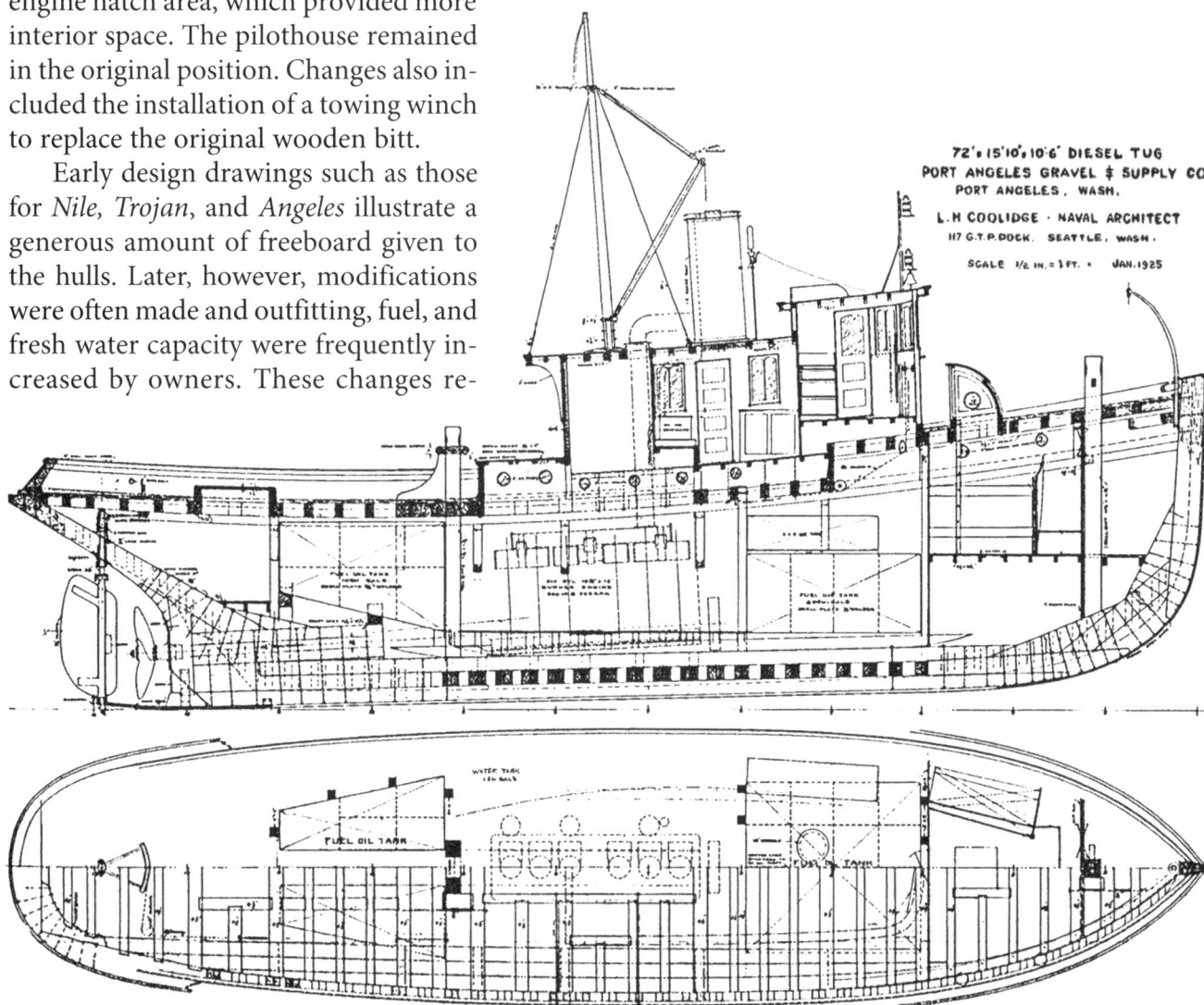

***Angeles* construction drawing, 1925. (With permission of Puget Sound Maritime Historical Society, Ship Plans Collection)**

167

In this midship section drawing, the handwritten note at right was penciled in by Leigh H. Coolidge and initialed LHC. The note suggests that 9/16-inch diameter carriage bolts would be better than the specified 1/2-inch bolts.

The lines drawing shows that the *Iver Foss* hull form had moderately hard bilges and a fair amount of deadrise. A pronounced V-shape in the bottom of the hull results in a deep draft, which then provides space to swing a large propeller for efficient towing at low speed.

If grounding should occur, however, a boat with a lot of deadrise and low door sills may be subject to flooding over the side when heeled on the beach during the ebb tide, as previously mentioned. *Iver Foss*, though, was built with high sills at the base of the deckhouse doors

Iver Foss was a favorite of mine. The tug had a deep hull with high bulwarks and good looking lines. The high, seagoing bow and a sheer that swept low at the stern for towing are similar to the form of the Mikimiki type tugs that Collidge designed much later for the United States Army Transportation Corps during World War II.

Construction Section drawing labels

NO. 6 CANVASS
7/8" x 4" T. & G.
BEAMS 2½" x 3" IN PILOT HOUSE.
COVERING BOARD 1¾" x 7½"
COVE 2½" x 2½"
FACIER ¾" THICK
PLATE 3½" x 4"
HOLDING DOWN RODS ⅝" GALV.
SHEATHING ⅝" x 4 T & G - OUTSIDE
            ⅝" x 4" - INSIDE

WINDOW SASH 1⅜" THICK - GLAZE WITH D.S. GLASS.
DOORS 1½" THICK - HEAVY, SOLID, BRONZE, RIM LOCKS

STANCHIONS 4" x 4"
HAND RAIL ¾" ROD

RAIL 3" x 9½"
3½" x 7½"
⅞" DRIFT BOLTS
(6) ⅝" GALV RING BOLTS ON EACH SIDE
3½" x 8½"
COVERING BOARD 3½" x 11½"
1¾" IRON BARK
2½" THICK
3½" THICK
PLANKING 2½" THICK - V.G. ON TOP SIDES.
PLANK FASTENED WITH ⅜" x 6" SPIKE
SALT STOP

CROWN 4"
5" x 6"
3½" x 5"
CAULKED SEAM
5" x 8"
COMBING 6" x 6"
DECK 2½" x 3½"
6½" x 9½"
⅝"
SHELF (3) 5½" x 10"
KNEES SIDED 6"
FASTEN WITH ⅝" IRON
CEILING 2½" THICK
⅜" x 6" SPIKE
7/16" x 10" SPIKE
½" CAR. BOLT
CEILING 4½" x 8½"
½" CAR. BOLTS

9/16 would be better LHC

4½" x 8½"
5" x 6"
6½" WIDTHS
11 BOLTS 6"
11½" x 13"
9" x 10½"
⅝" NUT BOLTS
GARBOARDS 3" x 13½", SQUARE FASTENED WITH 7/16" x 8" SPIKE
KEEL 9½" x 9½"
SHOE 2" x 9½" WITH 3 PLY SANDED ROOFING ON UPPER SURFACE.

FRAMES, DOUBLE 4½" FLITCH - SPACED 19"
FLOORS   "   5"
            " UNDER ENGINE SIDED 4"

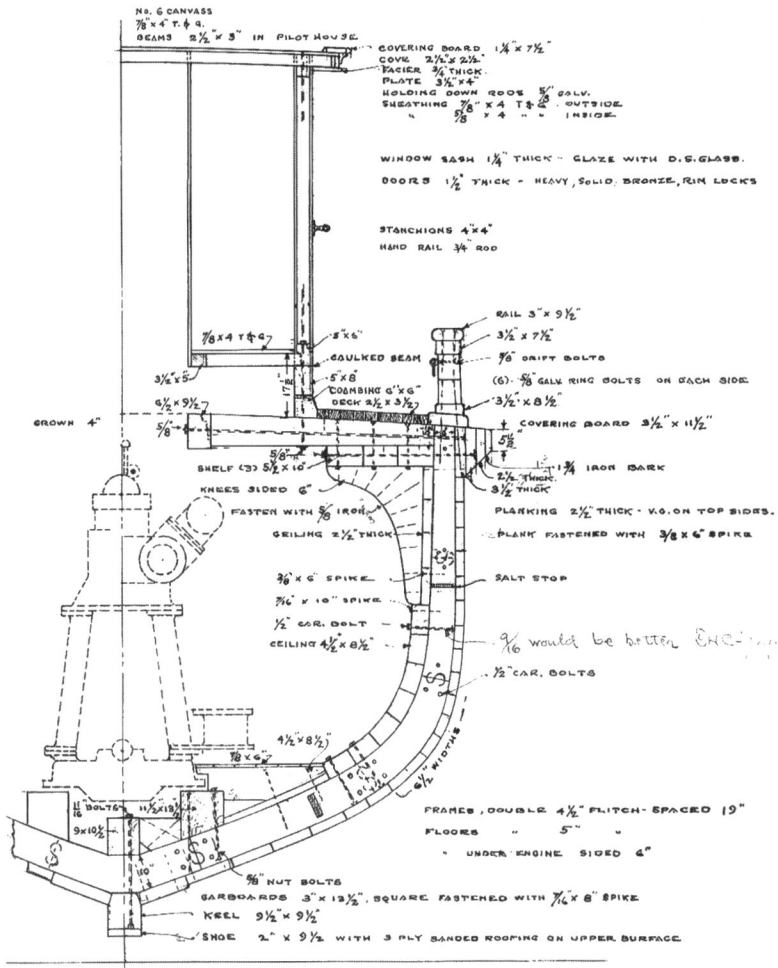

CONSTRUCTION SECTION
ALL SIZES ARE NET - FASTENINGS GALV'D.

Angeles midship section, 1925. (With permission of Puget Sound Maritime Historical Society, Ship Plans Collection)

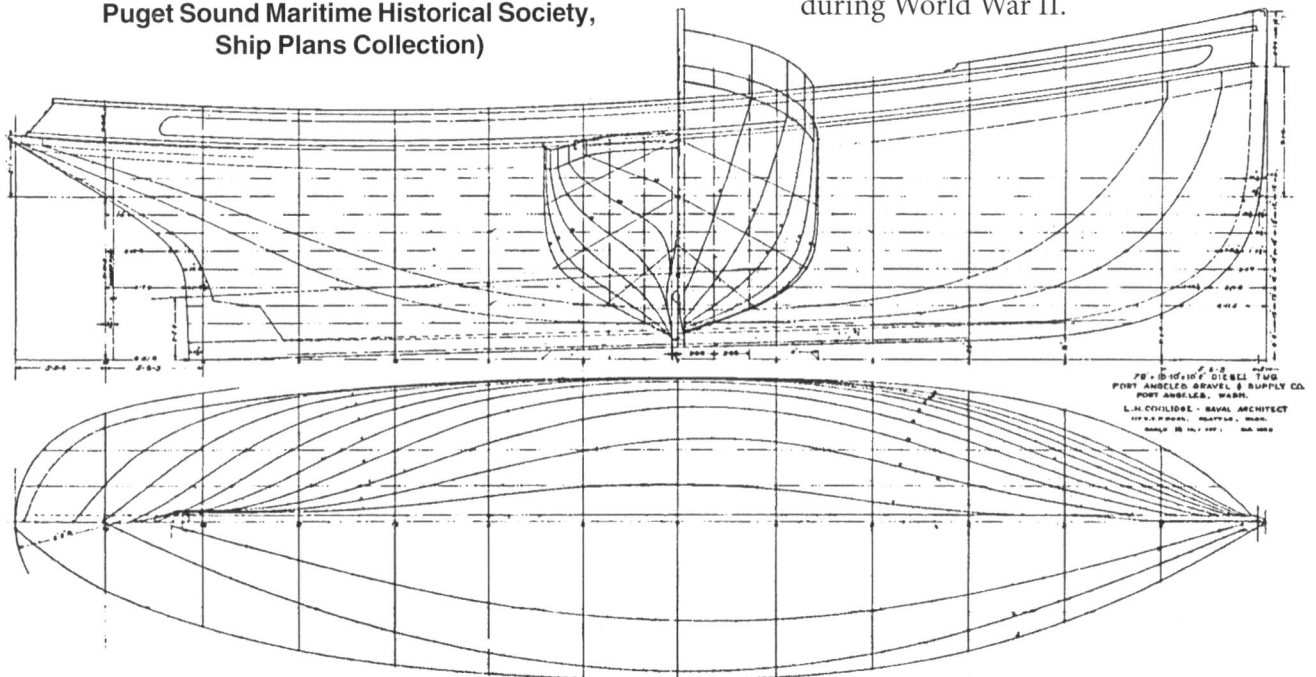

78' x 18' 10" x 10' 6" DIESEL TUG
PORT ANGELES GRAVEL & SUPPLY CO.
PORT ANGELES, WASH.
L.H. COOLIDGE - NAVAL ARCHITECT
SEATTLE, WASH.

Angeles lines, 1925.
(With permission of Puget Sound Maritime Historical Society, Ship Plans Collection)

Elaine Foss at the Ballard Locks, 1947. (From the author's collection)

In the photo above, *Elaine Foss* had left the Foss Pier and was entering the large lock at Ballard. *Elaine Foss* was a 60-foot wooden towboat built at St. Helens, Oregon, in 1926. The tug was powered by a six-cylinder, 250-horsepower Enterprise direct-reversing diesel engine but, occasionally, was somewhat problem prone. In an effort to reduce vibration, the engine was braced laterally from the cylinder heads to the sides of the hull by means of cables and turnbuckles. The tug's hull structure may have been built with framing that was a bit on the light side, resulting in insufficient stiffness.

Oswell Foss, built of wood at the Foss Tacoma yard in 1940, was 70 feet long with an eight cylinder, 450-horsepower, Enterprise direct-reversing diesel engine. In the photo below, *Oswell Foss* was heading north through Dana Passage toward Johnson Point with a log raft in tow. Henderson Inlet is at right in the background.

Oswell Foss in Dana Passage, 1950. (From the author's collection)

Here are two versions of a tug design, the first in the upper drawing and the second in the lower drawing, as proposed by Naval Architect H. C. Hanson for Foss Launch and Tug Company in late 1937. Both configurations were 70-feet in overall length.

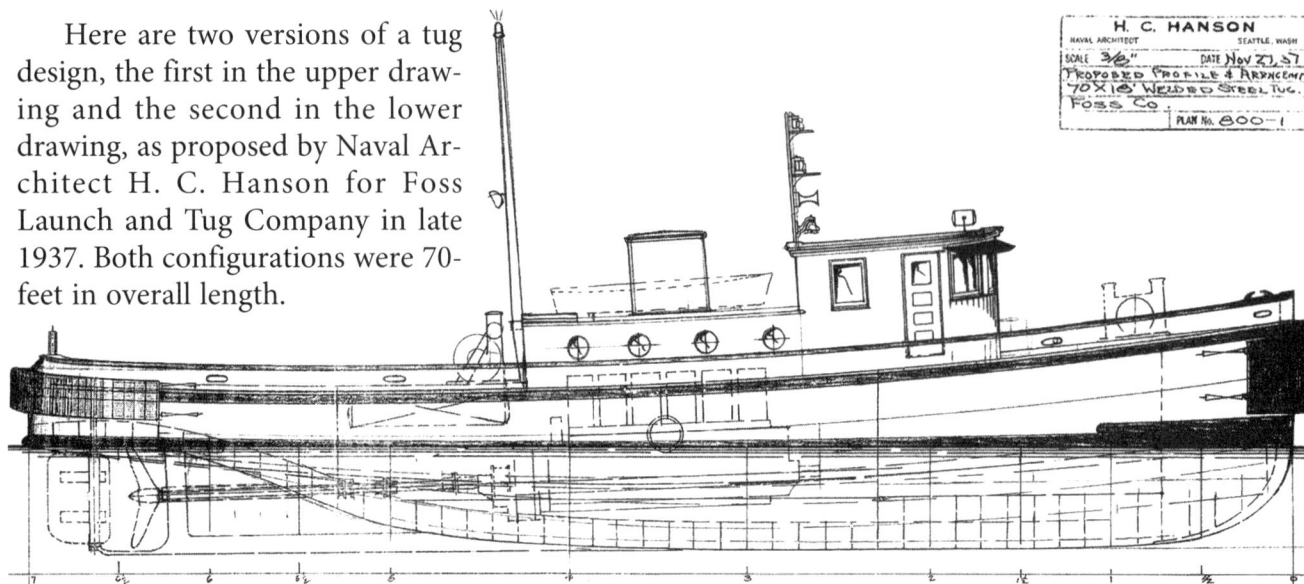

Proposed tug for Foss Launch and Tug Co., first version, outboard profile, 1937. (With permission of Whatcom Museum of History and Art, H. C. Hanson Collection drawing design 800)

So far as the I know, neither configuration was built precisely as shown in these drawings. This design can be compared, though, with the photos of *Oswell Foss* shown on the previous page and the next page. It is interesting to speculate that perhaps this second version was used as a reference for planning the construction of *Oswell Foss*.

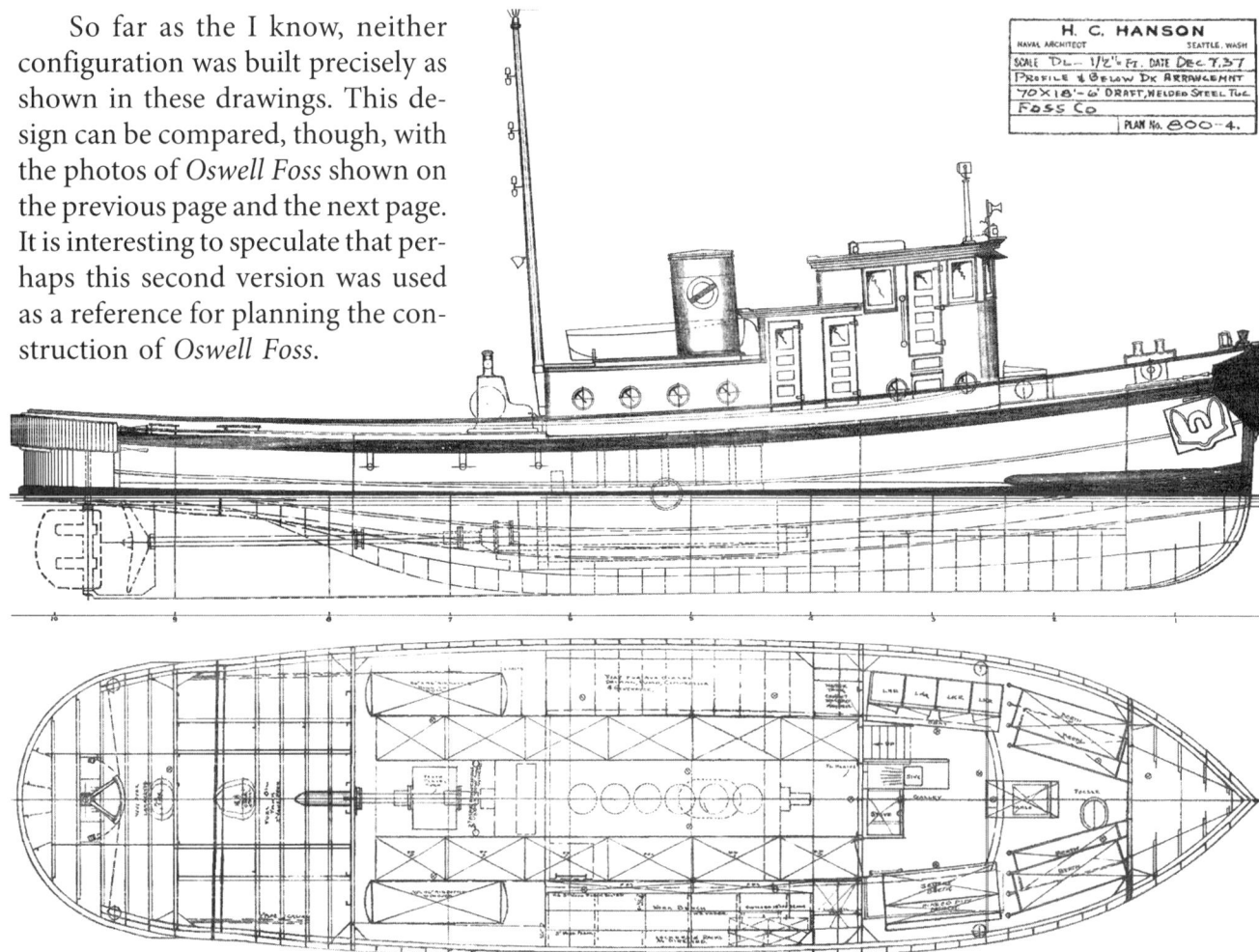

Proposed tug for Foss Launch and Tug Company, second version, outboard profile and below deck arrangement, 1937. (With permission of Whatcom Museum of History and Art, H. C. Hanson Collection design 800)

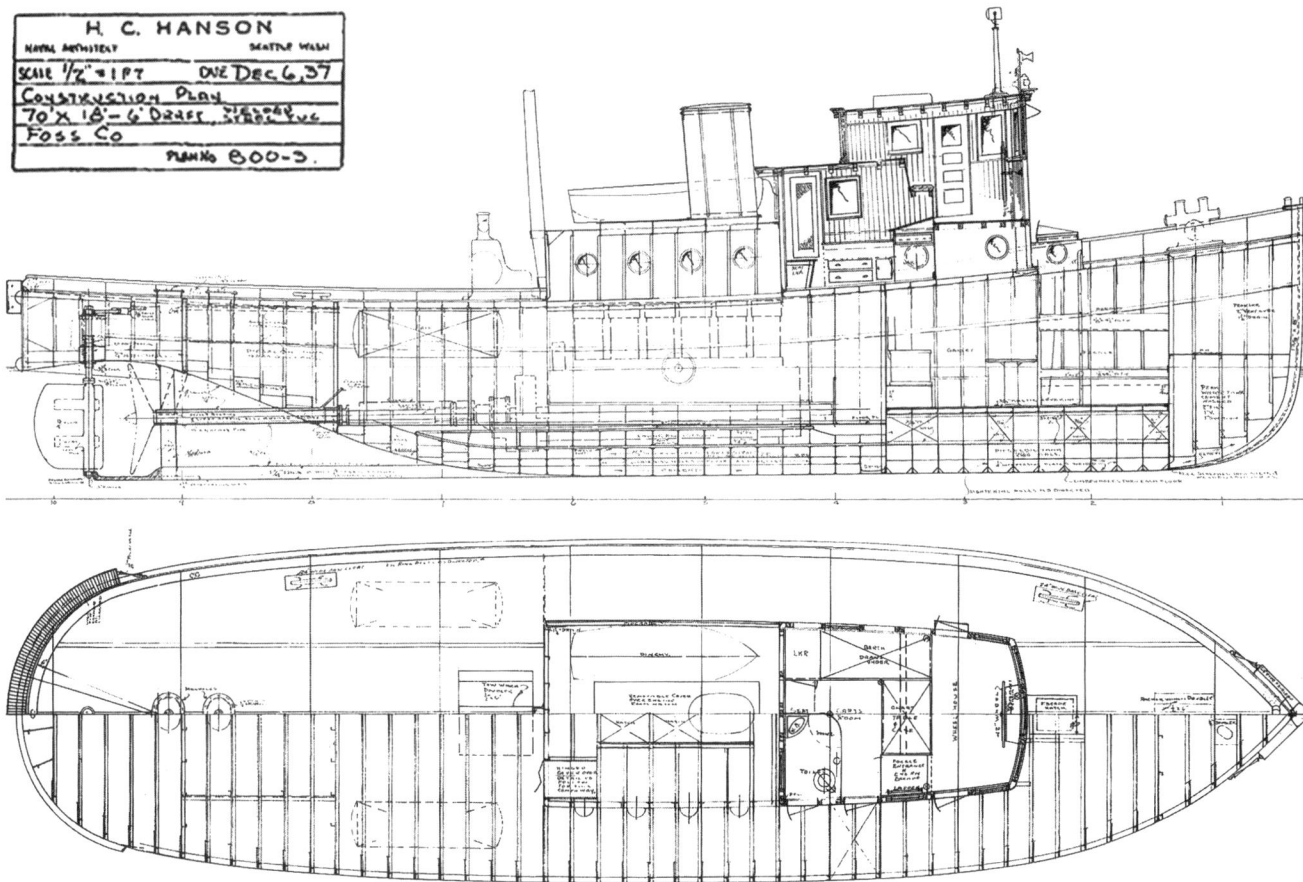

Proposed tug for Foss Launch and Tug Company, second version, construction plan, 1937. (With permission of Whatcom Museum of History and Art, H. C. Hanson Collection design 800)

Construction of *Oswell Foss* was completed a couple of years after Hanson's proposed design was done, but planning would have been underway at the time of these drawings. There are many similarities between Hanson's proposed design and *Oswell Foss*, but there are also a few differences. Rather than steel as shown on the proposal draw-

ings, *Oswell Foss* was built of wood and, for that reason, the underwater hull form would probably have been modified somewhat. The Foss Tacoma yard built several wooden tugs during the period from the 1920s into the 1940s, and the Foss shipwrights' experience in wooden boatbuilding, no doubt, influenced the choice of material.

Oswell Foss was about four feet longer than the Hanson design, the extra length probably needed to accommodate an eight-cylinder engine instead of the six-cylinder engine shown on the proposal drawings. In addition, *Oswell Foss*'s deckhouse was a few feet longer than the house in the proposed design, and access was provided on the port side rather than the starboard side. Other differences in appearance are minor. In any case, it is interesting to compare the Hanson design with *Oswell Foss*.

***Oswell Foss*, recently returned to Foss following U.S. Navy wartime service, at the Foss moorage in Tacoma, 1947. (From the author's collection)**

171

Employment of *Oswell Foss* as a unit of the Foss fleet was interrupted when the towboat, only a few months out of the shipyard, was requisitioned by the U.S. government during the military build up prompted by the threat of World War II. Following the end of the war, *Oswell Foss* was returned to Foss after six years of duty with the U.S. Navy. During the more than 30 years with Foss that followed the tug's release from the Navy, *Oswell Foss* was engaged in a variety of towing duties, primarily handling chip scows and logs but with additional work towing barges in Alaska waters and off the Pacific Coast.

In the photo above, *Drew Foss* and *Oswell Foss* were tending the big *Foss 300* steam powered floating crane during construction of the second Tacoma Narrows suspension bridge. On November 7, 1940, "Galloping Gertie" twisted in the wind and fell into Puget Sound. Following that calamity, a replacement suspension bridge, designed to withstand greater wind loads and pictured here, was opened for traffic in 1950.

Drew Foss, left, and *Oswell Foss*, right, with *Foss 300 crane* at the Narrows bridge, 1949. (From the author's collection)

Drew Foss, pictured below, was 53 feet long and built of wood at the Foss Tacoma yard in 1929. The towboat was originally powered by a Fairbanks-Morse diesel engine which was later removed and replaced with a 325-horsepower Caterpillar diesel engine.

Drew Foss could frequently be seen in the southern sound towing chip scows and lumber scows. A frequent assignment handed to the tug was working with the *Foss 301* dredge, pictured earlier in this chapter.

Drew Foss at the Foss Tacoma moorage, 1948. (From the author's collection)

In the photo at right, *Foss No. 15* was entering Olympia harbor to pick up a log raft. *Foss No. 15* was built of wood as the 63-foot-long, steam-powered tug *Elf* for Olson Tug Boat Company at Tacoma in 1902.

Elf had been built as a bridge deck tug, that is, a two-level arrangement in which the pilothouse was in place on top of the main deckhouse. Later, while working for Foss, the tug was given a 210-horsepower Enterprise direct-reversing diesel engine, a new towing winch and a new deckhouse as shown in the photos. "The Fifteen" had good lines and a clean running hull form.

In the middle picture, *Foss No. 15* had made up the log tow and was pulling the raft out of East Bay at Olympia. At low water, East Bay's exposed mud flats left only a narrow channel of shallow water remaining. As a result, at low tide, the log rafts were resting partially on the mud and access to the logs in East Bay by even the small harbor tugs had to wait until the water had risen several feet on the next flood tide.

When working in East Bay, a towboat the size of *Foss No. 15* required a water depth that would only be available at or near high tide. In the middle photo, it can be seen that the beach along East Bay Drive was covered with water, indicating that the tide was high. My boyhood home was near the area shown in the background of this photo.

At a higher stage of tide, there was water sufficient that the towboats could move out of East Bay directly north past Priest Point. The route along the shore at Priest Point was shorter than the westerly course over to the deep-water shipping channel that would have to have been followed at lower stages of tide.

Foss No. 15 entering Olympia harbor to pick up a log raft, 1941.
(From the author's collection)

Foss No. 15 pulling on the log raft that had been retrieved from the storage in East Bay at Olympia, 1941.
(From the author's collection)

Foss No. 15, with the log raft on the towline, heading north along the east shore of Budd Inlet, 1941.
(From the author's collection)

In the lower photo, *Foss No. 15*, with the log raft on the towline, had just cleared Priest Point and was continuing on north into deeper water where there was less chance of grounding. From this location, Dofflemyer Point and the entrance to Dana Passage are about five miles distant.

Foss No. 15 was one of the Foss fleet's more frequent visitors to southern Puget Sound. The towboat was engaged for many years towing slush pulp barges from Tacoma to the Rayonier plant at Shelton. During those years, "The Fifteen" was also busy handling lumber scows for the Simpson sawmill at Shelton, as well as towing logs in the Olympia area. In 1960, after the old Enterprise finally gave out from many years of hard work, a new 240-horsepower Washington diesel engine was installed as a replacement.

In the picture below, *Mathilda Foss*, with *Drew Foss* and *Foss No. 15* rafted outboard, was tied up at the Foss moorage in Tacoma. The 91-foot-long *Mathilda Foss* was built of steel by Willamette Iron and Steel Works at Portland, Oregon, in 1909. Originally steam-powered, the 375-horsepower vessel was to the order of the U.S. Army Quartermaster Corps and carried the name of *Capt. Gregory Barrett* at launch. The steamer then entered into service hauling freight and passengers.

After long service with the Quartermaster Corps, ownership changed, and the vessel put in a few years of use as a private yacht. During that time, the machinery was removed, and the inoperable *Capt. Gregory Barrett* was purchased by Foss Launch and Tug Company in 1936.

As had been done with many of the company's other boats, a rebuilding process was then undertaken to make the vessel ready for towing service. New accommodations were created, a 500-horsepower Enterprise diesel engine was installed, and new auxiliary machinery and deck outfitting were put in place. Renamed *Mathilda Foss*, the towboat remained in the service of Foss Launch and Tug for 20 years and completed a variety of towing assignments in local waters, the Strait of Juan de Fuca, Alaska, and out to the Pacific islands.

Left to right, *Foss No. 15*, *Drew Foss,* and *Mathilda Foss* at the Foss moorage in Tacoma, n.d. (Courtesy of Randolph Estvold)

Sandra Foss off Hyde Point, 1947. (From the author's collection)

In the photo above, *Sandra Foss* was heading north off McNeil Island with a log raft in tow. Tied alongside was *Foss No. 15.* The 77-foot-long *Sandra Foss* was built of wood as the steam-powered tug *Tyee* at Hoquiam in 1925. The original owner was Allman-Hubble Tugboat Company, and the tug was used for work in Grays Harbor and along the coast. Later, the towboat went to work for Foss after being refurbished with a new deckhouse and repowered with a 750-horsepower Enterprise direct-reversing diesel engine. *Sandra Foss* saw duty with the U.S. Army during World War II, working out of the Seattle Port of Embarkation. In the photo, the towboat's hull was still painted with wartime gray.

In the photo below, *Henry Foss,* with a log raft on a short towline, was in Budd Inlet approaching Olympia through the dredged channel. Originally built of wood as the PAF steamer *John Cudahy* at Ballard in 1900, the vessel was eventually acquired by Foss, and after renovation, which included the construction of a new deckhouse, the boat began work as *Henry Foss.* At 89 feet in length and resembling, but considerably larger than, *Sandra Foss,* the tug received a 1000-horsepower Enterprise diesel engine from Foss as part of the outfitting. The tug alongside *Henry Foss* is *Crosmor,* described previously in the book. At right in the photo, the Reserve Fleet of ships, located at Gull Harbor, is in the background.

The first *Henry Foss* in Budd Inlet, 1948. (From the author's collection)

175

Rustler ("Little Rustler"), 1930s. (Courtesy of Randolph Estvold)

Rustler ("Little Rustler")
with a pair of scows, 1930s.
(Courtesy of Randolph Estvold)

The 53-foot-long *Rustler* was built of wood at Hoquiam in 1887 for service in log-towing operations on the Chehalis River, bringing logs rafts from upstream down to the sawmills at Aberdeen and Hoquiam. The towboat was of fairly light draft to permit negotiating the shallow water of the river. *Rustler* had a series of owners, including R. J. Ultican Tugboat Company and several sawmills, but in 1925, the towboat was involved in a grounding incident on a Willapa Bay sand bar. At that time, Foss Launch and Tug purchased and salvaged the boat and brought it to Puget Sound.

After a renovation, which included the installation of a 100-horsepower Fairbanks-Morse engine, *Rustler* began working on a variety of jobs for Foss. Remaining with that company for more than 40 years, *Rustler* underwent two additional repowering jobs, receiving a 110-horsepower Washington followed later on by a 200 Cummins.

These photos were taken by Randy Estvold while a crewman aboard *Rustler*. Henry "Hank" Harder, a Foss captain and eventually dispatcher for Delta V. Smyth Tugs and Barges in Olympia, was also a crew member aboard *Rustler* at the time of the photos.

A second *Rustler* was added to the Foss fleet in early 1940, the tug retaining that name for one towing job to Hawaii before being renamed *Edith Foss*. During this period of only a few months, *Rustler* as described on the preceding page was known to crewmen as "Little Rustler" while the much larger and newly acquired *Rustler*, pictured at right, was nicknamed "Big Rustler."

The 82-foot "Big Rustler" was built of wood at New Orleans, Louisiana, in 1919 as a steamer for the U.S. government. R. J. Ultican Tugboat Company of Aberdeen bought the vessel in the 1920s and replaced the steam machinery with a new 425-horsepower Washington diesel engine. The tug received a major rebuild, which included a new deckhouse, before being put to work towing logs along the coast.

After Foss Launch and Tug Company bought "Big Rustler" in 1940, the tug was immediately dispatched on a towing assignment to Hawaii. Picking up three barges at San Francisco for use

Rustler ("Big Rustler"), 1940. (Courtesy of Randolph Estvold)

by General Construction Company on a project at Pearl Harbor, the tug then headed west for Hawaii. For the voyage, Oscar Rolstad was captain, and Richard Healy, former American Mail Lines master, served as navigating officer. Randy Estvold, whose photos are shown here, was also a crew member on that trip.

With three barges in tow, the towboat's fuel tank capacity was insufficient for the 2500-mile run to Hawaii, and so, before departing San Francisco, 99 drums of extra diesel oil were loaded onto the deck, as shown in the photo at left.

Under the weight of these drums of oil on deck plus full fuel tanks below deck, the tug's aft deck was awash. In fact, sea water sloshing on the aft deck was seeping down into the bilge at such a rate that the pumps were working full time until the engine burned off enough fuel to increase the tug's freeboard. The round trip was successfully completed when "Big Rustler" returned from Hawaii to the West Coast with a pineapple barge on the towline.

Rustler ("Big Rustler") at sea with drums of extra fuel on deck and three barges on the towline, 1940. (Courtesy of Randolph Estvold)

Edith Foss in Budd Inlet, 1948. (From the author's collection)

After putting in a year of towing for Foss, *Edith Foss*, ex-*Rustler*, was sold to Allman-Hubble Tug Boat Company of Hoquiam. The tug, renamed *Dauntless*, was then taken over by the U.S. government during World War II. After the war, Foss repurchased the tug and replaced the 425-horsepower Washington diesel engine with a 560-horsepower Union. In the photo above, *Edith Foss* was towing a log raft out of Olympia. From years ago, I can recall smoke rings rising from *Edith Foss*'s exhaust as the engine slowly turned at idle speed while the tug was pulling ahead on a spring line at Delta V. Smyth's moorage in Olympia.

The photo below is of *Edith Foss* outbound with logs in Budd Inlet. Chained along the port side of the raft were some extra boomsticks being transported. Sticks arranged along the sides of a raft to contain the logs are called "side sticks." Those oriented laterally to divide the raft into sections are known as "swifters." These boomsticks are generally of a length that will permit a raft to just fit within the 80-foot width of the large lock at Ballard. Swifters used in rafts made up for towing in rougher water may be placed on top of the logs and are then known as "top swifters."

For log towing in more open water, logs that had been taken out of the forests on the Olympic Peninsula were chained or cabled together into a huge monolithic mass, called a "crib," to withstand the swells in the Strait of Juan de Fuca and off the Washington coast. The Reserve Fleet of ships is at right in the picture.

Edith Foss, with logs on the towline, heading north in Budd Inlet, 1948.

Phillips Foss in Balch Passage, 1948. (From the author's collection)

The 75-foot wooden tug *Phillips Foss* was built at Oakland, California, in 1916 for use as a tender by Red Salmon Canning Company. After a series of owners, including Puget Sound Tug and Barge Company, Foss Launch and Tug Company purchased the tender in 1946, then put the boat to work on various towing jobs around Puget Sound for a period spanning 20 years. Power was supplied by a 300-horsepower, direct-reversing Atlas diesel engine that PST&B had installed.

In these photos, *Phillips Foss* is shown towing boomsticks on two separate, quiet, sunny days in southern Puget Sound. On pleasant days such as these, life can be pretty good aboard a tug.

Phillips Foss in Dana Passage, 1949. (From the author's collection)

Chris Foss, of 51-foot register length, was designed as *Crest* by L. H. Coolidge, and the tug was built of wood by the Sieverson yard at Seattle in 1925 for Wagner Tug Boat Company. The drawing below illustrates the construction and general arrangement of *Crest*.

The towboat was designed with a good deal of open deck space, and therefore, living quarters were quite minimal. The small deckhouse had room for a galley and a head, while the pilothouse was sufficiently spacious to allow for a single berth. Four additional berths were installed below in the fo'c'sle, accessed by a vertical ladder located just forward of the pilothouse. As shown on the drawing, the tug's propulsion engine was a six-cylinder Standard diesel engine of 8 1/2-inch bore and 12-inch stroke, producing 135 horsepower at 350 RPM.

Foss Launch and Tug Company purchased Wagner Tug in 1937, and *Crest* became *Chris Foss* in 1940. Over time, as frequently happens with boats, changes were made to the tug. The towboat's appearance remained as-built except that the deckhouse was increased in length by extending it aft over the low engine room trunk cabin, a modification similar to the change made for *Barbara Foss* as illustrated earlier in this chapter.

Crest was designed with a deep hull and a draft of about 7 1/2 feet at the aft end of the keel. This deep draft provided good water to the wheel but it was an unusually large dimension for a towboat of moderate size. It could be imagined that any changes over time, such as increased tankage, larger deckhouse, and heavier outfitting items, would very likely have added weight sufficient to increase the already-deep draft to an amount that precluded use of the towboat in the shallower waters of Puget Sound. As *Chris Foss*, the tug was engaged in towing logs and barges in Puget Sound waters for several years until, following a grounding at Dungeness Spit, the towboat was sold.

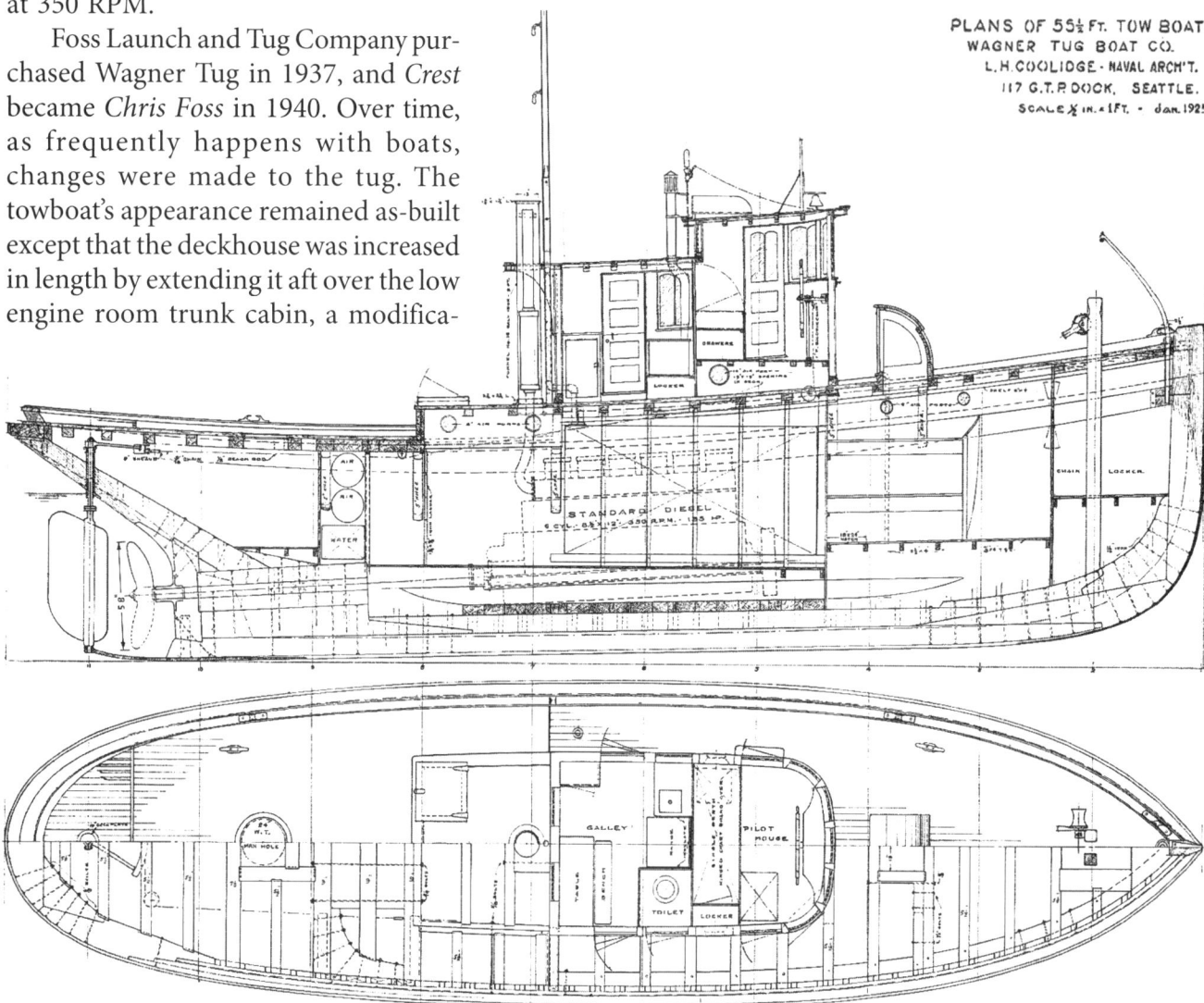

PLANS OF 55½ FT. TOW BOAT
WAGNER TUG BOAT CO.
L.H. COOLIDGE · NAVAL ARCH'T.
117 G.T.R DOCK, SEATTLE.
SCALE ¼ IN. = 1FT. - Jan. 1925

Crest structural profile and arrangement, 1925.
(With permission of Puget Sound Maritime Historical Society, Ship Plans Collection)

In the picture below, things were busy at Deception Pass. At the bottom of the photo, *Chris Foss* was tied to the aft end of a huge three-string log raft, under tow by *Martha Foss*, that was slowly exiting the east end of Deception Pass. Frequently, tail boat service for moving log rafts through the narrow confines of Deception Pass would also be provided by one of the Dunlap Towing Company tugs, called over from nearby La Conner. In the background of this photo, other log rafts under tow had cleared the pass and were on their way.

To handle the job of tail boat, per usual practice, *Chris Foss* was tied laterally to the aft end of the log raft so that the towboat's propeller thrust could be used to steer the tail end of the raft and keep it off the rocks that lined both sides of the pass, including, in particular, the rocky protrusion known as Gobbler's Knob on the south side. Oriented laterally, the towboat could go ahead or astern with the propeller, depending on which way the aft end of the raft needed to be moved, and rudder movement was not required. In this photo, *Chris Foss* was going ahead with the engine, as indicated by the propeller wash, to keep the raft from hanging up on the rocks off to port.

It can be seen that the port and center strings of logs under tow by *Martha Foss* are comprised of sections of logs enclosed by boom sticks that are floating in the water. The starboard string, however, has swifters mounted on top of the logs, creating a raft that is more suitable for rougher water than the other two strings.

Chris Foss, lower left, on the job as tail boat for a log raft under tow by ***Martha Foss*** at Deception Pass, 1946.
(With permission of Tacoma Public Library, Northwest Room)

Adeline Foss south of Hartstene Island, 1948. (From the author's collection)

The 72-foot-long *Adeline Foss* was one of the last steam tugs operating on Puget Sound. In the photo above, *Adeline Foss* was pulling on a log raft south of Hartstene Island near Olympia. *Adeline Foss* was built of wood for towing service at Tacoma in 1898 and was powered by a reciprocating compound steam engine or, as some called them, an "up and down engine."

Adeline Foss was originally named *Flosie* at launch and retained that name until the late 1930s when Delta V. Smyth, who had purchased the tug for operations out of Olympia, renamed the boat *Olympian*. For a time, Smyth had owned a much smaller boat, similar in appearance to his later tug *Parthia*, named *Olympian*. After *Flosie* became a member of the Delta V. Smyth Tugs and Barges fleet, *Flosie*, being the largest of Smyth's tugs, was no doubt thought of as the flagship. Smyth transferred the name *Olympian* to *Flosie* in recognition of the towboat's home port of Olympia.

The towboat, while carrying the names *Flosie* and *Olympian* in the earlier years, was listed in the U.S. government publication *Merchant Vessels of the United States* as having 175 horsepower.

After purchase by Foss Launch and Tug, the tug, renamed *Adeline Foss*, was also registered with 175 horsepower. However, earlier in the book, in the chapter "Delta V. Smyth Tugs and Barges," the towboat is noted as having received the 200-horsepower compound engine from the retired Lake Washington passenger steamer *Atlanta* in 1938. It is assumed that the change in horsepower was never recorded in the documentation.

Foss Launch and Tug acquired *Olympian* and another tug, *Alice,* from Delta V. Smyth in 1941. *Olympian* was then given the new name *Adeline Foss* while *Alice* acquired the name *Simon Foss*.

At the time of the above photo, *Adeline Foss* did not have many remaining days. Operating range, being at the mercy of insufficient fuel oil and boiler feed water-tank capacity, was limited, especially at slow speed while towing heavy log rafts. And, unfortunately, *Adeline Foss*, like the few other remaining steam tugs on Puget Sound, was very expensive to operate. So, a few months after the time of the above photo, *Adeline Foss* was retired and, following removal of salvageable items, the tug found herself in the bone-yard.

182

An incident of minor consequence, but indicative of the challenges of navigating these waters, occurred one morning a few years ago. I was at the wheel of a 36-foot-long twin-diesel powered boat of four feet draft on a course east from Shelton through Hammersley Inlet. Speed over the ground was low while bucking a flood tide. Suddenly the depth finder readings dropped rapidly, and I immediately reduced the speed of the engines to idle and released the clutches. Because of a piloting error, the boat had strayed from the "ditch", as local boatmen call it, and gently fetched up on the submerged flats of Skookum Point.

Rather than backing off the sand bar right away, I shut down the engines so that the cooling water pumps would not ingest sand and bits of clam shells into the raw water side of the cooling system. A cup of coffee was in order while waiting for the water to rise during the flood tide. About the time my coffee cup was empty, the boat slowly turned with the rising water and moved free of the bar. Restarting the engines, I was again on my way with only a bit of paint worn off of the boat's keel.

There are areas of Puget Sound where it is safest to navigate during a flood tide, even though an adverse current may have to be endured, so that, if grounded, the vessel will float off readily. However, professional captains, in attempting to meet schedules or to avoid bucking the tide, do not always have the benefit of an incoming tide.

When in treacherous waters, therefore, a towboat captain may occasionally find himself in a grounding situation with the water level dropping while the tide is on the ebb.

Duncan Foss was a 63-foot wooden ex-World War II YTL Class tug built at Newport Beach, California, in 1944. Foss Launch and Tug bought the towboat in 1951, and during an extensive renovation, *Duncan Foss* received a new deckhouse and a 400-horsepower Nordberg diesel engine. On one occasion, the skipper of *Duncan Foss* was not as fortunate as I was, and with the tide running out, the tug wound up high and dry next to the Simpson mill at Shelton, as pictured below.

On this occasion, *Duncan Foss* was working in close to the bank at the location of an old scow grid. Unfortunately, due to the dropping water level of the ebb tide, the aft end of the keel became trapped in the array of stub piles and timber caps, which restricted the tug's maneuverability. While the water depth continued to drop with the ebb tide, the tug, unable to escape, settled down and heeled over on the beach.

If the beach had been smooth, the towboat would probably not have suffered any structural damage from the grounding. However, as the bottom of the hull came to rest on the stub piles that were poking up through the beach, the hull was holed. Salvage was successful, though, and after repairs were made, *Duncan Foss* was active in the Foss fleet until 1972.

Duncan Foss on the beach at Shelton in the 1960s. (Courtesy of John Hurst)

Foss No. 8 at Port Angeles, 1963. (From the author's collection)

Foss Launch and Tug Company maintained a presence at Port Angeles for many years. The two small tugs shown here tended log rafts and carried out other towing assignments in the harbor at Port Angeles. *Foss No. 8*, pictured above, was 32 feet long and built of wood at Bellingham in 1935. *Nancy Foss*, also of wooden construction and shown in the photo below, was 45 feet long and built at Lopez in 1907. The horizontal line in the background of these photos is Ediz Hook.

Nancy Foss at Port Angeles, 1963. (From the author's collection)

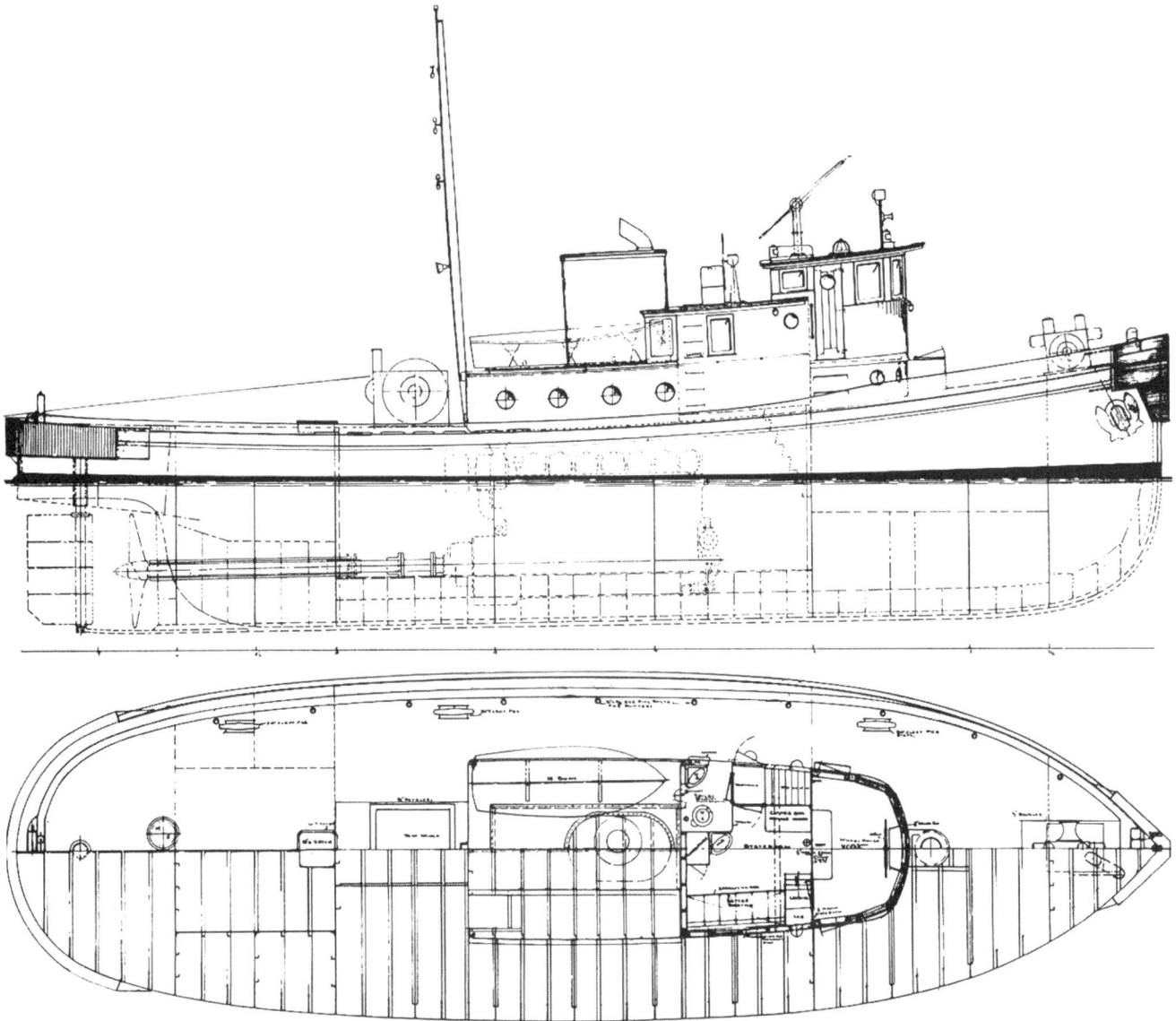

Brynn Foss outboard profile and arrangement.
(With permission of Whatcom Museum of History and Art)

This drawing illustrates the design by H. C. Hanson, Seattle naval architect, for a new tug to the order of Foss Launch and Tug Company in 1951. Of steel construction, the tug was 72 feet in overall length, 21 feet in beam, and over 9 feet in draft. Up-to-date amenities were installed for the crew, including an electric galley and heat.

The basic boat was built by Reliable Welding Works at Olympia, and machinery installation and finishing work were carried out by Foss in Tacoma. Upon completion, the tug was put to work in Tacoma performing ship-handling duties as well as a variety of other towing jobs. Power for *Brynn Foss* was a Nordberg six-cylinder, four cycle, 800-horsepower, supercharged diesel engine with direct drive to an 82-inch diameter propeller turning at 300 RPM. At the time, this amount of horsepower in a tug the size of *Brynn Foss* was impressive, but with the increasing size of ships calling, it was also becoming necessary.

To take care of the fairly high electrical load, two 60-kilowatt diesel generator sets were installed in the engine room, each a backup for the other. The towing winch was of Foss construction; it was not unusual for towing companies to build their own winches rather than purchase them from manufacturers in those days. Capacities of 12,000 gallons of fuel and 1,500 gallons of water were available, the fuel tanks being built integral with the hull.

Brynn Foss with a newly launched minesweeper built by the Puget Sound Boat Building yard at Tacoma, 1963. (With permission of Tacoma Public Library, Northwest Room)

Pictured above is *Brynn Foss* on the job moving a newly launched minesweeper. This 110-foot-long wooden minesweeper was one of a series built by the Puget Sound Boat Building yard at Tacoma for the U.S. Navy.

In the photo below, Foss Launch and Tug Company's *Carol Foss* was entering the locks at Ballard. At right in the background is the Lockhaven Marina, a fixture at that spot for many years and still in operation there.

Carol Foss entering the Ballard Locks, 1964. (From the author's collection)

One of Foss Launch and Tug Company's newer steel tugs during the period covered in this book, *Carol Foss* had a twin named *Shannon Foss*. Harold Hanson, Seattle naval architect, designed the boats, and the steel fabrication and assembly were done by Todd Shipyards, located at Harbor Island in Seattle, completing their share of the project in 1958. The tugs were 90 feet long, and each was powered by a Nordberg eight-cylinder, direct-reversing diesel engine of 1200 horsepower at about 300 revolutions per minute. The partially completed tugs were then towed to the Foss yard on the ship canal, and finishing work, including installation of the engine, was accomplished by the company's own skilled personnel.

By the time *Carol Foss* and *Shannon Foss* were being constructed, Foss had started the gradual process of retiring the old towboats and undertaking new construction. The earlier boats had worked hard for many years, and with wear and tear on the hulls and machinery, the maintenance costs were increasing to the point that it made sense to invest capital in new boats. In addition, the need grew for tugs with more horsepower and longer operating range. The barges being towed were growing in size and the ships that had to be handled in port were, by now, of much greater tonnage than the earlier cargo vessels; thus, the requirement arose for more installed horsepower and, along with that, greater fuel capacity. Important also were the improvements in crew com-

fort that could be provided by the increased space designed into the new boats.

In the decade of the 1960s, following the success of *Brynn Foss*, *Carol Foss*, and *Shannon Foss*, Foss Launch and Tug Company continued with a program to acquire new tugs to replace the aging boats and to augment the fleet. During this period, three C-class, eight D-class, three J-class, and three M-class tugs, all of steel construction, were completed and became familiar sights to observers around Puget Sound. These towboats ranged in size from 60 feet to 84 feet with 600 to 1700 horsepower in their engine rooms. The tugs were built by Martinolich at Tacoma and Albina Engine and Machine at Portland, Oregon.

A run suited to a J-boat was towing a railroad car barge between Seattle and the Simpson mill at Shelton, as shown in the photo below. With a relatively shallow draft and twin screws providing maneuverability, a tug such as the 60-foot *Julia Foss* was ideally suited to working in Hammersley Inlet and Oakland Bay, where the currents at mid-tide run fast, the tide range between high and low is extreme, with low water sometimes reaching minus three feet, and numerous sand bars are waiting to trap and ground a vessel.

Through new construction and conversion of vessels, as well as acquisition of smaller towing companies, Foss Launch and Tug continued to grow. By the end of the 1960s, Foss was operating approximately 100 towboats and 200 barges.

Julia Foss in charge of *Foss 117* railroad car barge in Hammersley Inlet, 1965.
(Courtesy of Elizabeth Wolf)

187

AMERICAN TUG BOAT COMPANY
Everett

American Tug Boat Company was founded in 1902 by Captain Harry Ramwell with the steam tug *R. P. Elmore* under ownership. The original colors for their towboats were black hull and dark red and white deckhouse. The colors were later changed to green hull, dark orange deckhouse, and black stack.

The American Tug moorage at Everett is at right in the upper photo shown below. In the photo, *Margaret S* was maneuvering while one of the twins, *Ann S* or *Janet W*, and *Elmore* behind, were tied to the pier. At left, the buildings with the large openings housed Everett Marine Ways. These ways were open to the weather for many years, as illustrated in the chapter "The Fishing Boats and Their Gear," and the buildings were constructed to permit the uninterrupted production rate required during World War II. A yard, owned by American Tug for hauling it's floating equip-

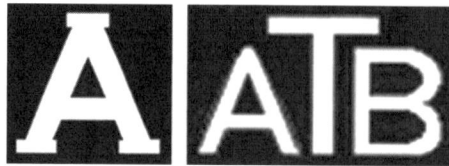

ment out of the water for maintenance, was at left of Everett Marine Ways. American Tug also owned American Pile Driving Company, involved with marine construction, pile driving, and dredging.

It is an unusual event when a towing company's tugs are all in the home port at the same time. The portrait shown in the bottom photo of the American Tug Boat Company fleet was taken by L. A. Eklund, the date of the photo being sometime after 1945 as indicated by the presence of four members of the fleet (*Condor, Gony, Ann S,* and *Janet W*) that had been surplused by the U.S. government following World War II. The boats, left to right, are *Manila, Orinda, Streamline, Argos, Forester, Peter, Sequoia, Boston II, Chickaloon, Margaret S, Magdalene, Condor, Gony, Gwylan, Irene, Elmore, Tillicum, Ann S, Janet W,* and *Mary D. Hume.*

American Tug Boat Company, right, and Everett Marine Ways, left, at Everett, 1949. (From the author's collection)

The American Tug Boat Company fleet, late 1940s. (Courtesy of Mary R. Jamieson)

R. P. Elmore and lumber schooners, n.d. (With permission of Everett Public Library, Northwest Room)

The steam tug *R. P. Elmore* is pictured above in this early photo while tending schooners that were loading lumber from scows. The schooner alongside *R. P. Elmore* appears to be heavily laden with lumber and deep in the water, the final loads of lumber having been hoisted onto the deck. The schooner just beyond, resting high in the water, was probably a recent arrival and had only just begun to load.

R. P. Elmore was built of wood at Astoria, Oregon, in 1890 as a cannery tender for Elmore-Sanborn Company. In 1898, Captain Ramwell purchased and outfitted the vessel for use as a tug in the service of his new company, American Tug Boat Company.

A funnel like *R. P. Elmore*'s extremely tall uptake was a common sight aboard other steam tugs as well. A tall funnel produced a good draft for the boiler's firebox, just as a tall chimney does for a residential fireplace. In 1922, *R. P. Elmore* was extensively rebuilt and the name was shortened to *Elmore*. In the process, the tug received a new 375-horsepower engine, the first full-diesel engine produced by Washington-Estep.

The wooden tugs *Forester, Boston II,* and *Manila* are illustrated below. The 50-foot *Forester* was built at Aberdeen in 1936, and *Boston II*, 53 feet in length, was built at Ballard in 1915. The smallest of the three at 42 feet in length, *Manila* was built at Seattle in 1913.

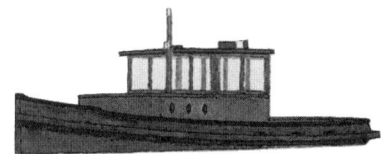

Manila

Forester

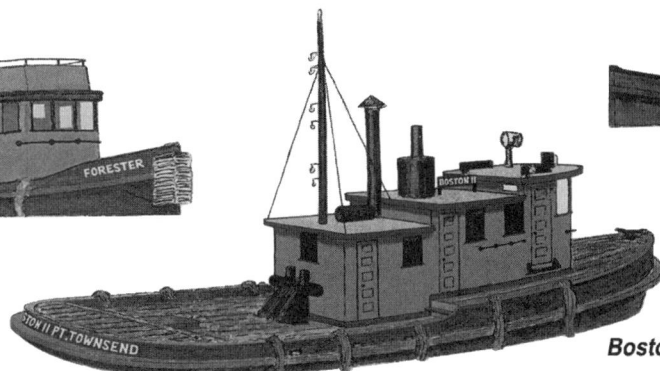

Boston II   N. KNUTSEN

189

Rosalie, n.d. (With permission of Snohomish County Museum)

One of the early tugs owned by American Tug Boat Company was *Rosalie*, pictured above. *Rosalie* was steam powered, 42 feet long, and built of wood at San Francisco, California, in 1898 for Alaska Commercial Company. Alaska Commercial was involved in barging activities on the lower Yukon River during the gold rush.

American Tug acquired the boat in 1905, and Robert Jamieson, at left in the photo above, eventually became the tug's master. *Rosalie* was primarily used as a harbor tug, moving scows and towing logs in Port Gardner Bay and the Snohomish River. In 1936, *Rosalie* was sold to Ecuadorian interests and hauled south aboard a Grace Line steamship.

In the photo on the next page, *Rosalie*, with wet decks, is pictured while rolling and pitching in rough water outside of Everett's harbor. On the next page, also, is one of the poems written by Bob Jamieson. This poem is included here courtesy of Mary R. (Lien) Jamieson, Bob's daughter-in-law. Bob Jamieson's son Floyd was Mary's husband, and Floyd eventually became captain aboard American's tugs, including *Chickaloon, Elmore, Gwylan, Irene, Margaret S,* and *Mary D. Hume.* Floyd's brother John also was a towboat man, and in fact, Mary herself worked for a time as cook and deckhand aboard American's towboats.

As described earlier, when working with log rafts, tug crew members routinely wear caulk boots with hobnails on the underside (frequently called "cork boots," "cork shoes," or just plain "corks") to provide safe footing when walking on logs. When out on the logs, Mary Jamieson did not have the benefit of secure footing because this type of foot attire was not available in her small size.

190

Rosalie in heavy-going off Everett, n.d. (With permission of Snohomish County Museum)

The Woes of Cap'n Bob

I'm sorry for Captain Bob Jamieson so woefully tried,
Fine weather for towing to him is denied.
At Stick Point on Whidbey Island he's destined to stay
And hang on boomsticks cause his logs got away.

No more on the market those hemlocks are found.
They're mixed with the driftwood that floats through the Sound.
I haven't the gale or the gall
To ask Jamieson to cheer up and smile.

I would rather approach him and whisper, "Old pal,
When next you are towing a raft in a gale,
Be wise, be watchful, not blind like an owl.
If you take many chances you'll be out on a foul."

"You brought on yourself this misfortune, you know,
By saying summer breezes can't break up a tow.
Before that announcement your ideas were great.
By making them public you sealed your own fate."

Such mistakes, say the owners, we cannot let pass.
Keep an eye on the weather when you see a low glass.

By Captain Robert Jamieson, tug *Rosalie*, 1930s (Courtesy of Mary Jamieson)

Black Prince, n.d. (With permission of Snohomish County Museum)

My father, Morris N. Knutsen Sr., who grew up in Snohomish, had fond memories and spoke often of *Black Prince*, pictured above. *Black Prince* was a wooden, shallow-draft, steam powered sternwheeler built by Robert Houston on the bank of the Snohomish River at Everett in 1901. The power plant consisted of two horizontal engines, one port and one starboard in line with the long connecting rods that drove the sternwheel cranks. These engines were supplied with steam from a former brickyard boiler. *Black Prince* had a hull length of 93 feet and an overall length of 112 feet, including the stern-wheel.

Originally, the sternwheeler was employed as a freight and passenger steamer on the Snohomish and Skagit Rivers by the appropriately named Snohomish and Skagit River Navigation Company. Eventually, *Black Prince* passed into the hands of

the Puget Sound and Baker River Railroad Company, and in 1922, the vessel was purchased by American Tug Boat Company for towing service in Everett's harbor and on the Snohomish River.

Black Prince was used primarily for handling log rafts in the shallow water of the river system. Frequently, to maintain more precise control when bringing logs downstream in the swift current encountered in river service, *Black Prince* would point the bow upstream and slowly back down the river with the log raft. The towboat was operated by American Tug Boat Company for 13 years until Captain Harry Ramwell, in the year when he passed away, signed the boat over to the Everett Yacht Club. The sternwheeler's deckhouse was then used as a yacht club meeting facility until 1956, when the structure was demolished and replaced with a new building.

American Piledriving Company piledriver *Tyee* under tow, n.d.
(With permission of Everett Public Library, Northwest Room)

In the early photo above, the American Piledriving Company piledriver *Tyee* was under tow with the assistance of a brisk tail wind. Ship handling in a wind can be problematic, particularly when maneuvering a vessel that has a lot of above-water profile area, such as an auto/passenger ferry or, in this case, an unwieldy pile driver. For a tug struggling mightily against the resistance of a floating object hanging on the towline, however, a breeze from astern can give a welcome push, especially when the tow has a lot of sail area, as the piledriver has.

The towboat in the photo above is believed to be American Tug Boat Company's steam tug *Gwylan* in the configuration that existed prior to the tug's modification, which resulted in the altered appearance as pictured in the photo below. In the photo below, the 69-foot *Gwylan*, built at Tacoma in 1902, is shown as lengthened and rebuilt in 1931.

Gwylan's rework included the construction of a new deckhouse and the installation of a 200-horsepower Atlas as a replacement for the steam plant. In this photo, *Gwylan* was at work with a log raft on the towline in Dana Passage north of Olympia. A tug with a tow tends to pivot around the towing bitt or winch when turning, and *Gwylan*'s long aft working space permitted placement of the winch well forward of the rudder, which would have made for good steering.

Gwylan in Dana Passage, 1948. (From the author's collection)

Ann S. at the Ballard Locks, 1963. (From the author's collection)

In the photo above, *Ann S.*, an 82-foot ex-YTB Class wooden U.S. Navy tug and sister to American Tug Boat Company's *Janet W*, was outbound in the large lock at Ballard with a barge in tow. In the photo below, the 67-foot-long *Gony*, ex-U.S. Army ST-396 built of wood at Stockton, California, in 1943 and a twin to American Tug's *Condor*, had Pioneer Sand and Gravel Company's scow *Pioneer No. 7*, loaded with sand and gravel, alongside in the big lock at Ballard. Both towboats had been surplused by the U.S. government after World War II.

Gony with *Pioneer No. 7* scow at the Ballard Locks, 1963. (From the author's collection)

194

Argos at Shilshole, 1963. (From the author's collection)

Argos, pictured above, towing a houseboat off Shilshole at Seattle, was 57 feet long and built of wood at Birmingham in 1914 for use as a passenger launch operating on routes between Tacoma, Dash Point, and Redondo. Originally, *Argos* was powered by a gasoline engine, but a few years later, the gas engine was replaced by a 100-horsepower oil engine that was eventually removed in favor of one developing 125 horsepower.

Following service as a passenger carrier, *Argos* passed into the hands of American Tug Boat Company for use as a tug. At the time of the photo,

American had sold the boat. In 1969, *Argos* sank, without any loss of crew, south of Wrangell Island in Alaska.

In the photo below, *Chickaloon* was running light in glassy smooth water. The 59 foot towboat was built of wood at Tacoma in 1924. *Chickaloon*, re-powered with a Caterpillar diesel engine in 1938, was among the earliest tugs to receive one of the smaller, lighter-weight, higher-speed diesel engines that were gradually replacing the large, slow speed, direct-reversing engines that had been in use for so many years.

Chickaloon, n.d. (Courtesy of Mary R. Jamieson)

Margaret S in Dana Passage, circa 1950. (From the author's collection)

The 56-foot-long *Margaret S*, pictured above pulling on a log raft in Dana Passage, was built of wood at Everett in 1910. At the time of the photo, the towboat was powered by a 155-horsepower Fairbanks-Morse diesel engine.

The current in Dana Passage runs fast, having a velocity at mid-tide of up to three knots; hence, it is important that a tug with logs on the towline, moving at no more than a knot or two, enter the pass in the direction of the tidal flow. Attempting to buck an unfavorable current when towing logs would result in no forward progress, or worse, the tug and tow could be set back.

In the photo below, *Arlyn Nelson* appeared to be a miniature tug when viewed against the backdrop of this rocky island in the San Juan Island group. *Arlyn Nelson*, at 57 feet in length and powered by a 90 horsepower, three-cylinder Atlas diesel engine, was built of wood at Sunrise Beach in 1914. The tug was used on a variety of assignments, including frequent runs towing gravel scows from the pit at Mats Mats.

Arlyn Nelson in the San Juan Islands, circa 1950. (From the author's collection)

At right is another picture of *Arlyn Nelson*, this photo showing the tug with fogged-over windows on a cold morning at Lake Union's Northlake. At the time of the photo, *Arlyn Nelson* had been sold by American Tug Boat Company, and the green and orange colors had been replaced with black hull and red and white house by new owners.

At right in the photo of *Arlyn Nelson* was *Iroquois*, at one time a passenger and auto carrier owned and operated by Puget Sound Navigation Company, the Black Ball Line, on a regular run between Seattle, Port Townsend, and Port Angeles. *Iroquois* was 209 feet long and built of steel at Toledo, Ohio, in 1902 for use in carrying passengers. Directly behind *Arlyn Nelson* in this photo was a U.S. Coast Guard 83 foot cutter, and just beyond the cutter was a power scow of a type frequently seen in Alaska.

Magdalene, pictured below, was a 60-foot-long wooden cannery tender when built at Tacoma in

Arlyn Nelson in Lake Union, 1963. (From the author's collection)

1914. Originally powered by a gasoline engine, *Magdalene* later received a 180-horsepower diesel engine while for many years in the employ of American Tug Boat Company.

Eventually, *Magdalene* changed ownership, as many other tugs did when business conditions warranted it, this time passing to Revilla Tug Service of Ketchikan, Alaska, for use as a pilot boat. The towboat then underwent rebuilding work, receiving in 1972 a 425-horsepower GM diesel as well as other new outfitting items.

Magdalene, circa 1946. (Courtesy of Mary R. Jamieson)

In 1937, Puget Sound Bridge and Dredging Company needed a tug suitable for assisting in a rock removal project on the upper Columbia River. For this purpose, a 63-foot towboat was built of wood at Bellingham to the order of PSB and D. The boat was named *Peter,* after a member of Puget Sound Bridge and Dredging's staff. A tunnel stern vessel of extremely shallow draft for operations in river water of little depth, the tug was powered by a pair of six-cylinder Superior direct reversing diesel engines of 260 horsepower each.

The drawings shown below and on the next page, by Seattle naval architect L. H. Coolidge, illustrate the design of *Peter*. Not every consideration in engineering lends itself well to calculation, and so it is in ship design. Compromises are usually required, and judgment must be exercised at every step of the design process in order to produce a result that is functional for the intended purpose. This is certainly true in the design of boats that are required to operate successfully in very shallow water.

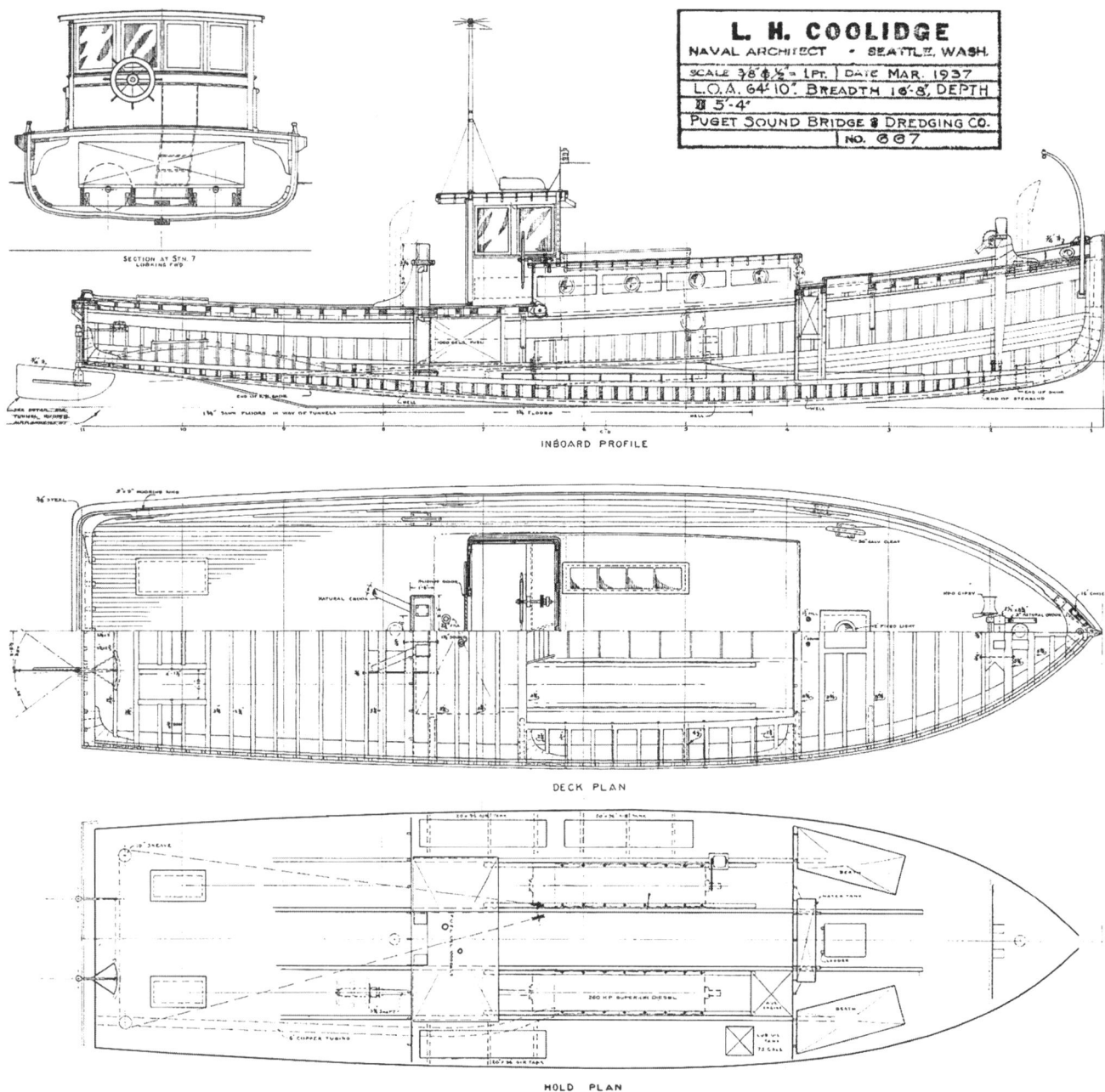

Peter arrangement and construction drawing, 1937.
(With permission of Puget Sound Maritime Historical Society, Ship Plans Collection)

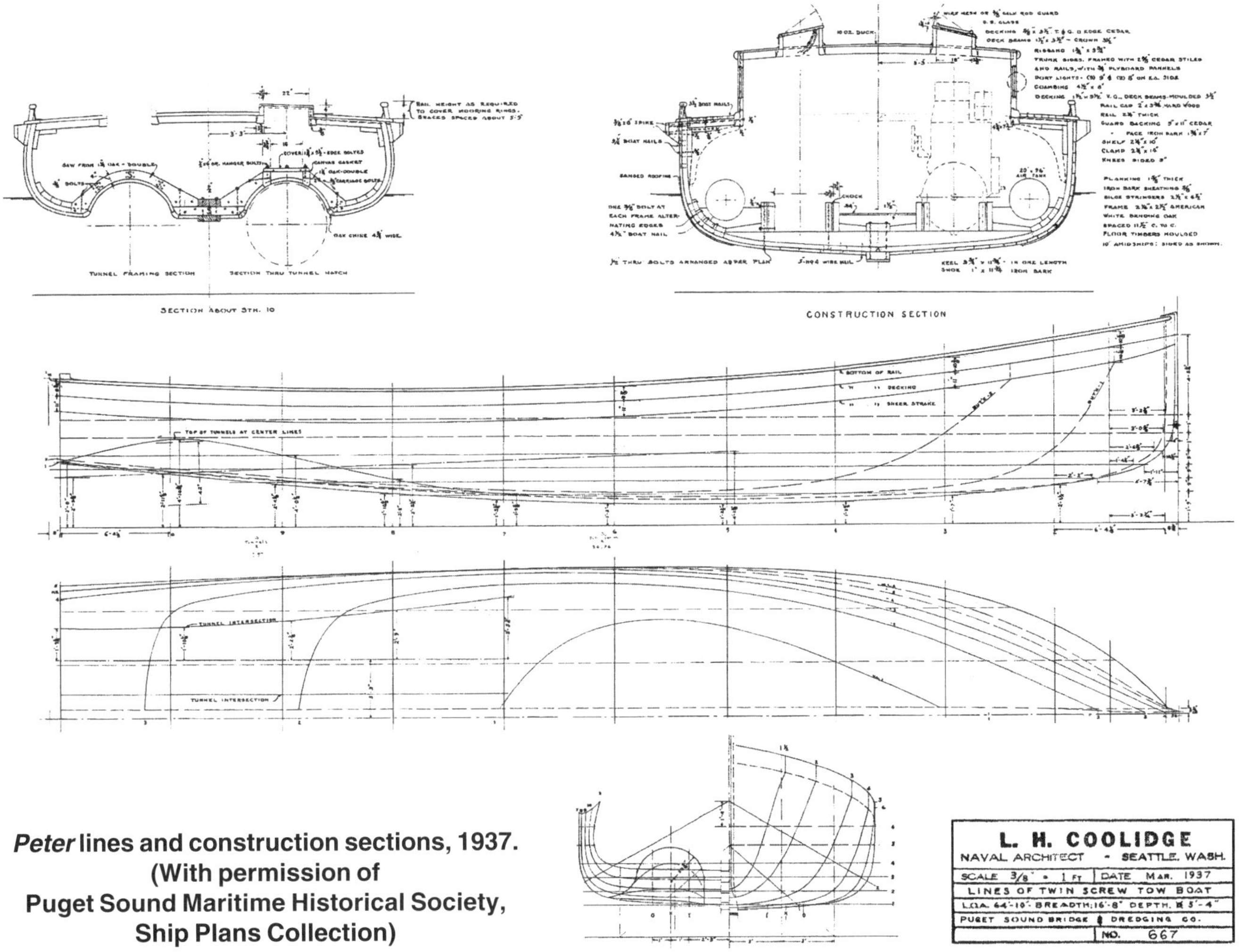
SECTION ABOUT STH. 10
TUNNEL FRAMING SECTION
SECTION THRU TUNNEL HATCH
CONSTRUCTION SECTION
L. H. COOLIDGE
NAVAL ARCHITECT - SEATTLE, WASH.
SCALE 3/8" = 1 FT
DATE MAR. 1937
LINES OF TWIN SCREW TOW BOAT
L.O.A. 64'-10" BREADTH 16'-8" DEPTH 5'-4"
PUGET SOUND BRIDGE & DREDGING CO.
NO. 667

***Peter* lines and construction sections, 1937. (With permission of Puget Sound Maritime Historical Society, Ship Plans Collection)**

Peter was intended for operation by a crew of two. Two berths were provided forward, but the design depth of a little over five feet did not allow for much else in the way of accommodation aboard this towboat. At a hull draft of about three and a half feet, the top of each tunnel at the location of the propellers was above the waterline. An effective rudder design would have an aspect ratio such that the height is considerably greater than the width. Due to *Peter*'s shallow draft, underwater space was limited, resulting in rudders with the height of the blades being only about one third the width, not unusual for a design of this type.

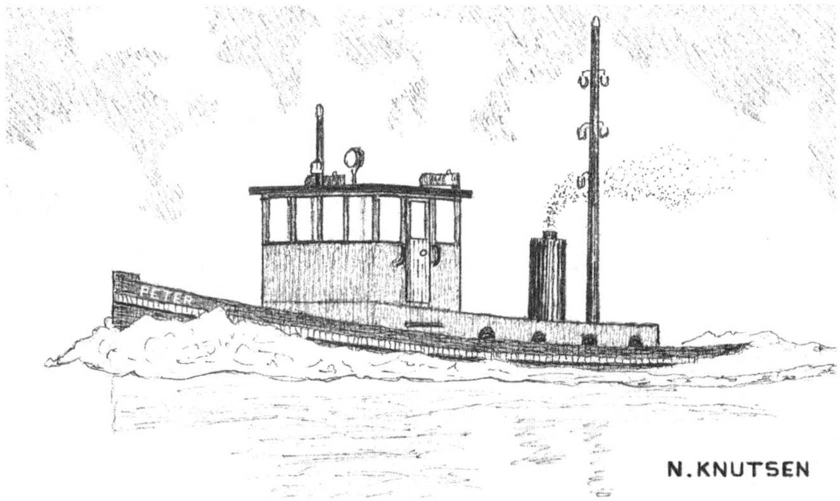
N.KNUTSEN

***Peter* as modified by American Tug Boat Company.**

After completion of the rock removal job on the upper Columbia River, ownership of *Peter* passed to American Tug Boat Company, which extensively reworked the towboat to the configuration as illustrated at left. The tug was then put to work handling log rafts in the harbor at Everett and the shallows of the Snohomish River.

Irene at Olympia, 1942. (From the author's collection)

In the photo above, *Irene* was in Olympia's harbor with a log raft alongside. *Irene* was a 73-foot wooden steam tug built at Tacoma in 1902 and later converted to diesel power.

In the photo below, *Mary D. Hume* was running light in Colvos Passage, locally referred to as the West Pass. This 98-foot wooden steam tug was built at Ellensburg, Oregon, in 1881. At the time of the photo, *Mary D. Hume*'s upper deckhouse was almost as long as the lower house. The upper deckhouse was later shortened, and the steam plant was removed and replaced with a 600-horsepower Washington diesel engine.

I can recall boarding *Mary D. Hume* from a small boat long ago while the tug was putting a steady pull on a log raft in Drayton Passage. In the engine room fidley at the main deck level, the engineer was comfortably seated while playing Scandinavian music on his accordion. Just below in the engine room, the big reciprocating steam engine was softly setting the rhythm for the music that was flowing from his accordion.

Mary D. Hume in the West Pass, 1949. (From the author's collection)

PACIFIC TOW BOAT COMPANY
Everett

George W, n.d. (With permission of Puget Sound Maritime Historical Society, negative 3268-3)

Pacific Tow Boat Company, owned by Louis E. Moe, was headquartered in Everett and house colors for their tugs were black hull, buff and white deckhouse, and black stack. The company was purchased by members of the Foss family in the late 1940s, and a few years later, the firm as a separate entity was integrated into Foss Launch and Tug Company as a subsidiary.

At a length of 93 feet and one of Pacific Tow Boat's largest tugs, *George W*, pictured above, was constructed of wood at Portland, Oregon, in 1889.

Originally built as the steamer *G. H. Mendell* for the Corps of Engineers, the vessel was acquired by the Columbia River towboat operator Shaver Transportation Company and rebuilt as the 480-horsepower *George W* in 1937, ownership of the tug later passing to Pacific Tow Boat.

The 61-foot, 200-horsepower tug *Lea Moe*, below, was built of wood at Tacoma in 1942. The date of the photo is unknown but, at the time, it is likely that *Lea Moe* was quite recent out of the building yard.

Lea Moe, n.d. (With permission of Puget Sound Maritime Historical Society, negative 427-1)

201

Chicamauga in Dana Passage, 1948. (From the author's collection)

In the photo above, the 60-foot-long *Chicamauga* was pulling a log raft through Dana Passage. *Chicamauga* was designed by Naval Architect L. E. Geary and built of wood at Seattle for Pacific Tow Boat in 1915. The original engine was a four-cylinder, 240-horsepower Nelseco engine, and in 1941, the tug was repowered with a 200-horsepower, direct-reversing Atlas diesel.

Sea Chicken with a string of boomsticks.

After many years of service with Pacific Tow Boat Company, the tug was renovated with a new deckhouse, including a raised pilothouse, and the name was then changed from *Chicamauga* to *Sea Chicken*. The rebuilt towboat is illustrated above.

As shown in the photo on the next page, three of Pacific Tow Boat's tugs were taking a rest at the company's home moorage in Everett. Left to right in the photo were *Sea Ranger, Sea Imp,* and *Sea Duke.* Pacific Tow Boat's largest tug *Sea Ranger,* 100 feet in length, caused *Sea Imp* and *Sea Duke* to appear rather small. The 350 horsepower *Sea Ranger,* ex-*Elmer Foss* pictured earlier in the book, was built of wood at Ballard in 1904.

In 1922, Pacific Tow Boat bought a wooden 46-foot hull that was under construction at Lopez Island and then completed the boat. Given the name *Sea Imp,* and with a 55 horsepower Atlas-Imperial diesel engine as power, the tug then worked for over 40 years until scrapped in 1963.

On an afternoon many years ago, while still a grade schooler, I paid one of my visits to the moorage of Delta V. Smyth Tugs and Barges Company in Olympia to admire the boats and watch the activities. It happened that Pacific Tow Boat's tug *Sea Duke* was in from Everett and tied to Delta Smyth's float. The towboat's crew asked if I would like a ride. To take a ride aboard an honest-to-goodness tugboat, well, of course the answer was yes without hesitation. The skipper backed the tug out of the moorage, turned, and headed north into the harbor.

202

The purpose of this short trip aboard *Sea Duke* was to check out the log rafts that were moored along Olympia's West Side and to locate the particular raft that the tug was scheduled to tow out of Olympia. An hour or so later, back at Smyth's moorage, I climbed over the tug's bulwark and on to the float, then rode off on my bike hurrying home to tell my parents all about it.

Being so young at the time, I was unaware that, many years before, Delta Smyth had rescued a derelict packet named *Victor II*. Renovation of *Victor II* was undertaken and, upon completion, Smyth operated this same vessel, later named *Sea Duke*, in towing service out of Olympia prior to Pacific Tow Boat's ownership of the boat.

Victor II was a 61-foot passenger/freight boat built of wood at Maplewood Beach in 1914. Gasoline engine powered and reportedly speedy, the vessel was used on a run between Allen, Vaughn and Tacoma. Unfortunately, in 1916, *Victor II* fell on hard times when the little packet was hit by a violent wind at Point Defiance. The vessel rolled over and went on the beach, with the lives of two passengers lost. Others aboard *Victor II* were res-cued by Olson Tug Boat Company's tug *Elf*, a tow-boat that was purchased a short time later by Foss Launch and Tug. Cargo had been stowed on *Victor II*'s upper deck, and it is possible that this heavy weight placed high in the boat raised the center of gravity by an amount sufficient to seriously degrade the stability.

Later, *Victor II* was hauled to Day Island, and after lying there for a few years, Delta Smyth bought the derelict and prepared the vessel for towing service out of Olympia. In the 1920s, the tug passed to Pacific Tow Boat Company, which undertook further rebuilding of the boat, including the installation of a 125-horsepower Atlas diesel engine. The towboat was named *Sea Duke*.

Sea Duke was not the best looking towboat on Puget Sound, but the tug worked successfully for many years in the employ of Pacific Tow Boat. The access to the pilothouse was via a vertical ladder on each side of the deckhouse. Climbing this ladder could probably be a bit of an adventure when the boat was rolling in even moderately lumpy water. *Sea Duke* was finally retired, set on fire and scuttled in Port Gardner in 1964.

Left to right, *Sea Ranger*, *Sea Imp,* and *Sea Duke* at the Pacific Tow Boat moorage in Everett, n.d. (With permission of Puget Sound Maritime Historical Society, negative 4824-3)

Baer at Olympia, 1942. (From the author's collection)

In the photo above, the Pacific Tow Boat tug *Baer* was running light in the harbor at Olympia. This towboat was 77 feet long and built of wood at Anacortes in 1912.

In the photo below, probably from the 1930s, Pacific Tow Boat's *Sea Vamp* was handling wooden scows piled high with lumber to be hoisted, by means of the ship's own cargo gear, aboard the steamship *Sunewarkco* at Everett. *Sea Vamp* was 50 feet long and built of wood at Seattle in 1923. *Sunewarkco*, 324 feet long, 3253 gross tons and 1500 horsepower, was built at Newark, New Jersey, in 1920. The cargo ship was owned by Portland-California Steamship Company.

Sea Vamp tending a scow loaded with lumber for the freighter *Sunewarkco* at Everett, n.d.
(With permission of Snohomish County Museum)

Lorens, n.d. (With permission of Puget Sound Maritime Historical Society, negative 2908)

The 49-foot *Lorens*, pictured above, was built of wood as a gasoline-powered cannery tender at Astoria, Oregon, in 1902. Later, a Fairbanks-Morse 45-horsepower semi-diesel powered the vessel, and still later, a 165-horsepower diesel engine was installed. In a manner similar to Elliott Bay Mill's log handling tug *Adelphus*, also an ex-cannery tender and pictured later in the book, the small trunk cabin was installed on the deck forward to house living accommodations for the crew. *Lorens* was destroyed by fire at Everett in 1957.

As described previously in these pages, crew accommodations were not spacious aboard many of the earlier towboats. Frequently, the fo'c'sle below deck was accessed via a small hatch and vertical ladder, there being insufficient space even for a sloping ladder. The space available below deck was sometimes barely able to house berths and a rudimentary galley. The captain usually had a small stateroom above the main deck. The upper deck house of *Sea Duke*, pictured earlier in this chapter, functioned primarily as the pilothouse, of course, but there was also a berth installed in the aft portion of the space. However, there was no bulkhead separating this sleeping area from the forward portion of the upper house where wheel watches were being stood; the two functions, sleeping and working, were in a single common space. Still, things could be gotten used to, and life aboard the towboats was pretty good.

In the photo below, *Thelma O* was handling log rafts at Everett. This 50-horsepower towboat was 45 feet long and built of wood at Seattle in 1912. *Thelma O*, although smaller in hull length and deckhouse size, was similar in appearance to *Sea Vamp*, pictured earlier in this chapter.

Thelma O, n.d. (With permission of Puget Sound Maritime Historical Society, negative 5980)

Sea Horse, from an H. C. Hanson design shown here, was built of steel at Seattle in 1949.

As noted in the drawing title block, the design was to the order of Foss Launch and Tug Company, but the tug was intended for operation by Pacific Tow Boat Company, a firm that Foss Launch and Tug had recently acquired.

The pilothouse location abaft the engine space, providing quick and easy access to the aft deck, was a logical arrangement for this type of towboat. As a day boat, only minimal crew accommodations were necessary; most day boats at that time did not even have so much as a head but this design provided a toilet that was located in a tiny compartment within the pilothouse.

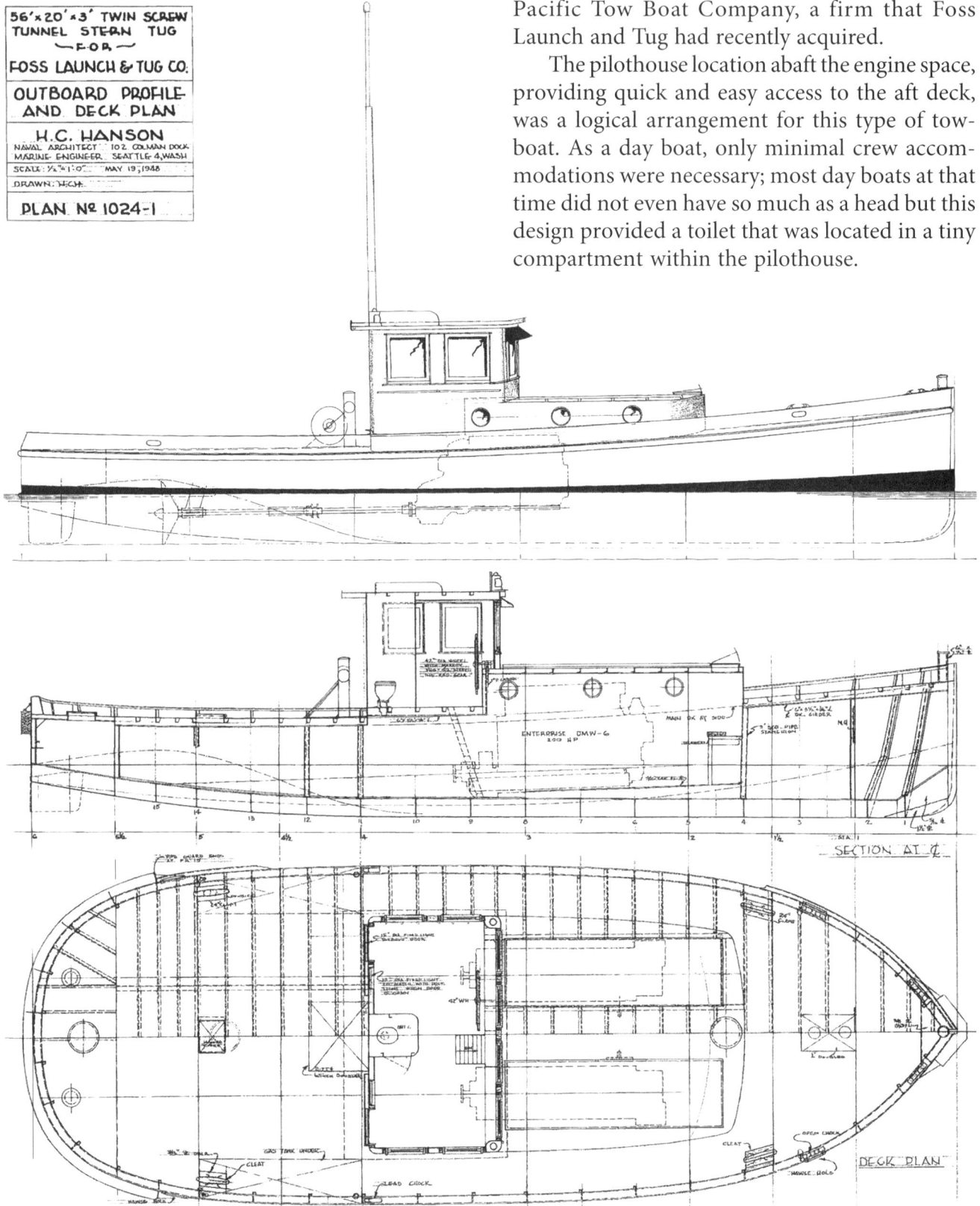

56' x 20' x 3' TWIN SCREW
TUNNEL STERN TUG
— FOR —
FOSS LAUNCH & TUG CO.
OUTBOARD PROFILE
AND DECK PLAN
H.C. HANSON
NAVAL ARCHITECT · 102 COLMAN DOCK
MARINE ENGINEER · SEATTLE 4, WASH.
SCALE : ½"=1'0". MAY 19, 1948
DRAWN: H.C.H.
PLAN № 1024-1

Sea Horse outboard profile, inboard profile and deck plan, 1948.
(With permission of Whatcom Museum of History and Art, H. C. Hanson Collection design 1024)

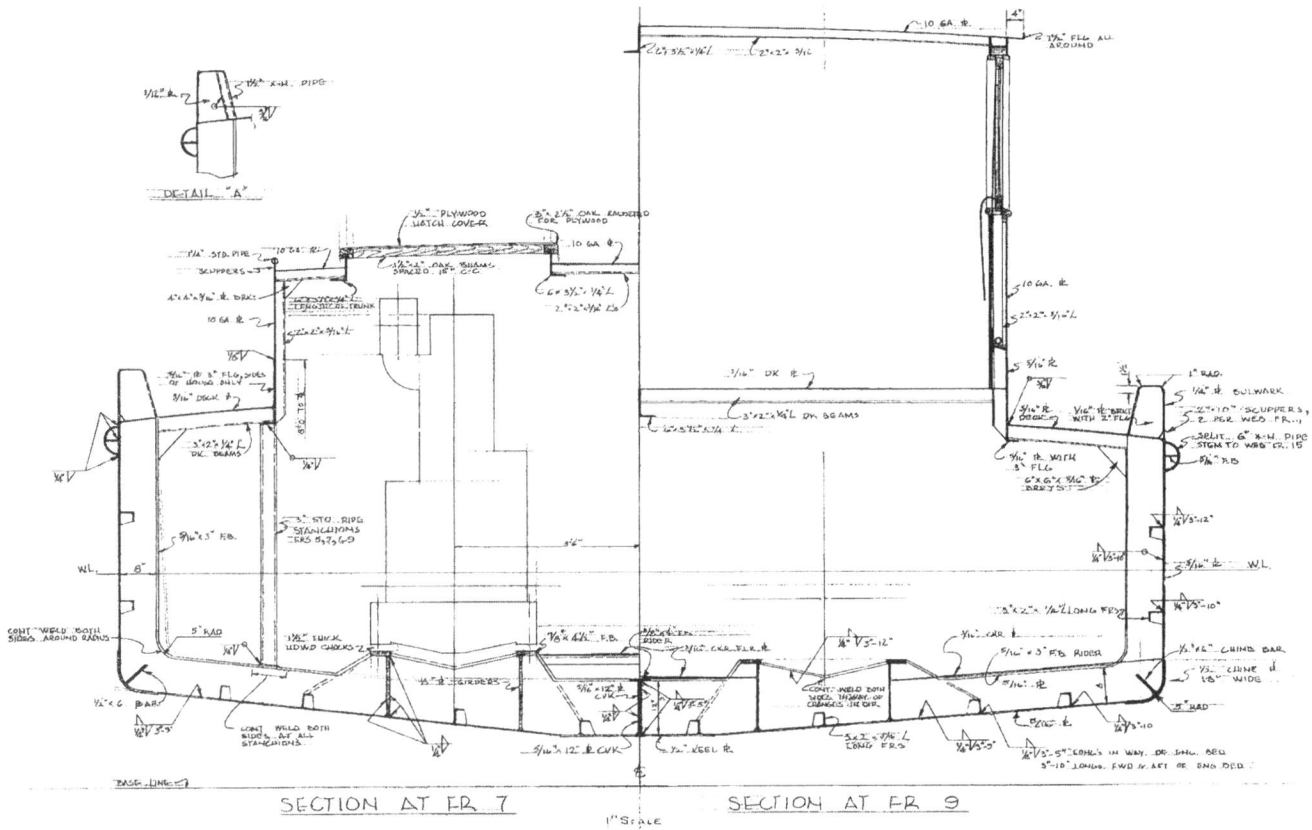

SECTION AT FR 7   1" SCALE   SECTION AT FR 9

Sea Horse construction sections, 1948.
(With permission of Whatcom Museum
of History and Art, H. C. Hanson
Collection design 1024)

With a draft of only three feet, *Sea Horse* was suited to handling log rafts in areas of shallow water at Everett and in the Snohomish River. A length overall of 56 feet and a broad beam of 20 feet provided the buoyancy necessary to achieve such a shallow draft.

The structural design of *Sea Horse*'s hull utilized widely spaced transverse web frames that supported longitudinal stiffeners. The deck, however, was framed transversely. A longitudinally framed hull can save weight as compared with a transversely framed hull, an important consideration for a boat with a very shallow draft.

Propulsion was provided by a pair of 200-horsepower Enterprise direct-reversing diesel engines driving twin screws in tunnels that provided a close fit to the propellers. Referring to the drawing on the previous page, engines with reduction

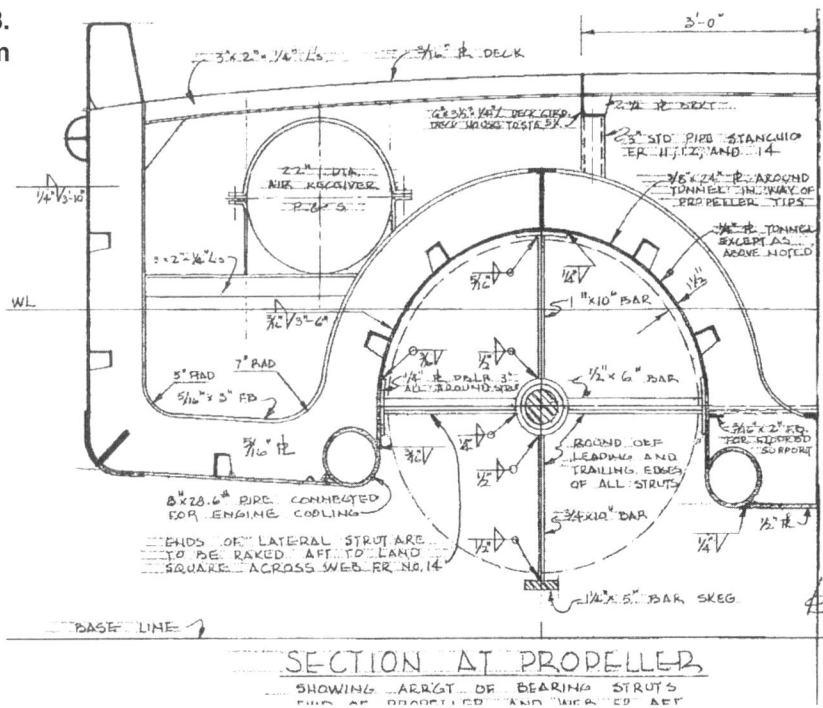

SECTION AT PROPELLER
SHOWING ARR'GT OF BEARING STRUTS

gears, smaller than the Enterprise engines, were outlined in the outboard profile, but the Enterprises as shown on the inboard profile were used instead. *Sea Horse*, with propellers of about four feet in diameter that powered a boat having a draft of only three feet, was an example of an extreme tunnel stern towboat.

207

DUNLAP TOWING COMPANY
La Conner

The Dunlap Towing Company has an interesting history. The company was founded in 1925 by Eugene Dunlap through the purchase for $10,000 of Anderson Brothers Towing, a La Conner based company, and renaming it Dunlap Towing Company. In the process, all three of Anderson's tugs, *Novice, Lilly,* and *Hustler,* were acquired by Dunlap.

These small tugs with their shallow drafts were well suited for operations in the various sloughs of the Skagit and Snohomish river systems. Not long after the purchase of Anderson Brothers Towing, the 50-foot wooden tug *Malolo* was built at Ballard as an addition to the Dunlap fleet, and this new, deeper draft boat was then available for assignments in more open Puget Sound waters.

In the early days, hay and oats were loaded manually aboard small barges at grain house landings that bordered the sloughs. These covered barges, capable of carrying 150 tons, were towed to the Albers Brothers Milling Company at Seattle. In addition, bales of straw, a by-product of the grain harvest, were hauled to chicken farmers in southern Puget Sound. Barges loaded with fish were also towed for delivery to Seattle.

In 1930, Dunlap Towing Company, like many other firms, found itself caught up in the hard times of the Great Depression. It was at this point that Dunlap entered the log-handling business by towing logs on the lower Skagit River. Other opportunities presented themselves, as well, to help in taking up the slack.

In 1936, Gene Dunlap was instrumental in convincing Washington state officials and the U.S. Army Corps of Engineers that Swinomish Channel should be dredged. The deepening of the channel was completed, and the improved navigation conditions provided an optional route to points north, such as Anacortes and Bellingham. In addition, the jetty between Goat Island and McGlinn Island was built, creating a channel and a protected bay for log storage and rafting.

The years during World War II were sometimes lean, but there were good times, too, with pulp logs being towed to Bellingham, cedar logs to the shake mills at Everett, and Douglas fir logs to Robinson Plywood at Everett. The log handling business was increasing rapidly. *Malolo* was repowered and, as new additions to the Dunlap fleet, the shallow draft tugs *Gerry D, Patsy D,* and *Martha* were built. In 1948, Dunlap bought Parker Towing of Mount Vernon. Into the 1950s, Dunlap purchased the Olympia Towing Company towboat *Crosmor* and, later, the Pacific American Fisheries tug *Vulcan.*

For a time, Dunlap Towing teamed up with Puget Sound Freight Lines towing freight barges by tug between ports on Puget Sound, augmenting Puget Sound Freight's declining fleet of small cargo ships. In addition to log handling, Dunlap hauled over 100,000 tons of rock by barge for the construction of the jetty at the new Shilshole Bay Marina. Another interesting tow consisted of bringing the old Bellingham Yacht Club building to La Conner for conversion into the Lighthouse Restaurant, still the city's best known and most frequented dining establishment.

In 1966, Dunlap began its first log yard operation by creating the Westside Yard on the shore of Swinomish Channel. Salt water dumping of logs by timber companies was on the decline, not only in the La Conner area but at Henderson Inlet, near Olympia, where Weyerhaeuser's log dump and booming area was ceasing operations. These changes were a matter of economics, and it is interesting to note that the Japanese, as an important customer, preferred to see their logs out of the water where the entire product could be viewed. Log scaling, measuring the size of logs, that had been performed on the water by scalers operating from a small, outboard-powered boat was now increasingly being done on dry land.

Novice, Gerry D, and *Martha,* left to right, at the Dunlap Towing Company moorage in La Conner, 1949. (From the author's collection)

The colors worn by Dunlap Towing Company's tugs were black hull, red and white deckhouse, and black stack. In this photo, three of the Dunlap Towing Company tugs were tied up between towing assignments. At left was *Novice,* a 42-foot wooden tug built at Anacortes in 1898. This boat had been with Dunlap since the beginning of the company. At center was *Gerry D,* a 35-foot-long wooden boat built at La Connor in 1941, and, at right, *Martha,* a 47-foot-long wooden tug built at La Conner in 1946.

Dunlap's boats were used primarily for handling logs, although over many years the company was involved in a variety of towing operations. As evidence that the towboats in the photo were log-handling tugs, though, wooden cleats can be seen fastened to each tug's deck to protect the deck planking from the nails on the bottom of the cork boots worn by the crew members. These wooden strips are expendable and much easier to replace when abraded than the deck planking would be. In addition, lying on *Martha's* deck on the port side is a pike pole, which is an important implement much used by log tug crew members. The freeboard of a Dunlap boat was designed to be quite low which made it easier to step onto and off of log rafts. In addition, greater freeboard was not really necessary in the relative calm of the waters where the boats normally operated. Most of Dunlap's boats were of limited draft to permit working in the shallow water of the area.

The Dunlap tugs were frequently called upon by other towing companies to act as tail boats, also. Tying on to the aft end of a log raft being towed by another tug through narrow Deception Pass, a tail boat assisted in steering log rafts through the narrow stretch of the pass to avoid hanging the raft up on the rocks flanking both sides of the channel.

At the top of the picture, a salmon fishing gillnet boat is in view while running south in Swinomish Slough. This type of boat is a bowpicker that utilizes a roller at the bow over which the net is set and retrieved, as opposed to a stern picker that works the net over the transom.

Dunlap Towing owned other boats, illustrated on the following pages, during the years covered here, also.

Although much of Puget Sound's maritime commerce is located in areas of deep water, a considerable portion of workboat activity also takes place in rivers and the shallow portion of bays. The drawing below illustrates the tunnel stern towboat *Martha*, also pictured in the photo on the previous page, designed by Edwin Monk Sr., Seattle naval architect, for the account of Dunlap Towing Company in 1945.

The towboat's overall length and beam were 52 feet and 13 1/2 feet, respectively. The boat's extremely light draft of 18 inches would seem to be about the minimum that could be allowed while still being able to deliver enough towing power for commercial service.

The boat was built with Douglas fir frames, Alaska cedar planking, and Douglas fir plywood for the deck and house. The propeller tunnel section, though, was fabricated of steel and bolted to the wooden portion of the hull. Propulsion power was provided by a pair of Chrysler gas engines driving twin screws. Forward of the engine room, a galley with range, sink, and icebox, berthing for two crew members, and a head were provided. Tank capacities were 200 gallons of fuel and 40 gallons of potable water.

The towboat was designed and outfitted for use in log towing on the Skagit River, an area of meandering channels and swift current that required a lot of skill on the part of the tug crew to avoid misfortune. For this purpose, a towing bitt was installed abaft the deckhouse, but in addition, a powered winch, with a length of steel chain wrapped on the drum, was located on the fore deck, a unique feature for use in Dunlap's specialized log-handling operation on the river.

When towing a log raft on the Skagit River, the length of chain was unwound from the winch drum, attached to the tail end of the raft, and allowed to drag on the river bottom. The drag of the chain on the bottom of the river slowed the speed of the tug and tow, thus assisting in maintaining control of the tow. Upon reaching tidewater, the towboat then retrieved the chain by stowing it on the winch, and the raft was then taken to the assigned destination.

As described previously in these pages, propellers operating in tunnels are not as efficient as propellers in more open water. Later on, Dunlap modified the stern of the towboat described here by lowering the shaft lines so that the propellers were operating in more open water.

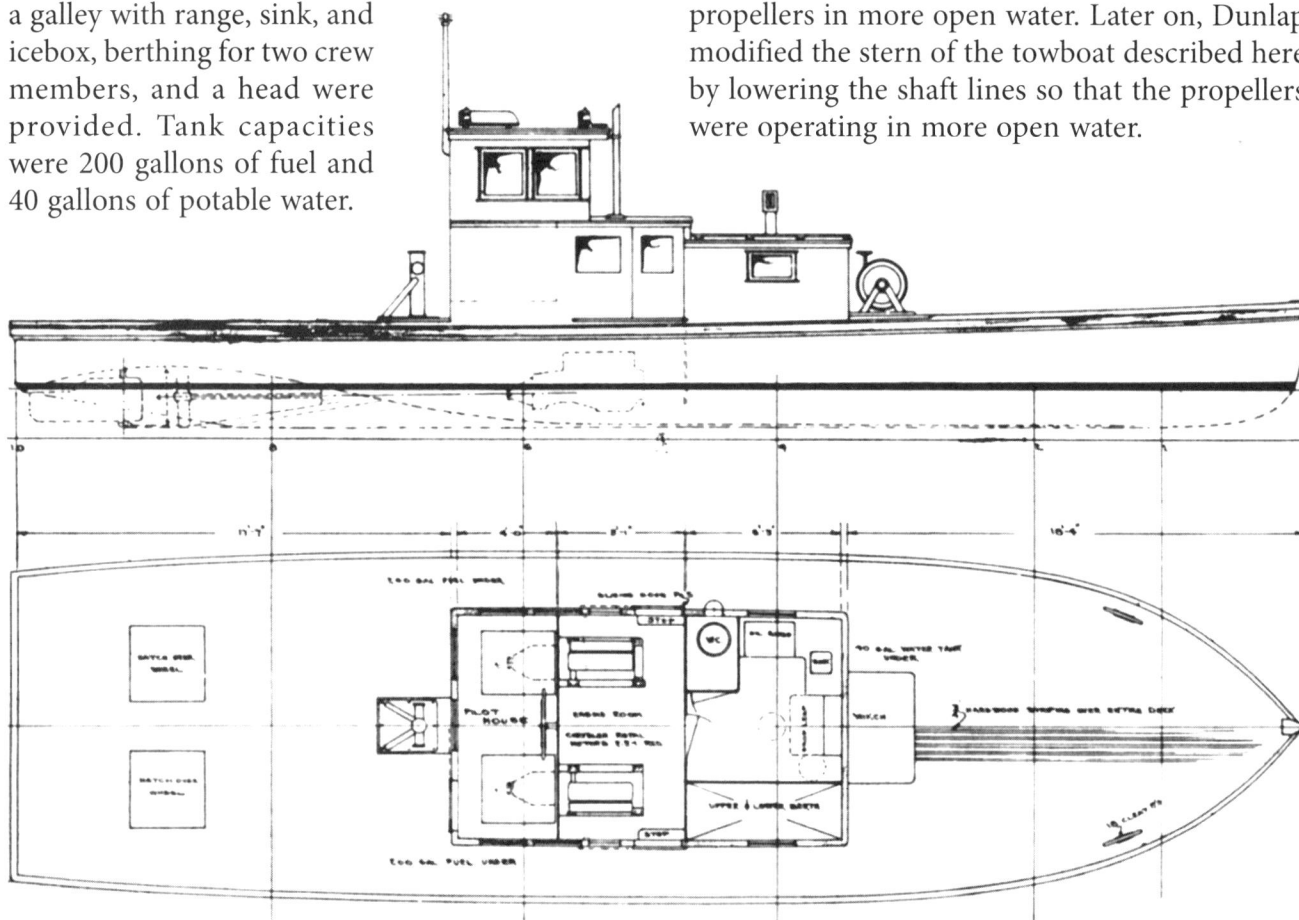

Tunnel stern towboat *Martha* for log handling on the Skagit River, 1945. (From *Pacific Motor Boat* April, 1945)

Malolo at La Conner, 1952. (From the author's collection)

Dunlap Towing's 50-foot tug *Malolo* was built of wood at Seattle in 1926 and was primarily engaged in handling log rafts. With more crew-accommodation space than the other Dunlap boats, *Malolo* was suitable for work outside of the local La Conner area.

Malolo at La Conner, 1949. (From the author's collection)

Skagit Chief at La Conner, 1952. (From the author's collection)

The 61-foot *Skagit Chief*, in the photo above, was originally built as a wooden sternwheeler at Everett in 1928. Later modified into a twin screw tunnel stern boat, the towboat was powered with a pair of 165-horsepower General Motors diesel engines. *Eathel*, one of the smallest towboats in the Dunlap fleet, is shown in the photo below, working with a string of logs.

Eathel at La Conner, 1949. (From the author's collection)

Ora Elwell, left, *Suzi*, right, and *W. T. Preston*, background, in Swinomish Slough at La Conner.

In the illustration above, *Ora Elwell* is shown pulling on a log raft in Swinomish Slough at La Conner with an assist from the diminutive towboat *Suzi*, at right. *W. T. Preston*, in the background, a big steam-powered combination snag boat and dredge operated by the U.S. Army Corps of Engineers, is described later in the book.

The 69-foot *Ora Elwell*, originally a steam-powered sternwheeler of 76 indicated horsepower, was built at Sedro Woolley in 1925. The vessel was designed with a shallow draft of only three feet for operation on the Skagit River. Eventually, *Ora Elwell* was rebuilt as a propeller-driven towboat, as shown here, similar in arrangements to *Skagit Chief*. The modification included the installation of a pair of 135-horsepower Atlas diesel engines driving twin screws in tunnels.

Little *Suzi*, perhaps the first towboat to be built of fiberglass, was built by Skagit Plastics Company at La Conner in 1956. With an overall length of 28 feet and a draft of 2 feet and propelled by a 150-horsepower Graymarine gasoline engine, *Suzi* was capable of a speed in excess of 15 knots when running light.

Vulcan, built by Commercial Boiler Works at Seattle in 1938, was a steel tug with a 72-foot length. Originally propelled by a 240-horsepower diesel engine, the tug was built for the Pacific American Fisheries operations located at Bristol Bay, Alaska.

Designed by Harold C. Hanson, Seattle naval architect, as the first welded steel cannery tender, the towboat was christened at launch by Dorothy Hanson, the designer's daughter. At the time of the photo at left, Dunlap Towing Company had recently purchased the tug for use in towing service.

Vulcan at the Ballard Locks, 1962. (From the author's collection)

213

BELLINGHAM TUG AND BARGE CO.
Bellingham

As was the case with many of the Puget Sound marine towing companies, Bellingham Tug and Barge had an interesting and colorful history. In 1914, Barney Jones, a log scaler, bought the tug *Peerless*, a 44-foot boat built at Bellingham in 1912 and pictured below in a photo by Jukes.

With Bloedel-Donovan Lumber Company as a client, Jones began towing logs that had been harvested from the forests of the Olympic Peninsula to the mills in Bellingham. The company continued to grow, and at one time the fleet consisted of thirteen tugs. Log towing continued to be the mainstay of the business for many years, but eventually, access to the remaining available timber was becoming more difficult, and as a result, the number of tugs was gradually reduced to seven.

For the remaining tugs, however, log towing, with destinations scattered all around Puget Sound, continued to be a big share of the company's business. Towing hog fuel and chip scows between British Columbia and Bellingham provided additional work, as did other towing assignments. Originally, most of the towboats were powered by steam, but as time went by, all of those tugs were converted to diesel power. Eventually, Bellingham Tug was nearly standardized on the make of engines with the installation of Atlas diesels in a large portion of the fleet.

Peerless, n.d. (With permission of Whatcom Museum of History and Art, negative 1996.10.1040)

Workboats at Bellingham, circa 1924.
(With permission of Whatcom Museum of History and Art, negative X3219.449)

In the photo by Sandison, above, Bellingham Tug and Barge Company's towboats were moored with three other workboats at Citizen's Dock on the Whatcom Creek waterway in Bellingham. Left to right in the picture were Bellingham Tug's steamers 153-foot *Daniel Kern* built at Baltimore, Maryland, in 1879; 141-foot, 1000-horsepower *Tyee* built at Port Ludlow in 1884; 116-foot *Richard Holyoke* built at Seabeck in 1877; and 90-foot *Prosper* built at Port Townsend in 1898. At left in the foreground, tied to J. H. Rife Piledriving Company's *Edna II*, is Bellingham Tug's little log tug *Automatic*. At center in the background is Nolte Sand and Gravel Company's 58-foot tug *Famous*, built at La Conner in 1901. *Mercury*, next to *Richard Holyoke*, was a tender for Chivak Packing Company.

The 56-foot-long wooden tug *Dividend*, pictured below, was built as the steamer *City of Olympia* by the Keton brothers at Olympia in 1898. Ownership passed to Pacific American Fisheries in 1900 for use as a cannery and fishtrap tender out of Fairhaven. *City of Olympia* is pictured, while working in that capacity, later in the book. Bellingham Tug bought and renamed the vessel *Dividend*, then installed a 180-hp diesel engine in 1929. Bellingham Tug's colors were black hull, burnt orange and white deckhouse, and black stack, but at the time of the photo, *Dividend* was painted World War II gray.

Dividend, n.d. (With permission of Puget Sound Maritime Historical Society, negative 197)

215

Richard Holyoke, n.d. (With permission of Anacortes Museum)

The steamer *Richard Holyoke* of 1877, pictured above and on the previous page, was one of the first deep-sea tugs built on Puget Sound. The tug was powered by a 20 and 36 x 24-inch compound engine and was built by Hiram Doncaster and William A. McCurdy.

After passing through a series of ownerships, *Richard Holyoke* became a unit of Bellingham Tug and Barge Company in 1923. The tug was em-ployed by Bellingham Tug and Barge for 15 years but was then put into layup and finally sold to Seattle owners who removed the steam plant, installed a 300-horsepower Fairbanks-Morse engine and modified the vessel for carrying freight in southeast Alaska. Later, while under South American ownership, *Richard Holyoke* was off Acapulco, Mexico, in 1947 when the vessel took on water and sank during a gale. In the photo above, *Richard Holyoke* was backed against a log raft, known as a "crib," while in the service of Bellingham Tug and Barge.

There is risk that a flat log raft would break up if transported in the swells of the ocean and the Strait of Juan de Fuca, so various schemes were used for strapping logs together into a solid mass for ocean towing. These rigs, assembled at the mouths of Olympic Peninsula rivers and elsewhere in the Pacific Northwest, went by names such as cribs, as mentioned above, "Davis rafts," "Benson rafts" and the 1000-foot-long "cigar rafts." Some of these monolithic log rafts were assembled with chain strapping in huge wooden cradles. An example of one type of log cradle is shown at left in this photo by Wilhelm Hester.

Log raft cradle under construction at Port Blakely, circa 1904. (With permission of University of Washington, Special Collections, negative UW11082)

216

In addition to moving logs in open waters by strapping them together to form rigid rafts, barges with cranes mounted on deck to load and unload logs have been used. Self-dumping barges have also been placed in service that are loaded by a shoreside crane. At the destination, ballasting a self-dumping barge with sea water on one side induces sufficient heel that the logs slide into the water. In reaction to the logs sliding off of the sloping deck, the heeled barge is actually kicked sidewise out from under the logs.

Towing a flat raft, consisting of logs floating freely within a corral of boom sticks, on the relatively protected waters of Puget Sound and delivering the raft intact to its destination is one thing, but attempting to do the same thing in the open waters of the Strait of Juan de Fuca or off the Wash-ington coast is quite another. Captain Ray Quinn, at the time in charge of the 1400-horsepower, Enterprise diesel powered Foss Mikimiki-type tug *Barbara Foss,* did indeed successfully tow a 64-section bundle raft from Esquimalt, British Columbia, across the open water of the Strait of Juan de Fuca to Port Townsend in December of 1949, perhaps a feat never before accomplished.

In making this tow, the course that was followed across the strait reduced, by an enormous amount, the elapsed time needed compared to that of the usual and more lengthy route through more sheltered waters to the east. By following the more risky but shorter route, Ray and crew were home from the trip in time for Christmas.

Prosper, pictured at left and below, was built of wood as a passenger steamer for operation between Seattle, Port Gamble, and Port Townsend. The vessel was purchased and converted to a towboat by Puget Sound Tugboat Company in 1907 for use in assisting sailing ships through the Strait of Juan de Fuca to the sawmills on Puget Sound.

Later, *Prosper*, still powered by steam, went to work in the employ of Bellingham Tug and Barge and, after several years of towing operations, the tug received a 350-horsepower Atlas diesel engine as a replacement for the steam plant.

Prosper off Dolphin Point, 1948. At the time of the photos, the steam plant had been replaced with a desel engine. (From the author's collection)

217

Barney Jr. at the Ballard Locks, 1964. (From the author's collection)

In the photo above, *Barney Jr.*, a 74 foot wooden tug built at Bellingham in 1926, was outbound and entering the large lock at Ballard. The stern of *W. T. Preston*, the U.S. Army Corps of Engineers steam-powered, sternwheel snag boat, is at left in the photo

At the time of the photo below, Bellingham Tug's *Intrepid*, painted in wartime gray, had arrived with a log raft and was temporarily anchored at Olympia. *Intrepid* was 86 feet in length and built of wood as the steamer *Charles Counselman* at Ballard in 1900.

Intrepid at Olympia, 1942. (From the author's collection)

At the time of the lower photo on the previous page, Bellingham Tug and Barge Company's 450-horsepower, oil-fired, steam-powered *Intrepid* was among the few remaining towboats on Puget Sound powered by steam machinery, others being *Adeline Foss*, *Kenai*, *Milwaukee*, and *Wanderer*. *Intrepid*'s series of ownerships and assignments illustrates the varied working histories associated with many of the Puget Sound tugs.

Gilkey Brothers Towing Company of Anacortes purchased *Intrepid* from Red Stack, a California towing company, that had been working the tug in the Hawaiian Islands. In 1936, Gilkey sold *Intrepid* to Delta V. Smyth Tugs and Barges for towing operations out of Olympia. Puget Sound Bridge and Dredging Company chartered the towboat from Smyth in 1939 for use in handling a dredge on a job for the U.S. Army Corps of Engineers at Valdez, Alaska. Along the way, American Tug Boat Company of Everett operated the tug for a time. During World War II, after the U.S. government requisitioned *Intrepid*, the tug was put to work towing barge loads of military supplies to Alaska. Eventually, the towboat passed to

Bellingham Tug and Barge Company and was finally dismantled at Anacortes in 1952.

Pictured below are two wooden, ex-World War II U.S. government tugs, the YTB class *Lummi Bay*, at left, and the LT class Mikimiki *Martha Foss*, at right. A large Union Oil tank ship was secured to the pier in the background.

The YTB class and LT class of towboats, built in large numbers for the U.S. government during World War II, were described more fully in the chapter "Some Notes on the Earlier Tugs," but specifically, the 1300-horsepower *Lummi Bay* was built by Everett Marine Ways at Everett in 1944 and the 1400-horsepower *Martha Foss* was built by Northwestern Shipbuilding Company at Bellingham, also in 1944.

Lummi Bay served in the fleet of Bellingham Tug and Barge Company while *Martha Foss*, as the name implies, was a member of the Foss Launch and Tug Company fleet. At the time of the photo, Bellingham Tug and Barge had been owned by Foss Launch and Tug since the late 1940s when the company was purchased from descendants of Barney Jones, the founder.

Lummi Bay and *Martha Foss* at the Union Oil facility in Seattle, 1963. (From the author's collection)

The 46-foot wooden tug *Bellingham Bay*, pictured at right, was built as *Salmon Scout* at San Francisco in 1937 for Bristol Bay Packing Company. Twenty years later, the boat was purchased for towing work by Bellingham Tug and Barge. Rebuilding work was undertaken by the Foss Launch and Tug Company yard in Tacoma and included the installation of a new deckhouse, shown here, as well as a Cummins V-12 turbocharged diesel engine capable of 400 continuous horsepower.

Bellingham Bay.

A longtime member of the Bellingham Tug and Barge fleet, *Shamrock II* was a 48-foot-long wooden tug built at Tacoma in 1916. As an indication of the slower pace then, the towboat was originally powered with only a small gasoline engine of 45 horsepower. At the end of *Shamrock II*'s working life, and after having been laid up for some time, the tug was donated to the city of Bellingham in the late 1950s for use as an eye-catching visitor reception center, as depicted in the photo below.

Shamrock II in retirement as a reception center at Bellingham, circa 1960.
(Courtesy of Anna J. Knutsen)

VESSELS EMPLOYED IN THE OWNERS' SPECIALIZED OPERATIONS

Most business firms that need marine transportation services contract it out to other companies that provide vessels for hire. Sometimes, though, it is advantageous for a firm to own one or more vessels to assist in the company's business activities, rather than requesting the service of others, if it is determined that a net economic benefit would accrue when all phases of activity are integrated under its own control.

On the shore of southern Puget Sound at the eastern edge of Nisqually Reach in an area that later hosted the town of DuPont, the Hudson's Bay Company established an outpost in 1833, which was known as Fort Nisqually. The company engaged in fur trading with the Clallam, Nisqually, Skagit, Snohomish, and Snoqualmie Indians, and the skins were then shipped from Puget Sound aboard sailing vessels. In 1835, a steamer was constructed in England for the company. The wooden vessel, a 101-foot sidewheeler, was named *Beaver*. Machinery was installed except for the sidewheels. The delivery passage from England was made under sail, and the wheels were installed at Vancouver up the Columbia River. A long and productive career ended in 1888 when *Beaver*, the first steamer to enter the Pacific Ocean, was wrecked on the rocks at the entrance to Burrard Inlet in British Columbia.

E. I. du Pont de Nemours and Company began manufacturing explosives at a facility constructed near the site of Fort Nisqually in 1910. The du Pont pier, built for loading and unloading cargo vessels, is shown in the photo below, looking north to Anderson Island and beyond.

The Du Pont pier, 1957. (With permission of Tacoma Public Library, Northwest Room)

To move freight between the du Pont explosives plant and the pier, company-operated trains traveled between the plant and the outer portion of the pier. The picture on the previous page shows that the du Pont explosives plant pier did not extend in a straight line from the shore but, instead, curved as it continued out from the beach. The railroad tracks were laid out along the shore to suit the topography of the land, and a large radius was required to continue the track onto the pier. Hence, a segment of the radius in the railroad tracks was on the shore, and the other portion of the curve was out on the pier.

The explosive plant's freighter *Dupont* was alongside the pier in the photos shown in these pages. *Dupont* was 60 feet long, 18 feet beam, and 71 gross tons. The little freighter was designed by Carl J. Nordstrom, Seattle naval architect, and was built of wood by Olson and Sunde at Seattle in 1930. Originally 135 horsepower, *Dupont* was later repowered with a 155-continuous-horsepower Caterpillar diesel engine in 1957. The new

Cat operated at 1225 RPM and, through a reduction gear, drove a 56-inch diameter by 46-inch pitch propeller at 320 RPM.

In addition to the new engine installation, a thorough renovation of *Dupont* was undertaken at Fishing Vessel Owners Marine Ways. The hull was recaulked, the vessel was repainted, a new exhaust system and upgraded engine controls were installed, and the 32-volt electrical system was rewired. Because *Dupont* frequently made long runs to Alaska, the storage of provisions was improved with new refrigerator/freezer equipment.

The explosives carrier shown here was actually the second vessel named *Dupont* to carry freight for E. I. du Pont de Nemours and Company. The first *Dupont*, 53 feet long and powered by a 30-horsepower gas engine, was built on Bainbridge Island in 1911. The second *Dupont*, built as a replacement for the earlier freighter, operated for many years until the vessel sank in the Gulf of Alaska in 1960; fortunately, the crew was rescued by the Mikimiki tug *Barbara Foss*.

Dupont at the Du Pont pier, 1957. (With permission of Tacoma Public Library, Northwest Room)

In the photo on the previous page, one of the du Pont battery-powered, narrow gauge trains was in position on the pier to deliver cases of explosives to the freighter *Dupont*. The photo below illustrates the transfer of explosives from the small freight cars to *Dupont*'s hold. Some of the materials used for making explosives were delivered in freight cars to the plant by Northern Pacific Railroad. Other commodities, such as sodium nitrate from Chile and sulfur, were brought to the pier by deep-sea ships.

Explosives manufactured at the "powder plant," as the du Pont facility was called by residents of the area, were in use all over the world. These explosives were employed in the logging industry, in construction of the Cascade Tunnel and Grand Coulee dam, for railroad and highway construction, for excavating the Panama Canal, and in mining projects in Alaska and the Philippines and other construction work around the world.

E. I. du Pont de Nemours Company built the town of DuPont to provide housing for the plant workers. The town was situated a safe distance from the explosive works, and homes and hotel rooms were rented by the residents, at reasonable rates, from the company. In later years, however, the homes were made available for sale at moderate prices to the plant personnel, and many of these homes are still in use by town residents. Businesses were established in town but, since du Pont owned the land and buildings, the business owners occupied space on a rental basis.

Occasionally, as might be expected in the process of manufacturing explosives, a fire or blast occurred which resulted in tragic injury or loss of life. DuPont was a closely-knit community, though, and entertainment, and social gatherings were organized by the citizens. The local beach was a popular attraction, and the pier offered an excellent platform for crabbing and fishing.

Loading explosives aboard *Dupont* at the Du Pont pier, 1957.
(With permission of Tacoma Public Library, Northwest Room)

223

Ruby VIII with a scow on the towline leaving Henderson Inlet, 1949. (From the author's collection)

Firms working with marine construction in the Puget Sound region frequently owned their own floating equipment for use on their jobs. Such a company was General Construction Company, involved with, and still contracting for, a variety of building projects. Depending upon the particular job at hand, a fleet of floating equipment for this type of work would include tugs, barges, cranes, piledrivers, and dredges.

Owned by General Construction, the 230-horsepower *Ruby VIII* was of steel construction and built by Reliable Welding Works at Olympia in 1944. As shown in the photo above, *Ruby VIII* was towing a loaded scow out of Henderson Inlet located a few miles north of Olympia. To the right in the distance, but out of the picture, the Weyerhaeuser log dump and rafting activity was in operation at that time; this tow may have been associated with that company's facility.

Ruby VIII was a hard-luck tug on occasion, having sunk once with the loss of the crew when, in a November storm, the towboat was towing a barge off Port Townsend. The tug was found lying on the bottom attached to the still-floating barge by the towline.

Testimony relating to the cause of the foundering was not available due to the loss of the crew members, but a reasonable assessment was that, for towing service, the stability of the vessel was not as good as it should have been. After being salvaged in Admiralty Inlet, *Ruby VIII* was delivered to Portland, Oregon, where the hull was widened by welding sponsons to the sides at the L. S. Baier and Associates yard. Following widening of the hull, the tug went back into service on the upper Columbia River.

The tug's register length was 52 feet, and the beam before widening the hull was 15 feet. Assuming a waterline length of perhaps 55 feet or so, the length to beam ratio was about 3.7, normally an adequate value unless it is coupled with a high center of gravity. The appearance of the towboat, with the two-level deckhouse, seems to indicate the possibility that the center of gravity was somewhat high.

Hull breadth that is insufficient to provide the stability that a relatively high center of gravity would require can result in disaster. Such a condition is especially dangerous in towing operations when the towline is not always directly astern but may be angled over the side when maneuvering, as in the *Leonine* incident described earlier in the book. Even worse, the circumstance is aggravated in rough water when the tug is rolling and the addition of a lateral pull by the towline would cause the vessel to heel, the roll angle then combining with the heel angle and possibly putting the deck edge under.

Peter M and *Steelhead* at the Ballard Locks, 1964. (From the author's collection)

In the photo above, Manson Construction and Engineering Company's 61-foot tug *Peter M* was at the Ballard Locks with a wooden scow in tow. Alongside was Manson's 47-foot tug *Steelhead*. Both boats were built of steel, *Peter M* at Seattle in 1950 and *Steelhead* at New Orleans, Louisiana, in 1943.

The 54-foot towboat *Norene*, pictured below, was built of wood at Everett in 1906 for working with log rafts on Hood Canal. The tug was originally powered with a gasoline engine but was later repowered with a diesel engine. At the time of the photo, the tug was owned by Larsen Construction Company.

Norene at the Ballard Locks, 1963. (From the author's collection)

Dredge *Townsend* at Olympia, 1947.
(From the author's collection)

Alfred at Olympia, 1947.
(From the author's collection)

Small freighters, such as those owned by Puget Sound Freight Lines, were of relatively shallow draft for operation to various ports around Puget Sound, but ocean-going cargo ships of a size such as *El Cedro* and *George Luckenback* required deeper water for navigation.

To accommodate deep-sea ships in Olympia's harbor, a channel was dredged and completed in 1911. The channel, in an outbound direction, runs north from the turning basin at Olympia's port pier, then angles northwesterly to Butler Cove on the West Side. At Butler Cove, the channel turns back to a direction of north by northwest and continues on into deeper water.

As any channel experiences a gradual accumulation of silt because of tidal currents and the discharge from rivers, it requires periodic maintenance by dredging in order to maintain suffi-

cient depth and width to accommodate the largest size of vessel that is expected to call.

The photos above show work underway in the Budd Inlet shipping channel in 1947. The dredge *Townsend* belonged to Puget Sound Bridge and Dredging Company. The tug *Alfred*, shown here tending a pile driver, also belonged to PSB&D. *Alfred* was somewhat different from most tugs in that the boat had a double ended hull, a pointed stern rather than the customary horseshoe-shaped stern. *Alfred* was 55 feet long and built of wood at Seattle in 1920. *Alfred* was similar to *Hornet*, both boats having been operated by Washington Tug and Barge for a number of years.

Blue Peter, pictured below, was Puget Sound Bridge and Dredging Company's beautiful yacht. The 86-foot yacht was built at Seattle in 1928 to a design by Naval Architect Ted Geary.

Blue Peter at the Ballard Locks, circa 1963. (From the author's collection)

In the photo at right, *Tom*, a 61-foot-long tug owned by Puget Sound Bridge and Dredging Company, is shown silhouetted against the late afternoon sun. *Tom* was built at Mare Island, California, in 1918 and, as shown here, the profile of the towboat's wake is of interest. The wake is large but, by the look of things, *Tom* had a clean running hull, with a wave crest at the bow and the second wave crest located at or just abaft the stern.

Tom in Elliott Bay, 1949. (From the author's collection)

Tom was probably at the theoretical maximum speed attainable for any displacement hull of similar length, that is, a hull with no dynamic lift such as a planing-type boat would exhibit. As determined from tank testing of ship models by William Froude at Torquay, England, in the late 1800s, the maximum speed a displacement hull can achieve, also sometimes referred to as "hull speed," is the limit at which any attempt to increase power so as to increase speed is futile due to the exponential rise in wave-making resistance.

This "speed-length coefficient" is the speed in knots divided by the square root of the waterline length in feet, and a well designed displacement hull can achieve a speed resulting in a coefficient of 1.34, as derived by Froude, or perhaps somewhat greater for an extremely narrow hull producing little wake. *Tom*, with a waterline length close to 65 feet, was probably capable of a speed of 10 knots or a bit more.

Even if pushed hard, not all hulls are able to attain the theoretical maximum speed length coefficient. The wave crest at the bow is normal for a displacement hull at any speed, of course, but the location of the second wave crest, for a vessel that is more resistant than *Tom*, would not be at the stern but would be forward of that point when running at top speed. In that case, at maximum speed, the second wave crest would be located alongside the hull, and a third wave crest would be at a point near the stern. It should be mentioned, however, that free running speed is not necessarily the most important criterion for the design of a tug; other considerations may override in the design approach.

For many years, Simpson Logging Company operated the 33-foot wooden tug *A. B. Govey* for juggling their log rafts in Oakland Bay at Shelton. Built by Blanchard Boat Works at Seattle in 1925, *A. B. Govey* had a double-ended hull. The tug was originally powered by a 100-horsepower Hall-Scott gas engine but later was upgraded with the installation of a 200-horsepower Cummins diesel.

Simpson operated other boats also, including the smaller tugs *Mud Hen* and *Number Eight*. In addition, boom boats were used to sort logs and move them to the log haul.

A. B. Govey at Shelton, 1947. (From the author's collection)

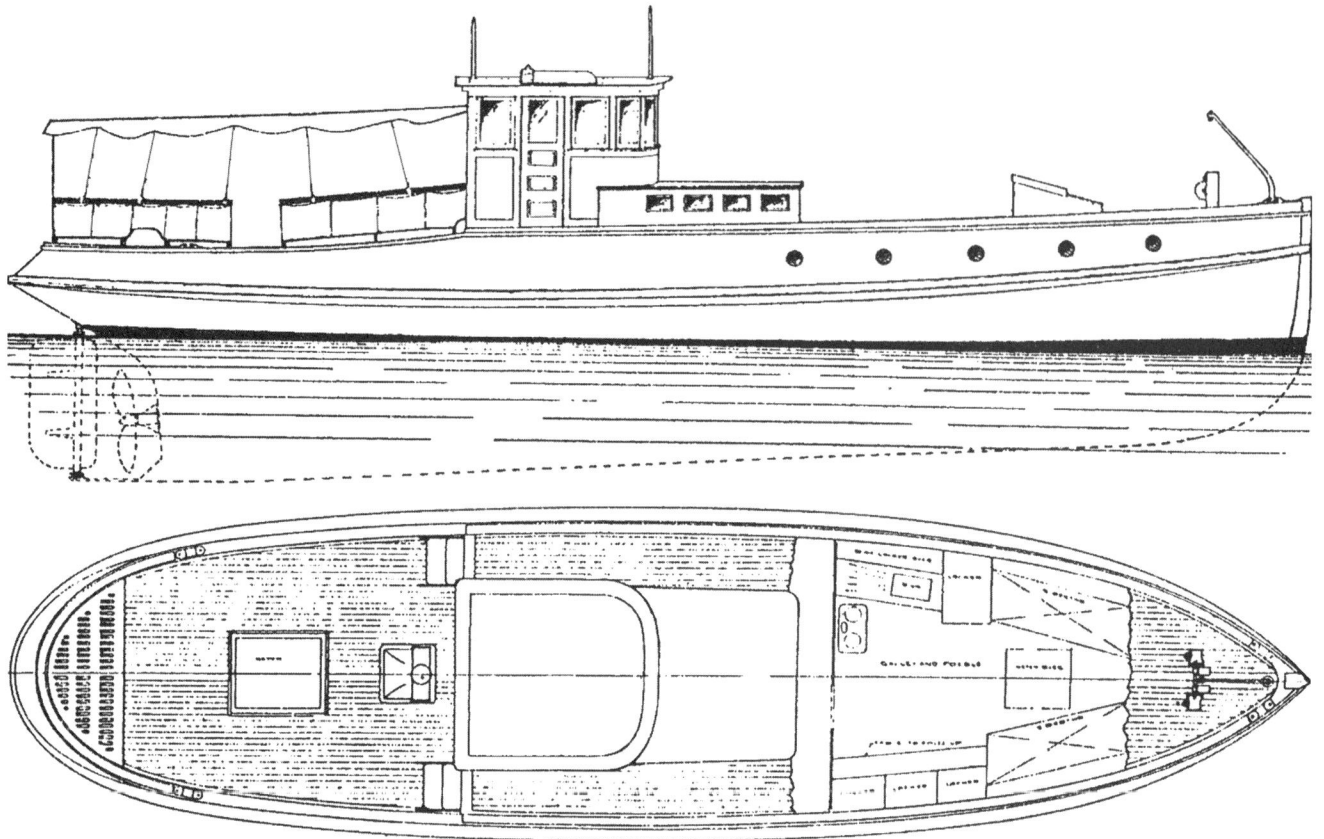

Stimson outboard profile and arrangement, 1914. (From *Pacific Motor Boat*, June 1914)

The 49-foot-long *Stimson*, constructed of wood at Seattle by Johnson Brothers and Blanchard in 1914, was built to the order of Charles D. Stimson for use in towing log rafts to his Stimson Mill Company, located at Ballard. The lumber used in building the tug was cut from tall, straight-grained trees and air dried at the Stimson mill before use. The towboat was built to replace Stimson's previous tug *La Paloma*, which had been destroyed by fire, and the design for *Stimson* was by L. E. Geary, West Coast naval architect.

Some of the most elegant yachts ever designed and built, as illustrated by the photo of *Blue Peter* in this chapter, came from the board of Ted Geary, but *Stimson* was not designed to win beauty contests. Functionality and suitability for the intended job determine a towboat's earning power, and good looks would do little toward making money in the towing business.

Stimson was powered by a Corliss gasoline engine of 80 horsepower, which was later replaced by a 110-horsepower, Atlas Imperial diesel engine, located below and forward of the wheelhouse. The arrangements of the tug were such that the boat could be operated single-handedly, if necessary, with the pilot house located abaft midship to provide good access to the aft deck and towline. *Stimson* primarily towed logs in Elliot Bay and Salmon Bay, but the design provided for living quarters below deck forward for more extended assignments elsewhere on Puget Sound.

Stimson was 50 years old in the mid 1960s when Mrs. Scott Bullitt, daughter of Charles D. Stimson, discovered that the tug had sunk. Mrs. Bullitt purchased the vessel and arranged for salvage. Raised from the bottom and afloat but leaking, *Stimson* was taken to Murray's Ocean Marine Yard where Mrs. Bullitt led the effort to have a complete renovation performed.

This rebuilding was no small task for it required a thorough cleaning of the once sunken boat, replacement of missing fittings and equipment, the fit-up of new timbers and planking in the extensively rotted areas of the hull and deck; as well as repair work needed to correct poorly performed repairs that had been undertaken by a series of owners over many years. Following a new paint job, *Stimson* was as good as new.

Adelphus in the Duwamish Waterway at Seattle, 1948. (From the author's collection)

A mill company tug of the same era as *Stimson*, *Adelphus*, pictured above, was owned by Elliott Bay Towing Company for use in log towing operations for the Elliott Bay Mill based on the Duwamish Waterway in Seattle. *Adelphus*' colors were green and white. The 56-foot-long boat had 100 horsepower and was built of wood at Seattle in 1911 as a tender for the Shaw Island Packing Company. Perhaps that amount of horsepower seems modest by today's standards, but for *Adelphus* and many of the towboats in operation at the time, it was sufficient for the job in the days when life moved a bit more slowly.

There is some uncertainty now about how the interior arrangements were laid out in *Adelphus*, but the limited size of the deckhouse and the smoke pipe extending out of the top of the forward trunk cabin indicate that the galley was forward down below. The smoke that can be seen emanating from the pipe in the photo would then be from the galley stove. The trunk cabin on the forward deck was added after the boat was placed

into towing service in order to provide additional accommodations for the crew.

Originally, in service as a tender for Shaw Island Packing Company, *Adelphus* had a considerable amount of clear deck space forward for handling cargo. This tug, with the towing bitt extremely far aft due to the deckhouse location, may have been suitable for towing log rafts, but steering while towing might have been a bit awkward if frequent maneuvering was required.

Adelphus was eventually lost while on a voyage to Alaska. Elliott Bay's other tug, *Louise No. 2,* was 60 feet long, had a two-level deckhouse, and was built of wood at Astoria, Oregon, in 1912. *Louise No. 2* was distinctive for the green shamrock painted on either side of the pilothouse.

As shown, this view is looking northeast from a point next to Spokane Street in Seattle. In the background is the Elliott Bay Mill. Near the base of the mill's smokestack, the ramped conveyer, used for hauling logs out of the water and up into the sawmill, is visible.

Pope and Talbot operated a huge sawmill at Port Gamble for many years. Located on northern Puget Sound near Juan de Fuca Strait, Port Gamble was immediately accessible to the sea. Extensive stands of timber on the Olympic Peninsula provided the logs to feed the hungry sawmill. At the beginning of the twentieth century, the harbor at Port Gamble would be found filled with log rafts, and many ships of various kinds, including sailing vessels, visited regularly to load lumber that had been produced at the mill.

Like DuPont as described earlier in this chapter, Port Gamble was a company town. Pope and Talbot owned the houses that were rented out to the mill workers and their families. The firm even owned the store where groceries and other items could be purchased by mill workers and their families on company credit. Port Gamble was, and still is, a picturesque town in a beautiful setting.

As the readily available Olympic Peninsula timber gradually became more scarce, logs had to be brought to the Port Gamble sawmill from other areas of Puget Sound, such as Bellingham, Hood Canal, Olympia, and Shelton. In 1951, Pope and Talbot commissioned a new wooden towboat to be built specifically for log towing. Designed by Seattle Naval Architect Edwin Monk Sr. and built by the Prothero Boat Company in Seattle, this tug, pictured below with logs on the towline, was named *P & T Pioneer,* and the boat was finished with a yacht-like appearance.

Per *Pacific Motor Boat Work Boat Journal* of September 1951, *P & T Pioneer* had a 65-foot length overall, a 20-foot beam, and a 7 1/2-foot draft. Propulsion power was provided by a Washington Iron Works diesel engine built at the plant on south Sixth Avenue in Seattle. The direct-reversing, six-cylinder engine produced 260 horsepower at 390 RPM. Auxiliary power was a General Motors two-cylinder diesel engine driving a generator to produce 30 kilowatts of electrical power. Tankage was provided for 5,000 gallons of diesel fuel, 110 gallons of engine-lubricating oil, and 1,500 gallons of potable water.

The exterior of the tug was painted white with black trim, and the interior was beautiful varnished wood. In the right photo, expendable cleats (strips of wood) are visible running fore and aft on the aft deck, a common installation aboard logging tugs, to protect the deck planking from being damaged by the sharp spikes on the bottom of cork boots that were worn by crew members when needed for working out on the log rafts.

Accommodations were provided for the usual inside boat crew of five, consisting of the skipper, mate, two deckhands, and a cook. Four berths were installed forward in the fo'c'sle, and a stateroom on the main deck was assigned to the skipper. As was customary practice aboard the tugs, the galley range was fired with diesel oil that was available from the tanks that also supplied the main engines. As mentioned previously in this narrative, most of the earlier towboats did not possess a shower. *P & T Pioneer* was designed and built with more attention to crew comfort, and as a result, the amenities even included a shower.

P & T Pioneer at the Ballard Locks, 1963. (From the author's collection)

In the upper photo on this page, *Nimrod* was anchored at Boston Harbor, located north of Olympia, with a small power boat tied alongside. Immediately in the background is Dover Point.

Nimrod was a 53-foot, double-ended towboat built of wood at Chuckunut in 1903 and, at the time of the photo, was owned by Olsen Towboat Company. Lewis Olsen used this tug, together with his other towboat, *Eau Claire*, for log salvage.

Eau Claire is shown in the lower photo with *Nimrod* and also later in the book. *Eau Claire* was a 34-foot wooden tug built at Seattle in 1909, and was a boat that had previously been operated by Delta V. Smyth Tugs and Barges for work in the harbor at Olympia.

Puget Sound's beaches catch a lot of driftwood because of extensive logging over a long period of time. When handling log rafts, sometimes things go wrong. Log rafts when under tow occasionally break up in rough water, a boom chain may break, or the end of an old boom stick may split out at the eye. Some of the logs then go astray and wind up on the beach.

These beached logs, if suitable for sawing into lumber, are valuable. To salvage a log from the beach, a towline is attached to the log, and the log is dragged from the beach and into the water by a tug. The salvaged logs are then usually contained within an enclosure of boomsticks and handled as a raft. In the Olsen operation, however, *Nimrod* and *Eau Claire* worked with a barge upon which a derrick had been rigged. The logs were hoisted out of the water and stacked onto the barge for transporting to their destination.

Nimrod anchored at Boston Harbor, 1948. (From the author's collection)

Nimrod, left, and *Eau Claire*, right, in Dana Passage, 1948. (From the author's collection)

231

Milwaukee at Seattle, 1949. (From the author's collection)

Milwaukee, a 107-foot, old-time looking steam tug, was built of riveted steel by Seattle Construction and Dry Dock Company (the ex-Moran yard) at Seattle in 1913 to the order of Chicago, Milwaukee, St. Paul, and Pacific Railway Company. The tug was assigned to towing railroad car barges between Seattle and the Bellingham terminal of Bellingham Bay and British Columbia Railway, a Milwaukee subsidiary. *Milwaukee* later towed a railroad car barge between Seattle and Port Townsend on a regular line haul run. *Milwaukee*'s engine was of the triple-expansion type with cylinder bores and stroke, in inches, of 15, 24, and 38 x 24. Steam was supplied at 150 psi by an oil-fired Scotch boiler to produce 900 horsepower.

The towboat's outboard profile drawing, shown below, shows the stern post supporting a rudder hinged with pintles and gudgeons, an arrangement typical of early steamers such as the 1916 tug *Wando* and the World War I U.S. Emergency Fleet cargo ship illustrated elsewhere in these pages. Later vessels utilized a cantilevered spade rudder or a rudder supported at its bottom in an extension of the keel called a "shoe."

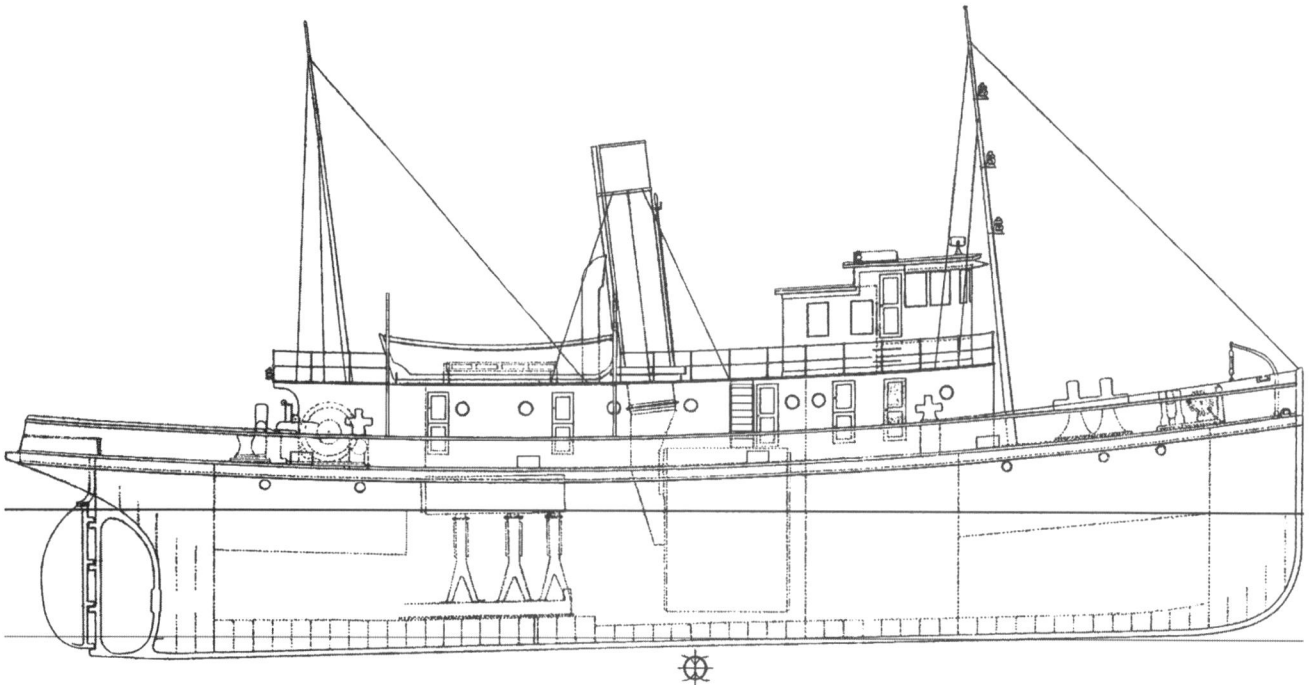

Milwaukee outboard profile, 1913.
(With permission of Puget Sound Maritime Historical Society, Ship Plans Collection)

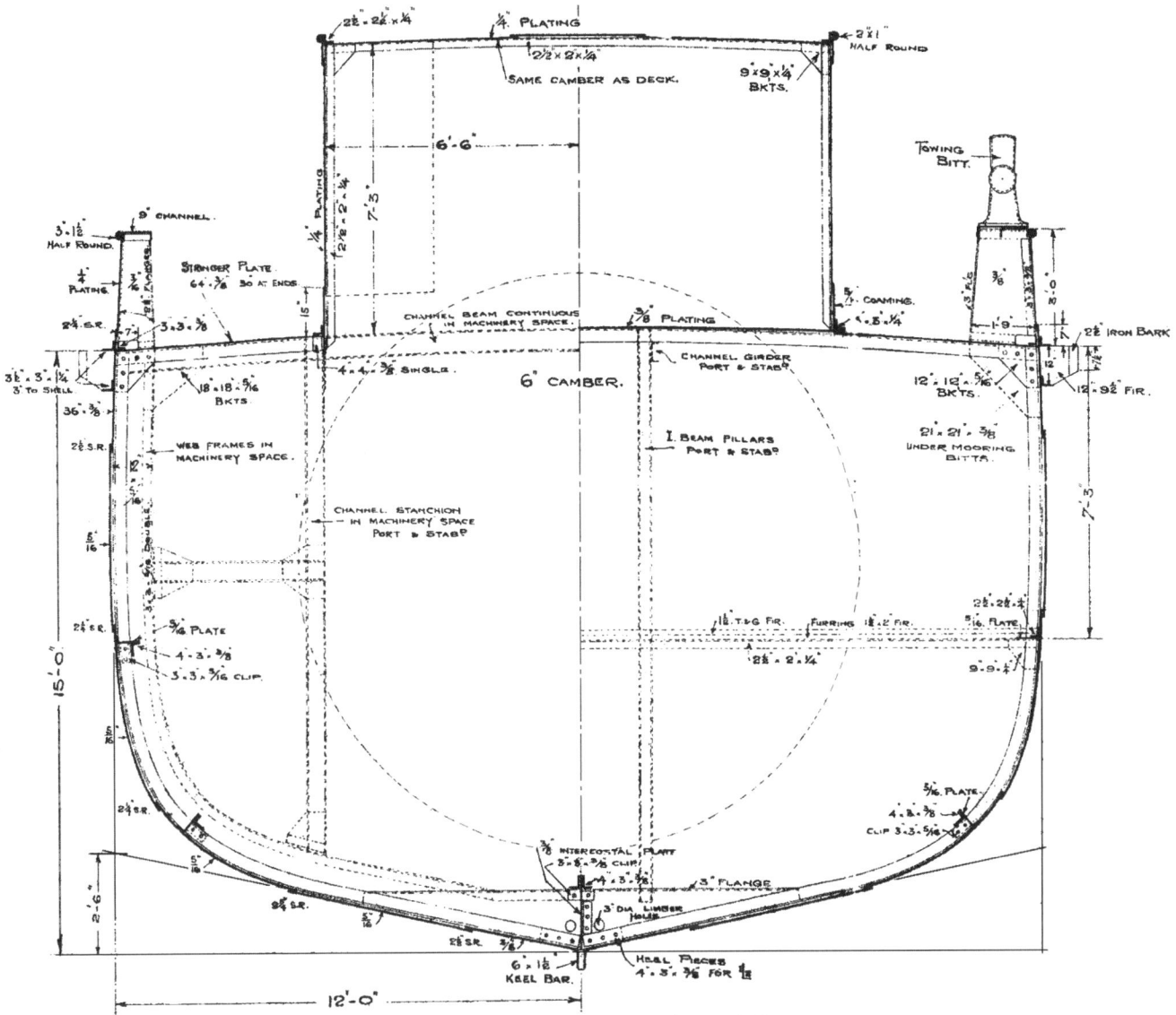

Milwaukee midship section, 1913.
(With permission of Puget Sound Maritime Historical Society, Ship Plans Collection)

The illustrations presented here are taken from the original design drawings as laid down by the builder in the spring of 1913. The midship section drawing indicates a full bodied hull with only a moderate amount of deadrise. The large circle indicated by a dashed line on this midship section drawing represents the Scotch boiler. As can be readily seen, this boiler was immense at about 14 1/2 feet in diameter. The triple-expansion steam engine, boiler, and uptake leading from the firebox to the funnel are outlined in the outboard profile drawing shown on the previous page.

Milwaukee maintained the railroad car barge runs for 42 years and was one of the last steam tugs on Puget Sound, but retirement finally arrived, and following a ceremony at the end of the towboat's last run, dismantling of the old timer was undertaken at Seattle in 1955.

SEATTLE CONSTRUCTION AND DRY DOCK COMPANY
ENGINEERS AND SHIPBUILDERS
SEATTLE, WASH

ORDER NO. A-7100	MILWAUKEE TUG	VESSEL NO. 76

Standard No. 3 with *S. O. Co. No. 15* at the Ballard Locks, 1963. (From the author's collection)

In the photo above, Standard Oil Company's 1000-horsepower tug *Standard No. 3* was alongside the 14,000-barrel *S. O. Co. No. 15* tank barge while inbound through the Ballard Locks. *Standard No. 3* was 93 feet long and built of steel at Slidell, Louisiana, in 1943.

Standard No. 3 served several ports around Puget Sound, including the Standard facility in Olympia. This tug moved petroleum products for many years on Puget Sound but was later retired and replaced by a new, larger tug which had considerably more power. Referring to the carrying capacity of *S. O. Co. No. 15* noted previously, a barrel is equal to 42 gallons, and it should not be confused with a drum, which is 55 gallons.

The Texas Company's tanker *Texaco California*, in the photo below looking north, looms large in Olympia's harbor. Log rafts are moored at left. At right in the distance is the Olympia Reserve Fleet of ships at Gull Harbor.

Tanker *Texaco California* approaching the pier at Olympia, 1964. (From the author's collection)

The Wyckoff Company was located on the south shore of Eagle Harbor, across the harbor from the town of Winslow on Bainbridge Island. This company was similar to Olympia Wood Preserving Company in the business of pressure treating wood with preservatives. Wyckoff operated the tug *Creosote*, named, obviously, for the petroleum preservative used for treating wood to ward off decay and marine borers.

Creosote, pictured below, was a 50-foot wooden tug built at Seattle in 1921, and company colors were black hull and green and white deckhouse. The tug was used to handle rafts of poles, the poles being straight logs from which the bark had been removed. At the Wyckoff plant, the poles were processed by pressure treating with preservatives. The debarked logs, after being pressure treated, were then suitable for use as telephone poles and pilings.

Creosote's deckhouse was located fairly far aft, and the forward portion of the main deck was raised to provide headroom for the accommodations below. The scuttle forward of the pilothouse provided shelter for entry to the spaces below. Access to these accommodations was via a sloping ladder, a common arrangement in the earlier days.

Unlike the more primitive anchoring arrangements aboard *Nile,* as described previously, *Creosote*'s anchor was stowed in a hawse pipe installed flush in the side of the hull forward. Utilizing the windlass on the foredeck, the anchor could be lowered simply by releasing the brake on the windlass and allowing the anchor and chain to descend by gravity. The anchor chain was wrapped a quarter turn on a pocketed sheave called a "wildcat," which simply freewheeled when dropping the anchor. The pockets in the wildcat matched the dimensions and spacing of the chain links. When lowering the anchor by gravity, the drop speed could be regulated by varying the application of the brake that was controlled by the handwheel on top of the windlass. For weighing anchor, the electric windlass rotated the wildcat, which hauled the chain in. The anchor chain was self-stowing by simply being lowered through the deck pipe and down into the chain locker.

Creosote in Salmon Bay at Seattle, 1963. (From the author's collection)

The Seattle fireboat *Duwamish*, pictured below in this early photo, was 113 feet long and built by Richmond Beach Shipbuilding Company in 1909. The vessel was accepted for service by the Seattle Fire Department in 1910. *Duwamish* replaced the 80-foot wooden fireboat *Snoqualmie* of 1890, at left in the picture. At the time of the photo, *Snoqualmie* was in a state of disrepair but was later renovated and put back into service.

As built for *Duwamish*, the stem raked aft to form a ram bow that was intended to sink a burning vessel if the fire could not be controlled. The bow was later rebuilt with a plumb stem. Construction of *Duwamish* utilized riveted steel, the steel decks then being sheathed with teak. Installed horsepower was 1100, obtained from a pair of vertical compound steam engines driving twin screws, which produced a speed of 10 knots. These engines were supplied with steam from four oil-burning watertube boilers, each of the twin funnels providing an uptake for a pair of boilers. Three American La France firefighting pumps provided 9,000 gallons of water per minute .

The U.S. Navy requisitioned *Duwamish* for World War II service in the Seattle area. During this period, the steam power plant was removed in favor of a diesel-electric arrangement driven by three 900-horsepower Cooper Bessemer engines. These engines drove water pumps capable of producing 22,800 gallons per minute maximum. One of the power plants could be switched between pumping and propulsion. With this engine powering the vessel, a speed of up to 14 knots could be attained.

Seattle fireboats *Duwamish*, center, and *Snoqualmie*, left, n.d.
(With permission of University of Washington, Special Collections, negative UW7733)

236

LT-130 in Elliott Bay, 1950. (From the author's collection)

Two United States Army Transportation Corps tugs of World War II vintage are illustrated here. At 115 feet in length, the welded-steel *LT-130*, shown in the upper photo, was nearly the same size as the U.S. Army Mikimiki type tugs, described previously. The 69-foot *ST-860*, shown in the lower photo, was also fabricated of steel.

Some of these towboats found their way into commercial towing service after World War II. For example, a government surplus tug similar to *LT-130* was purchased by Foss Launch and Tug Company and put to work as *Ellen Foss*. Eventually, a refurbishment of *Ellen Foss* was undertaken,

which included the replacement of the original 1200-horsepower, Fairbanks-Morse diesel engine with a 3600-horsepower, General Motors EMD turbocharged diesel engine.

ST-860 became American Tug Boat Company's *Judy S*, and Dunlap Towing Company's *Swinomish* was also originally of this U.S. Army ST Class. Following entry into the commercial towing business, however, *Swinomish* underwent some major rework, including construction of a modified deckhouse. *Swinomish*, pictured later in these pages, towed chip scows out of the Dunlap reload facility in Olympia.

ST-860 in Elliott Bay, 1950. (From the author's collection)

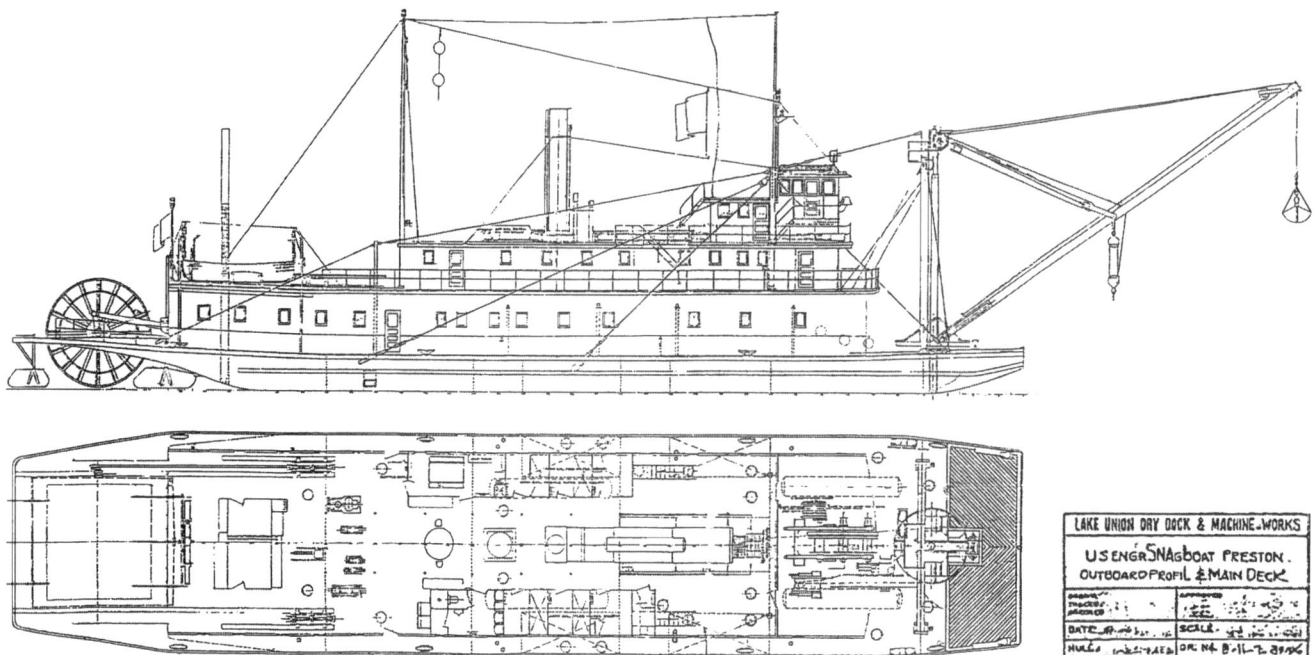

W. T. Preston outboard profile and deck plan, 1939. (With permission of Anacortes Museum)

W. T. Preston was built in 1939 by Lake Union Drydock and Machine Works at Seattle for operation as a snag boat by the U.S. Army Corps of Engineers. The purpose of this vessel was to keep the navigable waterways clear of obstructions. In this service, all manner of material, including debris caught in log jams, sunken logs, tree stumps that had been washed away in the rivers, and boats lying on the bottom, could be hoisted and placed on a barge for removal.

In this drawing, the lifting hoist is located at the halfway point on the boom while the bucket, used for dredging, is hanging from its hoist at the tip of the boom. What appear to be tall, vertical posts located forward and aft are known as "spuds." When *W. T. Preston* was required to maintain position at a job site, these spuds could be lowered to penetrate the bottom of the waterway, thus serving as an anchor, in a manner similar to the procedure used for positioning oil-drilling rigs that operate in shallow water.

Preston's hull was not built on land but, instead, was supported on top of a floating barge while under construction. The completed hull was launched by submerging the barge, after which the Corps of Engineers installed the deckhouse. *W. T. Preston* was built of welded steel and had a hull length of 138 feet, a beam of 34 feet, and a depth at side of 5 1/2 feet. The overall length, in-

cluding the sternwheel and its supporting structure, was 163 1/2 feet. The extremely shallow design draft of approximately 2 1/2 feet was an important feature that permitted the snag boat to operate in areas where the water was very thin indeed. Space at the main deck level was taken up with propulsion and auxiliary machinery, hoisting equipment, stores, and work spaces while the upper level housed crew accommodations.

Propulsion machinery consisted of two Gillette and Eaton double-acting, reciprocating steam engines, each rated at 170 horsepower. With a 14-inch bore and 72 inch stroke, these engines drove the 17-foot-diameter by 18-foot-wide wheel at 26 revolutions per minute, maximum.

As was standard practice for machinery arrangements in sternwheelers, the engines were placed on massive deck girders, one each port and starboard. Installed in a fore and aft, horizontal position, the engines drove the sternwheel by means of long connecting rods. The engines were supplied with steam at a working pressure of 180 pounds per square inch from an oil-fired locomotive type boiler. Since the steam machinery was non-condensing, the carriage of 8000 gallons of boiler feedwater, divided equally in two integral hull tanks, was necessary. Oil was fed to the boiler firebox from two tanks, also built integrally in the hull, with a combined capacity of 8000 gallons.

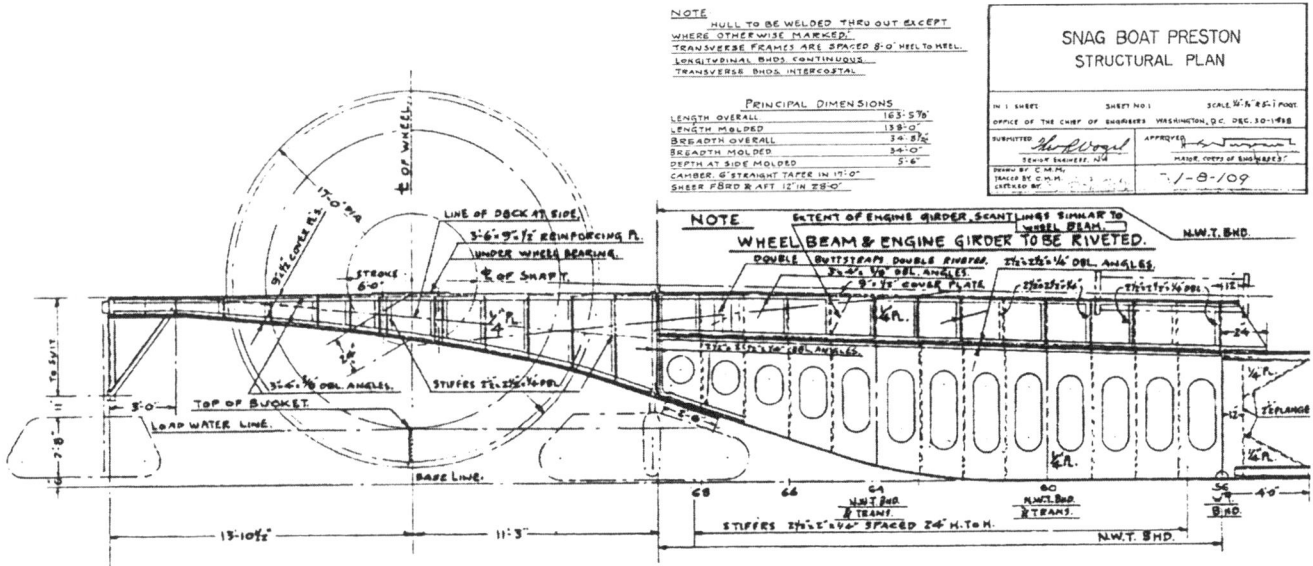

W. T. Preston wheel and rudder detail, 1938. (With permission of Anacortes Museum)

W. T. Preston's steering consisted of two rudders abaft the wheel and two rudders just forward of the wheel. In this arrangement, the rudders abaft the wheel could be used when moving ahead, just as in a typical propeller-driven vessel. However, the rudders forward of the wheel could aid greatly in maneuvering, particularly when backing; hence, these rudders, also frequently used by shallow draft propeller boats, have been called "backing rudders" or, sometimes, "monkey rudders." Power for operating *Preston's* rudders was supplied by a Washington Iron Works 11-inch-bore by 32-inch-stroke horizontal steam steering engine, placed transversely on the main deck and operating the rudders through connecting rods.

A sternwheeler might appear to be somewhat awkward in appearance, but in fact, such a vessel is quite capable of being maneuvered. Those who have ever observed the big steam sternwheel towboat *Portland* assisting ships on the Willamette River in Oregon, for example, would know that a sternwheeler can be surprisingly agile.

For *W. T. Preston*, the shape of the bow, as illustrated below, is identical to the shape of the stern. This form is similar to that of a barge except that the underwater shape of a barge is usually fuller aft than it is forward. The upward slope of the bottom at the end of this type of hull is known as "rake." The forward end of a barge is often called the "rake end".

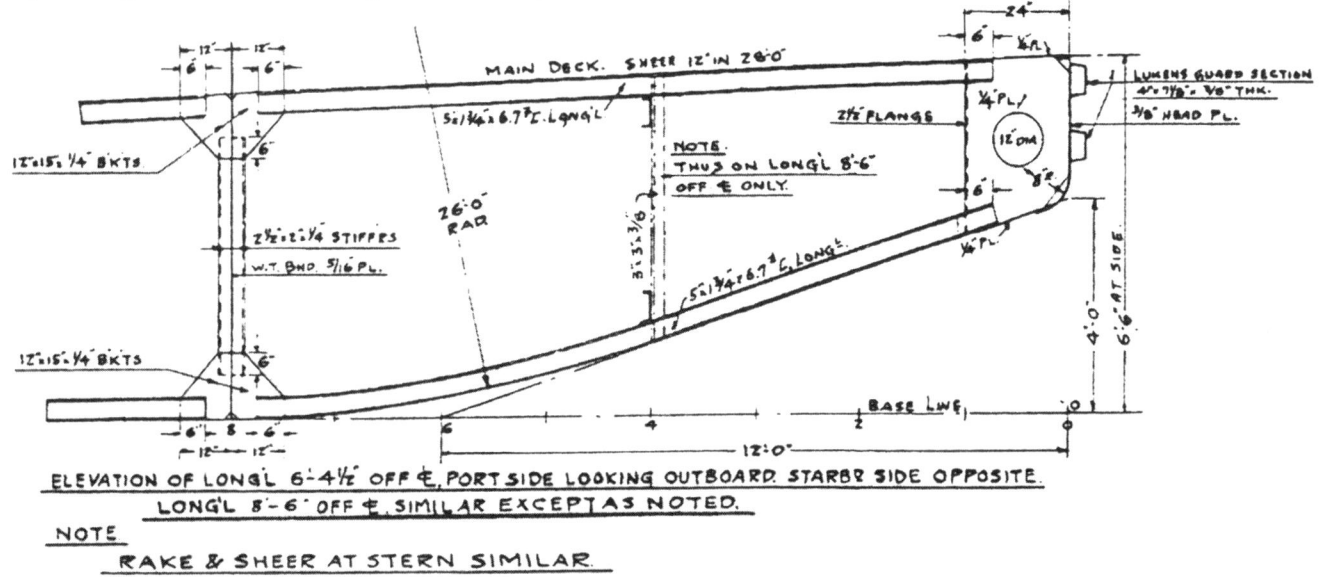

W. T. Preston section through the bow, 1938. (With permission of Anacortes Museum)

239

Over many years, there was a series of snag boats operating on western Washington rivers, such as the Skagit River and Snohomish River, by the Corps of Engineers beginning in 1895. *Skagit*, the first of these boats, worked from 1895 to 1914. *Skagit* was followed by *Swinomish*, in service from 1914 until 1929. Then the first *W. T. Preston* took over the work, this wooden hulled vessel remained in the employ of the Corps until 1939 when the second *W. T. Preston*, illustrated on the previous pages, was built and placed into river and sound service. This second *W. T. Preston* was outfitted with some of the components that had been salvaged from the first *W. T. Preston* after that boat's retirement, including the two propulsion engines, the sternwheel, and the funnel.

By 1960, *W. T. Preston*, the Port of Portland's steam-powered towboat *Portland* at work on the Willamette River in Oregon and the Canadian government's snag boat *Samson* in service on the Fraser River in British Columbia, were the only sternwheelers left in the Pacific Northwest. *W. T. Preston*, the last sternwheeler on Puget Sound, was eventually retired from service.

Following a competition between several cities for *W. T. Preston*'s acquisition, the snag boat was donated to the city of Anacortes. There the steamer was hauled out of the water. The transfer of the big sternwheeler from water to land was done only after much detailed study of the arrangements that would be needed to avoid causing any damage or distortion to the vessel. *W. T. Preston* remains today as an eye-catching public display on dry land near the water's edge.

The 80-foot *Rhododendron*, another United States government working vessel, is pictured below while tied up at Olympia's port pier. *Rhododendron*, officially classed as a lighthouse tender but frequently referred to as a buoy tender, was built of steel by Willamette Iron and Steel Works at Portland, Oregon, in 1934.

With a shallow draft and tunnel stern, the vessel was designed to operate on the Willamette and Columbia River systems but, later, was placed in service on Puget Sound. Power was supplied by twin 120-horsepower, Atlas diesel engines turning twin screws. Built to tend channel navigation markers, the vessel's lifting gear was used to hoist buoys out of the water and onto the deck for maintenance. The buoy tenders were named after tree and plant species, e.g., *Cedar*, *Fern*, and *Fir*, in addition to *Rhododendron*.

Rhododendron at Olympia, 1949. (From the author's collection)

HAULING FREIGHT AND PASSENGERS

The 212-foot, four-masted schooner *Wm. Nottingham*, pictured below, was designed by L. H. Coolidge and built of wood at Ballard in 1902 for use in general trade. The ship was one of numerous sailing vessels, both square-rigged and fore-and-aft rigged, that called at Puget Sound ports during the late 1800s and early 1900s. At the time when *Wm. Nottingham* was constructed, ships of sail still outnumbered steam ships.

The performance of square-rigged ships was heavily dependent upon wind direction, and at times, distance made good was logged only with great difficulty. On the other hand, fore-and-aft rigged schooners, such as *Wm. Nottingham*, had the advantage of being able not only to sail before the wind but also to tack successfully into the wind. These wind-powered vessels were the cargo carriers that arrived from the open sea and required the services of the big steam tugs, stationed near Cape Flattery, for assistance in entering the relatively confined waters of Puget Sound.

The principal cargo carried by these sailing vessels was lumber, poles, and piling, the poles and piling being straight, slender logs with the bark removed. Much of the sawn lumber transported was smaller to moderate sized that could be used for framing houses and other buildings, but large timbers, squared-off on the sides to be used for columns in buildings or for re-sawing, were also carried as cargo. These large squared-off timbers were known as "Japanese squares" when shipped for re-sawing in the Japanese mills but, in later years, were also called "cants" when re-sawn by Puget Sound mills. Lumber and poles were carried in the hold, but a considerable amount of the cargo was also carried on the weather deck.

Wm. Nottingham in Elliott Bay, n.d.
(With permission of Puget Sound Maritime Historical Society, negative 6397)

Beginning in the mid 1850s, millions of board feet of logs were gotten from the vast Pacific Northwest forests and turned into lumber by sawmills located at Apple Tree Cove, Port Gamble, Port Ludlow, Port Madison, Everett, Seattle, Tacoma, and elsewhere around Puget Sound. These ports and inlets were filled with windjammers, in from the sea to fill their holds and decks with lumber for shipment to the world. Many of these ships of sail had been built at yards on Puget Sound, such as the Hall Brothers.

By the end of the first decade of the 1900s, though, another type of "schooner" had appeared on the horizon, but these little ships were powered by steam rather than sail. These first steam-powered cargo carriers were, in fact, converted from wind-powered vessels by removing the sails and some of the rigging, adding a deckhouse, and installing a steam power plant and propeller. Nevertheless, the term "schooner" was still used to describe these newcomers. The steam schooners were not at the mercy of the wind and could navigate their way without assistance into Puget Sound.

Gradually, as a result, more and more cargo was being hauled by self-powered vessels, and the era of the wind ships was ending. With fewer sailing vessels needing assistance when calling on Puget Sound ports, the big steam tugs stationed at Cape Flattery were eventually no longer required, and they wound up out of a job, also. Where Puget Sound inlets were previously filled with sailing vessels that had arrived there to load cargo, space in ports, such as Eagle Harbor on Bainbridge Island and Lake Union in Seattle, was now occupied with idle ships of sail at anchor.

After giving way to the steam ships, *Wm. Nottingham* was out of work. For a time, the schooner operated as a cable laying barge. For this purpose, the main and mizzen masts were removed leaving the fore and jigger masts in place. In place of the two masts now missing, a midship deckhouse was installed.

Eventually, *Wm. Nottingham* was sent to the bone-yard at Nisqually Reach, as shown in the photo below. In this picture, I was operating the small power boat.

Wm. Nottingham on the beach at Nisqually, 1957. (From the author's collection)

Wapama, mid 1930s.
(With permission of San Francisco Maritime National Historical Park, negative B7.39085)

During the last years of the 19th century and the first part of the 20th century, the appetite for timber products throughout the world continued. The Pacific Northwest and the Redwood Coast of northern California held the forests that could supply these needs, and an endless procession of ships transported these cargoes to the assigned destinations. California was a voracious consumer of Washington and Oregon Douglas fir lumber, poles, and pilings, and Mexico provided an additional market for these wood products.

These cargoes of forest products had been transported by sailing ships, but the arrival of the steam engine started a trend that resulted in the conversion of sailing schooners to engine-powered vessels, as described on the previous page. By the addition of a steam engine and propeller, which created the "steam schooner," the wind-driven ships were gradually put out of work. As time went on, small lumber carriers were being built specifically to utilize steam power, and these new vessels continued to be referred to as steam schooners. More than 200 of these little ships operated in the "Scandinavian navy." *Wapama,* the only steam schooner still in existence, is pictured above in this photo by John W. Proctor.

Wapama was built by St. Helens Shipbuilding Company at the Columbia River town of St. Helens, Oregon, in 1915. Charles R. McCormick owned the shipyard, and *Wapama* was built for his own account. McCormick had become a ship owner in 1904, and by the mid 1920s, he owned over 70 steam schooners that were plying their trade along the Pacific Coast.

Wapama was built of old growth Douglas fir and had a length of 205 feet and a beam of 41 feet. *Wapama* was known as a "single ender," having a deckhouse aft and a hold and cargo handling gear in the forward portion of the vessel. "Double enders" were arranged with a midship deckhouse and cargo holds forward and aft of midship. After the stowage of cargo in the holds had been completed and the hatch covers were secured, pilings and additional lumber were usually lashed to the weather deck.

In addition to lumber cargoes, in the absence of air and highway travel, these schooners transported passengers to smaller ports that were not served by the larger passenger liners. Passage aboard the lumber schooners was available in either cabins or in steerage, and a dining salon was located on the main deck.

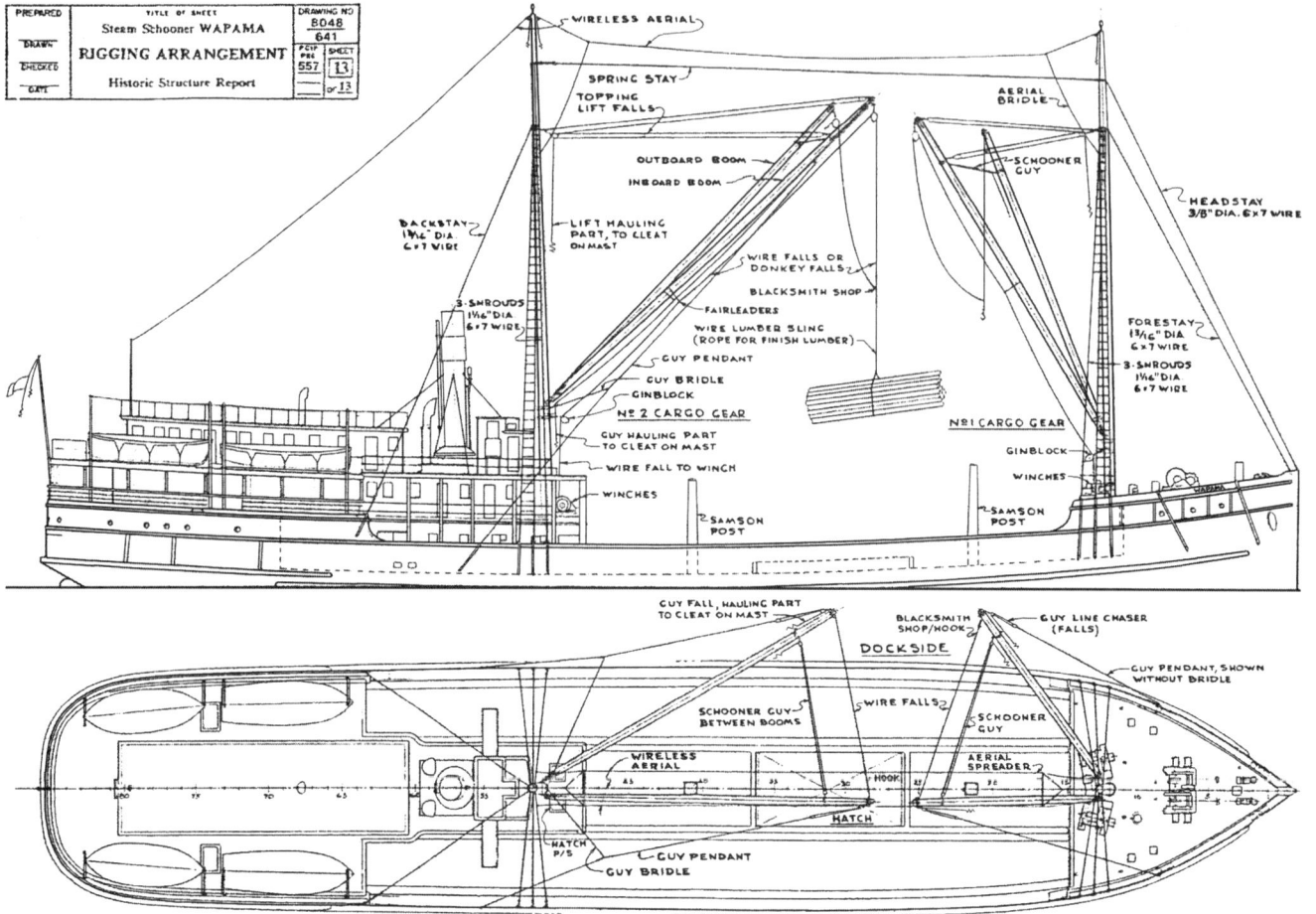

Wapama's rigging arrangement is illustrated above. The cargo handling gear consisted of two masts, one well forward at the foc's'le bulkhead and the other at the forward end of the deckhouse just abaft midship, with a pair of booms pivoting from the base of each mast.

Because of the presence of two booms at each mast, in the earlier days, the arrangement was known as "double gear." A similar cargo handling arrangement, known as "burtoning," was used in more recent years. With this system of double hoists attached to the load, the load may be picked up by either boom and then transferred laterally to the other boom for deposit at the intended location, a rapid method for handling cargo.

The rigging shown above indicates a single-point attachment between the hoist and the load. Picking up a load of lumber or poles at a single point was sometimes done, but it is difficult to accurately locate the pickup point over the center of gravity of the load so that the pile does not tilt excessively and slide out of the sling and spill. It could be dangerous if the hoist rigging is not made with a snug purchase so that a spill does not occur.

Frequently, two attachment points that straddle the center of gravity of the load are used, eliminating the need to accurately know the location of the center of gravity. A "crotch line" or a "spreader" is commonly used when hoisting lumber, as shown in the illustration at left.

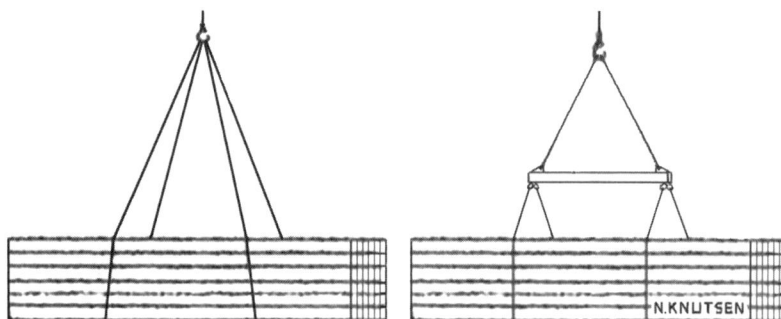

Hoisting with crotch line, left, and spreader, right.

244

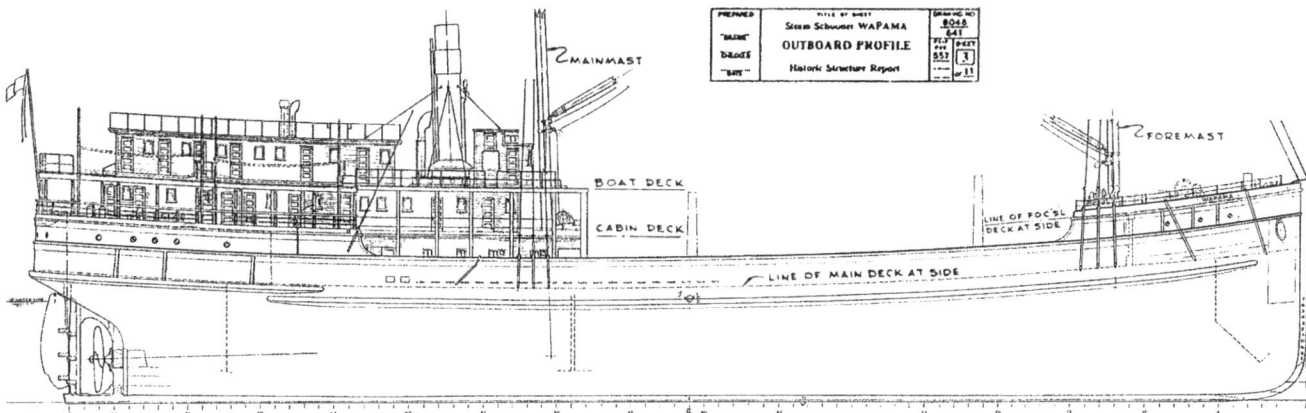

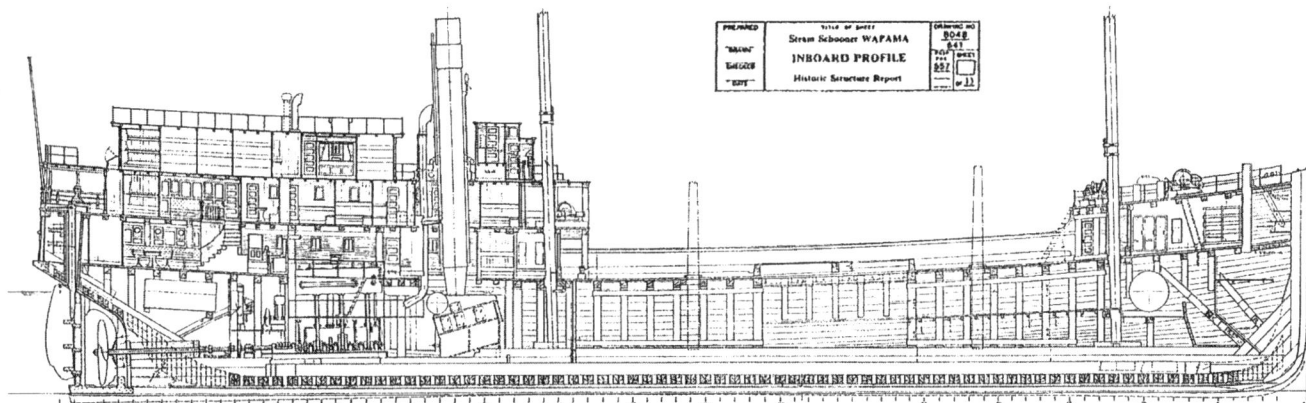

Wapama outboard and inboard profiles.
(With permission of San Francisco Maritime National Historical Park)

The outboard and inboard profiles for *Wapama* are shown above. Although this illustration is necessarily small, the load line marking can just be seen on the outboard profile at midship immediately below the main deck level at a draft of about 17 feet. An enlarged view of a load line marking, as painted on both sides of a ship's hull, is also illustrated with an explanation of the lettering.

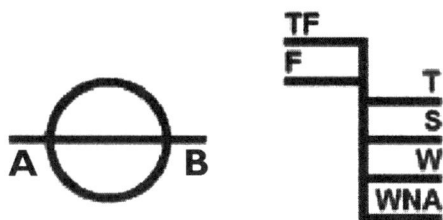

AB: American Bureau of Shipping
TF: Tropical Fresh Water Load Line
F: Fresh Water Load Line
T: Tropical Load Line
S: Summer Load Line
W: Winter Load Line
WNA: Winter North Atlantic Load Line

American Bureau of Shipping load line marking with explanation of lettering.

In the late 1800s, British statesman Samuel Plimsoll was central in framing legislation that was passed to improve safety of life at sea by preventing the overloading of ships. The result was the "Plimsoll mark," now referred to as the "load line," a mark that was required on both sides of a ship's hull to denote the lawful submergence level.

In 1929, by an act of the U.S. Congress, load lines for U.S. merchant ships were established in accordance with the International Load Line Convention. Load lines are administered by various classification societies around the world, the authority in the United States being the American Bureau of Shipping as denoted by the letters "AB" in the illustration above.

The summer load line "S" marks the fundamental draft to which a ship may be loaded, but the other marks apply when a ship is trading in a variety of other expected sea conditions. In tropical fresh water, the sea conditions are mild and a vessel may be loaded to the deepest draft indicated by "TF" on the load line. During winter in the North Atlantic ocean, the most severe and restrictive condition, a ship is limited to a draft no deeper than indicated by "WNA."

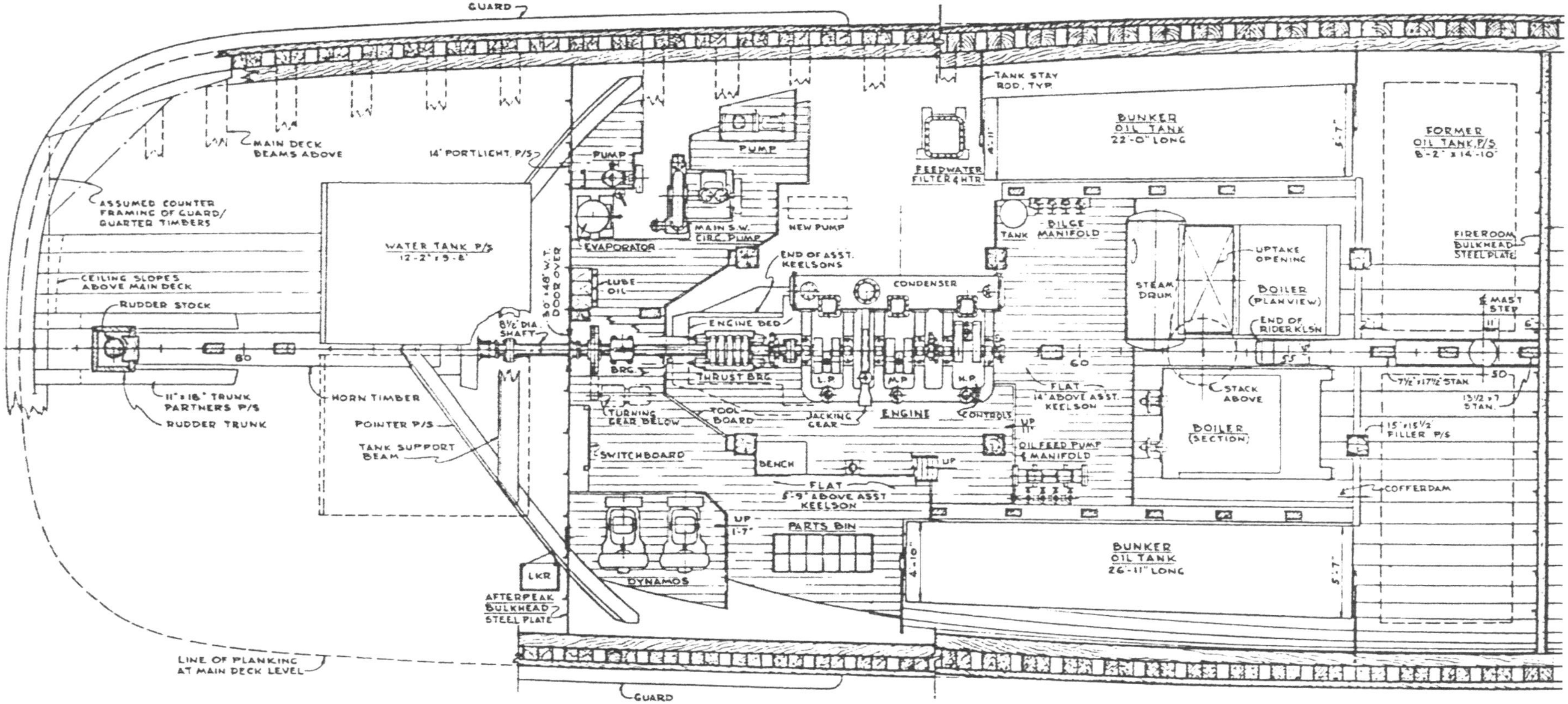

The arrangement of *Wapama's* engine room is shown above and at right. *Wapama* was powered by a three-cylinder, triple-expansion engine built by Main Street Iron Works in San Francisco, California. Two oil-fired water-tube boilers, built by the Babcock and Wilcox Company, were installed to supply steam to the main engine, auxiliary engines, cargo handling winches, and anchor windlass.

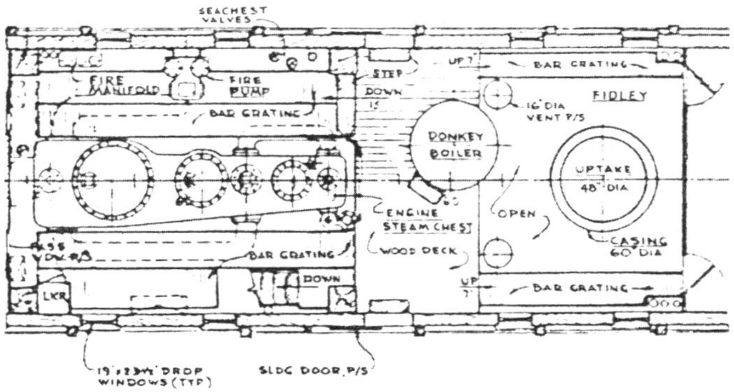

In the operation of a power plant such as that installed in *Wapama's* engine room, steam is drawn from the boiler-mounted drums to the engine's high-pressure-cylinder. The steam exhaust from the high pressure cylinder then passes to the intermediate (medium-pressure) cylinder and, from there, to the low pressure cylinder. The steam exhaust from the LP cylinder is then cooled and changed to water in the engine-mounted condenser for recycling as boiler feedwater.

Wapama engine room arrangement. (With permission of San Francisco Maritime National Historical Park)

Wapama upper engine room. (With permission of San Francisco Maritime National Historical Park)

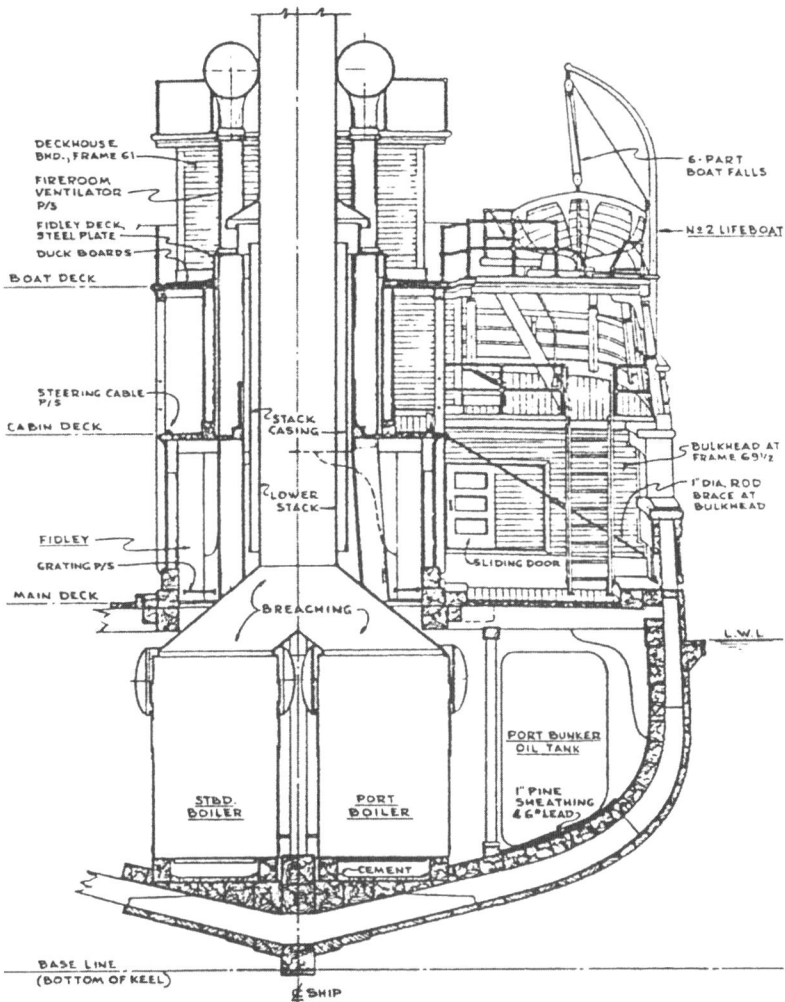

Wapama section at engine room boilers. (With permission of San Francisco Maritime National Historical Park)

In addition to the two main boilers, which supplied steam to the main engine, a donkey boiler was located in the upper engine room, as shown in the upper engine room arrangement on the previous page. The modestly-sized donkey boiler probably supplied, through the use of a pump, hot water for circulation to radiators that provided heat for the passenger and crew living spaces.

After a long career as a lumber carrier, *Wapama* passed through a series of ownerships before being abandoned, while carrying the name *Tongass*, against the shore in Lake Union. The ship languished forlornly in Lake Union until being rescued in 1957 by the San Francisco Maritime National Historical Park. With the original name *Wapama* restored, the vessel was towed to San Francisco, California. Following extensive renovation, *Wapama* was made available for public viewing along with other historic vessels that are moored in San Francisco's Maritime National Historical Park fleet.

Illustrations of *Wapama* that refer to San Francisco Maritime National Historical Park, shown on this page and preceding pages, are taken from drawings that were produced by the National Park Service during a survey.

The water from the condenser was next passed through a device, labeled "feedwater filter & htr" in the engine room arrangement shown on the previous page, to separate accumulated engine oil from the water. Aboard many early steam ships, the oil/water separator was a "hot well," a tank in which absorbent material was placed to remove engine oil from the condensate before it was injected into the boiler.

Flue gas from the port and starboard main boiler fire boxes passed through a Y-shaped uptake and then exited through a single funnel, as shown in the drawing above.

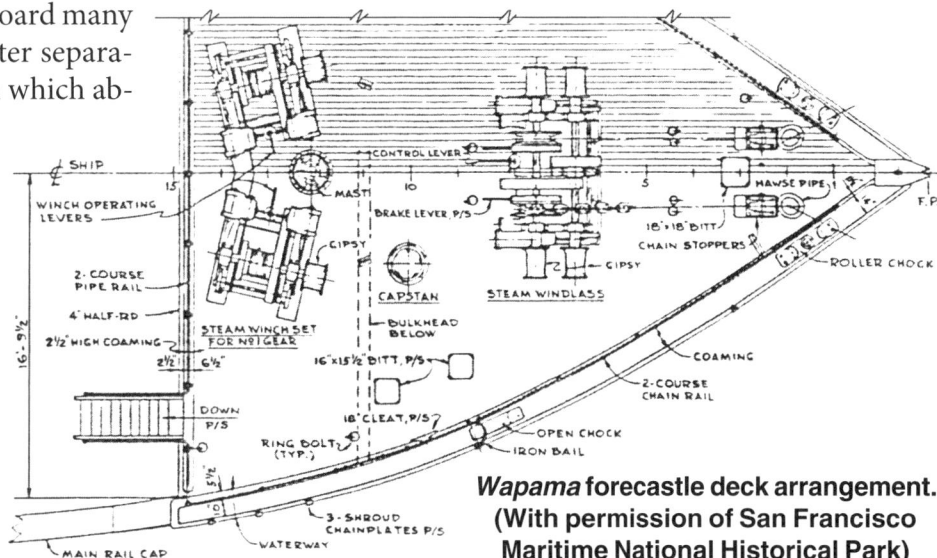

Wapama forecastle deck arrangement. (With permission of San Francisco Maritime National Historical Park)

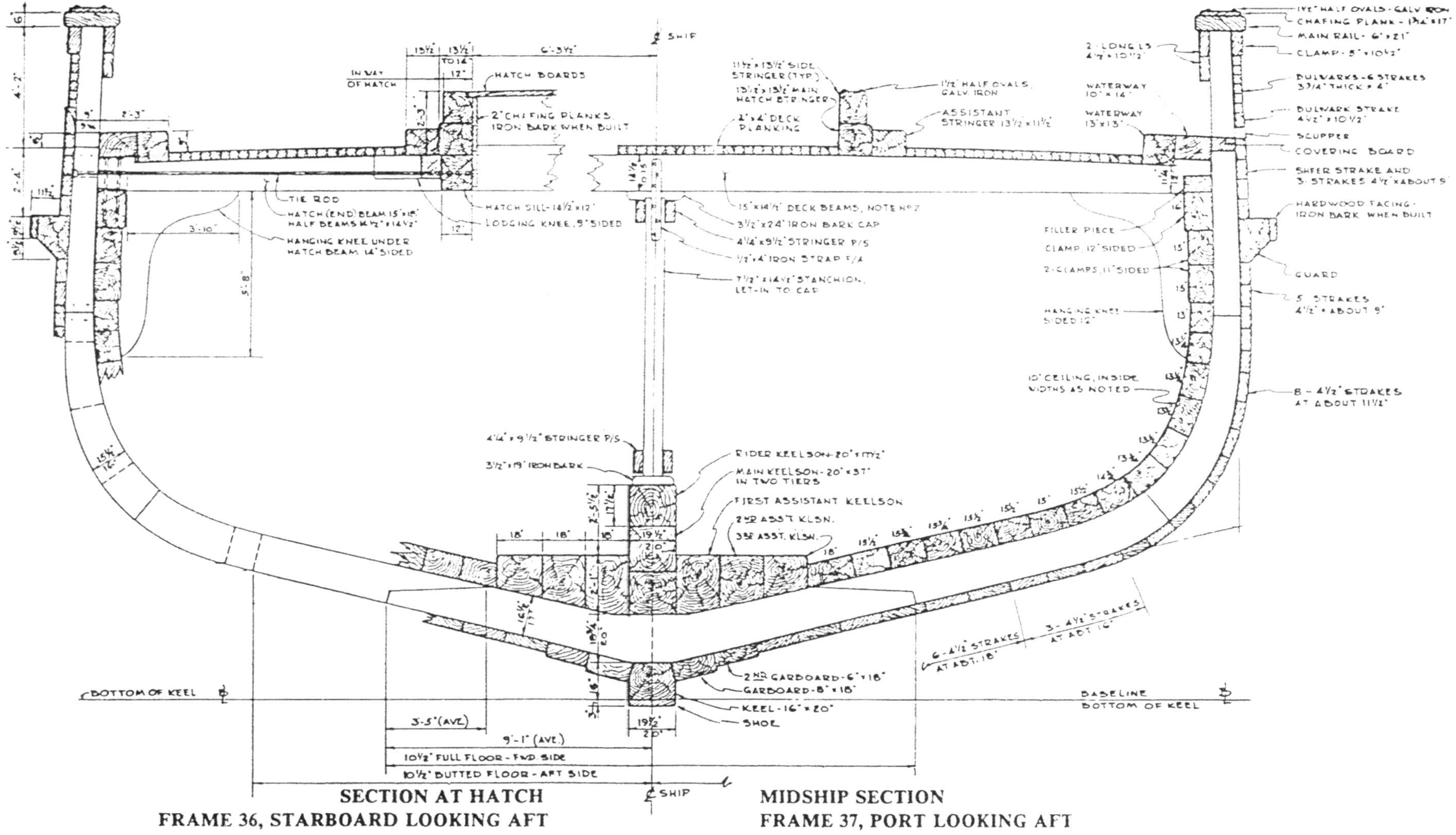

SECTION AT HATCH
FRAME 36, STARBOARD LOOKING AFT

MIDSHIP SECTION
FRAME 37, PORT LOOKING AFT

Wapama midship section. (With permission of San Francisco Maritime National Historical Park)

Over the years of enduring stress and strain while carrying cargo at sea, a ship might change shape somewhat. One such change is called "hogging" (hull bending with the ends deeper in the water than midship) or "sagging" (hull bending with the midship draft greater than the draft at the ends). A survey of *Wapama*, performed by the National Park Service in 1985, indicated that the vessel had hogged approximately a foot. To facilitate navigation in small ports having a shallow depth of water, steam schooner hulls were built with limited depth, and despite heavy scantlings intended to prevent permanent deformation of the hull, the vessels eventually tended to hog.

248

Quinalt loading at the Tidewater Mill in the Hylebos Waterway at Tacoma, 1921.
(With permission of Tacoma Public Library, Northwest Room)

Differing from the single-ended *Wapama* in the arrangement of machinery space and cargo holds, the double-ended steam schooner *Quinault* is shown in the Boland photo above. In this picture, the vessel was loading lumber at the Tidewater Mill in the Hylebos Waterway at Tacoma. *Quinalt* was built of wood at Portland, Oregon, in 1921 as a coastwise lumber carrier to the order of Hart-Wood Lumber Company.

Quinault, not much longer than *Wapama*, was 210 feet long, 1138 gross tons, and 625 horsepower compared with *Wapama* at 205 feet, 951 gross tons, and 825 horsepower. *Quinalt* was built with the machinery and main superstructure and deckhouse at midship, which made way for two separated holds, one forward and one aft. *Wapama*'s engine space and main superstructure and deckhouse were located aft, an arrangement that provided space for a hold forward.

Quinault and *Wapama* both were rigged with two masts for handling the cargo, with two booms at each mast to operate as a double gear system. The forward mast was stepped at the fo'c'sle bulkhead in both ships, but the aft mast was located at the aft end of the house in *Quinault* and at the forward end of the deckhouse in *Wapama*.

The Tidewater Mill, built on six acres of land located at the end of 11th Street on the east side of the Hylebos Waterway in Tacoma, began producing lumber in 1918. At least three fourths of the lumber was shipped by water, and the 750 feet of frontage provided moorage for loading two or more ships at a time. The steam-powered Tidewater Mill was one of the few mills on the Pacific Coast able to process the largest diameter logs that were brought in from the woods. Production capability was 100,000 board feet per day, and timbers up to 130 feet long could be sawn.

249

Mention was made earlier in these pages about the unique period in the first half of the 20th century when sailing vessels, steamers, and boats powered by internal combustion engines were all plying their trade at the same time. In the photo below, at left center, a steam-powered cargo ship was sharing space with a three-masted bark in Tacoma. Across the waterway, a four-masted bark was moored. The boat that was inbound through the channel was probably powered by an internal combustion engine, as evidenced by the absence of a tall funnel.

The picture illustrates well a typical collection of vessels that were driven by a mixture of propulsion methods, all operating in the same time frame. This was a period of many years duration rather than a happening that occurred in a brief moment of time. After steam power's initial appearance in ships' engine rooms, it was a century of transition in maritime commerce before steam-powered vessels completely displaced ships of sail. While both steam and sail power were in use, gasoline, semi-diesel, and diesel internal combustion engines were gradually showing up, in that sequence, on the scene. So, for a good many years, all of these means of propulsion were in simultaneous operation by commercial shipping.

Finally, commercial use of wind power vanished, but before working sail disappeared entirely, steam power had already started on its way into history, eventually displaced by the internal combustion engine. As time went on, internal combustion engines remained as the only source of power for commercial shipping.

Maritime activity at Tacoma, early 1900s.
(With permission of Tacoma Public Library, Northwest Room)

250

On April 6, 1917, the United States officially entered into World War I. By this time, the U.S. had been providing support for the war effort in a shipbuilding program that included a variety of moderate sized steam powered cargo ships, some built of wood and others of steel.

The steel vessel illustrated here, with a plumb bow, fantail stern, and good, old-time looks, was from a design by Albina Engine and Machine Works in Portland, Oregon. This style of ship was frequently seen in those days and has sometimes been referred to as a "three islander," with raised poop, bridge, and forecastle. The appearance of this ship might also be what a reader's mind's eye sees when a novelist or short-story writer describes a fictional "tramp steamer."

The freighters of this design had an overall length of 261 feet, breadth of 43 1/2 feet, and depth of 20 feet. Loaded design draft was 17 feet, 3 inches. These ships were nearly flat bottomed with only a slight amount of deadrise. With a full body, rather blunt bow, and moderate power, it could be imagined that the speed would not have been great. However, water transportation is well suited to the carriage of heavy loads in large quantities when speed is not of the essence.

After the Great War ended, some of these war-time cargo ships found their way into commercial service and could be seen on Puget Sound carrying all manner of freight, including lumber. Their appearance on the sound contributed to the demise, already underway, of the wind ships.

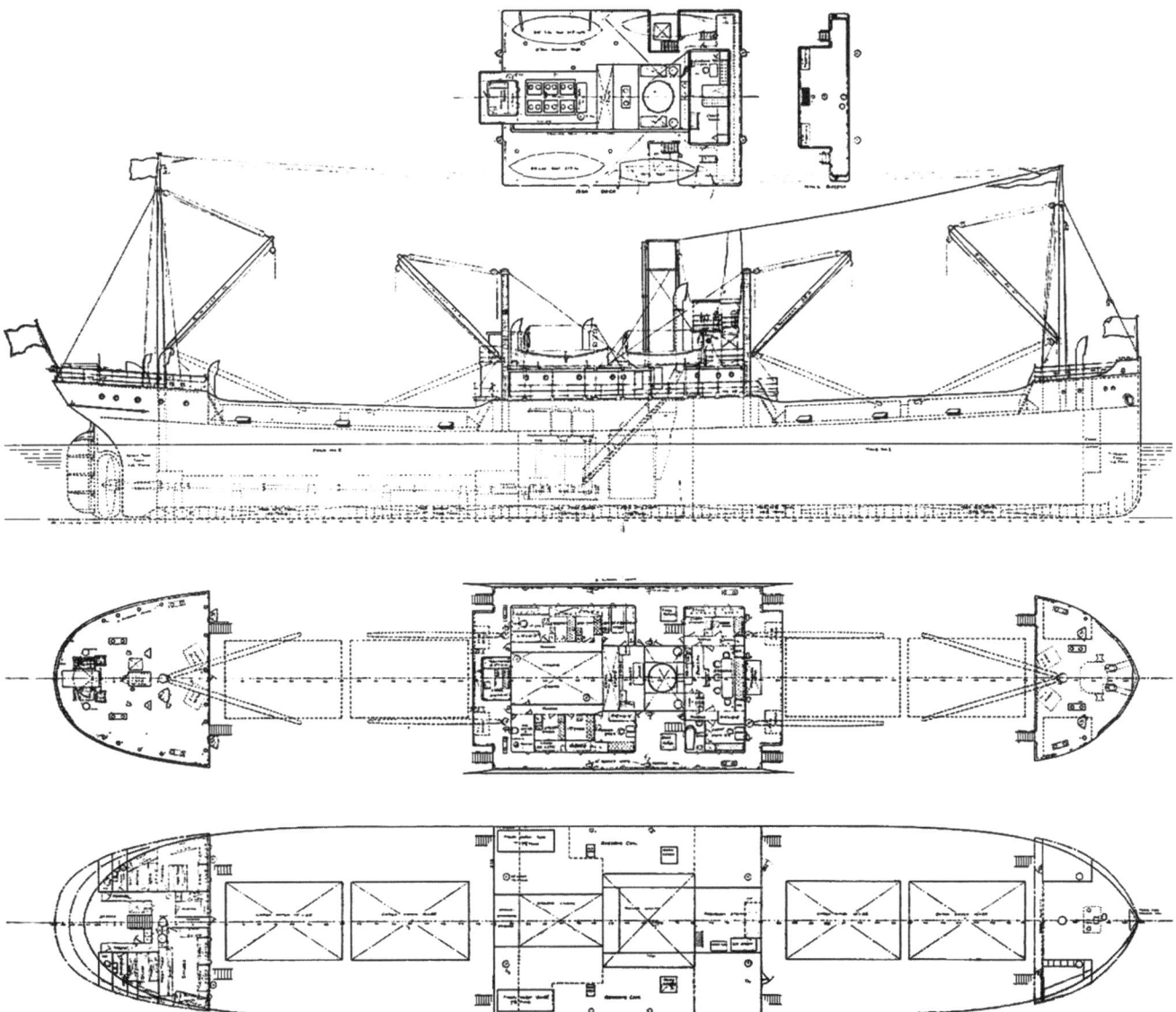

Cargo ship for U.S. Emergency Fleet, 1917. (From an Albina Engine and Machine Works drawing)

A triple-expansion steam engine, pictured below, designed by Albina Engine and Machine Works powered the freighter in the drawing on the previous page. The cylinder diameters, from high pressure to low, were 20 inches, 33 inches and 54 inches. With a stroke of 40 inches, this engine was rated at 1100 horsepower. A coal-fired boiler provided steam to the engine. In the illustration, the component at left is a Kingsbury thrust bearing, which, bolted to a foundation and connected to the propeller shaft, receives the thrust delivered by the propeller.

This engine was over 22 feet high from the mounting flange to the top of the cylinder heads and more than 25 feet long from the forward end of the engine shaft to the shaft-flange coupling at the aft end of the thrust bearing. Through an 11-inch diameter shaft, the engine drove a propeller of 14 feet diameter.

To equalize the stresses when multiple cylinders were used in a steam engine, it was desirable that the cylinders be capable of developing equal power. This was accomplished by sizing the bore of each cylinder so that, accounting for the steam pressure each cylinder received, with the greatest pressure being delivered to the smallest diameter cylinder followed by progressively lower pressures to the other, larger cylinders, the power output of the cylinders was uniformly proportioned. Sizing the cylinder bores in this way ensured that the forces were distributed evenly in the engine.

For ocean-going ships, the steam propulsion plants were not being superceded by huge diesel engines until the last half of the 20th century. For smaller vessels, such as tugs and passenger boats, steam power had almost disappeared by the mid 1900s. By that time, the steam-powered Puget Sound mosquito fleet of passenger vessels had virtually passed away. *Commander* and *Virginia V*, two steam-passenger vessels that remained in service longer than most, are described later in this chapter.

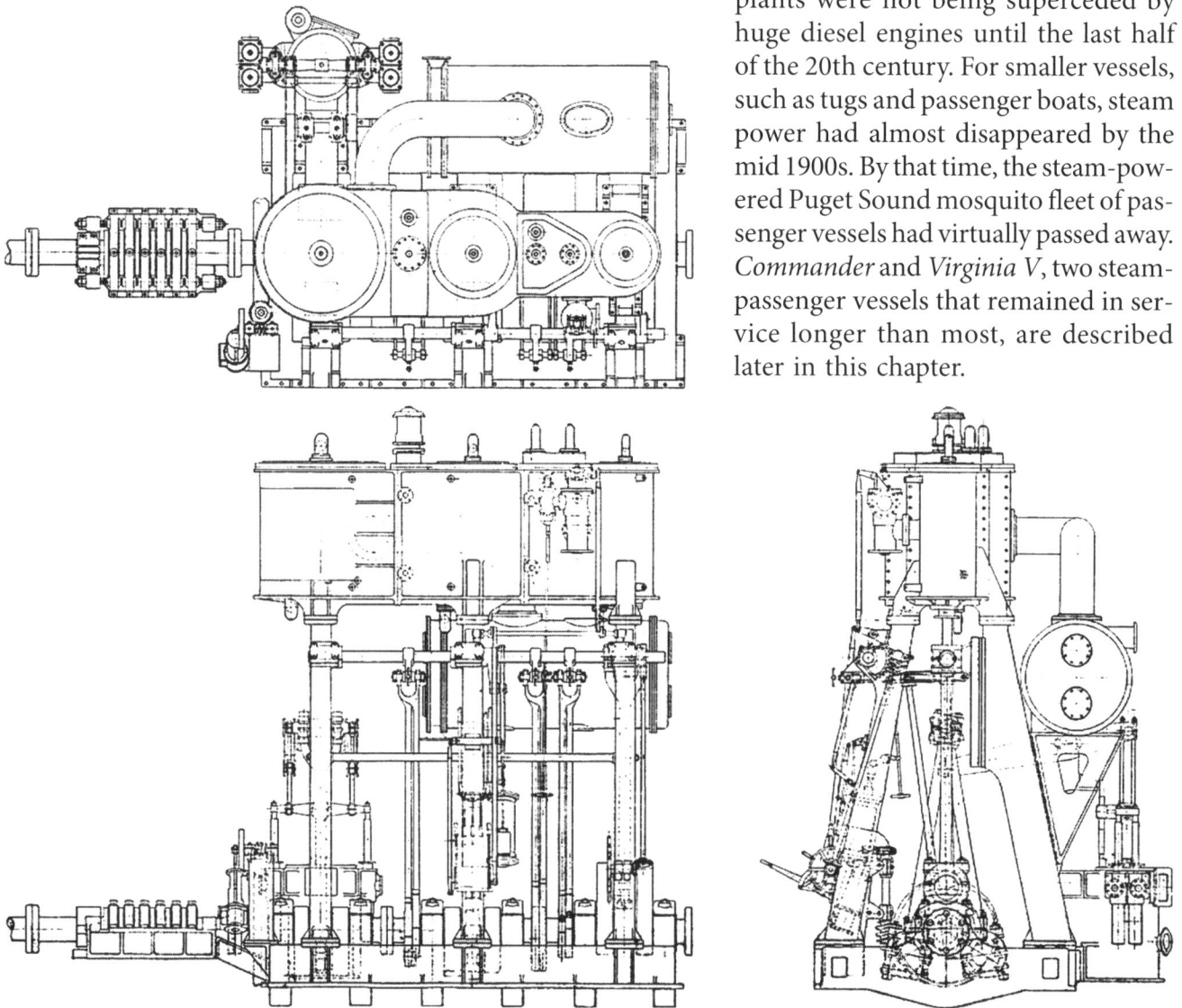

Steam propulsion engine for U.S. Emergency Fleet cargo ship, 1917.
(From an Albina Engine and Machine Works drawing)

Skookum Chief, 120 feet in length and operated by Puget Sound Freight Lines, was built of wood at Seattle in 1915. In the photo at right, *Skookum Chief* had exited Dana Passage and was passing Dofflemyer Point enroute south to Olympia's Percival Landing. As I recall, one of these freighters was adorned with potted plants which occupied a prominent position on the taffrail.

Percival Landing, at the foot of State Avenue in downtown Olympia, consisted of a pier and a warehouse used by Puget Sound Freight Lines as a freight handling facility. In the photo of Percival Landing below, looking north from Fourth Avenue, Puget Sound Freight Lines's *Skookum Chief* was approaching the pier to unload and load cargo. At left is the Olympia Yacht Club. In the distance, at the Port of Olympia pier, a freighter can be seen loading lumber from a scow moored alongside.

Puget Sound Freight Lines was founded by Captain Frank E. Lovejoy in 1919. His first vessel was the 65-foot-long freighter *Chaco,* powered by a Winton gas engine, on a charter basis from Sound Freight Lines. In 1920, Captain Lovejoy purchased *Chaco,* and thus, the little freighter became the first vessel owned by his company. Puget Sound's freighters, with their black hulls, orange

Skookum Chief off Boston Harbor, 1948.
(From the author's collection)

superstructures, and white deckhouses, were frequent visitors to Olympia and other ports around Puget Sound. These little ships also served several ports in British Columbia.

The cargo handling system was efficient. An elevator platform forward was used to move freight vertically between the cargo deck and the superstructure deck. Inside the vessel and at the pier, forklifts handled the palletized cargo, moving the pallets of freight on and off the ship. On land, the freight that had been brought in by water was delivered by truck to the ultimate destinations, and freight was picked up from clients by trucks and hauled back to the shoreside warehouse for loading aboard ship.

Puget Sound Freight Lines owned several freighters, including *Belana, F. E. Lovejoy, F. H. Marvin, Indian, Seatac, Skookum Chief,* and *Warrior.* The small ships were built with a flat bottom and a shallow draft so they did not require deep water for navigation into and out of Puget Sound ports. The speed of these vessels was not fast, but in the 1950s, *Belana* and *Skookum Chief* received some modifications that included reshaping of their sterns, which provided an extra knot or two of speed.

Skookum Chief at Percival Landing in Olympia, circa 1950.
(From the author's collection)

F. E. Lovejoy was the largest, as well as the newest, of the Puget Sound Freight Lines freighters and was only four years old at the time of the photo at right. In this photo, *F. E. Lovejoy* was off Boston Harbor enroute to Olympia.

Built of steel by Reliable Welding Works at Olympia, *F. E. Lovejoy*'s length of 170 feet and gross tons of 613 were much greater than *Skookum Chief*'s length of 120 feet and gross tons of 251. The installed horsepower of 1200 in *F. E. Lovejoy* was also much greater than *Skookum Chief*'s 360 horsepower. This power, together with a longer length and cleaner hull lines, gave the *Lovejoy* more speed than the other ships in the fleet.

As time went on, economics and age caught up with the little ships, and they were retired, one by one. The 106-foot-long PSFL vessel *F. H.*

F. E. Lovejoy off Boston Harbor, circa 1950.
(From the author's collection)

Marvin was built of wood at Everett in 1918. In the photo below, *F. H. Marvin* had been retired and was laid up on the beach at Henderson Inlet several miles north of Olympia. Eventually, the freighters were gone. Cargo was then hauled by tug and barge for a time, but finally, freight was only being handled by the company's trucks.

F. H. Marvin on the beach at Henderson Inlet, 1949.
(From the author's collection)

254

Skagit Chief at Seattle, 1948. (From the author's collection)

Besides Puget Sound Freight Lines, another shipping company was engaged in hauling freight on Puget Sound. Skagit River Navigation Company, of Mount Vernon, was owned by Mrs. Anna Grimison and operated *Skagit Chief*, shown in the photo above, on Puget Sound for many years.

The *Chief*'s sister sternwheeler was named *Skagit Belle*. *Skagit Chief* was built by Lake Union Drydock Company at Seattle in 1935, and *Skagit Belle* was a few years younger, taking to the water at Everett in 1941. Both freighters were about the same size at 165 feet in length and something over 500 gross tons. The two freighters were steam-powered and utilized a stern wheel for propulsion, similar to the sternwheelers operating at the beginning of the last century. The hulls were flat bottomed and of shallow draft to permit navigation in the Skagit River.

Skagit Chief foundered and sank in heavy seas off the entrance to Grays Harbor in 1956 while under tow by *Martha Foss*, never making it to a new life that had awaited as a floating restaurant in Portland, Oregon. In the 1960s, *Skagit Belle* sank while moored at her pier on Alaskan Way in Seattle. For a time, at least, it was a pleasure to have a pair of steam powered sternwheel freight boats operating on Puget Sound.

In 1919, Willis Nearhoff began operating three ferry boats between Mukilteo and Whidbey Island. In 1928, he sold out and purchased Horluck Transportation Company. A few months after that, Willis passed on, but his daughter Mary had been involved in the hard work and complexity of operating a fleet of boats and so was able to take over as manager and continue the activities of the firm.

As time went on, Mary, with the help of her mother, Bessie, husband, Fritz Lieseke, and other family members, was able to expand the business based in Port Orchard. *Carlisle II*, *Chimacum*, and *Concordia*, all 60-foot freight and passenger boats, made calls at Port Orchard, Annapolis, Retsil, Bremerton, Bainbridge Island, and the Puget Sound Navy Yard. The business grew to include a water-taxi service, and the company even entered into log handling with the 31-foot tug *Fritzy* and the ex-Navy LCVP *OK*.

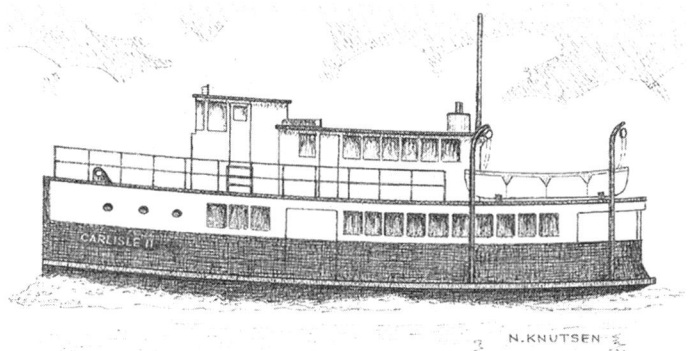

Carlisle II.

255

At right is a full-size reproduction of a ticket for passage in 1935 aboard the steamer *Commander*, a passenger and automobile-carrying vessel that was in operation between Seattle and Bremerton. The fares shown certainly seem small as compared with those of today, but of course, wages of that period were correspondingly low.

Commander was a fine looking ship, 184 feet in length, and built of wood by George R. Whidden at Bellingham in 1900. Originally named *General Frisbie*, the steamer, propelled by a four-cylinder, triple-expansion engine of 1000 horsepower, was to the order of Monticello Steamship Company headquartered in San Francisco, California. Newly built, *General Frisbie* was loaded with lumber and towed to San Francisco for installation of the engine, the charge for hauling cargo helping to defray the cost of the delivery trip.

In 1930, the ship, renamed *Commander*, was put on the Seattle-Bremerton run for Union Ferry Company, a joint venture with Puget Sound Freight Lines and Kitsap Transportation Company. In 1936, *Commander* was sold and rebuilt as a floating salmon cannery for use in Alaska. The steam plant was removed and replaced with a diesel engine, and accommodations were provided for cannery workers. In 1937, the floating cannery ceased operations, the machinery was removed, and the hull was towed to Kodiak, Alaska, and beached. However, the upper house was saved and became a private residence on the shore of Lake Washington near Sand Point.

The cylinders in most marine steam engines were oriented vertically, an exception being stern-wheelers, such as *Skagit Belle* or *Skagit Chief*, having engines laid out horizontally on deck and

Ticket (both sides) for passage aboard steamer *Commander,* 1935. (Courtesy of Anna J. Knutsen)

driving the wheel through long connecting rods. Most marine steam engines were double acting, that is, steam pressure powered the piston on the up-stroke as well as the down-stroke, and ranged from one-cylinder engines to multiple expansion engines with two or more cylinders.

In multiple-expansion engines, the steam was passed from cylinder to cylinder, each cylinder in succession being of increased diameter to utilize the decreased pressure of the exhaust steam from the previous cylinder. In triple-expansion engines, steam from the boiler was introduced first to the high pressure cylinder, then passed along to the intermediate cylinder and finally to the low pressure cylinder. From the low-pressure cylinder, the exhaust steam was passed along to a condenser for conversion back to boiler-feed water, thus conserving the makeup water that was carried on board in tanks.

256

The four-cylinder, triple-expansion type of steam engine installed in *Commander* was not commonly seen. A four-cylinder, quadruple-expansion engine could have been used, but the steam pressure needed from the boiler would have been greater than that required for a triple-expansion engine. On the other hand, at 1000 horsepower, a three-cylinder, triple-expansion engine would have had a low pressure-cylinder of very large bore with correspondingly massive castings. Therefore, no doubt as a compromise, a four-cylinder, triple-expansion engine was used having two low-pressure cylinders with castings of smaller and more manageable size.

Pictured below is *Virginia V*, a beautiful wooden 116-foot, steam powered vessel built at Maplewood near Olalla in 1922 for the Seattle-Tacoma route of the West Pass Transportation Company. On that run, the steamer also made stops at towns and settlements located along the western shore of Vashon Island. *Virginia V* was, and still is, the last of the old Mosquito Fleet steamers that carried freight and passengers to many locations around Puget Sound before new and improved highways furthered transportation by land.

At the time of the photo, this steamer was owned by Puget Sound Excursion Line, hence the large number of passengers on board. *Virginia V* was built by Vashon Island shipyard owner Matt Anderson to the order of Captain Nels Christensen to replace his *Virginia III* and *Virginia IV*. As was frequently the case in those days, drawings for construction of this vessel were minimal. At the time, many boats were constructed by builders without the use of drawings, the shipwrights working instead from a half model, for example, as well as by using an experienced and well-trained eye.

Virginia V's engine was built by the Seattle firm Heffernan Iron Works in 1904, one of two engines for use by the U.S. government. At the time, one of these engines was retained for powering a government vessel, but the other one was sold to the Lorenz brothers for installation in *Tyrus*, later renamed *Virginia IV* by Captain Christensen. When *Virginia V* was built, the Heffernan engine was removed from *Virginia IV* and installed in the new vessel. This propulsion machinery was a three-cylinder, triple-expansion engine with bore and stroke dimensions of 10 1/2, 16 3/4, 28 x 18 rated at 400 horsepower when turning at 175 revolutions per minute. Steam was supplied at a pressure of 200 pounds per square inch from an oil-fired boiler.

Virginia V at the Ballard Locks in the early 1960s. (From the author's collection)

257

In the earlier days, numerous deep sea passenger and cargo vessels, owned by various companies, were making calls on ports in Puget Sound. Of all of the ship operators, perhaps the company name best known to the public in the Pacific Northwest was the shipping firm Alaska Steamship Company, headquartered at Seattle.

Originally, the Alaska Steam flag consisted of a black ball against a red background. In 1927, however, the black-ball flag was transferred to Puget Sound Navigation Company, a subsidiary of Alaska Steam. After 1927, the Alaska Steam flag consisted of a design that retained the black ball against the red field but with the addition of a white letter A centered on the black ball and ringed with white, as pictured above.

Alaska Steamship Company was incorporated by a group under the direction of Charles E. Peabody in 1894 at Port Townsend. Without a ship at the time, Alaska Steam purchased and began operating the wooden steamer *Willapa*, pictured below, for twice-monthly service on the Seattle-Alaska route in 1895.

Willapa had been launched at Astoria, Oregon, in 1882 as the 100-foot *General Miles* for passenger and cargo service on the Columbia River and to ports on the Oregon and Washington coasts. Later, after being lengthened to 136 feet and renamed *Willapa* by one of the earlier owners, the packet was purchased by Alaska Steam while the vessel was on a Port Townsend-Neah Bay run. Following an extensive renovation, *Willapa* began working in the Alaska trade for Alaska Steam.

Aids to navigation were few in those days, and dead reckoning, based upon use of the compass, estimated speed, and knowledge of tidal currents, was relied upon in an effort to stay out of difficulty. Unfortunately, *Willapa*'s employment time with Alaska Steam was shortened when, three years after purchase, *Willapa* ran onto the rocks in British Columbia during a gale and was abandoned to the salvors.

Other ships followed *Willapa* in the service of Alaska Steam, vessels that were either owned or under charter. For many years, since highway and air transportation to Alaska did not exist, conveyance by water was the only method available for carrying freight and passengers between the Lower 48 and Alaska, a territory until statehood was achieved in 1959. Although there were economic downturns at times, accompanied by competitive rate wars that caused shipping companies to lose money, business was generally good.

During the Klondike stampede, gold prospectors with their outfitting gear and provisions were carried north from Seattle. Over the years, mail was delivered to post offices, and cargo was carried north for use in construction and mining, as well as for retailing by merchants to the increasing number of people in Alaska. On the return trips, gold bars were brought south to the assay office that had been established in Seattle, and copper was carried to the smelter at Tacoma.

Willapa at Juneau, Alaska, 1897. (With permission of University of Washington, Special Collections, negative UW23437)

Numerous cargo vessels were operated by Alaska Steam over the years, and in addition to a variety of freight that was regularly carried, an annual event was the transport of the salmon pack from Alaska to Seattle. The fishing was good in those days, and the annual pack of Alaska canned salmon could reach as much as 8,000,000 cases.

SS Aleutian, n.d. (Courtesy of Anna J. Knutsen)

In the mid 1950s, I was a deckhand aboard a Bristol Bay, Alaska, power scow. At the end of a summer fishing season, it was necessary to make ready the cases of canned sockeye salmon for transport by ship to Seattle. On schedule, an Alaska Steam cargo ship anchored in Bristol Bay, at the eastern edge of the Bering Sea, to await the arrival of the season's sockeye salmon pack.

Meanwhile, at the cannery, the salmon pack was loaded aboard a power scow for transport out to the ship. The power scow, manned by the regular crew with the assistance of Eskimos, transported the cases of canned salmon out to the ship. The cases of canned salmon were then moved from the deck of the power scow and into the freighter's hold by means of the freighter's hoisting gear for transport to Seattle.

Early in the 20th century, Alaska Steam began catering to the growing number of people who desired a trip north purely for pleasure, in addition to those who were traveling to Alaska for business purposes. To attract the traveling public, more attention was being paid to appointments aboard the ships for the comfort of the passengers. One of the passenger ships, the 400-foot *Aleutian* pictured in the postcard at the top of the page, was the second liner by that name in the Alaska Steam fleet. The first *Aleutian* struck the rocks and sank near Kodiak, Alaska, in 1929. The second *Aleutian* was built at Philadelphia, Pennsylvania, in 1906 and was purchased by Alaska Steam soon after the first *Aleutian*'s mishap.

The cover of a 1938 dinner menu, for use by passengers aboard Alaska Steam's liner *Alaska*, is shown half-size at left. The painting depicts two Aleut sailing canoes at sea.

SS *Alaska* dinner menu cover, reduced size, 1938. (With permission of University of Washington, Special Collections, negative UW23438)

Princess Marguerite at Lion's Gate in Vancouver, British Columbia, n.d. (Courtesy of Anna J. Knutsen)

Princess Marguerite, depicted above in this postcard picture (vessel name is misspelled in the postcard note), was actually the second passenger steamship of that name. Before this second *Princess Marguerite* was placed in service, two three-funnel ships had been built in Scotland in 1925 for use by the Canadian Pacific Railway. One of these ships was named *Princess Kathleen*, and the other was called *Princess Marguerite*.

These twin-screw turbine steamships were sisters, 350 feet long and, with 12,250 horsepower, were capable of attaining a speed of 22 knots. In 1942, *Princess Marguerite* was torpedoed and sunk in the Mediterranean Sea while in service as a British troopship. In 1952, *Princess Kathleen* met her demise due to poor visibility triggered by a rain squall while the steamship was on a run between Juneau and Skagway in Alaska. Off course, *Princess Kathleen* ran onto the rocks, eventually slid off, and sank. All passengers were landed safely, but salvage of the ship was impractical, and *Princess Kathleen* was declared a loss.

In 1949, two new steamships were built by the Fairfield Company at Glasgow, Scotland, for use by the B.C. Coast Service of Canadian Pacific. These ships were named *Princess Marguerite* and *Princess Patricia*. The vessels were 373 feet in length, powered by twin-screw, turbo-electric drive, and reached a speed of 23 knots on trials. Steam was provided at 320 pounds per square inch by four oil-fired water-tube boilers. The ships were intended for day service and, therefore, only limited stateroom space was provided. Because of this, however, areas were opened up for spacious and comfortable accommodations for 2000 passengers. Anyone who sailed aboard a "Princess" ship, for example, on the Seattle-Victoria, British Columbia run, would recall the feeling of being aboard an honest-to-goodness steam-powered passenger liner, where the ambience and relaxation during the voyage was worth more, perhaps, than the time spent at the destination.

The demand for passenger ferries to be put into service on Puget Sound was increasing, as well. A number of the photos that follow, credited to the Society of Naval Architects and Marine Engineers, are from a paper *Puget Sound Automobile Ferries: Their Evolution and Design* that was read by Seattle naval architect George C. Nickum before the society in 1965.

One hundred years ago, vast areas around Puget Sound had not yet been developed for industry and habitation. There were, however, those avant-gardes and speculators who saw the potential for profit, and one such person was C. D. Hillman. In 1907, Hillman set out to develop an area a few miles north of Olympia known as Boston Harbor. Purchasing several thousand acres there, Hillman began promoting the sale of five-acre lots.

With few roads existing in the horse-and-buggy days, Hillman brought potential buyers to the landing at Boston Harbor by steamboat. Since a fare was not charged for this service, thousands of people made the trip. Some were just along for the ride, and not everyone purchased a building site, but many did put money down on property. Glowing assertions were made by Hillman regarding the desirability of building a home at Boston Harbor, but many of these claims were also greatly exaggerated. By 1911, Hillman was in trouble with the law, and faced with charges of fraud, his promotion of the properties ceased.

In addition to the enterprise at Boston Harbor, C. D. Hillman was engaged in land development deals elsewhere around Puget Sound, as well. One such operation was located at West Seattle, where Hillman's West Seattle Land and Improvement Company was active in the real estate business. To provide transportation for prospective property buyers, *City of Seattle*, pictured below, was used on the run across Elliott Bay. *City of Seattle* was 122 feet long and built at Portland, Oregon, in 1888. Although vehicles could be carried on the deck of Mosquito Fleet steamers using special handling arrangements, the steam-powered, side-wheel vessel *City of Seattle* was distinctive for being the first ferry in operation on Puget Sound that permitted conveyances to be routinely driven on and off. Propulsion power was provided by two 16 x 20 inch single cylinder engines of 135 horsepower each, supplied with steam at 100 psi. With an engine at each sidewheel, the port and starboard wheels could be rotated in opposite directions when maneuvering.

By 1911, much of the land had been bought up at West Seattle, and the street railway system had been extended. *City of Seattle* continued on this run until 1911, but with decreased need for service, the vessel was sold to California owners. News that the ferry service had been discontinued resulted in public protests, however, and another ferry, named *West Seattle* and also operated by the land company, continued the service from downtown Seattle to West Seattle. Eventually, this ferry service was taken over by the city of Seattle, operating at a loss but maintaining amicable relations with the public.

City of Seattle, n.d. (With permission of the Society of Naval Architects and Marine Engineers)

Whatcom, n.d. (With permission of the Society of Naval Architects and Marine Engineers)

The photos here provide an example of the changes that many Puget Sound vessels underwent during the course of their working lives. The steamer *Whatcom*, shown above, was originally the 169-foot-long *Majestic* built at Everett in 1901 for Thompson Steamboat Company. Propulsion power was provided by a triple-expansion engine with bore and stroke dimensions of 18, 30 1/2, 51 x 24 inches. Eventually, still carrying the name *Whatcom*, the steamer was in service on the Seattle-Bellingham run for Puget Sound Navigation Company. Later, *Whatcom* was converted into the ferry *City of Bremerton*, pictured below, for use on the Seattle-Bremerton route, replacing the speedy steamer *Bailey Gatzert*. As modified, the ferry could handle both autos and passengers.

City of Bremerton, n.d. (With permission of the Society of Naval Architects and Marine Engineers)

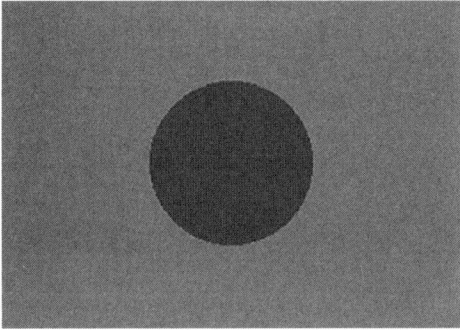

Puget Sound Navigation Company house flag.

Puget Sound Navigation Company, known as the "Black Ball Line," was formed as a subsidiary of Alaska Steamship Company in 1900 to operate the 136-foot steamer *Rosalie* between Puget Sound and Victoria, British Columbia. In 1903, a consolidation with La Conner Trading and Transportation Company resulted in a greatly enlarged number of steamers owned by Puget Sound Navigation. Joshua Green, who with other investors had operated La Conner Trading and Transportation, became president of the company.

In 1927, Joshua Green, retired and in time, control of the company passed to Alexander Peabody, the son of Charles E. Peabody, one of the founders of Alaska Steamship Company. The house flag shown above was transferred to Puget Sound Navigation by Alaska Steam, the parent company, in 1927, and it consisted of a black ball placed against a red background; hence the familiar name Black Ball Line. Prior to 1927, the house flag flown by Puget Sound Navigation had consisted of a red star on a white diamond against a blue field, from a design by Mrs. Green.

In 1906 and 1907, the fleet was upgraded with the purchase of the Great Lakes steamers *Indianapolis* (180 feet, 1500 horsepower), *Chippewa* (200 feet, 2100 horsepower), and *Iroquois* (214 feet, 1500 horsepower), all built at Toledo, Ohio. These vessels brought speed and an enhanced sense of luxury to the passengers. *Indianapolis* was scrapped in 1938, but *Chippewa* and *Iroquois* continued in operation for a good many years, the latter being rebuilt in 1951 as a diesel-powered freight vessel for operation between Seattle, Port Townsend, and Port Angeles.

Although *Indianapolis*, *Chippewa*, and *Iroquois* were fast, they could not keep up with the famed passenger steamer *Flyer* that was owned by Columbia River and Puget Sound Navigation Company. The 170-foot, fine-lined *Flyer* was built of wood at Portland, Oregon, in 1891 and was immediately placed in service on Puget Sound. As recorded in *Lewis and Dryden's Marine History of the Pacific Northwest*, *Flyer's* engine was triple expansion with cylinder dimensions of 21, 30 and 54 x 30 inches, which powered a run between Seattle and Tacoma, a distance of 28 miles, in about an hour and a half. The vessel was capable of such speed while only taking out 1200 horsepower from the engine.

Rather than continuing to compete with such a speedy steamer, Puget Sound Navigation Company purchased *Flyer* from Columbia River and Puget Sound Navigation Company in 1911 and continued with the operation of the vessel on Puget Sound. In 1928, a new highway was opened between Seattle and Tacoma, which encouraged increased travel by automobile, putting many steamers such as *Flyer* out of a job. In 1929, *Flyer*, after metal items had been removed for salvage, was towed to Richmond Beach and burned.

President Green had begun the practice of replacing aging steamers, as well as those that had been involved in mishaps, with newer vessels. The company continued to purchase additional vessels as the years went on, and any unit of the fleet that did not prove to be profitable in service was sold. Gasoline, semi-diesel, and full-diesel engines were gradually replacing steam plants as propulsive power. Competition between operators in the business of Puget Sound water transportation was intense, and many small companies went out of business or were swallowed up by larger firms. In 1935, Puget Sound Navigation Company bought the extensive holdings of the cargo and passenger line Kitsap County Transportation Company. In eliminating KCTC from competition, Puget Sound Navigation was well on the way to holding a near-monopoly in the business of carrying freight and passengers on Puget Sound waters.

Eventually, though, new highways were being built, and an increasing number of vehicles were rolling off of the assembly lines, causing pressure on the earnings of passenger and freight steamers, as well as on railways. A trend emerged that led to replacement of the Puget Sound passenger and cargo vessels with vehicle/passenger ferries that catered to the needs of highway travelers.

Quinault, n.d. (With permission of the Society of Naval Architects and Marine Engineers)

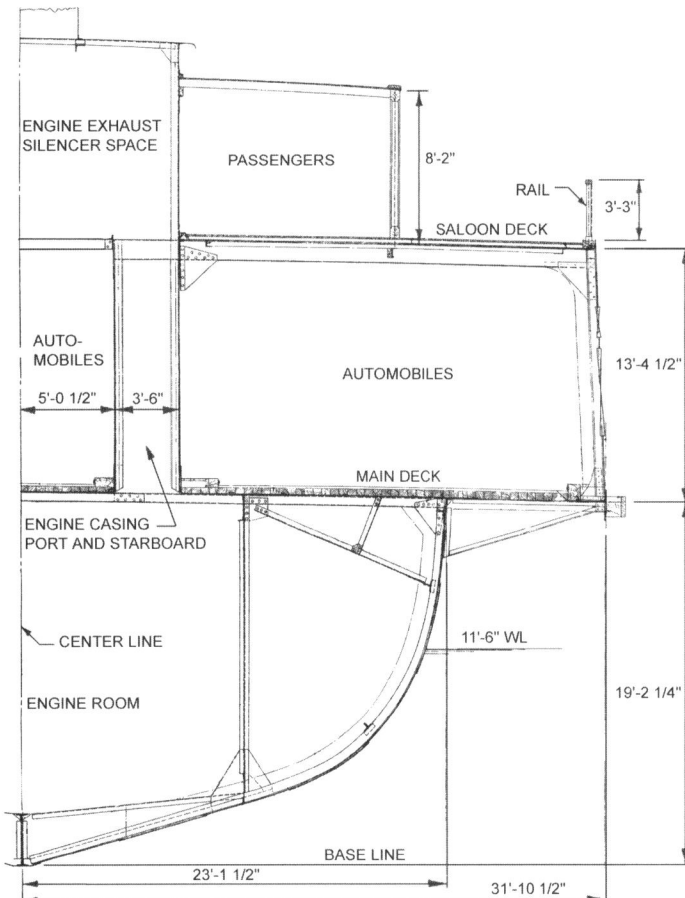

Steel-electric ferry midship section, n.d.
(From a W. C. Nickum and Sons Company drawing,
with notes by the author)

A variety, and sometimes odd assortment, of passenger and freight vessels operated on Puget Sound for many years. However, with increasing auto travel in the Puget Sound area, as well as buildup of personnel at the Puget Sound Naval Shipyard in Bremerton, there was a need for auto/passengers ferries that were specifically configured for moving larger numbers of passengers and cars.

It happened that, from 1937 to 1940, a California fleet of ferries was being phased out and replaced by the new San Francisco Bay bridges. Captain Alexander Peabody purchased six ferries, all built in the Bay area in 1927, for his Puget Sound Navigation Company. Modernized, widened and reworked to accommodate the larger autos that were on the roads at the time, these 258-foot-long car ferries with their steel hulls, steel and wood superstructures, and diesel-electric propulsion became known as the "steel-electrics" and were renamed *Enetai*, *Illahee*, *Klickitat*, *Nisqually*, *Quinault,* and *Willapa*.

Quinault is pictured above, and a typical transverse section through the hull and superstructure of the riveted steel-electric ferries, prior to widening, is illustrated at left.

Chetzemoka, n.d. (With permission of the Society of Naval Architects and Marine Engineers)

In addition to the steel-electrics, Captain Peabody brought five 240-foot, 40-car wooden ferries north, under tow by the Puget Sound Tug and Barge tugs *Active, Commissioner,* and *Neptune,* from the Bay area. These were known as the "Golden Class" ferries because of their names *Golden Age, Golden Bear, Golden Poppy, Golden Shore,* and *Golden State.* Although temporary wooden barriers were attached to the forward end of the vessels to ward off boarding seas, *Golden Bear* was a wreck at the end of the voyage. The other four ferries, however, were placed into Puget Sound service and renamed *Chetzemoka,* pictured above, *Elwha, Kehloken,* and *Klahanie.*

To further expand Puget Sound Navigation Company's operations, two steam-powered ferries, *San Mateo,* pictured below, and *Shasta* were brought north under tow by Puget Sound Tug and Barge's *Goliah.* At 217 feet in length, each of these steel ferries was powered by a 1400-horsepower, triple-expansion engine having cylinder dimensions of 19, 32, 54 x 36 inches.

San Mateo, n.d. (With permission of the Society of Naval Architects and Marine Engineers)

An example of a wooden ferry was the double-ended *Kitsap*, built by Lake Washington Shipyards Corporation at Houghton in 1925 for Kitsap County Transportation Company. The midship section drawing for this vessel is shown at left. Passenger seating was provided by sturdy wooden benches, but the shape of these benches left something to be desired in the way of creature comfort. *Kitsap*'s hull form was designed with a knuckle, or chine, located below the waterline. Each transverse frame was cut from two straight lengths of wood with a joint at the knuckle. The 159-foot *Kitsap* was propelled by a Washington-Estep diesel engine of 600 horsepower.

The ferry entered service on the Fauntleroy-Vashon-Harper route. Ownership of *Kitsap* passed to Puget Sound Navigation Company when Kitsap County Transportation was purchased by Puget Sound Navigation in 1935. In 1962, *Kitsap* was sold to the Oregon Highway Commission for operation across the Columbia River between Megler and Astoria, Oregon.

Vashon, pictured below, was noteworthy as being one of the few ferries of the time that had a V-shape hull form, an underwater shape that was similar to the hull form used in the design of the new Puget Sound ferries that came along much later. *Vashon* was 191 feet long and was built for Kitsap County Transportation in 1930 by the same yard at Houghton that built *Kitsap*. *Vashon* was assigned to the Seattle-Vashon-Harper route. In addition to being known for the V-section hull form, this vessel was also the largest ferry in operation on Puget Sound at that time. Propulsion was provided by a 930-horsepower Washington diesel engine.

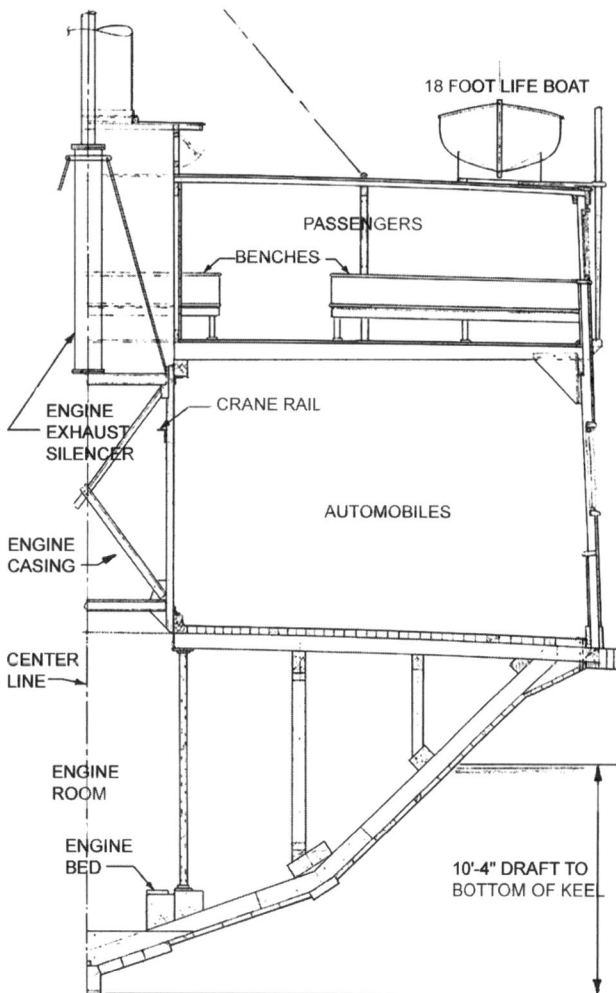

**Kitsap midship section.
(From a W. C. Nickum and Sons Company drawing, with notes by the author)**

Vashon, n.d. (With permission of the Society of Naval Architects and Marine Engineers)

Different in appearance from the other ferries in the Puget Sound fleet, and probably distinct from any other vessel ever built, was the auto/passenger ferry *Kalakala*. In this postcard nighttime picture of *Kalakala*, Seattle is brightly illuminated in the background.

It might be assumed, from the streamlined and futuristic appearance, that the ferry was newly built at the time the postcard was being viewed by tourists, but that would only be partially correct. In fact, the 265-foot *Kalakala* was built of steel as *Peralta* by Moore Drydock Company at Oakland, California, in 1927, but with a totally different superstructure from that shown.

Peralta, powered by a Westinghouse steam turbo-electric power plant of 2600 horsepower, was used for carrying passengers between San Francisco and Oakland. In 1933, the Oakland terminal was seriously damaged by fire, and *Peralta* was caught in that blaze. In that year, Captain Alexander Peabody, of Puget Sound Navigation Company, bought the damaged ferry and had the vessel towed north to Puget Sound.

Stripped down to the bare hull, the ferry was outfitted with a new streamlined superstructure at Lake Washington Shipyard. Renamed *Kalakala* and fitted with a new 3000-horsepower Busch-Sulzer diesel engine, the ferry was touted as capable of a speed of 16 knots or more. In fact, however, some years later, the new ferry *Evergreen State* could

Kalakala, 1937. (Courtesy of Anna J. Knutsen)

overhaul *Kalakala* while traveling at only 15 knots. The Chinook name *Kalakala* means "Flying Bird" but, with her shiny, contoured superstructure, the vessel acquired many nicknames, with the most common monicker heard being "Silver Slug."

The ferry may have given passengers a smooth ride during the earlier period when the vessel had been powered by a finely balanced, rotating steam turbine. Unfortunately, the big Busch-Sulzer reciprocating engine that replaced the steam turbine, combined with hull structure that probably lacked sufficient stiffness, induced an uncomfortable amount of vibration into the hull and decks.

In 1951, the state of Washington bought Captain Peabody's company, and the system evolved into a pattern of routes as shown at left. *Kalakala* remained on the Seattle to Bremerton route for a time but eventually took over the Port Angeles to Victoria shuttle run. Later, moored in Alaska after being retired from carrying passengers, *Kalakala* became a king crab processing plant, a factory of very unusual architecture indeed.

Washington State Ferry System auto/passenger routes. (From Washington State Department of Transportation literature)

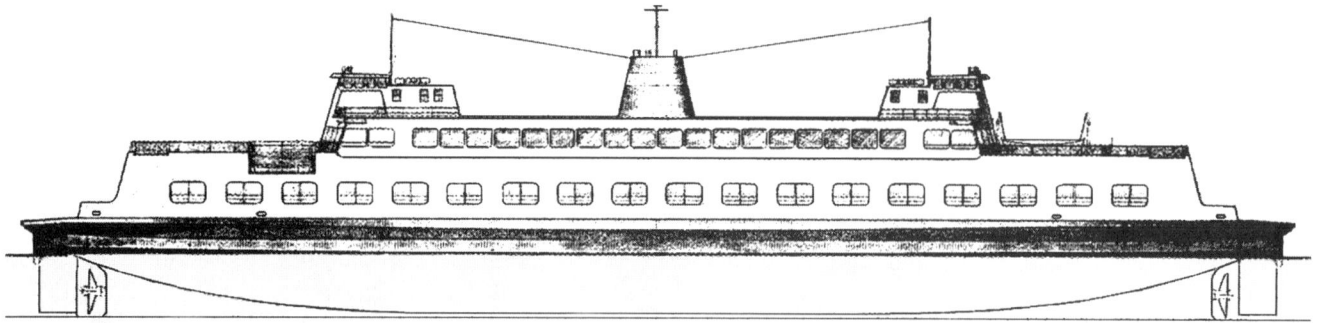

Evergreen State Class Washington state ferry, 1953. (From a W. C. Nickum and Sons Company drawing)

Following purchase of Puget Sound Navigation Company by the state of Washington, modernization of the cross sound ferry system was begun in 1953, and the illustration above, an outboard profile from a drawing by the Seattle design firm of W. C. Nickum and Sons Company, shows the appearance of the new ships. *Evergreen State* was built by Puget Sound Bridge and Dredging Company at Seattle in 1954, and four years later a contract was awarded to the same firm for *Klahowya* and *Tillicum*, of the same class.

William C. Nickum began his career as a ship designer while working in East Coast shipyards. In 1916, he moved to Seattle where further experience was gained at Seattle Construction and Drydock and at the Todd Tacoma shipyard. W. C. Nickum and Sons Company was established as a design office by William C. Nickum at Seattle in 1925, and in 1935 his sons George C. and William B. became partners in the firm. For many years, the company was involved with the design of a variety of vessels, including the Puget Sound auto/passenger ferries.

At 310 feet in overall length and with diesel-electric propulsion of 3200 horsepower, passengers aboard an *Evergreen State* class ferry could be transported at a speed of up to 16 knots. Of double-ended design, as were most of the Bay Area ferries excepting *Kalakala*, propulsion power and a propeller were installed at each end of the vessel so that the ferry would not have to turn around at the slip to make a return trip; the captain would simply move to the pilothouse at the other end of the ferry to navigate.

A diesel-electric propulsion plant consists of a diesel engine driving a generator, which, in turn, provides current to an electric motor. The electric motor is connected to the shaft, which drives

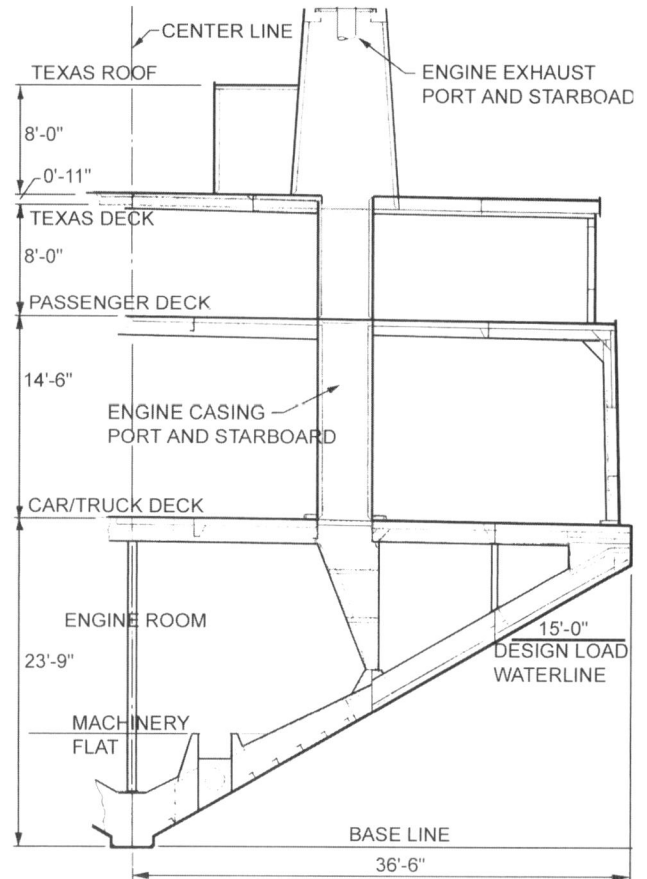

Evergreen State Class ferry midship section, 1950s. (From a W. C. Nickum and Sons Company drawing, with notes by the author)

the propeller. In a double-ended ferry, an electric motor is installed at each end. One or more engine/generators, installed at midship, can supply electricity to the motor at either end. This method of propulsion had been used aboard some of the earlier ferries, and the reliability had been proven, while also exhibiting superior controllability during close quarter maneuvering, when approaching the terminals, for example. Good reasons had been established, then, for installing this type of propulsion in *Evergreen State*, also.

The *Evergreen State* Class of ferries started a long-term trend in modernizing the state's ferry fleet. The year 1967 saw the completion of the even larger 382-foot-long *Hyak* series of diesel-electric powered, double-ended ferries that became known as the Super Ferries. These new ferries, *Hyak* and sister ships *Elwha*, *Kaleetan*, and *Yakima*, similar in appearance to *Evergreen* State, were built by National Steel and Shipbuilding Company at San Diego, California, to a design by W. C. Nickum and Sons Company.

As described previously, a double-ended ferry has a propeller at each end, with the wheel at the trailing end providing the propulsion. If no power were given to the propeller at the forward end, it would simply rotate, or "windmill," in the water flow. It was found, though, that an increase in efficiency of at least 10% could be achieved by applying just enough power to the forward propel-

ler so that it would turn at a no-thrust speed, i.e., neither exerting thrust to pull the vessel along nor windmilling while dragging in the water flow.

The midship section for the *Hyak* class of vessels is depicted below and shows the V-form of the hull similar to that of *Evergreen State*. In addition to the benefit of more economical construction, as compared with a molded hull form having round bilges, the characteristics of stability and of flooding due to damage for the V-form hull are very good, considerations that are particularly important for a vessel that carries passengers.

Although the V-form hull requires somewhat more propulsion power than a molded form at a given speed, the difference is not great. *Hyak*'s double-deck arrangement for automobiles outboard of the engine casings can be seen in the drawing. The 'tween deck height at centerline accommodates large trucks, permitting the carriage of any long-haul truck having the maximum height that could travel under the overpasses on the interstate highways.

The *Evergreen State* Class ferries can carry 100 cars and 1200 passengers, the *Hyak* class 160 vehicles and 2600 passengers. Beginning with *Kalakala*, more attention was being paid to passenger comfort.

A galley for food and drink preparation was installed aboard the *Evergreen State* class ferries and also in later designs. Instead of wooden bench seating as used aboard the early ferries, more consideration was being given to furnishings. Seat spacing aboard the new ferries was great enough that no one but an unusually tall passenger could prop his or her feet up on the opposite seat. For the new ferries, the window sills were lowered to permit seated passengers to comfortably view the scenery, and tables used by card players, who were not gazing out the windows anyway, were moved toward centerline.

The operating speed of the *Hyak* Class ferries was set at 19 knots. A higher speed could have been attained, but the 19-knot speed provided economical operation while maintaining a favorable schedule. The *Hyak* Class ferry crossing time between Seattle and Bremerton of 45 minutes was an improvement over the time of more than an hour needed by previous auto/passenger ferries for this run.

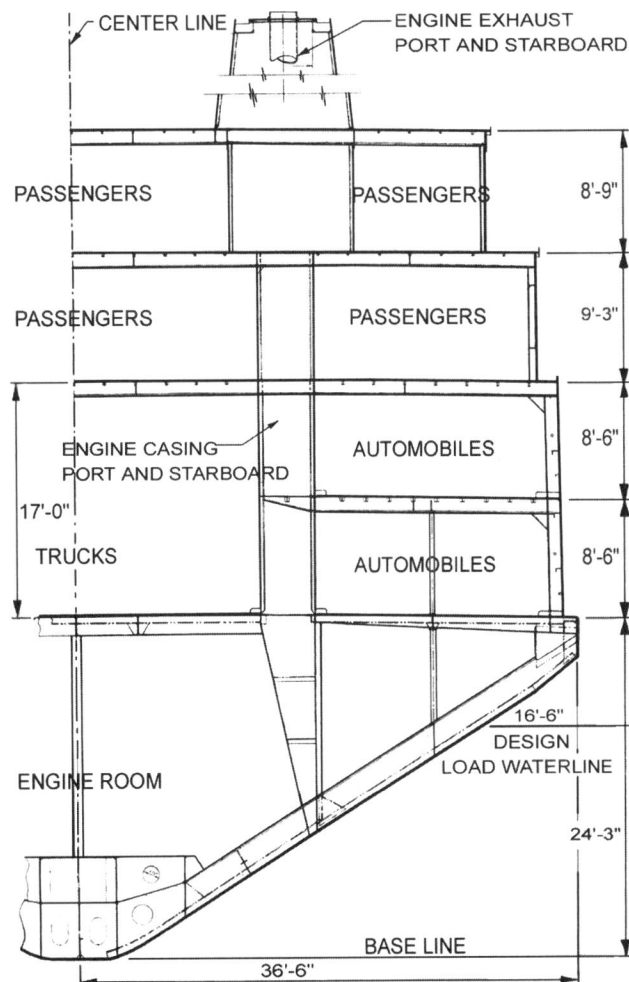

***Hyak* Class midship section, 1960s. (From a W. C. Nickum and Sons Company drawing with notes by the author)**

Although diesel electric propulsion was initially seen on Puget Sound when the Black Ball Line purchased the "Golden" Class ferries and brought them north to Puget Sound in the 1930s, this type of propulsion had been in use for many years before. The development of diesel-electric propulsion was begun by the Winton Engine Company, in coordination with the United States Navy, in 1913. The first installation was made in the collier *Jupiter*, which later was converted to become the aircraft carrier *Langley*. Success with diesel-electric power led to its use by the Navy, particularly as propulsion in submarines and tugs. Electric propulsion was also used in battleships, the generator being driven by a steam turbine.

Diesel-electric propulsion also saw use in civilian applications in the early years, the first being the Nathaniel Herreshof-designed yacht *Elfay* of 1919-pictured below. *Elfay*'s auxiliary propulsion system consisted of a six-cylinder, 115 horsepower Winton diesel engine turning at 450 revolutions per minute. This engine was directly connected to a 75-kilowatt direct current generator which, in turn, operated a 90-horsepower electric motor that drove the propeller shaft.

Schooner *Elfay*, with-diesel electric auxiliary power, 1919. (From General Motors Cleveland Division literature, 1940s)

The Winton Engine Company eventually became the Cleveland Engine Division, later known as the Electro-Motive Division, or EMD, of General Motors, and development of diesel-electric propulsion continued. These two-cycle, medium-rpm engines are in widespread use as propulsion in vessels of all types, as well as for powering diesel-electric locomotives. Smaller, higher speed, two-cycle engines are produced by General Motors as Detroit diesels and see use in a variety of applications, including boats and trucks.

Diesel-electric drive has advantages in many applications. Flexibility in arrangement of machinery is available with this type of propulsion, and since the engine/generator is not connected to the propeller shaft, this unit can be located where convenient, near midship in most cases. The electric drive motor is usually located as close to the propeller as possible to minimize the propeller shaft length. There is no mechanical connection between the engine/generator and the electric motor; instead, electrical current is simply delivered to the motor via cables, which can be routed along a convenient path. Control of the propeller rotation speed is superior, varying from zero to maximum-rated rpm, an important consideration for the maneuverability of a tug or ferry.

The drawing, from General Motors Cleveland Division literature of the 1940s, at the top of the next page, illustrates the application of diesel-electric drive in a tug. This tug, of overall length 103 feet, was built of steel to a design by Tams, Inc. The 12-cylinder General Motors diesel main engine produced 1200 horsepower. The engine was directly connected to a direct current generator that turned at 800 revolutions per minute, supplying current to an electric motor that provided 1000 horsepower. The motor drove, through a reduction gear, a three-blade bronze, 8-foot-10-inch-diameter propeller at up to 200 rpm.

The arrangement of propulsion machinery in the *Hyak* Class ferries, as laid out by the designers W. C. Nickum and Sons Company in the 1960s, is shown in the drawing at the bottom of the next page. Since the ferry is double-ended with a propeller at each end, two propulsion systems are provided, but the propulsion components at one end can be electrically switched to work together with those at the other end.

The arrangement of diesel-electric propulsion machinery in a tug as described on the previous page is illustrated immediately below, and the arrangement of the diesel-electric machinery for the *Hyak* Class ferries of the 1960s is shown at the bottom of the page. Because both ends of *Hyak*'s hull are pointed, there is not really a bow or stern, but instead, the ends of the ferry are simply numbered. In the drawing, the No. 1 end is shown, and the No. 2 end is similar and opposite.

The machinery at one end of the double-ended hull is duplicated at the other end. Each of the two engine rooms provides space for a pair of General Motors 16-cylinder EMD diesel engines, each driving a generator, plus auxiliary machinery. In total, then, there are four engine/generator sets in the vessel. A 7000 horsepower electric motor drives a fixed-pitch propeller at up to 180 revolutions per minute, through a reduction gear, at each end of the hull. The double-ended ferry, with the underwater hull form the same at both ends, can travel at up to maximum speed in either direction.

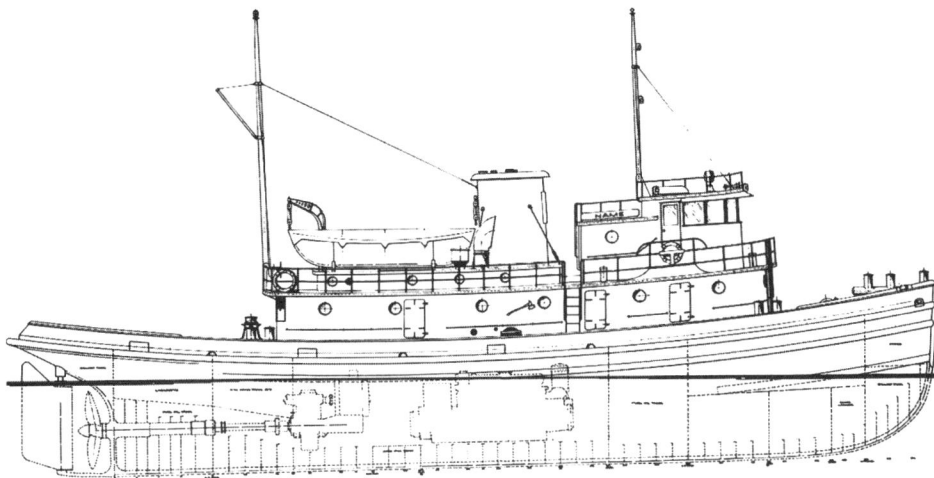

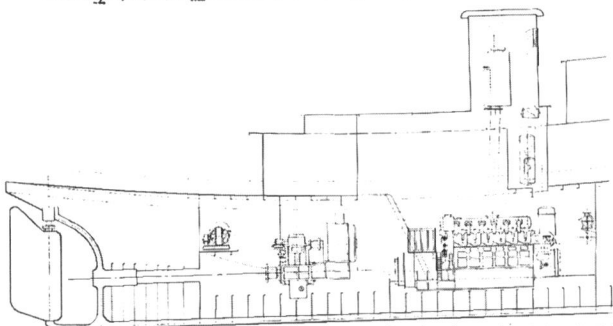

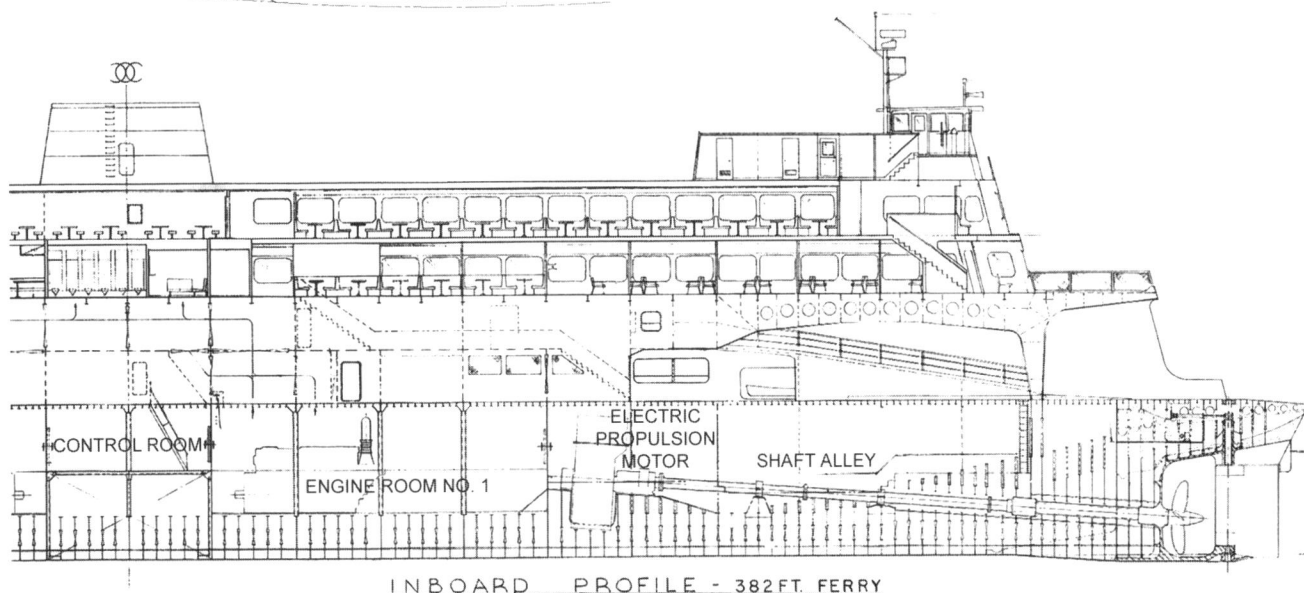

Diesel-electric tug outboard profile and machinery arrangement. (From General Motors Cleveland Division literature, 1940s, with notes by the author)

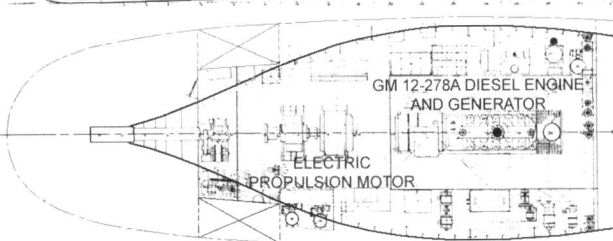

Diesel-electric powered *Hyak* Class ferry inboard profile, 1960s. No. 1 end is shown, No. 2 end is similar and opposite. (From a W. C. Nickum and Sons Company drawing, with notes by the author)

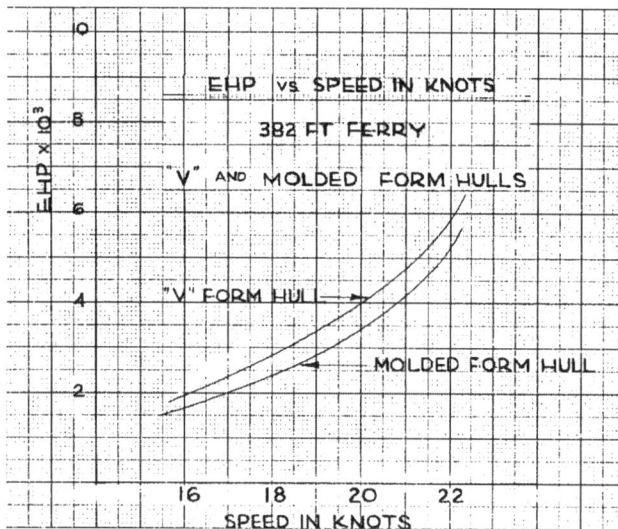

Speed and power curves for V-form and molded form *Hyak* Class ferry hull designs, 1960s. (From a W. C. Nickum and Sons Company graph as derived from towing-tank model test data.)

Speed and power curves are shown above for two hull forms, a V-form and a round bilge-molded form, that were worked out by W. C. Nickum and Sons Company during the design process for the *Hyak* Class ferries. These curves were derived from model testing done in the towing tank at Wageningen, Holland.

At a speed of 19 knots, for example, EHP is a bit over 3300 horsepower for the V-form hull and just over 2800 hp for the molded form hull. EHP is shorthand for effective horsepower, which is derived from the resistance of the hull moving through the water. Actual installed horsepower needs to be considerably greater than effective horsepower to account for efficiency losses in the propulsion system.

Although the propulsion efficiency of the V-form hull design as model tested in the tow tank was less than that of the molded form, the V-form was selected for the *Hyak* Class ferries. As design work continued, it was found that the stability of the molded form vessel was insufficient. With the increase in beam that would have been required for the molded form the hull efficiency would have been reduced, and much of the propulsion advantage that had been indicated in tank testing would have gone away. In addition, the simplified construction inherent in the V-form versus the more complex shape of the molded form was an advantage in construction cost saving.

All things considered, the V-form hull works well for a ferry. Nonetheless, if all other factors are equal, a trade-off between construction cost and life-cycle operating cost is examined when designing a ship. Designing for economical construction is important, but other considerations also have an influence on the final design.

Washington State Ferries continued with the construction of new vessels to replace those that were being retired. The population in the Puget Sound region was increasing, improved highways were being constructed, and more people were traveling by automobile. It was time to continue building new ferries.

Of modest size, *Hiyu*, pictured on the next page, was also from the drawing boards of W. C. Nickum and Sons Company and built of steel by Gunderson Brothers Engineering Corporation on the Willamette River at Portland, Oregon, in 1967. The ferry is 162 feet in overall length and carries 40 automobiles and 200 passengers.

Designed for use on routes of short distance and transit time, such as the Point Defiance-Tahlequah route for which the vessel was originally intended, the ferry does not require a galley for food preparation. Although *Hiyu* is much smaller than the other ferries in the Washington State Ferries system, the rounded ends of the vehicle deck in plan view are identical to those of the larger ferries to fit the pattern of pilings that form the slip at each end of the route.

The 860-horsepower twin engines aboard *Hiyu* drive the propellers through a gearbox and clutch arrangement for a speed of 10 knots. The engine clutched to the trailing propeller provides the major propulsion power. The other engine, however, is connected to the leading propeller and turns at approximately idle speed. This arrangement provides good efficiency as compared with allowing the leading propeller simply to drag in the water and windmill. The engines alternate their roles in providing propulsion depending on which direction the double ended ferry is traveling.

As indicated on the *Hiyu* vehicle deck arrangement as illustrated on the next page, trucks are loaded in the two lanes between the engine casings, and automobiles are handled outboard of the casings, with space provided for two auto lanes on each side.

Hiyu auto/passenger ferry outboard profile.
(From Washington State Ferries literature).

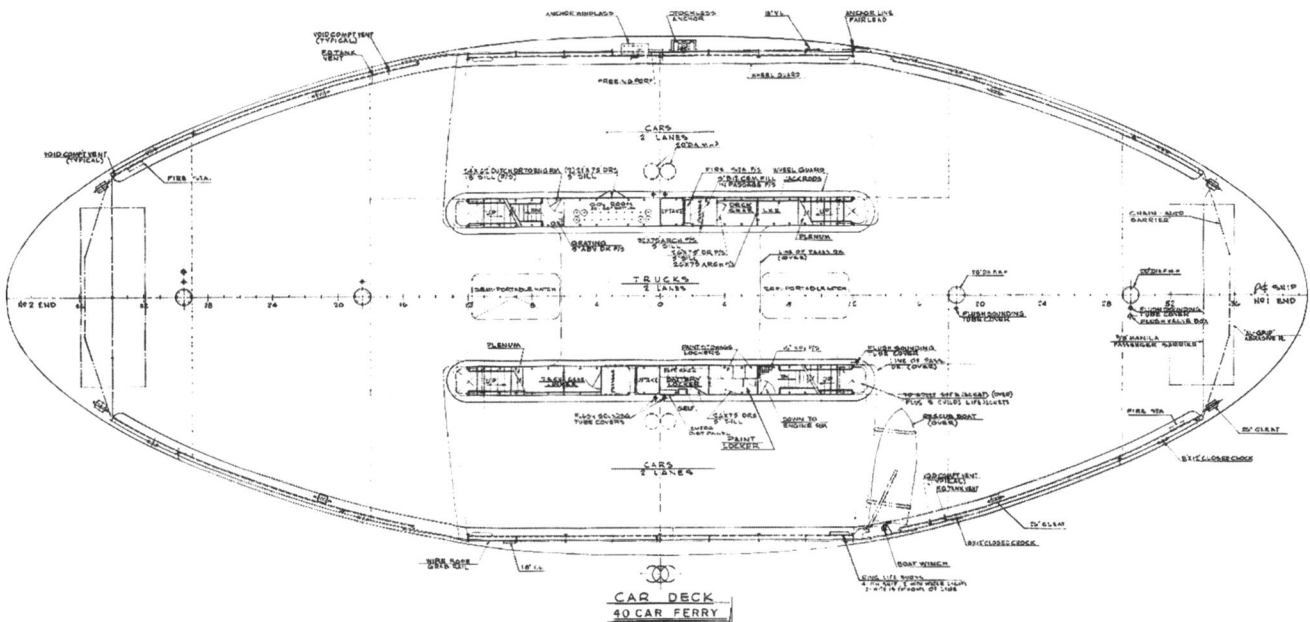

Hiyu vehicle deck arrangement, 1960s.
(From a W. C. Nickum and Sons Company drawing).

Because of their weight, heavy trucks are loaded along the centerline to minimize vessel heel as they are driven aboard. Autos, being of lighter weight, are parked outboard of the casings but are received aboard in a sequence that alternates from one side to the other also to minimize vessel heel during loading.

The twin engine casings aboard modern ferries work out well for loading trucks and autos. The steam-powered ferries of early days were arranged with a single casing located on centerline, which meant that trucks and autos all were parked outboard, although trucks could be moved aboard in the lanes closest to centerline. The single casing aboard the steam ferries was necessarily larger than a modern casing because the uptake from the boiler firebox was more bulky than the exhaust pipe of a diesel engine. In addition, since the boiler and firebox were located on centerline, the casing, from a practical standpoint, had to be located on centerline; the large firebox uptake could not readily be routed anywhere else.

A casing for a modern diesel-powered ferry needs space only to accommodate a sloping ladder for access to the engine room, the engine exhaust and clearance for pulling the engine pistons, which is a much smaller volume than an early boiler uptake. Other spaces can also be built in a casing and given over to such needs as storage lockers, fire fighting equipment, routes for piping and electrical runs, and aboard the larger ferries, toilet facilities may even be installed.

273

Just as the beautiful scenery in the Puget Sound area has graced illustrations on postcards, the big, glamorous cross-sound ferries have been the stuff of postcard pictures also. Toiling in out-of-the-way places around Puget Sound, however, were the small ferries that never gained fame but were much appreciated by the people who lived in the areas served by these little vessels.

Many residents in areas where a small ferry was essential for getting somewhere else looked upon the boat as their own, and as a matter of fact, in some instances the local residents did own the ferry. At another location, a small ferry might be owned by an individual who also worked as captain aboard the boat, in the same way that the 50-foot passenger steamer *Mizpah* was owned and captained by Volney Young in southern Puget Sound in the first decade of the last century.

Such a ferry was *Acorn*, having overall dimensions of 64-feet-10-inches length and 25-feet beam. *Acorn*, illustrated in the H. C. Hanson design drawing below, was built of wood at Seattle in 1924 for Mrs. Berte H. Olson for use on a route between Camano Island and Whidbey Island in northern Puget Sound. The small deckhouse supplied upper engine room space, and the centerline location provided transverse weight balance while allowing cars to be placed on deck port and starboard. Accommodations for passengers in the deckhouse were not necessary for the short transit time across Saratoga Passage, a distance of only a mile and a half or so.

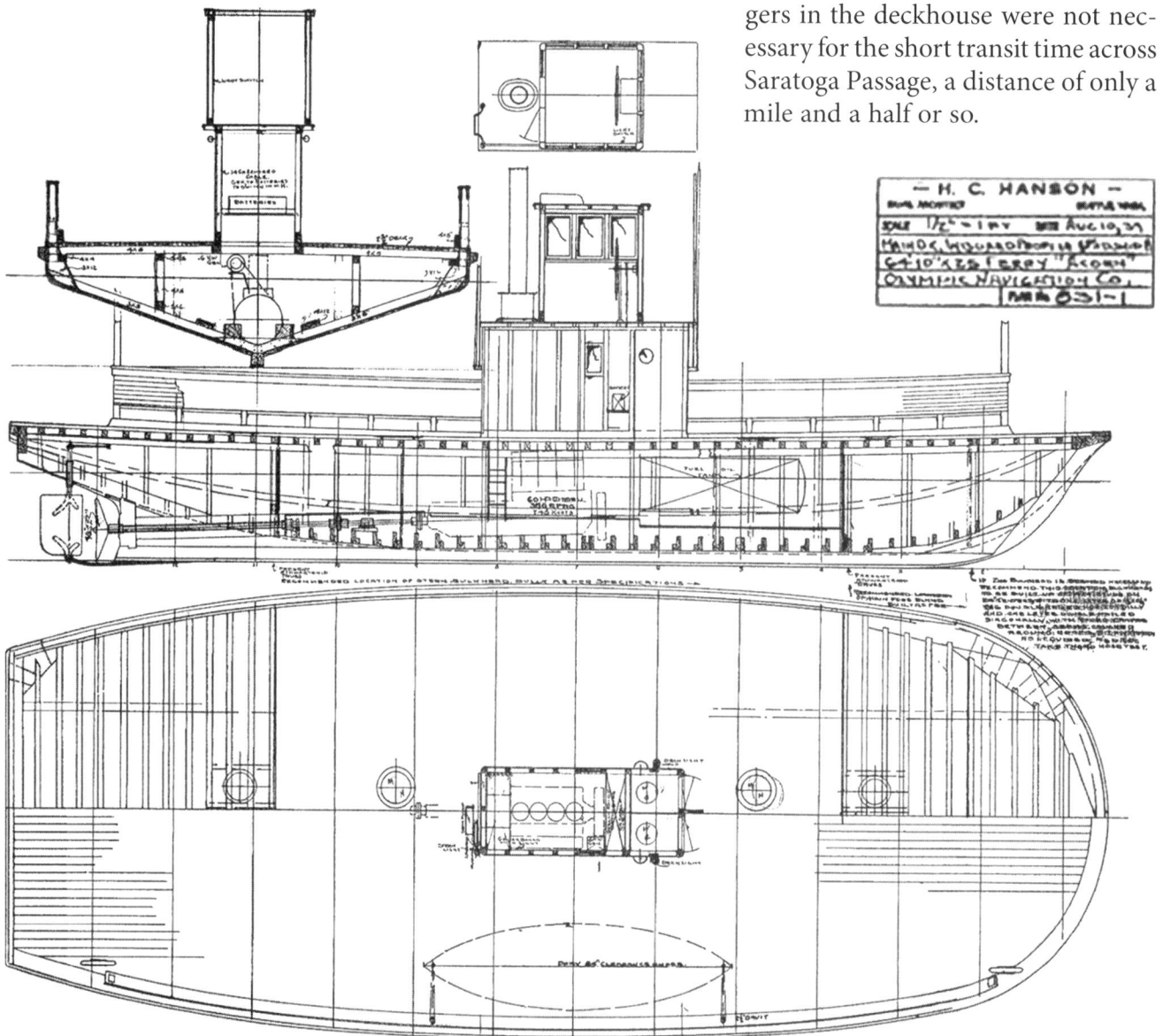

Acorn, 1924. (With permission of Whatcom Museum of History and Art, H. C. Hanson Collection drawing 831)

Only a moderate amount of propulsion power was required for the short distance traveled on the route *Acorn* was assigned to, since high speed was unnecessary to maintain a reasonable schedule. Hence, the diesel engine installed in *Acorn* was a mere 60 horsepower obtained while turning at less than 400 revolutions per minute. Judging from the length and beam of *Acorn*, perhaps up to eight automobiles of a size that was in use at the time could be accommodated.

It can be seen from the drawing on the previous page that the hull cross section was a V-shape, similar to that used for the large ferries designed by W. C. Nickum and Sons Company 30 years later, which greatly simplified construction. It may also be noticed that the fuel tank was located in the hull forward of midship; as the fuel was burned by the engine, although the weight of the vessel would have decreased and the bow would have risen, the stern would have maintained a constant draft, a good feature that preserved sufficient propeller immersion in the water.

Mrs. Olson also operated a ferry on a route that crossed Deception Pass. This ferry consisted simply of a scow towed by a gas boat, but this run was discontinued when the bridge across Deception Pass was constructed in 1935.

In 1936, Mrs. Olson began to use *Acorn* and another small vessel named *Clatawa* for a ferry operation that crossed Hood Canal between Port Gamble and Shine. This route had been purchased from Captain Peabody of Puget Sound Navigation Company. Mrs. Olson sold the activity back to Captain Peabody in 1950, who then relocated the route to a course between Lofall and South Point. This run was discontinued in 1961 when a new floating concrete bridge was completed to span Hood Canal. *Acorn* was then purchased by Hat Island Development Company for service between Everett and Gedney (Hat) Island.

Privately owned auto/passenger ferries operated in various areas of southern Puget Sound, also. Pictured below is *City of Steilacoom*, 91 feet long and built at Gig Harbor in 1924. *City of Steilacoom* was originally propelled by a 200-horsepower Fairbanks-Morse engine, but later, in 1951, the ferry was repowered with a 270-horsepower Caterpillar diesel engine.

City of Steilacoom, n.d. (With permission of Puget Sound Maritime Historical Society, negative 2704–4)

The Skansie brothers, Andrew, Joseph, Mitchell, and Peter, were commercial fishermen and in 1912 they established Skansie Shipbuilding Company at Gig Harbor. The yard then operated successfully for many years, and during one period, from 1912 to 1929, it was reported that over 180 purse seiners and cannery tenders, as well as other types of vessels, were built.

Washington Navigation Company, with Mitchell Skansie as president, was established in 1926 to operate ferries that eventually provided passenger and automobile carrying service on routes connecting Tacoma, Gig Harbor, Steilacoom, Anderson Island, McNeil Island, and Longbranch. One of the ferries operated by Washington Navigation was *City of Steilacoom*.

Much later in *City of Steilacoom*'s working life, the ferry was in service for Pierce County and ran between 6th Avenue in Tacoma and Fox Island. In 1962, the ferry was sold to Webb School of California and moored in the San Juan Islands as a facility for a boys' school located there. *City of Steilacoom* was finally retired and dismantled at Steilacoom in 1975.

Perhaps one of the shortest ferry runs on Puget Sound was the route that crossed Pickering Passage between Hartstene Island and the mainland in southern Puget Sound, a distance of no more than a half mile. The first series of ferries that made the Pickering Passage crossing were built of logs and powered by automobile engines. The log ferries operated on the Pickering Passage crossing from 1922 until the early 1930s when the little vessel *Hartstene*, a self-propelled wooden scow, was built and put into service on the route.

Hartstene certainly was not a fast boat, requiring close to a half hour for the short crossing of Pickering Pass. Vehicles were taken aboard and off-loaded right on the beach by means of a ramp that could be raised and lowered by a hoist. The ramp hoist was attached to a boom, which, in turn, was supported from a wooden frame and wire rope back stays. *Hartstene* is pictured below not long before being retired from service and replaced by a new ferry.

The new ferry which replaced *Hartstene* was a higher speed vessel built of wood by Henry Long at Olympia in 1945. The new boat was named *Hartstene II* and was about the same size as *Acorn*. *Hartstene II* could carry eight cars and, in a manner similar to the earlier ferry, utilized a ramp for handling vehicles on and off the beach, although the operating gear for raising and lowering the ramp was better engineered than what had been used aboard the previous *Hartstene*. By this time, the sand and gravel on the beach at each end of the run had been paved over. *Hartstene II* remained in service, charging fifty cents per car transported, until 1969 when a bridge was constructed across Pickering Passage.

Hartstene, 1945. (With permission of Mason County Historical Society)

THE FISHING BOATS AND THEIR GEAR

In at least one respect, the occupation of fishing is similar to gold prospecting—the chance to strike it big, to be a "highliner." There were fish, a lot of fish most of the time, in the waters of the Pacific Northwest and Alaska during the first half of the 1900s.

The illustration at right, from an early postcard titled "Seining on Puget Sound, Washington," depicts boats and methods that seem rather primitive by the standards of today. The date of the postcard is unknown, but judging by the size and type of boats being used, the attire worn by the fishermen, and the handling of the skiff and net entirely by hand, the postcard probably displays a scene from a time not long into the 1900s before World War I.

Seining on Puget Sound, n.d. (Courtesy of Anna J. Knutsen)

The floats depicted in this illustration are cork discs, having a hole in the center through which the cork line is passed. These corks were usually about five inches in diameter and two inches thick. Even after cork floats were replaced with cylindrical or ellipsoidal-shaped cedar or plastic floats, the float line was still frequently referred to as the "cork line." The hollow glass balls that would occasionally wash up on the beaches in the Pacific Northwest were net floats that had broken away from Japanese fishing nets but were not a type in use by American fishermen.

In those days, many of the boats that fished in Puget Sound were small and similar to those in the picture. The net boat appears to have only modest shelter, and therefore, the crew would not have ventured very far from home in seeking the fish. The rowing skiff at lower right was used to assist in the handling of the net.

In the first half of the 20th century, there was a huge demand for boats capable of seeking and collecting the sea life that was, and to a lesser extent still is, so abundant in the waters of the Pacific Northwest and Alaska. The yards on the shores of Puget Sound were busy supplying the boats that could take on the job of catching fish.

Boatbuilders such as Birchfield Boiler Works, Jones-Goodell, Kazulin-Cole, J. M. Martinac Shipbuilding, Martinolich Shipyard, Peterson Boat Building, Puget Sound Boat Building, Tacoma Boat, and Western Boat Building Company at Tacoma; the Skansie brothers at Gig Harbor; Ballard Marine Railway, Norm Blanchard, Bryant's Marina, Commercial Marine Construction, Vic Franck, Grandy Boat Company, Hansen Boat Building, Hydraulic Supply, Jacobsen Boat Company, Monson Boat Company, Olson and Sunde, Frank Prothero, Sagstad Shipyard, and Tregoning Boat Works at Seattle; Fletcher Bay Boat Works at Bainbridge Island; Fishermen's Boat Shop and Everett Marine Ways at Everett; Wheeler Shipbuilding at Anacortes; Bellingham Shipyard and Wrang Shipyard at Bellingham; and Jenson and Sons at Friday Harbor were all builders of boats for service in the fisheries.

Boats were also home-built by fishermen for their own use. Most of the vessels of the time were built of wood, although some were fabricated from steel and aluminum. Fiberglass had not yet found much use in commercial boat building.

Everett Marine Ways, 1929. (With permission of Everett Public Library, Northwest Room)

The photo above, taken by Juleen and looking from the water side up the hill toward the city, is a view of Everett Marine Ways located at the foot of Hewitt Avenue near American Tug Boat Company in Everett. As will be noticed in the photo, much of the area behind the shipyard was a residential neighborhood of single-family homes and apartments. In this picture, the painted letters on the end of the building at right in the photo, just above the seiner *Glacier*, spell out "MACHINISTS—SHIP CARPENTERS—CAULKERS."

Hauled out, as shown in this photo, side by side at extreme left were the purse-seiners *Congress*, *Marysville*, and *Sunset*, left to right. Just left of center, *Pardner* was cradled on a railway. Right of center, *Giant II*, a cargo carrier, was on another marine railway. At extreme right, *Tatoosh* and *Glacier*, both purse-seiners, were on the blocks. At center in the background, a new hull can be seen under construction. Just beyond this new hull, the lettering on the end of the building identifies it as being home to the Harbor Saloon.

All of these boats hauled out in the yard for maintenance were of wooden construction, and most were of early vintage, having been built in yards at Gig Harbor, Tacoma, and Seattle around the time of World War I or before. On the other hand, the seiner *Glacier*, at the extreme right in the photo, was built at Gig Harbor in 1927 and was, therefore, nearly new at the time of the photo. The seiners on the blocks in this photo ranged in length from 46 feet to 59 feet. The 65-foot *Giant II*, powered with a 75-horsepower Kahlenberg engine, was built as an explosives freighter at Seattle in 1912 for Giant Powder Company.

Propulsion power installed in the fish boats was not a lot by today's standards, frequently 50 horsepower or less. At the time many of these work boats were built, diesel engines had not yet found their way into use so most were powered by gasoline engines or semi-diesel engines. These engines were slow speed and built for heavy service and, in the horsepower range noted here, would likely have had less than four cylinders.

278

The photo by Juleen shown below was taken on the same day as the picture on the previous page and is a different view of Everett Marine Ways, looking from a location at the upper part of the ways toward the water. The powder freighter *Giant II* is at left in the picture, and three of the seiners can be seen at right. The nearest of the three seiners, *Sunset*, is also pictured on the next page while afloat and out on the job. The double-ended boat *Pardner* is just to right of center, and it appears that this vessel may have been in the process of receiving a new deckhouse at the time of the photo. The chain hoist mounted on stout framing just abaft *Pardner's* deckhouse indicates that some heavy lifting was being done, perhaps the removal and replacement of the engine.

The new boat under construction that was in the background of the photo on the previous page is in the foreground in this view. The hull fram-ing appears to be complete, half of the deck beams have been laid in, and planking of the hull has begun. When planking a hull, the last strakes to be attached to the frames are usually some of those intended for the bottom. Delaying the installation of a few bottom planks leaves an opening for sweeping wood shavings and dust out of the hull. The husky stem and closely spaced sawn frames bespeak a hull that would likely have been intended for application in commercial work.

The shipyards were busy in those days, and in the area of the yard that is included in this photo, there are 13 workers in view. These were people skilled in the art of wooden shipbuilding. A variety of hand tools can be seen in the photo, but the only indication that a power tool might have been in use is what appears to be a discarded rotary sanding disc at the bottom of the picture to right of center.

Everett Marine Ways, 1929. (With permission of Everett Public Library, Northwest Room)

Purse seiners, 1931. (With permission of Everett Public Library)

N. KNUTSEN

Peugh.

Pictured above are photos taken by Juleen showing wooden seine boats in operation. The two upper pictures show *Empress* and *Hercules*, classic purse seiners of the day. At the lower left, the wooden seiners *Sunset*, *Limited*, and *Elector* are shown rafted with the power schooner *Dorothy* at the Fisherman's Packing Company scow.

The diesel-powered *Dorothy* was 93 feet in length and built of wood at Seattle in 1914. This power schooner had a variety of occupations in her career, including voyages as an Alaska trading vessel, as well as halibut fishing and cod fishing in the Bering Sea along with the schooners *Azalea*, *Sophie Christenson*, and *Wawona*. Eventually, *Dorothy* was modified and wound up working as a gold dredge on the coast of Oregon.

The picture at lower right shows crewmen unloading salmon from the hold of a seiner. The crewman in the seiner's hold was using a peugh to toss the fish up onto the deck of the receiving vessel, and just right of center, a salmon can be seen in midair flight on its way out of the hold and over the deck edge.

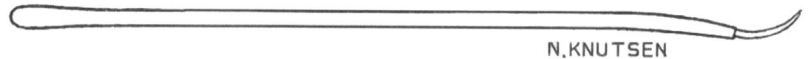

A peugh, illustrated above, has a handle about five feet long with a sharp tine on the end. The tine is inserted into the fish, and the fish is then pitched up onto the deck of the receiving vessel. The tine on the peugh produces a small hole in the fish, but with care, it can be inserted into the head to avoid damage to the edible portion, if necessary. However, a peugh is usually used for fish that are intended to be canned rather than those meant for processing into steaks and fillets. The hold can also be unloaded by "brailing," which involves filling a basket with fish and then, with the boat's rigging, hoisting and swinging it over the side to the shoreside facility or receiving vessel.

Much is learned through practice, and this is true when using a peugh. Years ago, I was a deckhand aboard a power scow at Bristol Bay, Alaska. Some of the young Aleut women, using outboard powered skiffs and gill nets, fished commercially for salmon. It was the local custom, passed along from season to season, that the deckhand aboard the power scow would climb down into the women's skiff and pitch the fish up onto the deck of the scow. The young women could certainly have done that; after all, they had arrived at the power scow with a boatload of fish, and netting those fish had taken skill, strength, and work. Because of the leverage available when using a peugh, the first fish that I pitched with the peugh went over the power scow and out into the water on the other side (though lost, the high-flying salmon was included in the women's fish tally anyway). Getting the feel of it, and backing off on the swing of the peugh quickly corrected the problem.

Power scows have provided a frequently used method for hauling fish from the catcher boats to the cannery. In addition, a power scow has the advantage of also being able to haul freight. The drawing of a power scow shown below is from a 1951 design by H. C. Hanson, and the configuration is representative of a typical power scow of the time.

The power scow depicted in this drawing, named *Tonsina*, was designed for employment in the New England Fish Company's Alaska operations. The vessel had a documentation length of 62 feet, an oveall length of 66 feet, a beam of 22 feet, and was built of steel by Hydraulic Supply Company at Seattle. Two Caterpillar diesel engines totaling 160 horsepower drove a pair of 36-inch diameter propellers. The power scow's draft was quite shallow at just over three feet.

A commonly used method for unloading fish from a power scow, and less time-consuming than brailing, consists of simply flooding the deck with water and sluicing the fish out through an opening in the side rail. Passing overboard with the water flow, the fish would drop over the side and be carried by a conveyor at the side of the pier up into the cannery. In this drawing of a power scow, at midship the small rectangle in the side rail represents the gate that could be opened for sluicing fish over the side onto a conveyor.

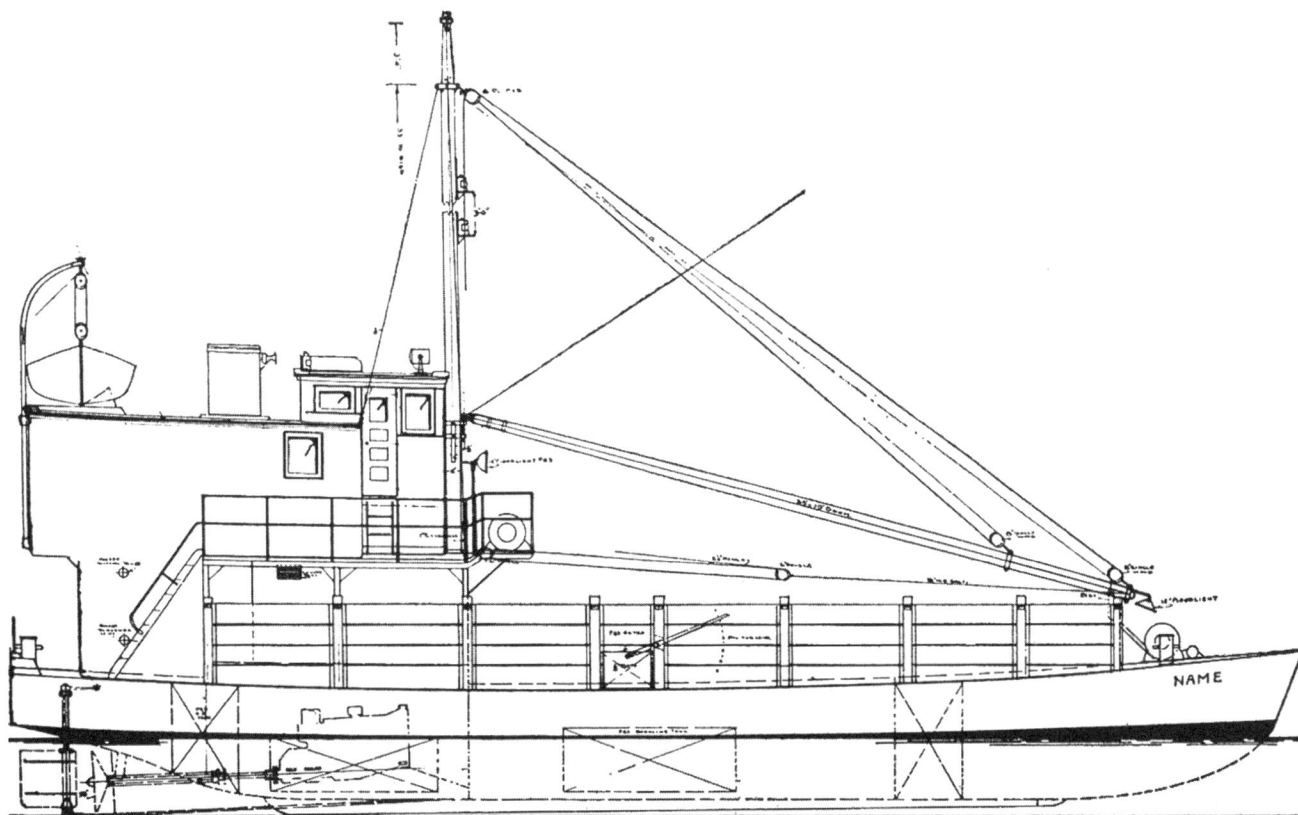

Tonsina outboard profile, 1951. (With permission of Whatcom Museum of History and Art)

Illustrations of fishing gear that follow are as depicted in *Commercial Fishing Gear of the United States*, published by the United States Department of the Interior, Fish and Wildlife Service in 1961.

Purse seines have long been used for catching a variety of fish, including menhaden on the East Coast, herring on the Pacific Coast, sardines on the Oregon and California coasts, and after supplanting the hook-and-line method of fishing, tuna in the warmer waters offshore from the Pacific Coast. The purse seine is also widely used in the Pacific Northwest and Alaska for harvesting salmon, a species also caught by use of other types of nets, as well as by hook and line.

When deploying the purse seine, or "making a set," the first step is to surround a school of fish with the net, which is hanging vertically in the water like a fence. The web may be the order of 1800 feet long by 40 feet deep. In this operation, one end of the net is attached to the power skiff, which, after casting off from the seiner, holds one end of the net in position while the seiner proceeds ahead in a circle around the fish with the seine feeding out over the stern. The line of corks, or floats, at the top edge of the net are buoyant at the surface of the water while the

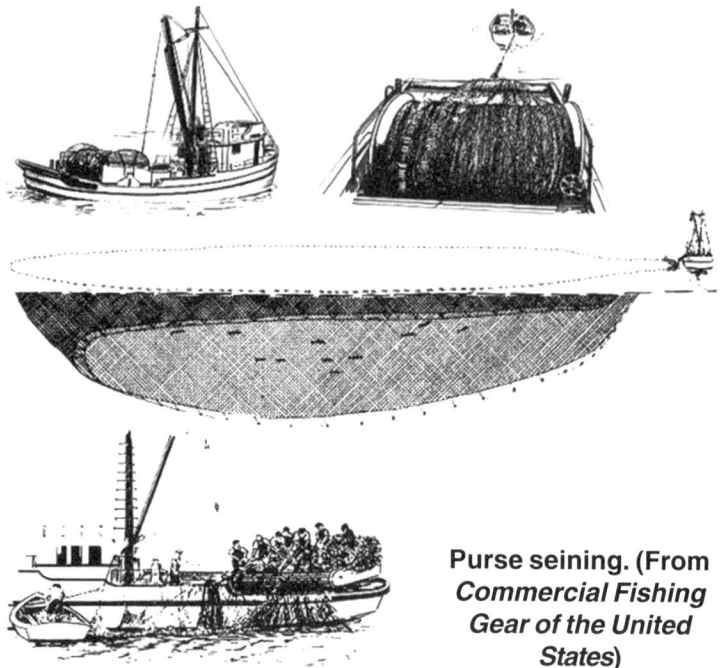

Purse seining. (From *Commercial Fishing Gear of the United States*)

weights spaced out along the line at the bottom of the net, called the lead line, cause the net to hang vertically in the water like a fence. The "purse string," which had been fed through rings along the bottom of the net, is then hauled in and closes the bottom of the net so that the fish cannot escape by sounding, and the net forms a dish shape and is said to be "pursed up."

A drum seiner, with the net spooled on the winch drum, is shown in the upper part of the illustration above. The drum seiner deploys the net and also retrieves the net over the stern.

Traditionally, boats have utilized a turntable at the stern for stowing the net as shown in the lower portion of the drawing at the top of the page and in photos that follow. The turntable has a powered roller at the outboard edge, and the table can be rotated. When making a set, the net is fed out over the stern, and when hauling the net, the table is turned so that the roller is at the side of the hull, as shown in the drawing.

For many years, retrieval of the net required several crewmen to pull the net in by hand, as shown in the illustration at the top of the page. In the 1950s, however, a fisherman by the name of Mario Puretic patented a device known as a powered block, shown in operation at left and manufactured by Marine Construction and Design Company in Seattle. The powered block reduced the amount of labor involved in net retrieval.

Purse seine Power Block. (From *Commercial Fishing Gear of the United States*)

The powered block is essentially a large hydraulically powered pulley attached to the end of the boom. The net is fed up and over the sheave, and the free portion of the net drops straight down to the deck. The wrap of the net over the sheave of nearly 180 degrees provides purchase sufficient that the net can be hauled in entirely by the powered rotating sheave, thus eliminating most of the manual labor that had previously been involved in net retrieval.

Purse seiners at Gig Harbor, 1948. (From the author's collection)

Further hauling on the purse string, while as much of the net is hauled in aboard the seiner as possible, causes the dish shape of the net to become smaller until it virtually becomes a bag. In a good haul, several thousand salmon may be in the net. The salmon can then be removed from the net, which is still in the water, and transferred into the seiner's hold by brailing.

A fishing method known as "round-hauling" is used by small boats. When round-hauling, one end of the net is anchored and the boat sets the net by pulling on the free end and returning to the anchored end, thus encircling the fish. The round-haul net is similar to but smaller than the seine used by the larger purse-seiners.

Some of the fish boats worked in various areas of Puget Sound and the San Juan Islands, thus remaining in local waters year-round. Many other boats fished at more distant locations off the Pacific Northwest coast, Alaska, or elsewhere but, in the off-season, maintained a home base in the quiet of Puget Sound harbors.

A group of purse seiners at rest between fishing seasons is pictured above, a few of the numerous fish boats that typically lay at anchor in the protected inlet of Gig Harbor while awaiting the next year's fishing. A quiet time between seasons provides a period for repairing and maintaining the boats, engine room, deck machinery, rigging, and nets.

In the photo at left, the 59-foot wooden seiner *Fort Bragg*, built at Los Angeles, California, in 1919, was headed west while negotiating the swift, swirling currents of water in narrow Deception Pass.

Purse seiner *Fort Bragg* outward bound through Deception Pass, 1949.
(From the author's collection)

Purse seiner *Western Maid* north bound in Swinomish Slough, circa 1950. (From the author's collection)

In the picture above, *Western Maid*, with a documentation length of 70 feet, was a wooden purse seiner built at Tacoma in 1934. In the photo, *Western Maid* was heading north through Swinomish Slough at La Conner.

The seine, not on board at the time of the photo, would be stowed on the turntable at the stern and deployed and retrieved over the roller when fishing. The turntable could be rotated to place the roller in line with the net as it is paid out and hauled back in. The power skiff, as pictured in the photo, was lashed down on the turntable in the normal carrying location and could be lifted and handled over the side by the boom. The skiff would have been lashed down on top of the net if the net had been stowed on the turntable. At the time of the photo, a powered block would probably have been hanging from *Western Maid*'s boom, but the device was not in existence yet. As a result, after making a set, the net would have been retrieved by hand, the old-fashioned way.

Western Maid was fairly large as purse seiners go. The purse seiners that fish for salmon are generally around 50 feet or longer in length, but smaller seiners are also in use. For example, beach seiners, which fish very close to shore as the name implies, are sometimes no more than 40 feet in length. A beach seiner requires a very shallow draft and, usually, a tunnel stern for working in the shallow water next to the beach.

On the following pages is a fine looking 1935 design for a seiner by Naval Architect H. C. Hanson. This seiner, of 56-feet overall length and 15-feet beam, was smaller than the boat pictured above, but the arrangements were essentially similar. In fact, a stretched-out version of the seiner shown in these design drawings would bear a close resemblance to *Western Maid*.

The earlier seiners featured a pipe rail at the flying bridge, as in these design drawings, and frequently canvas was attached to the rail to form a barrier against spray driving over the bow when heading into a heavy chop. In the first decade or two of the 1900s, many seiners did not have a flying bridge but, instead, featured an outside steering wheel installed at the forward end of the pilothouse at the main deck level, in addition to the wheel inside the pilothouse. This outside wheel was attached to the same shaft as the inside wheel, the shaft penetrating the forward end of the pilothouse. *Western Maid*'s flying bridge dodger was probably made of plywood and, likely, a later addition. The wind screen at the forward end of the dodger was usually made of glass or plexiglass.

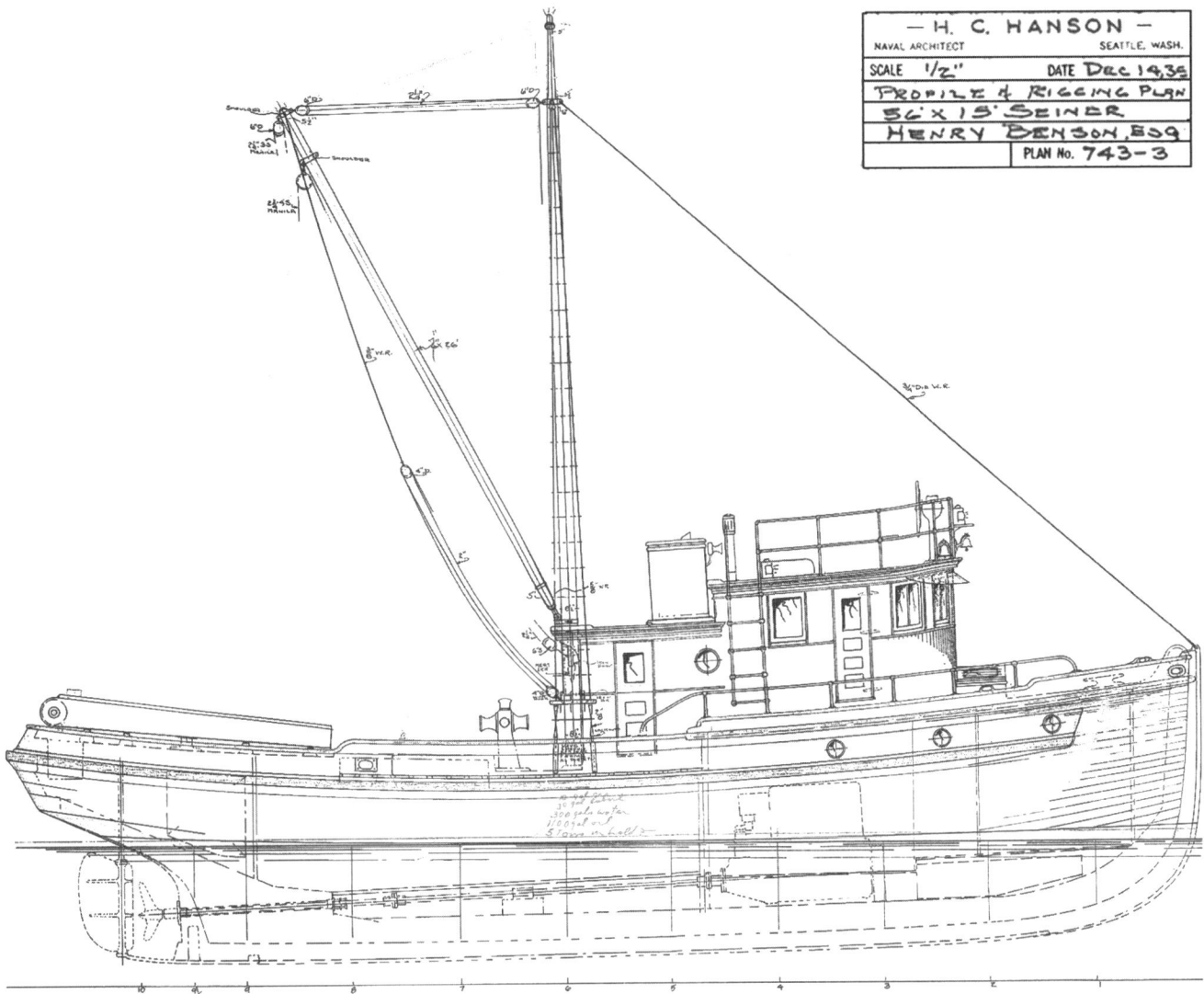

Seiner outboard profile, 1935.
(With permission of Whatcom Museum of History and Art, H. C. Hanson Collection design 743)

The outboard profile for the 1935 seiner designed by Harold Hanson is shown above. On the side of the hull, five lines of handwritten notes read "10 gal gas, 30 gal lub oil, 300 gal water, 1100 gal oil, 5 tons in hold." At another location on the original drawing of the outboard profile is another handwritten note, not shown here, that reads "engine wt 11,000 lb." These values are needed to predict the weight of the boat. The hull lines are then laid out so that the amount of buoyancy matches the weight.

The drawing on the next page illustrates the interior layout and structural arrangements for the 1935 Hanson seiner design. The fish hold occupies most of the hull length from just forward of midship and on aft, leaving the forward portion of the hull for crew accommodations and engine room, the usual arrangement aboard a seiner. The living spaces are not large but are adequate for extended periods. A stateroom, galley, and head are located at the main deck level, and eight berths are provided below in the fo'c'sle. Both the galley and head are accessed from outside on deck.

The engine room is forward of the hold, and because a long shaft is needed to connect to the propeller, an intermediate shaft bearing, located about halfway between the engine and the stern bearing, is indicated on the drawings. This intermediate bearing is needed to prevent shaft whipping. If supports for a rotating shaft are too far apart, severe vibration, or whipping, could be induced in the shaft. This vibration would eventually cause the shaft to break, and other mechanical components could fail as a result.

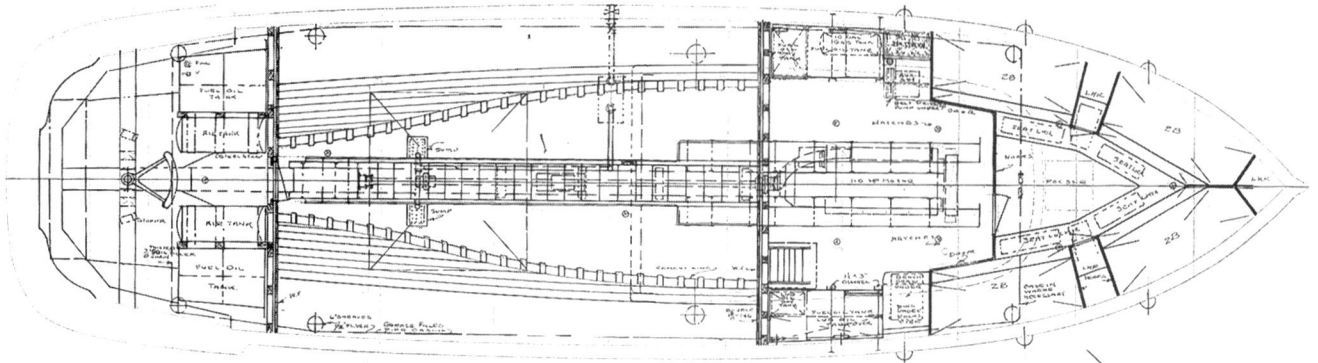

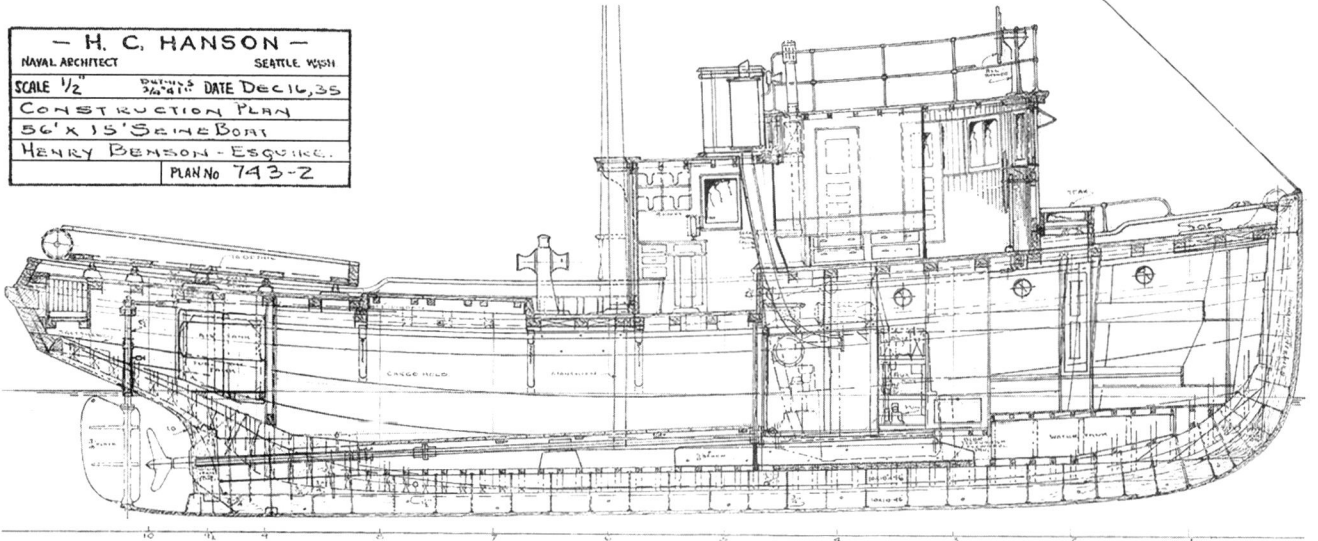

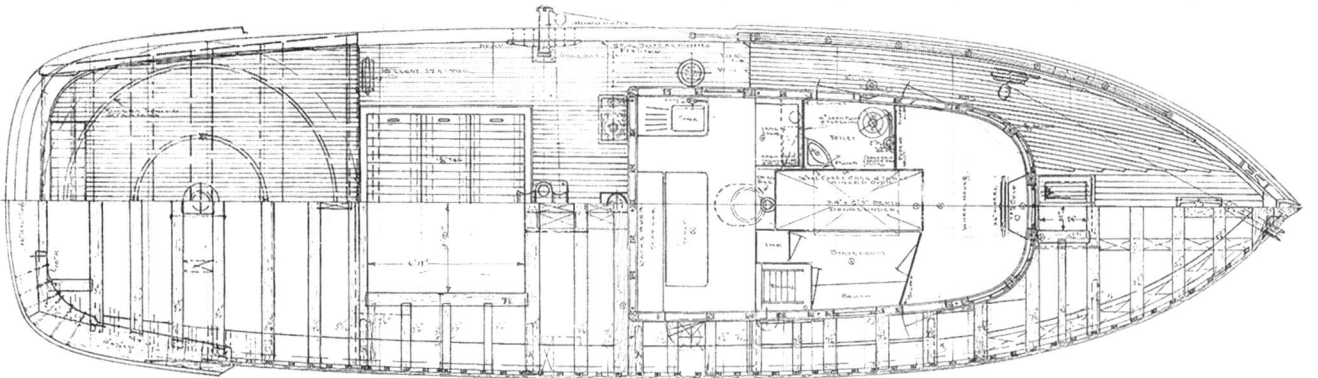

Seiner inboard profile, arrangements and construction, 1935.
(With permission of Whatcom Museum of History and Art, H. C. Hanson Collection design 743)

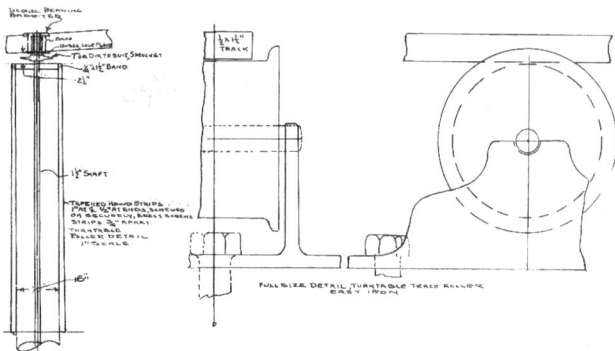

Seiner turntable net roller and track roller detail.
(From drawing above)

At left are details of the track rollers, mounted on the deck, that support the turntable and the net roller, over which the net is set and retrieved, attached to the aft end of the turntable. Two steel tracks are fastened to the underside of the turntable in concentric circular patterns as shown in the drawing above. The track rollers are mounted on the deck and spaced at 5-foot intervals around two concentric circles in line with the circular tracks on the underside of the turntable. The turntable can then be rotated about its center pivot.

The seiner's scantlings are shown in this Hanson section drawing. The transverse frames are of steam-bent white oak. These frames extend up through the deck and are planked, a frequently used method to form bulwarks. Another method for assembling bulwarks is the use of solid wood cut to shape, in which case the hull frames rise only to the underside of the deck. Hull planks are fairly heavy but not quite as thick as used in a typical tug. The hull planks above the waterline are not as wide as those below the waterline. The planks above the water experience alternating wet and dry conditions, and therefore, width is limited, as is done with a wooden planked deck, to prevent opening of hull seams due to swelling and shrinkage of the planks.

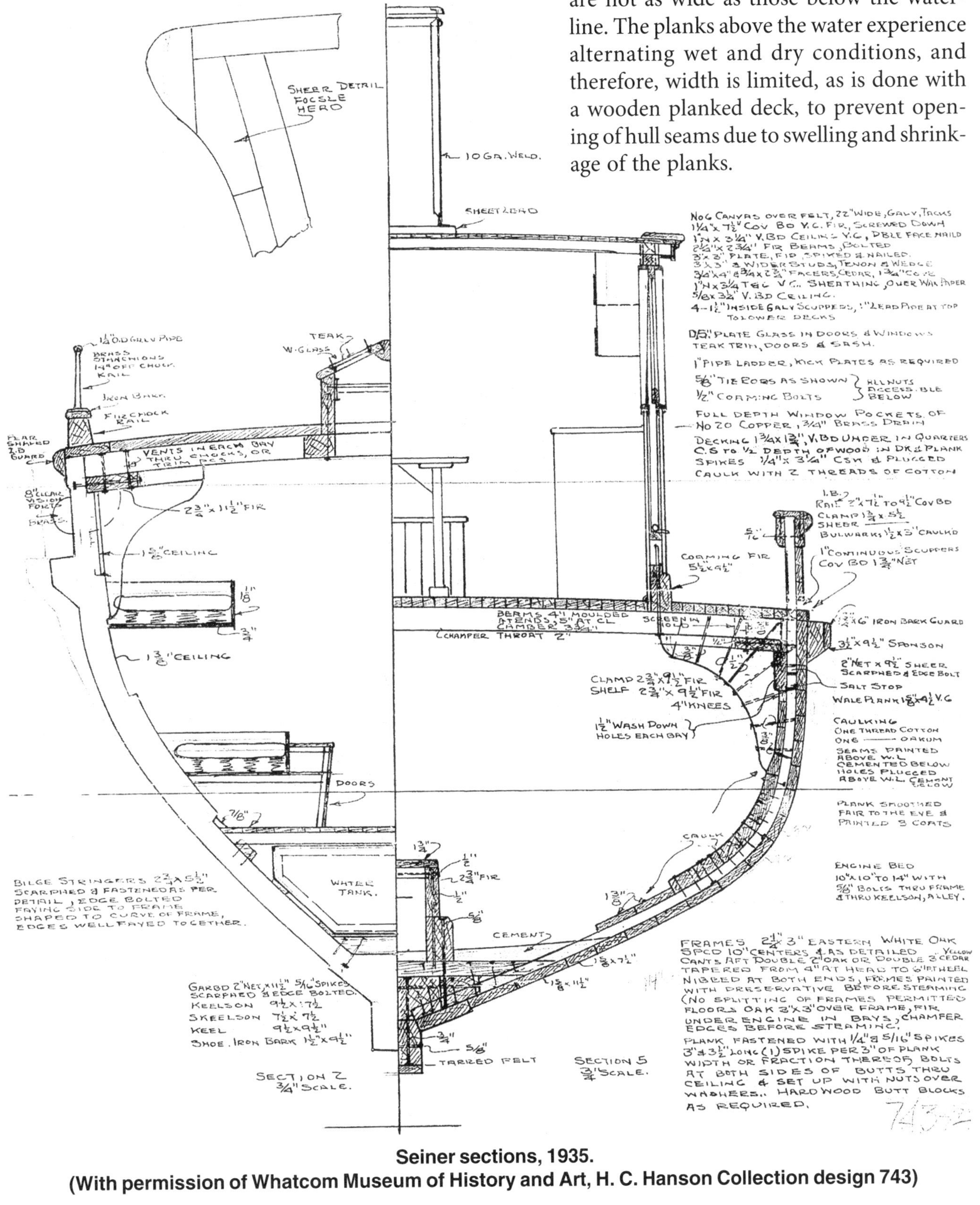

SHEER DETAIL
FOCSLE HEAD

10 GA. WELD.

SHEET LEAD

No 6 CANVAS OVER FELT, 22" WIDE, GALV. TACKS
1¼" x 7½" COV BD V.C. FIR, SCREWED DOWN
1" x 3¾" V. BD CEILING V.C., D'BLE FACE NAIL
2¼" x 2¾" FIR BEAMS, BOLTED
3" x 3" PLATE, FIR, SPIKED & NAILED.
3" x 3" 8 WIDER STUDS, TENON & WEDGE
3/8" x 4" & ¾" x 2¾" FACERS, CEDAR, 1¾" COVE
1" x 3¾" T&G V.C. SHEATHING OVER WALL PAPER
5/8 x 3½" V. BD CEILING.
4-1½" INSIDE GALV SCUPPERS, 1" LEAD PIPE AT TOP
TO LOWER DECKS

D/5" PLATE GLASS IN DOORS & WINDOWS
TEAK TRIM, DOORS & SASH.

1" PIPE LADDER, KICK PLATES AS REQUIRED

5/8" TIE RODS AS SHOWN   ALL NUTS
½" COAMING BOLTS   ACCESSIBLE BELOW

FULL DEPTH WINDOW POCKETS OF
No 20 COPPER, ¾" BRASS DRAIN

DECKING 1¾ x 1¾", V. BD UNDER IN QUARTERS
C.S. TO ½ DEPTH OF WOOD IN DK & PLANK
SPIKES ¼" x 3½" CSM & PLUGGED
CAULK WITH 2 THREADS OF COTTON

1.B.
RAIL 2¾" x 7½ TO 9½" COV BD
CLAMP 1¾ x 5½
SHEER
BULWARKS 1½" x 3" CAULKD
1" CONTINUOUS SCUPPERS
COV BD 1¾" NET

COAMING FIR
5½" x 9½"

2" x 6" IRON BACK GUARD
3½" x 9½" SPONSON
2" NET x 9½" SHEER
SCARPHED & EDGE BOLT
SALT STOP
WALE PLANK 1⅝ x 4½ V.G.

CAULKING
ONE THREAD COTTON
ONE ──── OAKUM
SEAMS PAINTED
ABOVE W.L.
CEMENTED BELOW
HOLES PLUGGED
ABOVE W.L. CEMENT
BELOW

PLANK SMOOTHED
FAIR TO THE EYE &
PAINTED 3 COATS

ENGINE BED
10" x 10" TO 14" WITH
5/8" BOLTS THRU FRAME
& THRU KEELSON, ALLEY.

FRAMES 2¼" & 3" EASTERN WHITE OAK
SP'C'D 10" CENTERS & AS DETAILED   Yellow
CANTS AFT DOUBLE 2" OAK OR DOUBLE 3" CEDAR
TAPERED FROM 4" AT HEAD TO 6" AT HEEL
NIBBED AT BOTH ENDS, FRAMES PAINTED
WITH PRESERVATIVE BEFORE STEAMING
(NO SPLITTING OF FRAMES PERMITTED)
FLOORS OAK 3" x 3" OVER FRAME, FIR
UNDER ENGINE IN BAYS, CHAMFER
EDGES BEFORE STEAMING.
PLANK FASTENED WITH ¼" & 5/16" SPIKES
3" & 3½" LONG (1) SPIKE PER 3" OF PLANK
WIDTH OR FRACTION THEREOF, BOLTS
AT BOTH SIDES OF BUTTS THRU
CEILING & SET UP WITH NUTS OVER
WASHERS. HARDWOOD BUTT BLOCKS
AS REQUIRED.

1¼" O.D. GALV PIPE
BRASS
STANCHIONS
14" OFF CHUCK
RAIL
IRON BKR.
FIRE CHOCK RAIL

FLARE
SHAPED
1.B.
GUARD

VENTS IN EACH BAY
THRU CHOCKS, OR
TRIM PCS

8" CLEAR
VISION
FOC'L
BRASS

2¾" x 1½" FIR

1⅝" CEILING

1⅛"

1⅜" CEILING

TEAK
W. GLASS

CLAMP 2¾ x 7½ FIR
SHELF 2¾" x 9½" FIR
4" KNEES

1½" WASH DOWN
HOLES EACH BAY

BEAMS 4½" MOULDED
& ENDS 5" AT CL
CHAMBER 3¾"
CHAMFER THROAT 2"

SCREEN MOLD

DOORS

BILGE STRINGERS 2¾ x 5½"
SCARPHED & FASTENED AS PER
DETAIL, EDGE BOLTED
FAYING SIDE TO FRAME
SHAPED TO CURVE OF FRAME,
EDGES WELL FAYED TOGETHER.

WATER
TANK.

7/8"

¾"

2¾" FIR

1"

GARBD 2" NET x 11½" 5/16 SPIKES
SCARPHED & EDGE BOLTED
KEELSON 9½" x 17½"
SKEELSON 7½" x 7½"
KEEL 9½" x 9½"
SHOE. IRON BARK 1½" x 9½"

CEMENT

TARRED FELT

SECTION 2
¾" Scale.

SECTION 5
¾" Scale.

Seiner sections, 1935.
(With permission of Whatcom Museum of History and Art, H. C. Hanson Collection design 743)

287

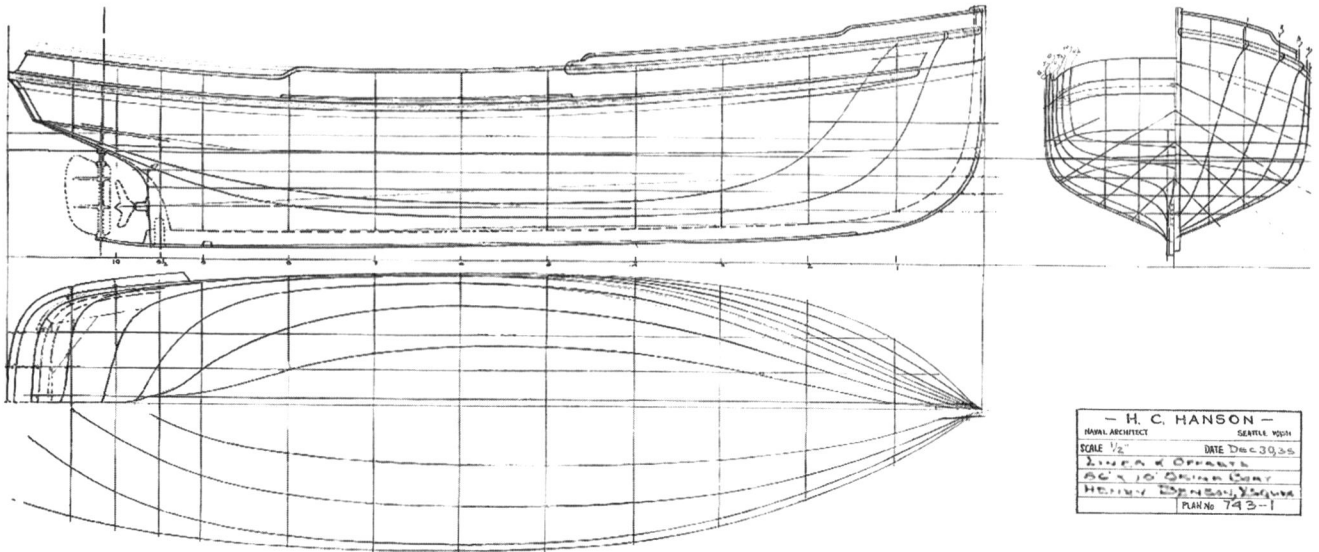

Seiner lines, 1935.
(With permission of Whatcom Museum of History and Art, H. C. Hanson Collection design 743)

The lines drawing for the seiner as designed by Harold Hanson is illustrated above. The boat was given a sweeping sheer, and the underwater body features a generous amount of deadrise. The lines drawing, as well as drawings on the previous pages, indicate a lot of freeboard, but as shown, the seiner is only in a moderately loaded condition. The stern of a purse seiner is necessarily quite broad to accommodate the turntable.

The drawing on the next page shows a purse seiner design by Walter C. Howell, naval architect. Built of wood by Wrang Shipyard Company at Bellingham in 1950, the seiner had an overall length of 52 feet 8 inches, a beam of 15 feet 6 inches, and a draft aft as designed of 6 feet 4 inches. The draft of a commercial fishing boat will vary significantly depending upon the load being carried, however, and seiners have sometimes arrived with a load of fish heavy enough to nearly put the aft deck awash.

The engine specified for the Hanson seiner was 110 horsepower. The Howell-designed seiner shown on the next page, built 15 years after the Hanson boat, was powered by a 165-horsepower General Motors diesel engine and achieved a speed of just under 10 knots when moderately loaded. An increase in engine power over the years was typical of boats of all types. In the first ten or twenty years of the last century, a fish boat of this size might have had no more than 50 horsepower in the engine room. Hull frames on 10-inch cen-

ters were white oak, and the planking was 1 5/8-inch thick Douglas fir. These scantlings were similar to those of the Hanson seiner. Tanks were provided for carrying 870 gallons of diesel oil and 400 gallons of fresh water.

The layout and crew accommodations of the Howell design were typical of Pacific Northwest purse-seiners. Besides the wheel and controls located in the pilothouse, a second control station was located above on the bridge. This flying bridge included a plywood dodger and wind deflector.

The galley and dinette were located in the deckhouse just abaft the wheelhouse, and two berths, upper and lower, were on the starboard side in the same space. Two portlights, one for each of these berths, were installed in the side of the deckhouse. Berths located in the galley area would be far from ideal, to say the least, but space aboard a fish boat was limited. The head was accessed from outside on deck, convenient to the open working space aft, but in any case, the interior area was sufficiently limited that space for inside access to the head could not be afforded.

Below, in the fo'c'sle, six berths were provided. As was done in the seiner design shown on this and previous pages, the fo'c'sle was separated from the engine room by a bulkhead, a luxury when compared with the situation aboard some of the earlier boats that had sleeping quarters below deck in common with the engine space, with no partition of any kind.

Walt Howell's design for a purse seiner, shown below, is essentially similar to seiners built years before but is more modern in appearance. Though space is limited, the accommodations provide sufficient comfort for time spent at sea.

Walt, now deceased, and I had some things in common. Although beauty is not a requirement for a vessel that has to make a living, Walt, as do I, had an appreciation for a good-looking, heavily built, sea-going boat. The drawing below demonstrates Walt's gift for creating an attractive and able boat capable of doing some hard work. Sea-going fish boats are not fast, but toward the other end of the speed spectrum, Walt and I, as owners of E-type Jaguars in the earlier days, also had an appreciation for high performance cars.

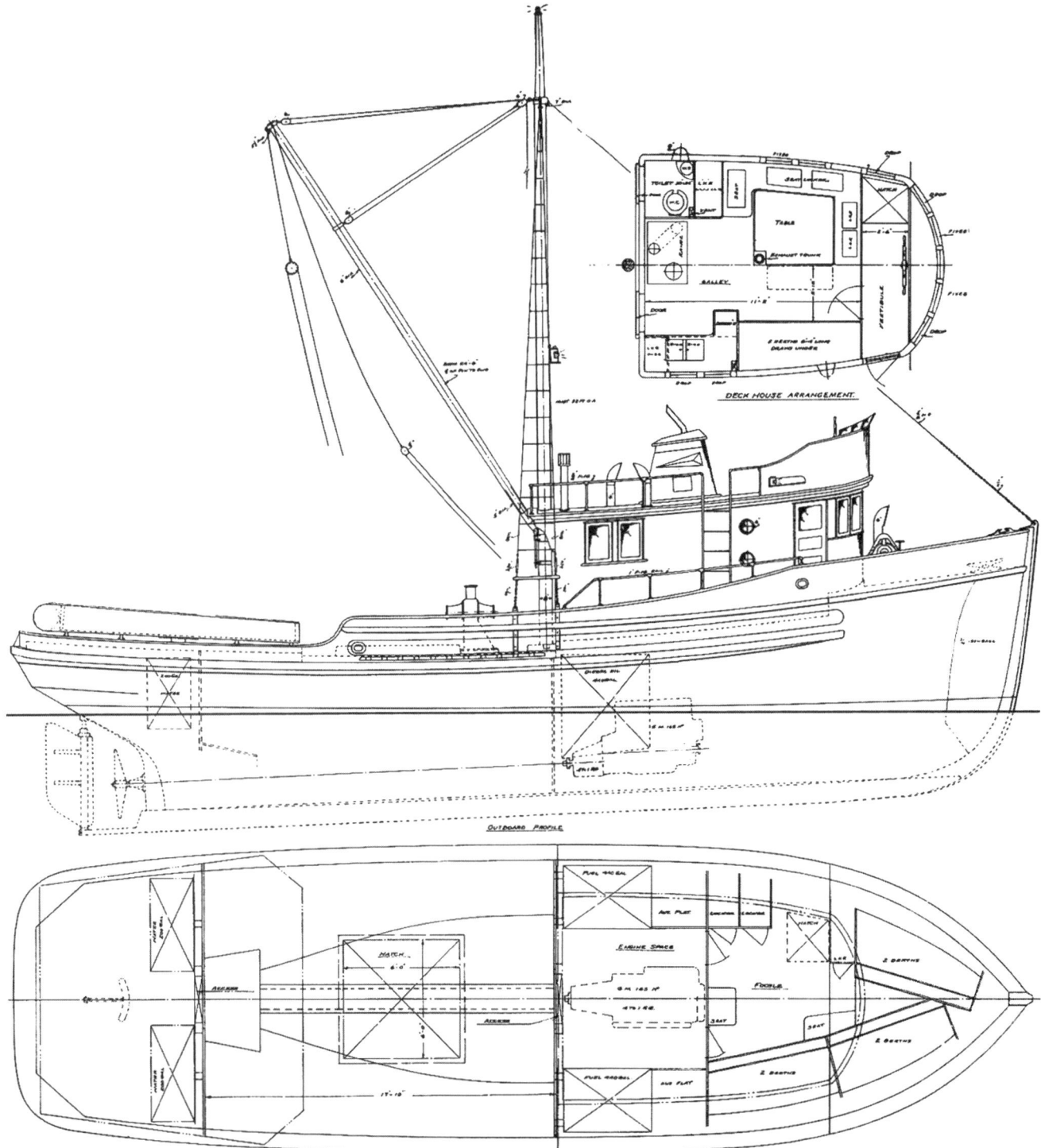

Seiner outboard profile and arrangements, 1950. (From *Pacific Motor Boat*, January 1950)

289

Another type of net fishing, quite different from purse seining, involves the use of what is known as a gill net. The boats that utilize the gill-net method of fishing are usually not large, and three of them are shown in this photo.

The gill-netters in the photo are "stern pickers," as distinct from "bow pickers" that handle the net over the bow. The boats as shown were using powered drums that could be rotated to set and retrieve the net over the stern, as well as to stow the net. Many small boats are not equipped with powered equipment, and the net is set and retrieved manually over a roller. A net may be "picked" by lifting a section of webbing from the water and removing a trapped fish, or it may be picked as the net is pulled in.

The illustration below shows the arrangement of a gill net after being set. The net depicted here is a drift net, that is, it floats freely and moves with the current. If the ends were anchored to the bottom, it would be known as a "set gill net." A gill net is deployed to hang in the water from

Gillnetters in the Ballard Locks, 1964. (From the author's collection)

the buoyancy of the cork line at the top edge while weighted down by the lead line at the bottom edge. The gill net's mesh size is matched to the size of the species being pursued so that a fish, swimming into the net, can only penetrate through the net as far as the back part of the fish's head, where the gills are located, because the larger middle section of the fish prevents further travel. On the other hand, the fish cannot back out because the gills become caught in the web. Fishing at night or in muddy water can be productive for fishermen since the fish are prevented by the low visibility from detecting the gill net.

A gill net is hundreds of feet long and perhaps 12 feet deep, the precise dimensions dependent upon the laws that regulate commercial fishing in a particular area. The mesh size, to suit the species sought and also to comply with the law, is checked by pulling taut two diagonally opposite corners of an opening and measuring the distance between the knots, a method known as "stretch measure." For example, if the web opening were square with a stretch measure of 5 1/2 inches, this opening would be 2 3/4 inches on each side.

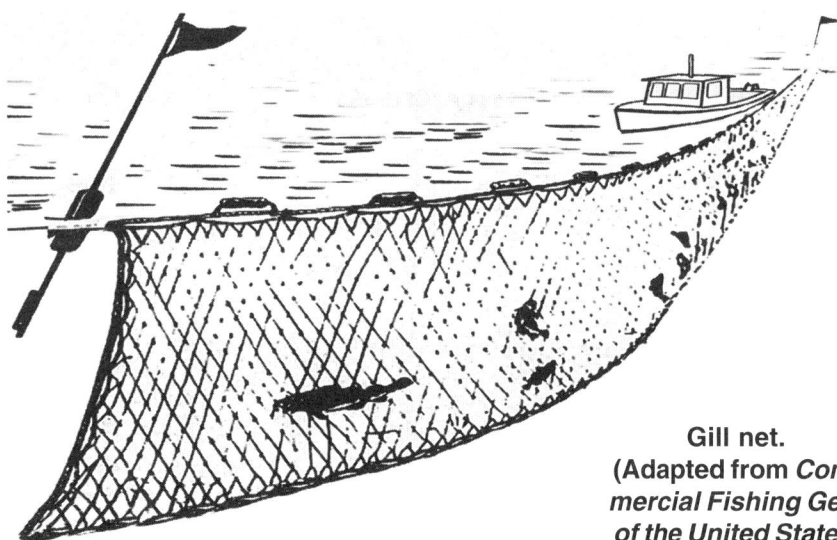

Gill net.
(Adapted from *Commercial Fishing Gear of the United States*)

290

At right, the drawing shows a salmon caught in a gill net. In the illustration, the salmon has penetrated partway through the net but is trapped by the webbing fibers caught under the fish's gill covers.

Occasionally a large fish can become entangled in a gill net that was intended for smaller fish. At Bristol Bay, Alaska, the gill net mesh was sized for sockeye, or red, salmon that were averaging 10 pounds in weight. In one instance, an Aleut boy in an outboard skiff had caught a king salmon in his net. I was aboard a power scow, and dropped a line down to the young man in the skiff so that he could pass it through the gills, and the fish was hauled up on deck. At the cannery, the king salmon weighed in at a whopping 60 pounds, fetching a premium price to boot.

The jaunty looking gill-netter illustrated below, a stern picker designed to handle the net with a power drum, was from the boards of W. H. Dole,

Salmon caught in gill net.
(From *Commercial Fishing Gear of the United States*)

naval architect. At the time the drawing was done, Heine Dole was living aboard his sailboat *Chantey* at the Olympia Yacht Club. The boat depicted in the drawing was 36 1/2 feet overall length by 10 feet beam and utilized plywood planking. A Packard eight gas engine, driving a 22-inch-by-18 inch propeller through a 2 to 1 reduction gear, gave the planing hull a top speed of around 20 knots when moderately loaded. Accommodations were designed for a crew of two.

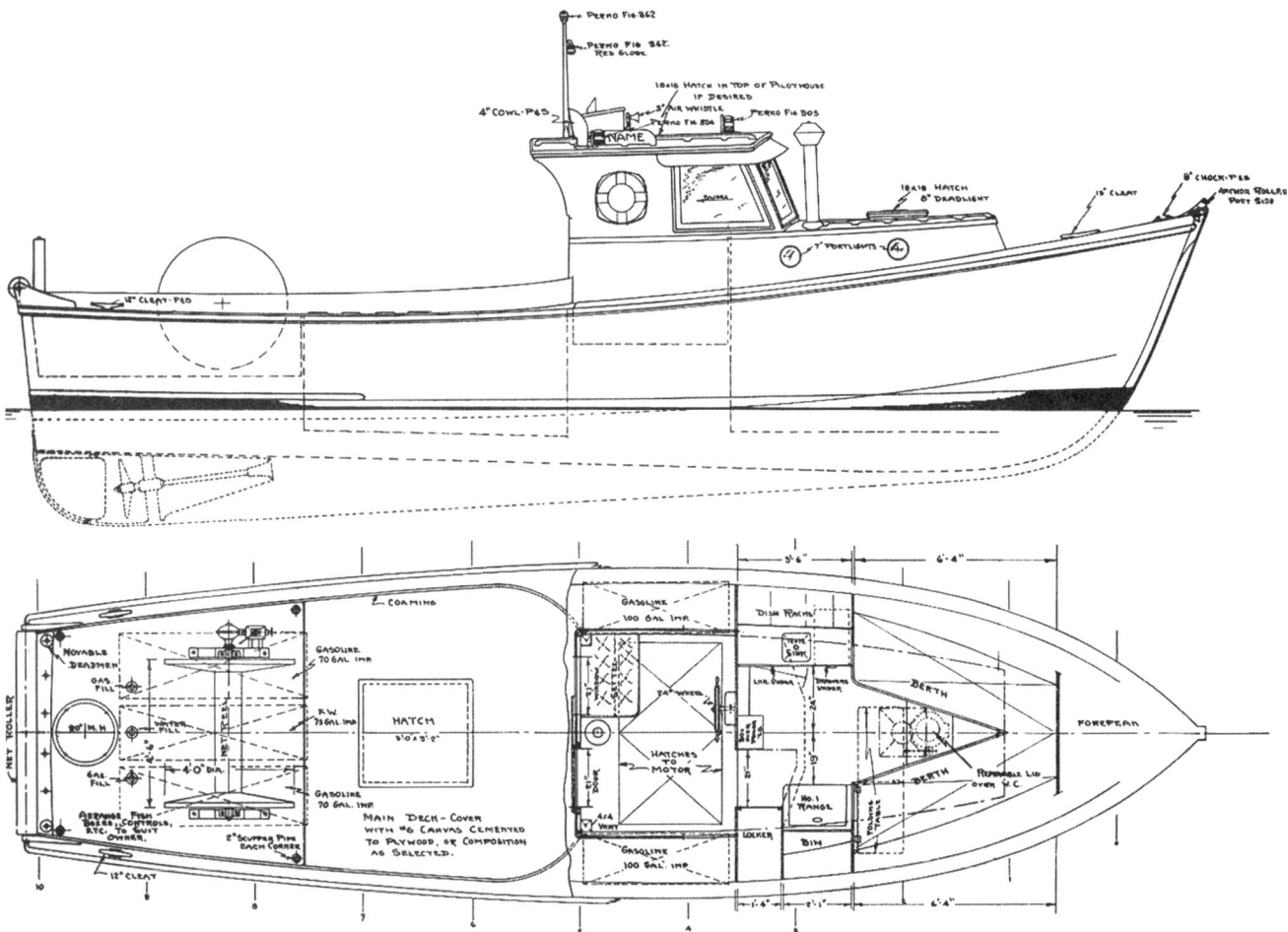

Gill-netter, 1949. (With permission of W. H. Dole)

One of the oldest methods of catching salmon in the Pacific Northwest was the "reef net" system, and this form of fishing may be unique to the Puget Sound area. The San Juan Islands were discovered and named by Spanish explorers around 1790, but Native Americans, using reef nets between the sand spits and reefs, had been fishing in those waters long before that time.

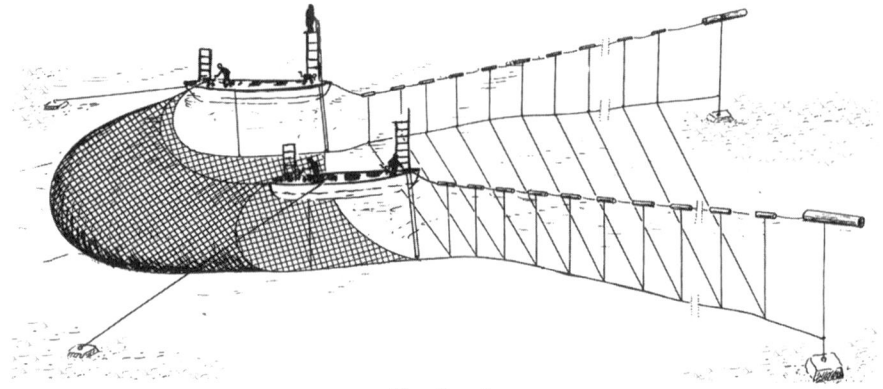

Reef net.
(From *Commercial Fishing Gear of the United States*)

Using a reef net was a tricky proposition and required much skill and experience. Originally, the Native Americans would support a horizontal mat in the water between reefs at a depth just below the top of the reefs. The salmon, swimming over a reef, would then drop over the crest of the reef and on down to a depth just above the mat. When the school was observed passing over the mat, the mat would be quickly raised out of the water, thus trapping the fish.

A more modern version of the reef net is shown above. A wedge-shaped pattern of vertical and horizontal lines is shown at right in the illustration. Fluttering strips were attached to these lines, and the fish were guided toward the netting. The rest of the operation was quite similar to the ancient method; when a school was moving over the horizontal portion of the net toward the curved bunt, the edge of the horizontal portion of the net was raised to trap the fish, just as the mat was raised in the earlier days.

The reef net was supported from two skiffs, one on each side. Fish activity at the net was observed from the height of a tower by a man in each skiff. At the proper moment, the fishermen quickly descended from the towers and raised the edge of the net to trap the fish.

The type of fixed entrapment gear pictured below, constructed of a series of pilings driven into the sea bottom along which fiber netting or chicken wire fencing is attached, was called a pound net. The long leader, extending toward shore into the distance at upper right, directed the migrating salmon toward the heart, at the middle of the picture. The heart, in turn, led the fish into the rectangular enclosure, called the pound, crib, or pocket, at lower left, which then held the trapped fish.

In the photo on the next page, *City of Olympia* is shown alongside a scow while tending a pound net. *City of Olympia* was 56 feet long and built of wood by the Keton brothers at Olympia in 1898. Initially in Alaska service, ownership of the vessel passed to Pacific American Fisheries at Fairhaven in 1900. Steam powered, the cannery tender was fitted with a 9, 18 x 14 compound engine by PAF in 1906.

Later on, *City of Olympia*, with a different deckhouse and repowered with a 180 horsepower diesel engine, was operated in towing service for many years by Bellingham Tug and Barge Company as *Dividend. Dividend* was pictured earlier in the book.

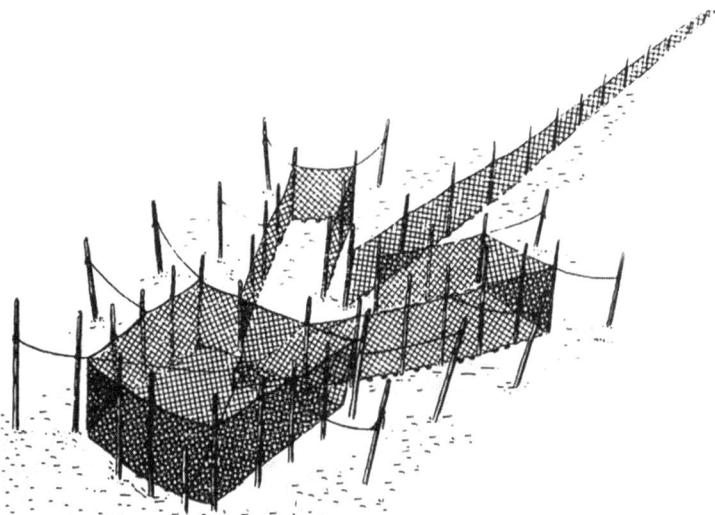

Pound net.
(From *Commercial Fishing Gear of the United States*)

City of Olympia tending a pound net before 1917. (With permission of the Anacortes Museum)

As previously mentioned in the book, usage and ownership might change several times in the life of vessels or their machinery. The compound

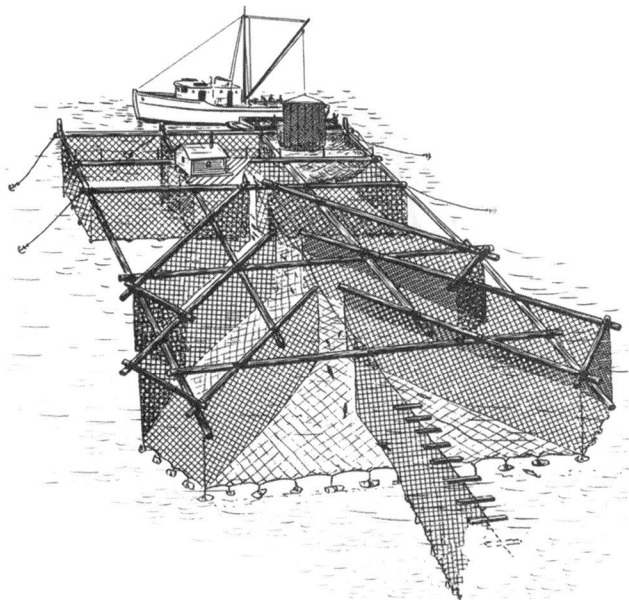

Floating salmon trap. (From
***Commercial Fishing Gear of the United States*)**

steam engine that had been installed in *City of Olympia* by Pacific American Fisheries in 1906 was removed and installed in the new PAF cannery tender *Nile* of 1917. This steam engine was later removed from *Nile* and installed in Bellingham Tug and Barge Company's tug *Dividend* (ex-*City of Olympia*). *Nile* and *Dividend*, both pictured earlier in the book, were later powered by diesel engines.

The floating fish trap was similar in operation to the pound net. In some areas of Puget Sound and Alaska, the conditions precluded the use of pilings, essential to the construction of a pound net, giving rise to the floating salmon trap. The picture at left depicts a floating salmon trap, although various versions of this arrangement were in service. Instead of pilings driven into the bottom, an anchored structure of floating logs and vertical pipes was used. Permanent fish traps, such as pound nets and floating salmon traps, were declared illegal by the state of Washington in 1937 and were outlawed by Alaska when that territory became the 49th state in 1959.

Troller off Westport, 1963. (From the author's collection)

Conditions at sea are not always calm and serene, as evidenced by the photo above showing a Pacific Northwest salmon troller, with the poles up and stowed, in heavy going. Fishing seasons are limited in length so, if at all possible, a skipper would put to sea in dirty weather and get the gear working rather than losing precious time.

Many salmon trollers were operated single handed. A friend of mine operated a troller off the Washington coast by himself, and to catch a few hours of sleep at night, he would set the auto pilot on a westerly course and head out on a slow bell into the swells, leaving the beach safely astern. In the morning, he would turn and steer back closer to shore and put his gear down again.

The drawing below illustrates the arrangement used for trolling gear. A double set of poles is shown, but a single set may also be used. The poles are stowed vertically alongside the masts when not in use and swung out to the sides when fishing. The lines are made up of stranded stainless steel, galvanized steel, or bronze wires. These lines are attached to the trolling poles with shock-absorbing springs and, with a fish on, are hauled in by means of small winches called "gurdies."

Shiny lures with a hook attached are fastened to the end of the lines with swivels and wire leaders. Lead weights, varying from 10 to 40 pounds or more in weight depending upon the desired fishing depth, are used to sink the lures below the surface of the water. The lead weights are usually spherical in shape, hence, the term frequently used for a weight is "cannonball."

Troll-caught Chinook and coho salmon are cleaned on board the boat and then kept moist. If the fish must be held for more than 24 hours, they are iced. Cleaned salmon caught by hook and line, intended for the dinner table, can command a higher price than those that may be scarred when caught in a net.

Troll gear. (From *Commercial Fishing Gear of the United States*)

This boat, designed by H. C. Hanson, was 42 feet in overall length, 11 1/2 feet in the beam, and representative of the classic Pacific Northwest wooden fishing trollers in use around 1940. A slowly moving boat having a broad stern tends to broach in a following sea, which makes course holding difficult and can be dangerous if the boat is thrown broadside to the seas; hence, many trollers were double ended, i.e., they were built with a pointed stern in a manner similar to, but more blunt than, the hull form at the bow.

The boat shown here was double ended at the waterline, but to facilitate use as a combination boat, the sides at the stern were flared out to provide sufficient width at the deck to permit also other types of fishing. The boat depicted in this design was a bit larger and had more space for accommodations than many of the Pacific Northwest trollers. A bulkhead separated the living accommodations from the engine space. Note the gaff-rigged steadying sail that could be raised if needed.

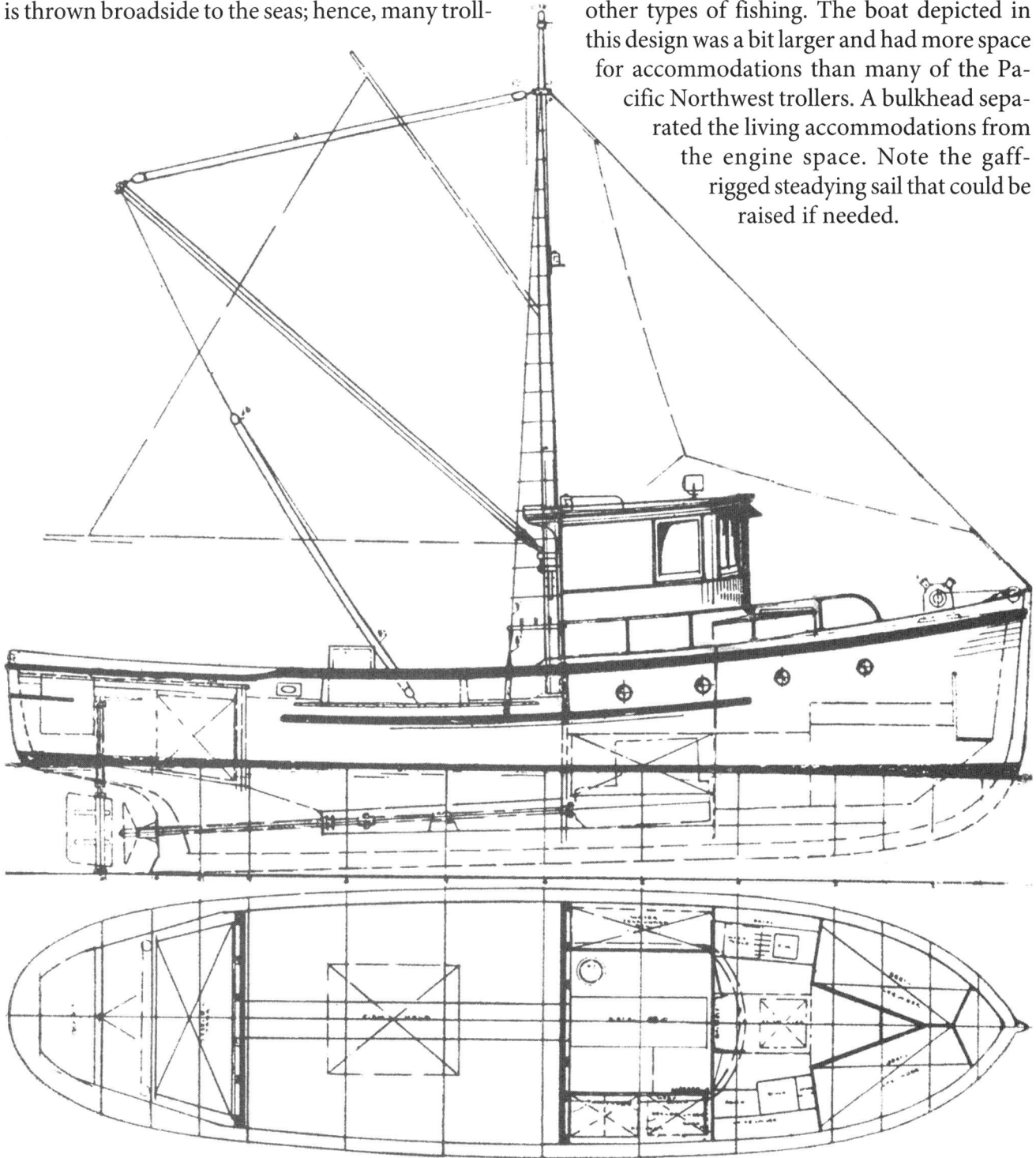

Troller outboard profile and arrangement, 1940.
(With permission of Whatcom Museum of History and Art)

At Port Madison, 1949. (From the author's collection)

As stated earlier, rather than engaging a professional yard, it was not unusual for the owner to undertake the construction of a wooden boat, who would then operate the vessel himself. In the idyllic setting on the shore of Port Madison at the north end of Bainbridge Island pictured above, a traditional double-ended wooden troller was under construction while sheltered by the roofed structure at right. Though the upper portion of the hull frames have not yet been trimmed off, the planking was nearly complete.

In those days, there were not so many mass-produced, cookie-cutter boats, and hence, most of them had unique appearances that reflected the owner's preferences, requirements of functionality, or sense of aesthetics. Behind every one of these individualized craft there was probably an interesting, but perhaps untold, story. The history of the boat hauled out on blocks at left in the picture above is not known, but it appears that the configuration of the vessel may simply have evolved in stages of construction, perhaps by the owner, over the years as was the case for the development of many boats at that time.

In addition to salmon and other species of fish, tuna have been traditionally harvested commercially by means of the hook and line, as depicted at right. In this illustration, two-man poles are being used to land the tuna, but the number of poles per man may vary from one to four. Tuna are not fished commercially in Puget Sound and, in fact, have rarely been seen in those relatively cold waters, but especially for a period of time during the middle of the 1900s, Tacoma became a center for the construction of tuna boats or, as they were sometimes called because of their stylish appearance, tuna clippers.

Tuna thrive in areas of the sea where the water temperature is 60 degrees or a bit more or less than that, depending on the particular type of tuna. The water temperature in Puget Sound is generally less than 50 degrees, much cooler than required for tuna habitat. Hence, schools of tuna are usually found in the warmer waters 60 miles off the West Coast and beyond. Commercial tuna-fishing vessels frequently range long distances out into the Pacific Ocean, as far as the Pacific Islands and Australia.

Tuna fishing with hook and line. (From *Commercial Fishing Gear of the United States*)

296

Yolande-Bertin, 1949. (With permission of Tacoma Public Library, Northwest Room)

In the photo above, the yacht-like *Yolande-Bertin*, built by Tacoma Boat Building Company in 1949, is shown on a trial run. *Yolande-Bertin* was 106 feet long and propelled by a 550-horse-power Washington diesel engine. *Yolande-Bertin* was built for hook-and-line fishing, the standard method of fishing for tuna at a time before purse seine fishing had found its way into that fishery a number of years later.

Hook-and-line tuna fishing involved the use of a combination of live bait and lures. The first step, then, was to find the bait fish and collect them. From a perch in the crow's nest high up on the mast, a crew member could watch over the sea surface and observe the air for bird behavior that would give telltale clues that indicated small fish in the area. Once found, the bait fish were encircled with a net and then brought aboard. The bait fish were kept alive in tanks, containing circulating sea water, on deck at the aft end of the boat as shown in the photo above. The boat then headed out to sea.

Like the search for bait fish, the tuna were found by observing, from the crow's nest, the water and watching for bird activity. Spotting a school of tuna, the boat moved into that area, and a crew member, known as a "chummer," threw live bait into the sea. The tuna were attracted to the live bait and became frenzied in their feeding, and once the tuna were feeding, the fish would then hit on artificial bait. Crew men with ten-foot poles then began fishing with artificial squid lures, as illustrated on the previous page.

The stern of a hook-and-line tuna boat had very low freeboard and the aft deck was awash, so the fishermen wore hip boots. When a tuna hit the lure, the leverage of the pole was used to throw the fish overhead and onto the deck, much like unloading salmon from a fish boat by use of a peugh. The hook was barbless so that the tuna could readily be shaken off of the hook, and the lure again put into the water. If the tuna ceased biting on the lure, bait fish were then placed on the hooks, and fishing could continue.

Tuna seining with the powered block. (From *Commercial Fishing Gear of the United States*)

Commercial salmon fishing methods have utilized two different techniques, either a net or a hook and line, that have been in continual use side by side for a long period of time. Net fishing for tuna, though, did not become important until the advent of the powered block method of handling a purse seine in the 1950s. Prior to that time, hook-and-line fishing was the method in use for harvesting tuna as described on the previous pages, but the powered block and purse seine largely supplanted hook and line gear.

A tuna seine net is similar to but much larger than a salmon seine net, and the two are handled in much the same way. The tuna net may be up to 2700 feet long by 300 feet deep, is very heavily made and would be extremely cumbersome, if not impossible, to handle manually. The invention of the powered block, which could manage a large net, was instrumental in furthering the feasibility of seine fishing for tuna. The illustration above demonstrates the use of the powered block in retrieving a tuna purse seine.

Besides the hook-and-line gear used when fishing for salmon and tuna, other hook-and-line methods of commercial fishing have also been used, particularly for catching bottom fish. The drawing below depicts longline gear or, as it has frequently been known on the Pacific Coast, "setline" gear. The equipment consists of a very long line, laid out on the bottom of the sea, to which is attached a series of short lines having baited hooks on the free end.

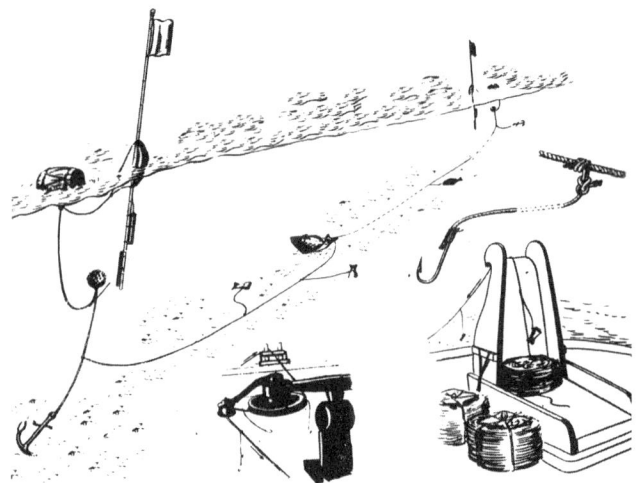

Longline or setline fishing gear. (From *Commercial Fishing Gear of the United States*)

The main portion of a longline assembly, known as a "ground line," that lies on the bottom of the sea is made up of skates, each skate being about 300 fathoms, or 1800 feet, long. The skates are connected together to form an assembly called a "string" or a "set." The short lines, or gangions, attached to the ground line every 15 feet or so are leaders to which the baited hooks are fastened.

Commercial fishing for cod and halibut as done by sailing schooners made use of a number of small boats known as "dories," similar to those that were in use on the Grand Banks. A dory was a seaworthy craft, 16 to 19 feet in overall length, with a sweeping sheer, a flat bottom, and a narrow stern having a transom called a "tombstone" because of its shape. Originally propelled by the use of oars, a time-honored method sometimes known by various names such as "Swedish steam" or "Norwegian steam," the dories were later powered by outboard or inboard motors.

At the fishing grounds, the dories, each carrying one or two fishermen outfitted with gear, were lowered into the water. The mother ship was miles away from the first dory when the last dory was set out, so a doryman led a lonely life while fishing from a small boat at sea. In addition, the doryman's boat-handling skills were sorely taxed when the wind and waves rose.

The dory fishermen were equipped with either handlines having two baited hooks on each of them or, in later years, skates of gear that would be laid out on the sea bottom. After lowering the last dory into the water, the mother ship then headed back to the location of the first dory to begin retrieval of the boats, hopefully loaded with fish by then, in the same order in which they had been released. The fish were then taken aboard, cleaned, and salted down in the hold. The amount of fish caught varied from season to season, but in good times, a schooner could return with more than 400,000 cod in the hold.

A dory is prominent in the illustration shown below. This picture is from the 1880 watercolor painting *Boys in a Dory* by Winslow Homer. The painting was done by Winslow Homer while he was residing in Gloucester, Massachusetts, in the summer of 1880. Homer's residence that summer was the lighthouse on Ten Pound Island in Gloucester Harbor. In the painting, a two-masted schooner is in view beyond the rocky point.

***Boys in a Dory* by Winslow Homer, 1880.**

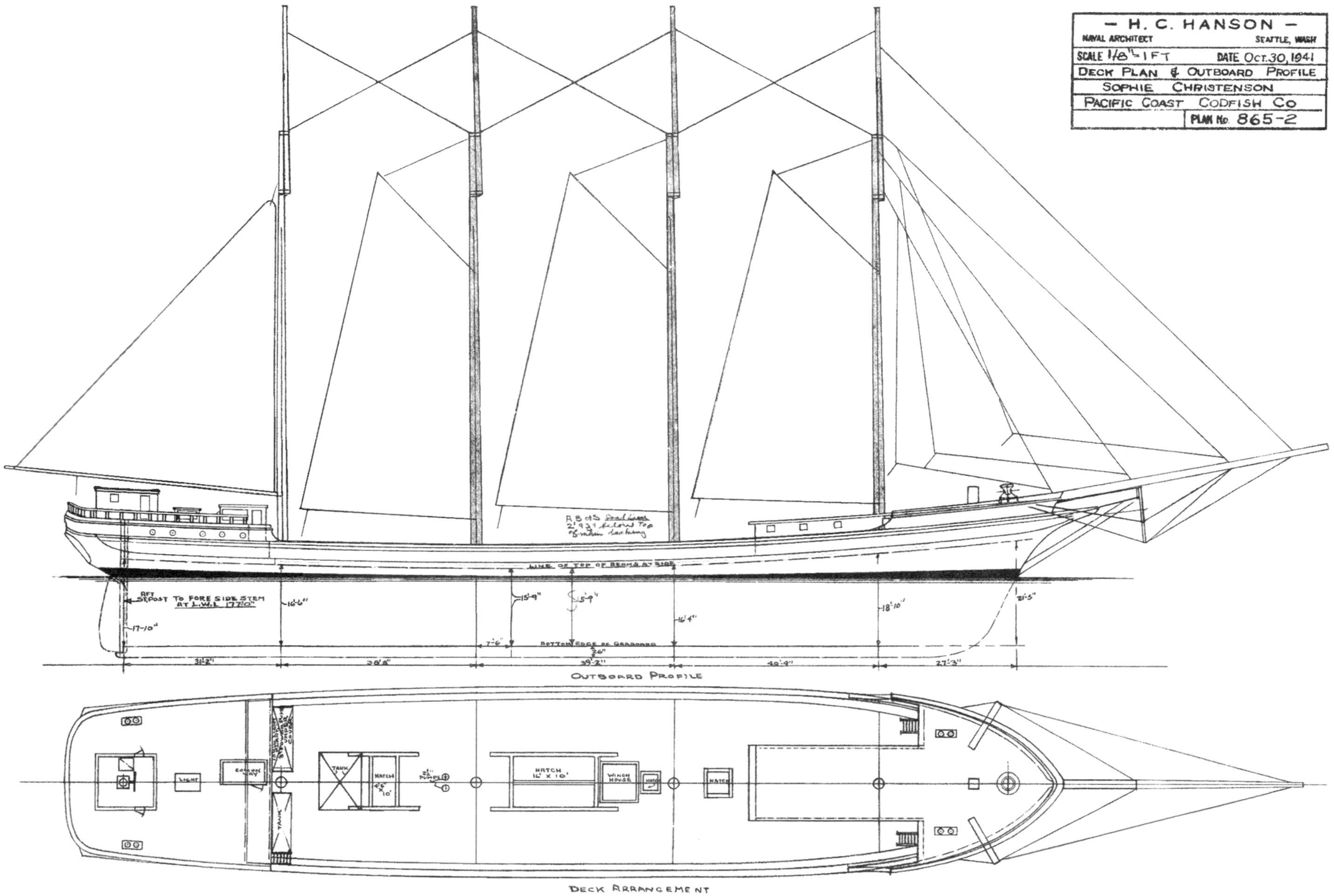

The 1901 schooner *Sophie Christenson* deck plan and outboard profile drawn in support of a refit in 1941.
(With permission of Whatcom Museum of History and Art, H. C. Hanson Collection design 865)

DECK ARRANGEMENT

OUTBOARD PROFILE

— H. C. HANSON —
SEATTLE, WASH

NAVAL ARCHITECT	
SCALE 1/8" = 1 FT	DATE OCT. 30, 1941
DECK PLAN & OUTBOARD PROFILE	
SOPHIE CHRISTENSON	
PACIFIC COAST CODFISH Co	
PLAN No. 865-2	

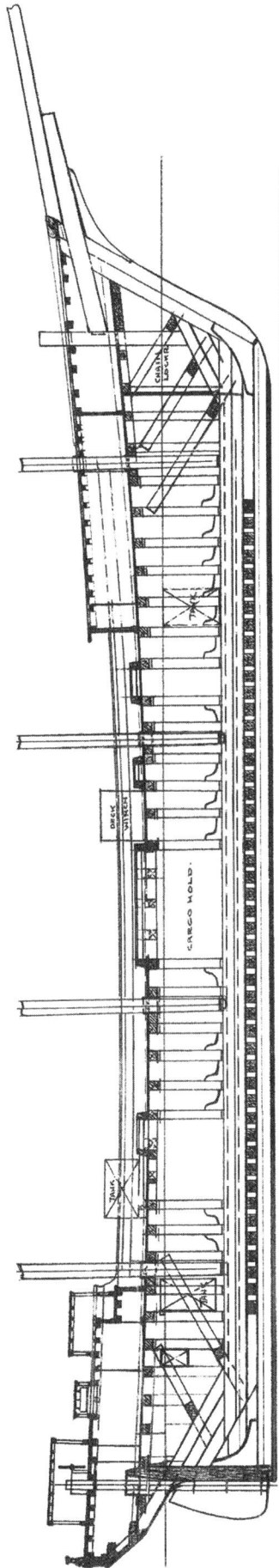

INBOARD PROFILE.

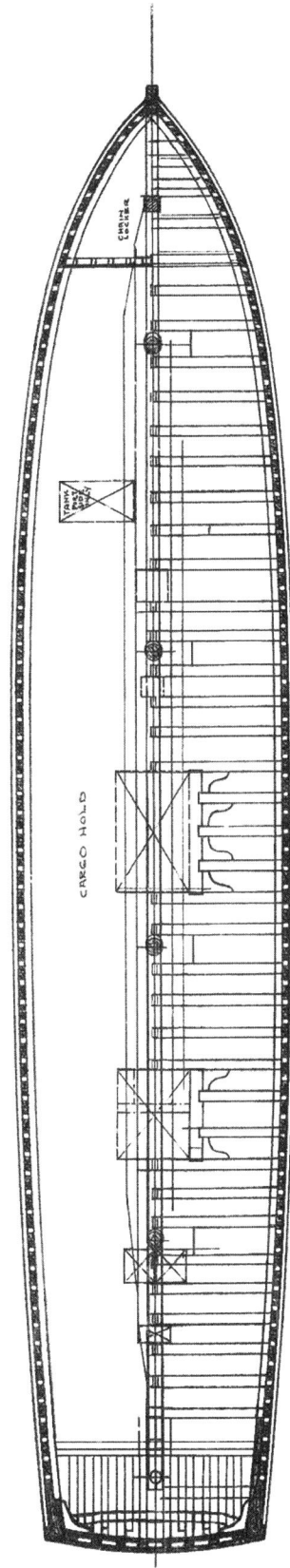

CARGO HOLD.

BEAM FRAMING.

CARGO HOLD

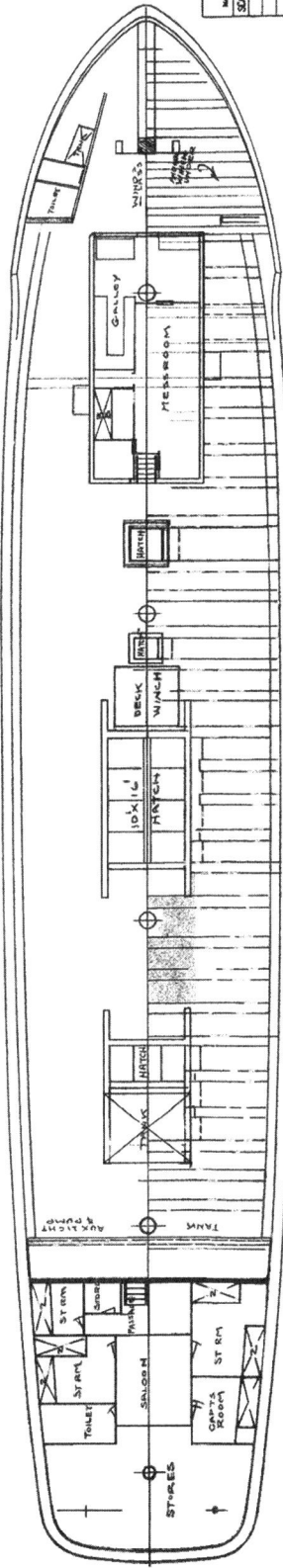

FOCSLE & POOP ARRANGEMENT.

— H. C. HANSON —
SEATTLE WASH.
NAVAL ARCHITECT
SCALE 4" = 1 FT.   DATE OCT. 30, 1941.
CONSTRUCTION PLANS
SOPHIE CHRISTENSON
PACIFIC COAST CODFISH CO.
PLAN No 865-3

The 1901 schooner *Sophie Christenson* construction plans drawn in support of a refit in 1941. (With permission of Whatcom Museum of History and Art, H. C. Hanson Collection design 865)

Sophie Christenson was built of wood by the Hall Brothers yard at Port Blakely in 1901 and then carried lumber and other cargo for a series of owners. After being purchased by Captain J. E. Shields in 1925, the schooner continued to carry cargo before entering the Bering Sea codfishery. At the time the drawings on these pages were generated, *Sophie Christenson* had 40 years of hard work behind her.

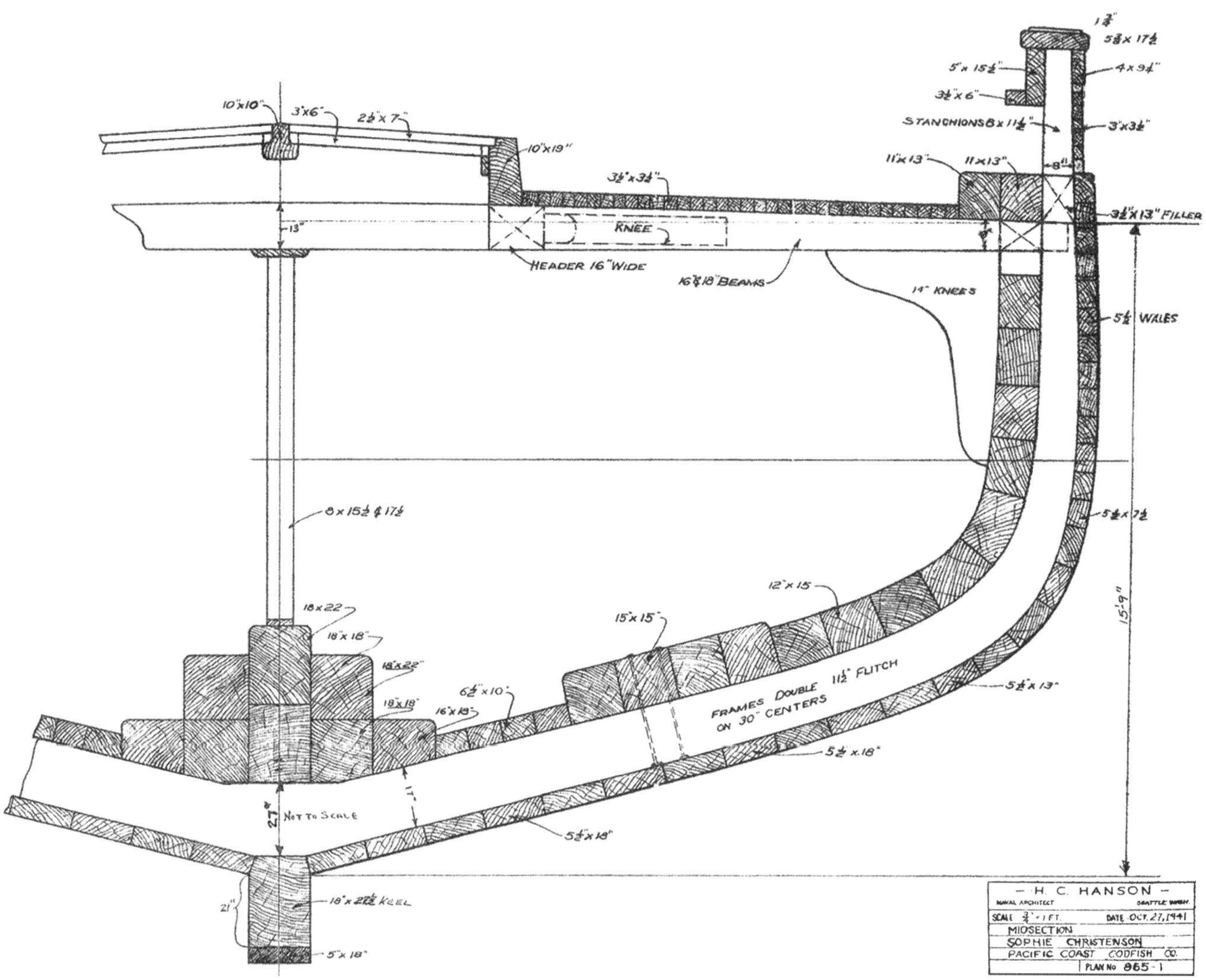

10"x10" 3"x6" 2½"x7" 10"x19"

1¾" 5⅝"x17½"
5"x15½" 4"x9¼"
3½"x6" 3"x3½"
STANCHIONS 8x11¼"
11"x13" 11"x13" 8"
3½"x3½" 3½"x13" FILLER
KNEE
HEADER 16" WIDE
16&18" BEAMS
14" KNEES
5½" WALES
13"
8x15½ & 17½
18x22
18"x18"
18"x22"
18"x18"
6½"x10"
16"x19"
15"x15"
12"x15"
FRAMES DOUBLE 11½" FLITCH ON 30" CENTERS
5½"x13"
5½"x7½"
15'-9"
5½"x18"
27" NOT TO SCALE
17"
5½"x18"
21"
18"x22½" KEEL
5"x18"

— H. C. HANSON —
NAVAL ARCHITECT SEATTLE WASH.
SCALE ¾" = 1 FT. DATE OCT. 27, 1941
MIDSECTION
SOPHIE CHRISTENSON
PACIFIC COAST CODFISH CO.
PLAN No 865-1

The 1901 schooner *Sophie Christenson* midship section drawn in support of a refit in 1941. (With permission of Whatcom Museum of History and Art, H. C. Hanson Collection design 865)

The drawings above and on the previous two pages were associated with a 1941 refit, including new masts being stepped, that involved the American Bureau of Shipping. To provide evidence of seaworthiness, ABS is the classification agency for approval of ships registered in the United States. Other countries also have classification societies, such as Lloyd's Register in the UK, Det Norske Veritas in Norway, Germischer Lloyd in Germany, and so forth. The drawings shown here are useful when determining seaworthiness.

As indicated on the outboard profile drawing, a measurement was taken showing a register hull length of 177' 0", and in addition, hull depths were obtained at a series of locations along the length. These dimensions were probably recorded during a survey. Having dimensions such as these plus the arrangement drawings and the midship section scantling drawing, from which hull strength is evaluated, the maximum allowable operating draft to ensure safety at sea can be arrived at. On the outboard profile drawing, at midship just above the bulwark, is a handwritten note that reads "AB of S loadline 2' 9 3/4" below top of main decking," the location of the loadline mark as assigned by the American Bureau of Shipping.

Perhaps what first catches the eye upon viewing *Sophie Christenson*'s midship section drawing are the massive hull scantlings. Hull planking used in building *Sophie Christenson* was 5 1/2 inches thick, and ceiling planking was 12 inches thick. The underwater planks were 18 inches wide, and keelson timbers were up to 18 x 18 inches. Because large old-growth, fine-grain trees are no longer available in quantity, it is doubtful that such a ship could be duplicated today

Black Shield, ex-*C. A. Thayer*, early 1950s. (Courtesy of Anna J. Knutsen)

Into the early 1900s, boats powered by steam engines or internal combustion engines began to join the fishing fleet. Even so, the days of sail did not end then but, instead, continued into the mid 1900s as a few schooners such as *Alice, Azalea, C. A. Thayer, Charles R. Wilson, Fanny Dutard, John A, Sophie Christenson,* and *Wawona* pursued the Bering Sea cod.

The postcard above, from the early 1950s, illustrates the 156-foot *Black Shield*, the former Bering Sea cod-fishing schooner *C. A. Thayer*. As *Black Shield*, the vessel was in retirement and reduced to acting as a tourist attraction on Hood Canal. *C. A. Thayer* was built of wood on Humboldt Bay in California in 1895 as a lumber carrier and freighter.

In 1925, *C. A. Thayer* was purchased by Captain J. E. Shields for service in the Bering Sea cod fishery. In the early 1940s *Sophie Christenson* and *C. A. Thayer* were taken over by the U.S. government for service during World War II, and at the end of the war, the schooners were returned to Captain Shields. During a survey, though, *Sophie Christenson* was found to be in a deteriorated state, and after salvable items were removed, the vessel was scrapped.

However, *C. A. Thayer* was in better condition than was *Sophie Christenson*, and a determination was made that repairs for the vessel were economically feasible. The masts in the above photo were not the schooner's original masts but, instead, are three of *Sophie Christenson*'s masts that were removed and stepped in *C. A. Thayer* during the refit. Following this work, *C. A. Thayer* sailed north again to fish for the Bering Sea cod.

C. A. Thayer's last voyage to the Bering Sea was in 1950, and after four years of layup at Poulsbo, the vessel was sold to Charles McNeal, who renamed the schooner *Black Shield* for display at his McNeal's 101 Attractions on Hood Canal. In 1957, the state of California purchased the vessel, and following repairs and carrying her original name *C. A. Thayer*, the ship was delivered under sail for permanent exhibition on the waterfront in San Francisco, California.

The first engine-powered cod and halibut fishing boats evolved from sailing schooners that were fishing in areas of the north Pacific Coast around the turn of the last century. Some of these schooners had been brought around the Horn from the New England Grand Banks. Like the first engine-powered steam schooners that were engaged in the coastwise carriage of lumber and poles, the first engine-powered halibut schooners had been built as sailing schooners. As converted to engine power, the appearance was similar to a Grand Banks type of sailing vessel except that a pilot house was constructed on the aft deck and an engine and propeller were installed.

Later, engine-powered halibut boats that came out of the shipyards were newly designed but still featured two masts and an aft location for the deckhouse; thus, some of the appearance of the old sailing schooners was preserved and these vessels were referred to as halibut "schooners." Such a boat was the longline halibut schooner *Yakutat*, pictured on the next page. *Yakutat* was 71 feet long and built of wood at Seattle in 1913. The longline was set and retrieved over the stern chute visible in the photo of *Yakutat*. Although sails were not required for powering *Yakutat*, steadying sails in a fore and aft position could be hoisted, which greatly reduced rolling in beam seas.

**Yakutat, n.d. (With permission of
Puget Sound Maritime Historical Society, negative 7248–2)**

In the photo at left, the halibut schooner *Yakutat* of 1913 was running light with no fish in the hold, as indicated by the large amount of aft trim. It is obvious that, because of the aft trim with the bow high in the water, forward visibility from the pilothouse was restricted.

The 1942 wooden halibut boat illustrated below and on the next pages was from the boards of Naval Architect H. C. Hanson. In this design, some features of the form were replicated from the halibut schooners of a much earlier time.

If the arrangement had been reversed, with the deckhouse located aft and the hold forward, the boat would resemble an earlier halibut schooner such as *Yakutat* of 1913. For this design, though, the forward location of the deckhouse was in keeping with the trend underway toward the middle of the 1900s.

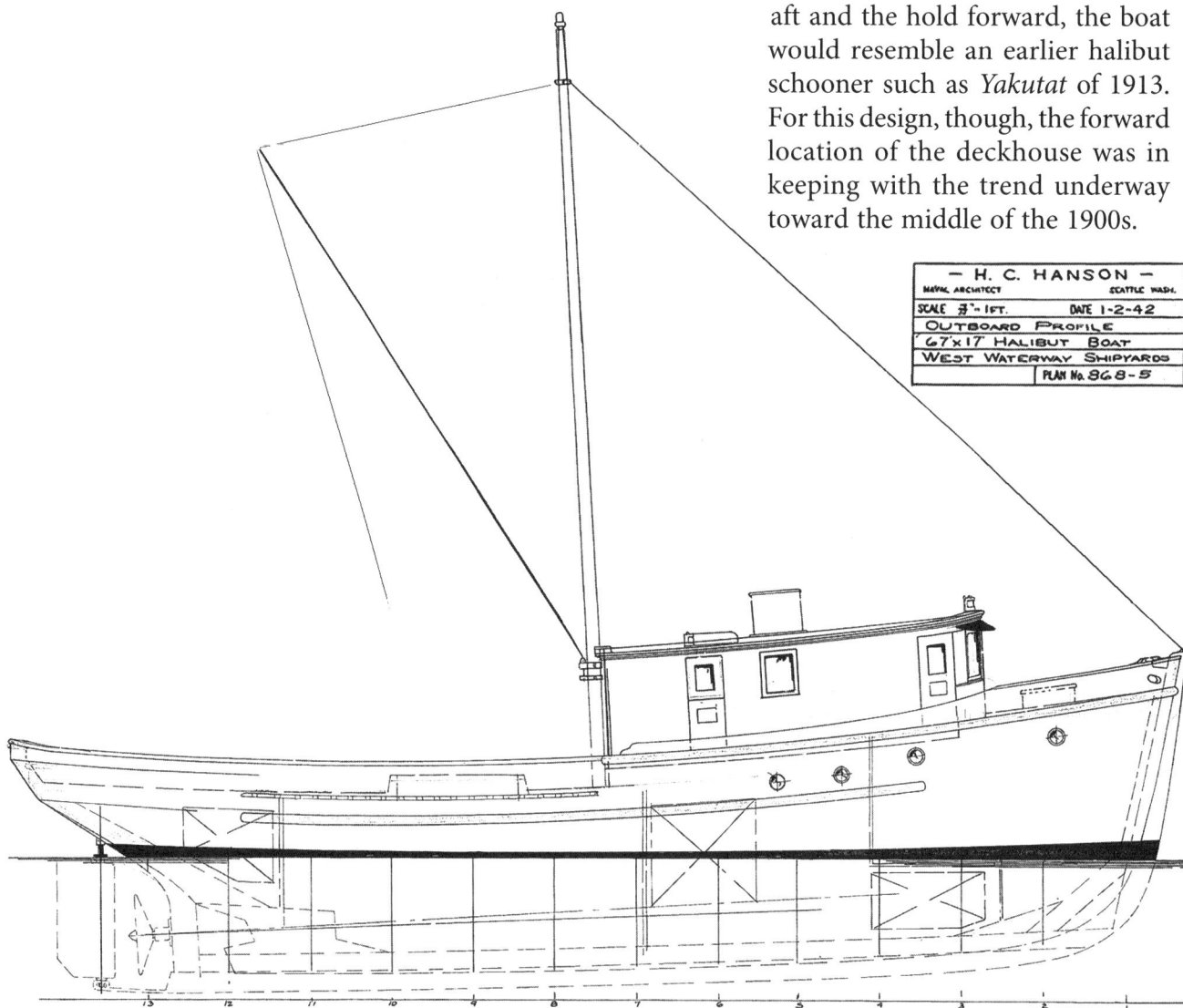

**Halibut boat outboard profile, 1942.
(With permission of Whatcom Museum of History and Art, H. C. Hanson Collection design 868)**

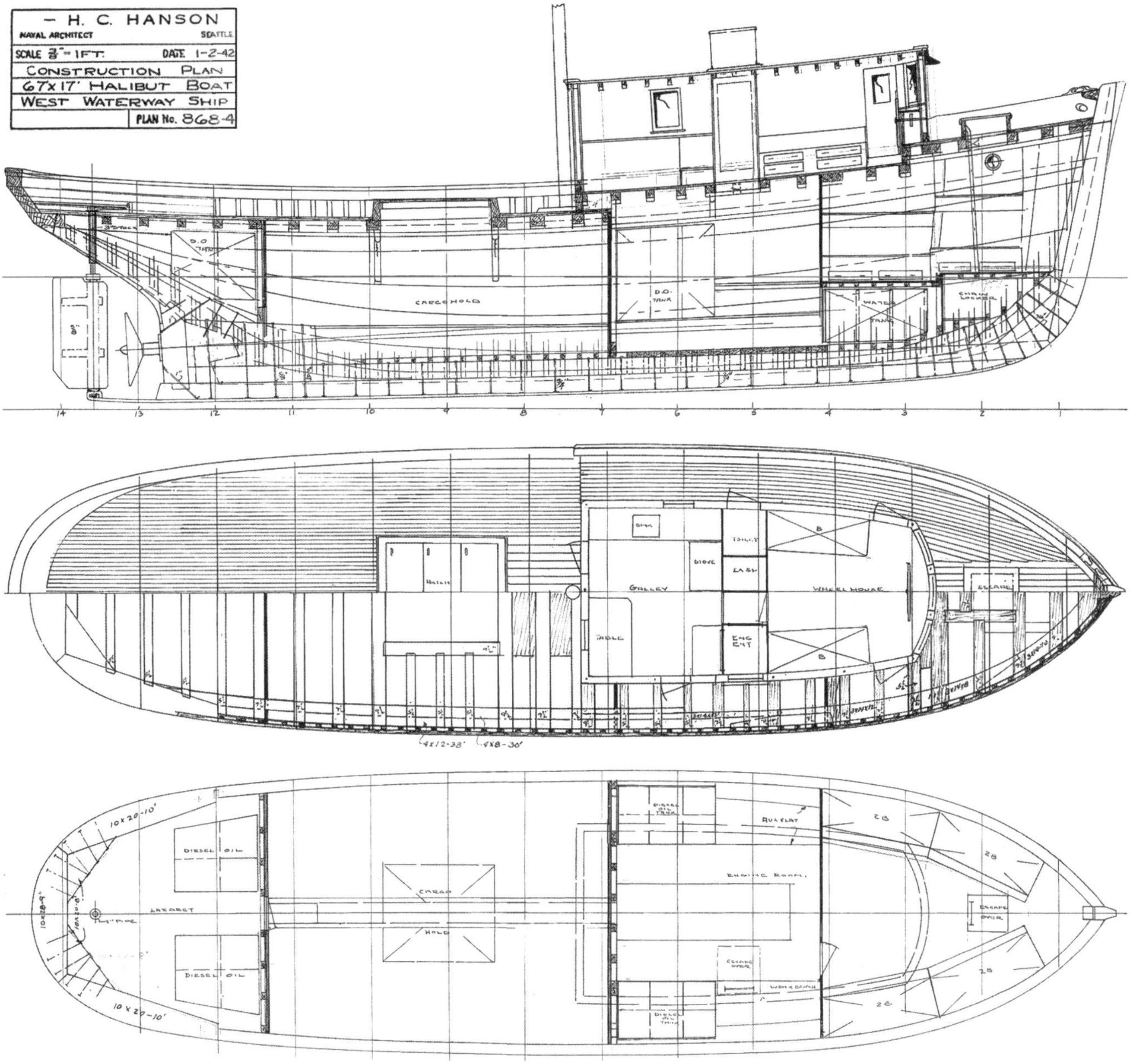
H. C. HANSON
NAVAL ARCHITECT SEATTLE
SCALE 3/8" = 1 FT. DATE 1-2-42
CONSTRUCTION PLAN
67 x 17' HALIBUT BOAT
WEST WATERWAY SHIP
PLAN No. 868-4
CARGO HOLD
GALLEY
WHEEL HOUSE
ENGINE ROOM

Halibut boat inboard profile, arrangements and construction, 1942.
(With permission of Whatcom Museum of History and Art, H. C. Hanson Collection design 868)

Overall dimensions of the 1942 Hanson halibut boat were 67-foot length and 17-foot beam. Living accommodations in the vessel were somewhat limited because of the large amount of space given over to the hold, engine room and working deck area.

Quarters were provided for a crew of ten with two single berths in the pilothouse and eight berths, stacked in pairs, in the fo'c'sle. The fo'c'sle was accessed via a hatch on the fore deck and a near-vertical ladder. This space was not large, and little provision was made to admit light and air. In fact, some inexperienced crew members who were not used to the tight quarters might have had to endure feelings of claustrophobia, at least for awhile. Still, the fo'c'sle provided a welcome place of rest for crew members who were between periods of grueling labor and long hours of fishing. The galley and head were in a more appealing location on the main deck, both spaces being accessed from outside on the weather deck.

The hull form of the Hanson halibut boat is illustrated by the lines drawing shown on the next page. The shape of the overhanging stern is reminiscent of the schooners that were at work on the Grand Banks many years before.

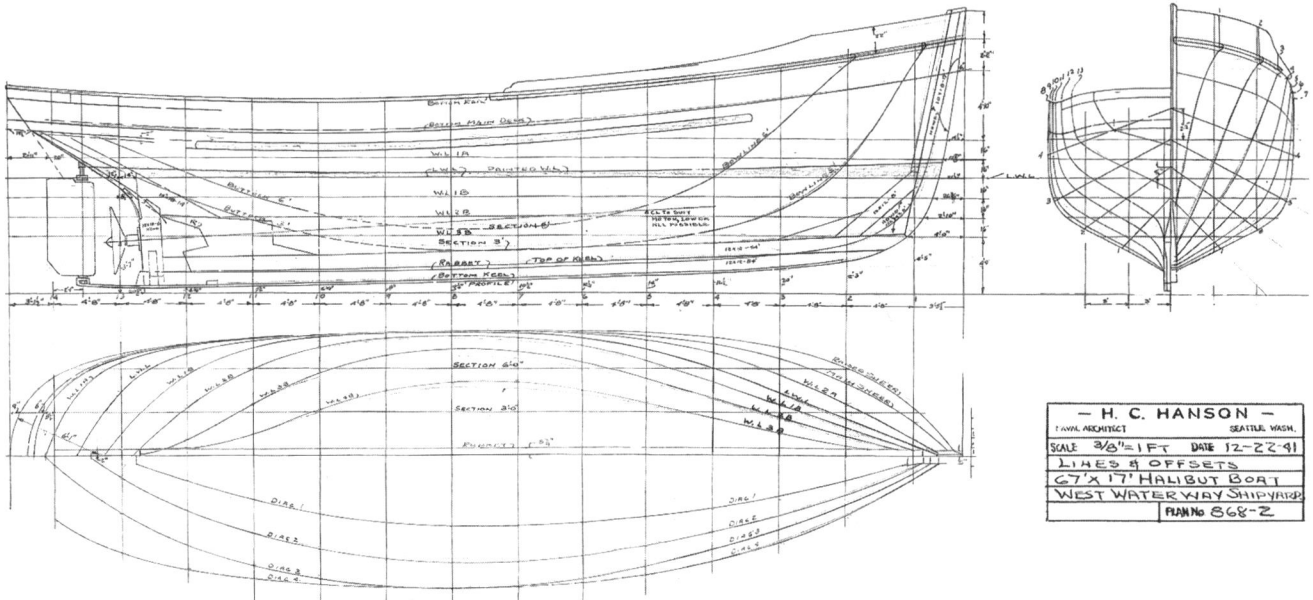

Halibut boat lines, 1942. (With permission of
Whatcom Museum of History and Art, H. C. Hanson Collection design 868)

The hull form of the 1942 Hanson halibut boat is shown in the lines drawing above. The load water line, labeled LWL, as drawn, allows for a generous amount of freeboard. In practice, with a bonanza catch of fish in the hold, the boat probably sat deeper in the water at times.

The Native Americans of the North Pacific coast have fished for halibut many centuries. In the late 1800s, commercial fishing for halibut in the North Pacific was first engaged in by men of Norwegian ancestry. Halibut are prized by diners and, accordingly, command a high price.

Halibut are the largest of the flatfishes, the females ranging up to eight feet or more in length and several hundred pounds in weight, while the males are much smaller. Halibut are known to exist in water depths of more than 3000 feet, but most are caught in much shallower water.

Another method of bottom fishing, known as trawling, is one in which a net is towed along the sea bottom. Although the intent of bottom trawling is to harvest only a specific type of fish, the net is not capable of discrimination in what is actually scooped up so, unfortunately, a variety of illegal or unmarketable sea creatures in the net's path is caught, also.

Most of this unwanted sea life does not survive the trawling operation and is simply thrown overboard as scrap. In addition, damage to the fragile sea bottom from dragging the net, which may take millennia to repair itself, if ever, also results from this type of fishing. Hence, restrictions on bottom trawling have been put in place at many locations in the world in order to preserve the sea bed in its natural state.

The beam trawl, pictured below, is a bag-shaped net that is dragged along the sea bottom by the towing vessel. The beam trawl takes its name from the wooden or metal transverse beam at the forward edge that acts as a spreader to keep the mouth of the bag open.

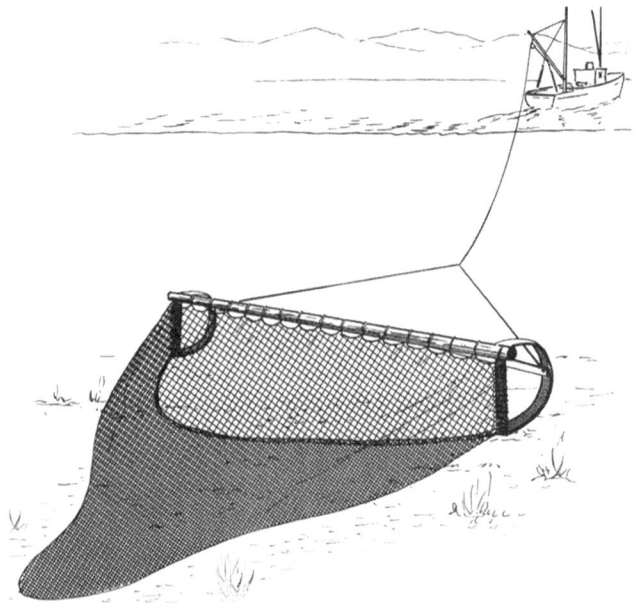

Beam trawl. (From
Commercial Fishing Gear of the United States)

A variation on the beam trawl is the "otter trawl," shown at right. Instead of a spreader beam attached at the net bag opening, two otter boards or doors, one at each side of the forward edge, keep the forward end of the bag spread open laterally.

The two doors, simply plane surfaces, are usually built of wood and are about three feet wide by six feet long. Oriented with a long edge down, the doors are angled outward when the trawl is towed over the bottom at a speed of two or three knots. When under tow, water pressure against the angled doors keeps the net spread open.

Rather than utilizing a frame at each side of the net opening as the beam trawl does, the mouth of the otter trawl is kept open vertically by buoys attached at the upper edge. The closed, trailing end of the trawl is known as the "cod end," a term handed down from the cod fishery in New England and so called because the caught fish would

Otter trawl. (From *Commercial Fishing Gear of the United States*)

be in that portion of the bag. Periodically, the trawl is hauled aboard, and the fish are removed.

Deep Sea, pictured below and, at the time, larger than most trawlers, was built of steel for Deep Sea Trawlers, Incorporated, by Birchfield Boiler Works at Tacoma in 1947. The East Coast-type trawler was 130 feet long and, powered by a 1200-horsepower General Motors diesel engine, achieved a speed of 14 knots. Hold capacity was available for 420,000 pounds of frozen king crab and/or frozen filleted sole.

Deep Sea at Seattle, 1948. (From the author's collection)

The best known and most highly utilized of the crab species in the Pacific Northwest is the Dungeness, and the crab pot is the most common method for catching them. Pots, in various sizes and designs, are also used for trapping other species of crab, the largest pots being those used in catching the enormous king crabs that inhabit the bottom of the Bering Sea.

Two versions of the Dungeness crab pots are illustrated at right. A crab pot consists of a metal frame enclosed with galvanized wire mesh. The pot can be baited, frequently with the bait enclosed in a mesh or perforated container to prevent it from being consumed by the crabs, and lowered to the sea bottom where it rests until hauled aboard. Detecting the bait, crabs enter the pot through a small hole that is sometimes in the form of a funnel-shaped opening but are trapped because they are simply not able to work their way back out through this opening. A keg or other type of buoy, floating on the surface of the water and tethered to the crab pot, identifies the location for later retrieval of the pot.

A commercial crab boat would likely put to sea with pots stacked high on the deck. Metal crab pots are heavy, and the pile of pots would have a high center of gravity. Most commercial Dungeness crabbing is done off the Washington and Oregon coasts and a boat, when negotiating a harbor entrance, must deal with waves that tend to pile up chaotically on the bar. In northern waters, the boat and the load of pots can ice up, which would add even more weight to the burden being carried. In the interest of trapping as many crabs as possible, there has also been a tendency to carry

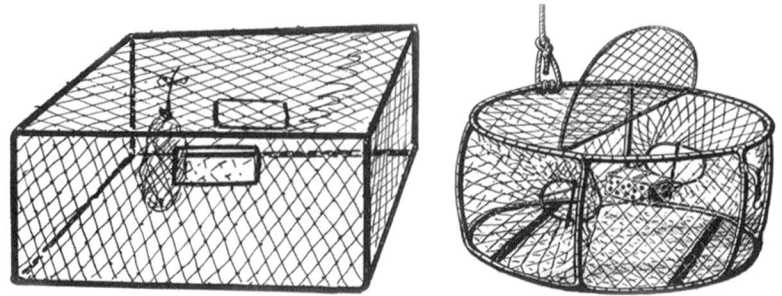

Dungeness crab pots. (From
*Commercial Fishing Gear of the United States***)**

a greater number of pots on board the boats than might be prudent. Due to the weight being carried and the high center of gravity of the load, together with frequently adverse weather conditions, a number of crab boats are lost every year. For many years, the safety of the earlier boats was not regulated by the government, but today any crab boat over an established minimum length and built, or substantially modified, after a certain date, all as specified by the U.S. Coast Guard, is required to have a stability analysis performed by a naval architect for approval by that agency.

The early settlers in the Pacific Northwest were introduced by the Native Americans to the abundant and succulent clams and oysters that grew in the shallow waters of the salt water inlets. All manner of implements are used to harvest clams and oysters, including hand tools such as various types of hoes, rakes, shovels, and tongs. At commercial farms, where oysters are commonly grown on strings suspended in the water from rafts, for example, the oysters are harvested by simply pulling the lines out of the water and detaching those oysters that have matured.

At large commercial oyster beds that are in an area of sea bottom that does not have any obstructions, the dredge is employed. Dredges may take various forms, but the illustration at left shows the essential features. This device is towed along the sea bottom and scoops up the oysters. Periodically, the dredge is hoisted aboard by the towing vessel, and the contents are emptied on the deck. The towing vessel, also referred to as a dredge, is usually smaller than but similar to *Tonsina* that was pictured earlier in the chapter.

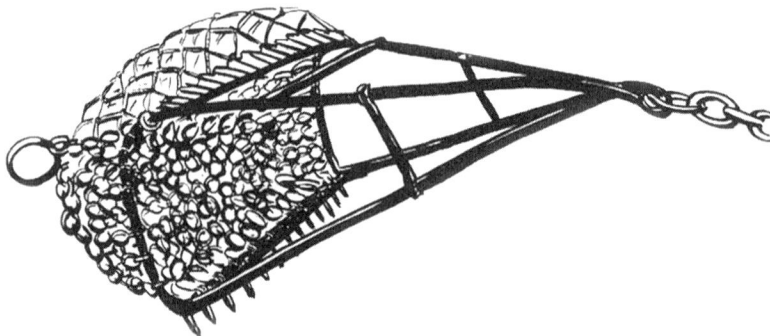

Oyster dredge. (From
*Commercial Fishing Gear of the United States***)**

A BRIEF LOOK AT RECENT TIMES

The mining of sand and gravel continues today at Steilacoom under ownership of Glacier Northwest rather than Pioneer. Rayonier is pretty much gone, but the Simpson mill is still in production in Shelton at, perhaps, less capacity than in the earlier days. Although Reliable Welding Works is still operating in Olympia, as Reliable Steel in the production of tanks and other products, it is no longer in the business of building ships. As described earlier in the book, by the 1960s, the wood-products industry was changing, and that situation was evident in Olympia.

The shipping of logs was becoming more common than the shipping of finished lumber. Unfortunately, one by one, the mills and plants were being shut down and dismantled. In the earlier years, many students who dropped out of high school in Olympia, or those who graduated but were not continuing on to college, could find jobs in the lumber mills and plywood plants, but those jobs are gone now. Eventually, Georgia Pacific took over Washington Plywood, and the plywood plant and sawmill operated under the GP logo for a time. A decline of manufacturing, similar to that taking place in southern Puget Sound, was occurring in other areas of Puget Sound, as well.

Hardel Plywood was still producing wood products in the early 1990s but then met an untimely and disastrous end. On Labor Day weekend during Olympia's Harbor Days in 1996, my wife, Sharon, and I were aboard our 36-foot wooden boat *Baby Grand* moored at Percival Landing. Out on deck, while sipping coffee at about five o'clock in the cool of the fall morning, we could see flames on Olympia's West Side shore glowing in the darkness. The Hardel Plywood plant was on fire.

Within a short time, the flames became huge. In the light of the flames, sheets of veneer could be seen drifting high into the air, fluttering and turning end over end, carried aloft by the hot updrafts of the fire. A gentle north breeze delivered ash to Percival Landing and beyond, where the boats and everything around were sprinkled with the powdery residue. Warmth was felt as the air from the north passed over the flames and was conducted to Percival Landing, as if from a giant circulating air-heating system. In a short while, the plywood plant was gone.

In the 1990s, ships were still calling on Olympia to pick up cargo, but not in the numbers seen in the 1950s and before. In the recent photo below, the Philippine registered cargo ship *Pino Gloria*, quite different in appearance from the freighters of earlier times, is pictured while loading logs at the Port of Olympia.

Pino Gloria at Olympia, mid 1990s. (From the author's collection)

Interspersed with log-carrying ships operated by various companies, ships operated by Sunmar Shipping Lines began to load containerized cargo at the Port of Olympia in the 1990s. The destination for the cargo was Russia, but with the collapse of the Soviet Union and the Russian economy, Sunmar was forced to cease operations in 1998. To support Sunmar's operations, the Port of Olympia had purchased two large container-handling cranes from the Port of Los Angeles. With Sunmar gone, the cranes have been sitting idle much of the time, though the cranes are also capable of handling other tpes of cargo.

Olympia is more distant from the open sea than Seattle and Tacoma are. This additional distance causes an increase in voyage time for a ship operator, a disadvantage to Olympia as a port of call. But fortunately for the Port of Olympia, logs are still being shipped from Olympia several times a year. The military has also utilized the Port of Olympia for handling cargo shipments, as well as for moorage of temporarily inactive vessels.

The now idle container cranes at Olympia's port pier are indeed big, and perhaps they appear extra large because they are in the setting of a small harbor; in the larger ports of Seattle and Tacoma, the cranes would not be as noticeable. Several years ago someone wrote a letter to the editor of Olympia's newspaper, the *Olympian*, complaining about the unsightly appearance of the large container cranes sitting atop the Port of Olympia pier. Perhaps there were others who shared the letter writer's opinion.

Growing up in Olympia when it was a working harbor and the sawmills were turning out finished lumber while operating double shifts, and being young at the time, I assumed, perhaps naively, that Olympia would always be like that. Percival Landing and the yacht moorages of today present a pleasing appearance, but I do miss that busy working harbor of a long time ago. Whether or not the now-dissolved arrangements between the Port of Olympia and Sunmar had made good business sense when originally implemented is not explored here, but I do not look upon the cranes at the Port of Olympia as being all that unsightly. Instead, I see them as an indicator that some marine commerce has still been going on in Olympia's harbor.

In recent years, Dunlap Towing Company has had a wood chip reloading operation, log raft storage, and several small tugs on Olympia's West Side, as pictured here. Scows towed by Dunlap tugs haul the wood chips to pulp and paper mills, such as Port Townsend Paper Company and Pope and Talbot's plant at Nanaimo, British Columbia. The company is still headquartered at La Conner but their operation in Olympia acts as a reminder of the bustling industry that once lined the shores of the harbor there. In the photo below, a Dunlap Towing Company chip scow at Olympia was in position for loading.

Dunlap Towing Company's facility at Olympia, 1996. (From the author's collection)

Swinomish at Olympia, early 1990s. (From the author's collection)

In the photo above, Dunlap Towing's *Swinomish* was lying at Percival Landing in Olympia. *Swinomish* has been employed in towing the Dunlap chip scows, including the one pictured on the previous page. A hometown visitor at the time of the photo, the 69-foot *Swinomish* was built of steel as the U.S. Army *ST-166* by Reliable Welding Works at Olympia in 1943.

Swinomish, known under previous ownerships as *Bronco*, *Pacific Rocket*, and *Gary Foss*, was acquired by Dunlap in 1974 and refurbished, with a modified deckhouse included in the work. The modified deckhouse can be compared to the house as originally built for this particular group

of tugs as in the photo of *ST-860* shown earlier in the book. This type of tug design, one of several different configurations included in the U.S. Army ST Class, was known for uncomfortable rolling characteristics at sea due to the slack bilges designed into the round bottom hull.

At right in the photo below, Dunlap's log handling tug *Yokeko* was at the log storage on the West Side of Olympia. The 73-foot wooden tug *Irene* was tied to the logs at left in the background of this photo. Built at Tacoma in 1892, *Irene* was a long-time member of American Tug Boat Company's fleet but had been sold into private ownership at the time of the photo.

Irene, left background, and *Yokeko*, right, at Olympia, early 1990s. (From the author's collection)

311

Cedar King at Olympia, 1996. (From the author's collection)

In the photo above, Dunlap Towing's 345-horsepower *Cedar King* was moving along Olympia's West Side with a log raft in tow. The 40-foot tug was built of steel at Olympia by Reliable Welding Works in 1970 as a replacement for *Johnny Jr.* in operation at the time for Olympia Towing Company. The photo below shows two Dunlap bulldozer tugs at Olympia's West Side.

Dunlap boom boats at Olympia, early 1990s. (From the author's collection)

P & T Pioneer at Olympia, 1993. (From the author's collection)

A few of the elderly towboats were still earning their keep on Puget Sound, and *P & T Pioneer* of 1951 was still looking good as a working tug at the time of the photo above. In the picture, the towboat is seen pulling a bundle raft of hemlock logs out of Olympia's West Side log storage. A couple of years after the photo was taken, Pope and Talbot, the original owner of *P & T Pioneer* and still the owner at the time of the photo, closed its big sawmill at the beautiful little town of Port Gamble. Among the assets sold by Pope and Talbot was *P & T Pioneer*.

Because everything nowadays must be done with high output and lowest possible input to meet modern demands, most of the old towboats were unable to keep up and are gone now. With the declining wood products industry, the number of tugs based in Olympia went nearly to zero.

Capital City Tug Company went away, but the tug *Virgo Young* remained for awhile under the ownership of Olympia Boom Company. Delta V. Smyth Tugs and Barges was bought out by Foss Launch and Tug Company. The ex-Smyth tugs *Hoonah, Parthia*, and *Rufus* were employed for awhile by Foss after purchasing Smyth's firm, but the other towboats were sold or otherwise disposed of. Later on, ship handling duties in Olympia harbor were taken care of by towboats based in Seattle and Tacoma. Olympia Towing Company's tug *Crosmor* was purchased by Dunlap

Towing Company of La Conner. Still later, Olympia Towing Company was acquired by Dunlap.

Towing companies were disappearing elsewhere around Puget Sound, also. In addition to buying Delta V. Smyth Tugs and Barges, Foss Launch and Tug Company bought the assets of Pacific Tow Boat Company, as well as Bellingham Tug and Barge Company. Dunlap Towing Company purchased the remaining assets of American Tug Boat Company. Olson Tug Boat Company and Tacoma Tug and Barge Company eventually disappeared, as did Pioneer Towing Company and Washington Tug and Barge.

Foss Launch and Tug Company became Foss Maritime Company and has continued to operate, although under a series of different ownerships. Puget Sound Tug and Barge Company and Cary-Davis Tug and Barge ultimately consolidated as Crowley Maritime Corporation, which is still very much in business. Other firms currently in the towing business are Fremont Tugboat, operating a long time at its Lake Union location, Brix Towing and Olympic Tug and Barge. In these more recent years, Island Tug and Barge and Western Towboat have developed into sizable firms, while Manke Lumber's fleet of well-kept tugs is at work handling their logs and other towing activities. But fewer tugs are in operation on Puget Sound today, and most of the marine towing companies that were busy in the earlier years are gone.

Wanderer on the beach at Nisqually, 1957. (Courtesy of Morris N. Knutsen Jr.)

Most of the early towboats, no longer able to work, eventually had to be laid to rest. The photo above shows the big steam tug *Wanderer*, stripped of outfitting items and last owned by Foss Launch and Tug Company for many years, in the boneyard at Nisqually Reach. In the photo, I was operating the small power boat. This flat-bottom, tunnel-stern skiff, powered with a 10-horsepower air-cooled inboard engine, was designed and built by me for beachcombing.

The photo below shows the remains of *Wanderer* 28 years after the upper photo was taken. At the time of the photo, nearly all of the hull was gone, with only some heavy bottom framing and keel timbers left as a reminder that a large wooden vessel had once occupied this spot.

Wanderer on the beach at Nisqually, 1985. (Courtesy of Morris N. Knutsen Jr.)

314

Of the few earlier tugs still afloat, even fewer are still in commercial towing service. Some of the retired towboats were bought by individuals for their personal use but have deteriorated or sunk due to a lack of resources to make repairs and provide proper maintenance. However, others that are still in operating condition are in use as yachts or workboat/yachts today.

The amount of time, energy and money required to restore and maintain an aging vessel cannot be overemphasized, as more than one owner has found. Prior to embarking on a vessel renovation, the budget needed to do the job must be known. Estimating the cost accurately is very difficult, and as a result, the cost tends to creep up due to the discovery of additional problems as the work progresses. This applies not only to individual owners. Groups such as preservation societies and museums have also frequently underestimated the cost of repairs that an old ship might need. In addition, when refurbishment has been undertaken, enormous problems may then arise in assembling the funds necessary for completing the work.

One case in point, of many that could be cited, involved *Mary D. Hume*, a large wooden tug that had been operated by American Tug Boat Company for many years out of Everett and later by Crowley Marine. As mentioned previously in the book, *Mary D. Hume* was built at Ellensburg, Oregon, in 1881. The town of Ellensburg has since been renamed Gold Beach.

In 1978, the towboat was retired and, under the tug's own power, delivered back home to Oregon by a Crowley crew. The vessel had been donated by Crowley to the Curry County Historical Society and the Port of Gold Beach. *Mary D. Hume* was to be moored at the mouth of the Rogue River across the water from the Hume estate, the tug having been named after the wife of steamboat operator and fish cannery owner R. D. Hume. Due to neglect, *Mary D. Hume* now lies hopelessly sunk in the shallow water at the mouth of the Rogue River.

After many years of service working for Delta V. Smyth Tugs and Barges out of Olympia, the tug *Sand Man* was finally sold in the mid 1950s. There followed a series of owners, but the tug has remained in the Olympia area since that time. The photo below shows the retired tug moving slowly between the log raft storage and the beach on Olympia's West Side.

Sand Man at Olympia, 1992. (From the author's collection)

In the photo of *Sand Man* on the previous page, the boat was riding high in the water, indicating that the fuel and water tanks were not full or that some of the tanks were no longer in use. As a working tug, *Sand Man* sat deeper in the water and operated with less freeboard. Built by Crawford and Reid at Tacoma in 1910, *Sand Man* had eventually become, by now, another example of a wooden vessel that finally deteriorated after so many years of operation.

As stated before, properly taking care of an old vessel requires lots of tender loving care. *Sand Man* had sunk more than once, as have other elderly vessels, and a considerable amount of dry rot had accumulated over the years, despite attempts to maintain the tug. There is obviously a strong desire to preserve a boat like *Sand Man*, and many people can empathize with that. But the challenges are great and so, when funds are limited, it can become a losing battle.

Other vessels have been put on display out of the water such as the clipper ship *Cutty Sark* in the United Kingdom, the polar exploration ship *Fram* in Oslo, Norway, the sternwheeler *W. T. Preston* at Anacortes, and Bellingham Tug and Barge Company's towboat *Shamrock II*, which functioned as a tourist reception center at Bellingham after retirement, to name a few. However, dry-land display would have to be properly done or eventually the condition of a ship could worsen even out of the water. In fact, a wooden vessel's condition while afloat may already have deteriorated to a point where even dry-land display might no longer be feasible.

Ultimately, help for *Sand Man* arrived in the form of funding. Possession of the vessel was signed over from private ownership to the Sand Man Foundation. This was eventually followed by grants and donations, and restoration was undertaken. After removal of the deckhouse, as well as the Caterpillar diesel engine that had been installed by Delta Smyth in the 1940s, the hull was towed from Olympia to Port Townsend, hauled out at the Port Townsend Boat Haven, and placed under protective cover and in the care of personnel from the Port Townsend Shipwrights Co-op. Rework of the deckhouse and overhaul of the Caterpillar diesel engine was done at Olympia. Rebuilding is now complete, and *Sand Man* is operational again in the water, though not with the original Frisco Standard engine.

The appearance of the tug is as originally built except that, during the restoration, the bulwark at the stern was not rebuilt to full height. During *Sand Man*'s working life, the bulwark was at full height all around. After the tug had been sold by Delta Smyth, a new owner apparently cut the bulwark height down at the horseshoe stern, perhaps as an expediency during a repair. For unknown reasons, this later modification was repeated in the restoration rather than adhering to the original configuration as a working towboat. Photos on succeeding pages illustrate some of the restoration work undergone by *Sand Man*.

Wooden shipbuilding requires the ultimate in craftsmanship. Unlike house construction, with its straight lines and angles, wooden ships consist primarily of curved pieces, and very little aboard a vessel is square to the world. Boat building requires the precise fit of one part to another, primarily for strength and integrity but, as well, for appearance. Perhaps only cabinet and furniture making equals the fine work required in the construction of a boat.

The Northwest School of Wooden Boatbuilding has been in operation for twenty years, with locations at Port Townsend and Port Hadlock. This school has an experienced faculty dedicated to teaching the skills necessary for undertaking an extensive renovation such as the one that *Sand Man* underwent. An associate degree from the school requires 1440 hours of work, in the classroom and in the shipyard, over a period of nine months.

The author spent some time at Port Townsend visiting with two of the shipwrights, Ben Tyler and Benedikt "Bene" Hoffmann, who were involved with the reconstruction of *Sand Man*. Both are graduates of the Northwest School of Wooden Boatbuilding, and as members of the Port Townsend Shipwrights Co-op, these gentlemen also have a lot of practical boatbuilding experience under their belts. Ben Tyler has taught at the Northwest School of Wooden Boatbuilding. In addition to being a skilled shipwright, Bene Hoffmann has been to sea as a licensed ship master. Other members of the Shipwrights Co-op have been working on *Sand Man*, as well.

Bow view of *Sand Man* undergoing restoration at Port Townsend, 2001. (From the author's collection)

In the photo below, Ben Tyler was removing large iron boat nails that had attached hull plank-ing, by now decayed, to *Sand Man*'s frames for more than 90 years.

Stern view of *Sand Man* undergoing restoration at Port Townsend, 2001. (From the author's collection)

Sand Man undergoing restoration at Port Townsend, 2001. (From the author's collection)

The hull structure in the lower portion of *Sand Man*'s hull was generally found to be good. The structure above the turn of the bilge, however, had deteriorated. The upper framing was removed, and new sawn frames were installed, the shapes made by patterning from the old frames. At each location, the new frames were actually double, installed in pairs sistered together.

In the photo above, new planking was being installed to the sides of the hull. The wood used was vertical-grain Douglas fir, 1 3/4 inches thick, just as was applied in the original construction of *Sand Man*. This wood was obtained from old-growth trees that grew slowly, which resulted in fine grained planks. Most of the hull planks were bent cold when being installed to the shape of the hull. At locations where the planks required more severe bending or where they needed to be twisted, the planks were first steamed and then installed hot to increase the flexibility.

When planking a hull, the planks usually cannot be installed while maintaining a constant width as obtained from the sawmill. Because the planks cannot be bent in the stiff edgewise direction, they need to be sawn to shape. The process followed to measure for and determine the required shape of a plank is termed "taking spilings." Optionally, a plank shape can be obtained by using the old plank as a pattern. The edges of the resulting sawn shape will be curved, and the width will vary along the length in order to fit up to the adjacent plank.

For *Sand Man*, instead of using nails, the new hull planks were fastened to the frames with four-inch-long, galvanized steel screws. Two screws were used to attach each plank at the frames, while three screws were installed at the ends of each plank. The screws were countersunk to recess the heads, and the holes were then plugged with Douglas fir bungs.

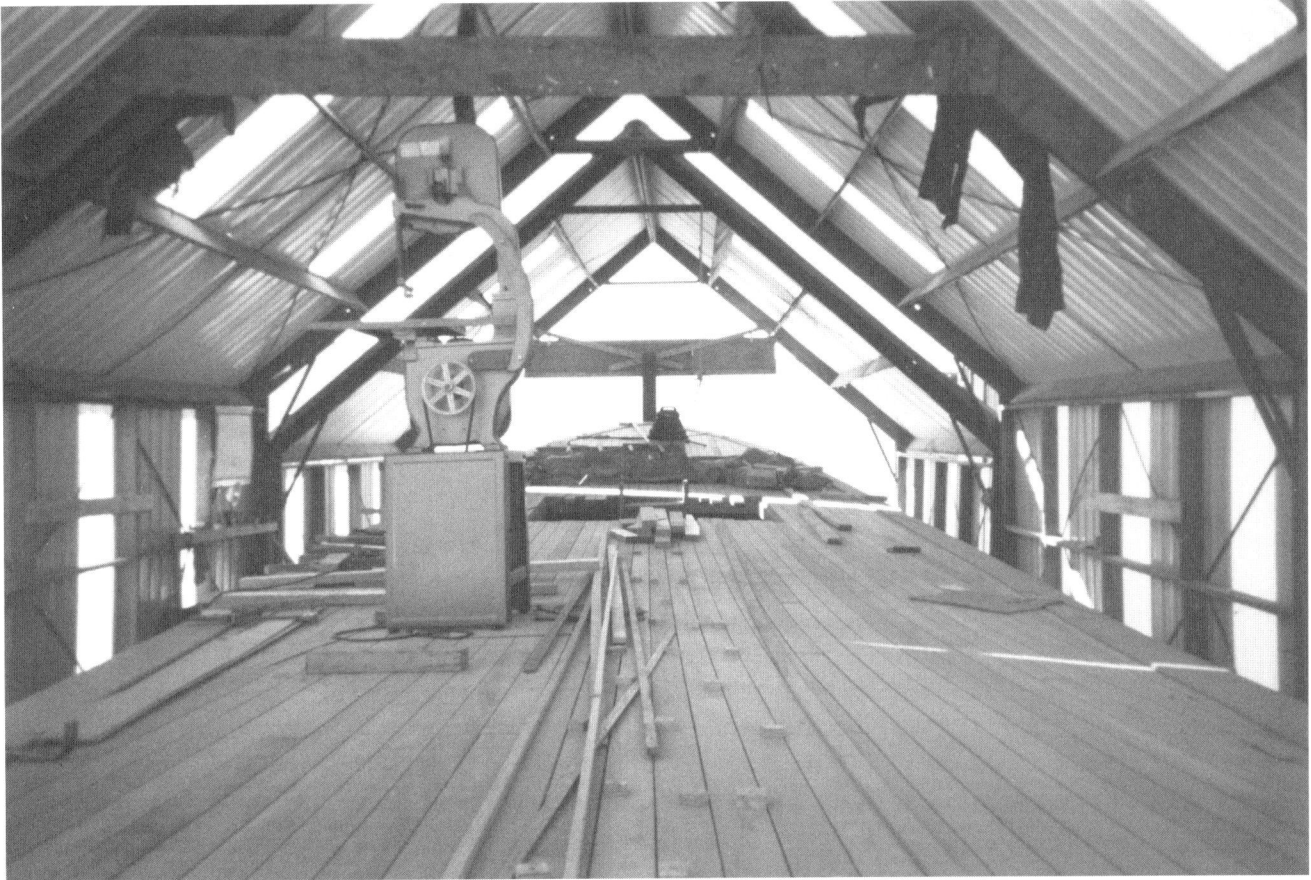

Sand Man undergoing restoration at Port Townsend, 2001. (From the author's collection)

Because of deterioration, *Sand Man*'s entire deck and bulwark had to be removed. As shown in the photo above, looking toward the bow, a new deck was being installed using fine grain, old-growth Douglas fir. In the photo, a band saw for use in cutting lumber to a curved shape is resting on deck portside. *Sand Man*'s new bulwarks (not yet fitted at the time of the photo), for example, were to be made up of solid wood blocks cut to curved shapes.

The deck seams, as well as the hull seams, had not yet been caulked at the time of the photo. The edges of the hull and deck planks are beveled to a depth of approximately 3/4 of the thickness so that, when the planks are installed, there exists a V-shaped groove between each pair of strakes. To make the hull and deck watertight, the seams must be caulked. Using a mallet and tapered caulking irons, cotton strands are tapped into the tapered grooves. The cotton strands are very fine and can be pushed deeply into the V-shaped grooves. This step is followed by tapping oakum strands into the seams. The oakum is much more coarse than the cotton and, therefore, would be incapable of being forced into the extreme recess of a seam. On the other hand, because of the relative coarseness, the oakum fills a seam more readily than would cotton. Oakum is stranded from the hemp plant and then is soaked in pine tar. Finally, the seams are payed with marine pitch to seal out moisture.

The use of a mallet and caulking irons to fill the seams with cotton and oakum strands requires a great deal of skill. Tapping the strands too hard can result in the material being pushed through beyond the recess of a seam, thus tending to force the planks apart. On the other hand, insufficient force would result in a seam not being filled in a firm manner. The art of caulking, then, can best be learned by doing it, and an experienced caulker will know by feel and sound of the mallet when a seam has been properly filled.

In addition to new hull and deck planking, the ceiling on the inside of the hull frames, as well as many other structural components, had to be replaced due to deterioration, also.

319

A new stem for *Sand Man*'s bow, left, and a grown knee, right, for installation in *Sand Man*'s hull, 2001.

(From the author's collection)

In the photo at left above, a new sawn stem had been installed in *Sand Man*'s bow during the rebuild. The photo at right above shows what is known as a "grown knee," a curved piece of wood in which the natural grain flows around the L-shape of the component, thereby resulting in a strong structural member. This piece was cut from a hackmatack tree in New England. A knee can be installed to reinforce the joint between two structural members, such as the connection between a deck beam and a hull-side frame.

Other elderly tugs that had earned their keep on Puget Sound were able to avoid the bone-yard and are still in operation but, like *Sand Man*, are under private ownership. A number of these remaining towboats have had deckhouse modifications made to improve the living spaces, as well as repairs to correct the deficiencies of old age. Although many of these towboats have been repowered while in private ownership, a few still retain the big, slow-speed, direct-reversing diesel engines that had been installed many years ago.

Some of the boats have been renamed by new owners while others have retained the names they carried while employed in commercial towing. Whether carrying new names or old, all of these have been illustrated previously in the book or are pictured in this chapter.

Crosmor, formerly in commercial service for Olympia Towing Company as well as Dunlap Towing Company, has been sighted on Puget Sound as *Big Toot*. *Iver Foss* is now *Merilyn* and under new ownership. The tug *Prosper* eventually be-

came *Odin*. *Shannon Foss*, twin to previously described and pictured *Carol Foss*, was sold to private interests and renamed *Judi M*.

Other retired tugs have retained the names that had been used while working in commercial service. Some of these towboats are *Arthur Foss*, *Bee*, *Chicamauga* (*Sea Chicken* for a time during the towboat's working career), *Creosote*, *Elmore*, *Favorite*, *Henrietta Foss*, *Irene*, *Lorna Foss*, *Malolo*, *Nancy Foss*, *Oswell Foss*, *Palomar*, *Parthia*, *R. A. McDonald*, and *Tillicum*.

A tug that retained a portion of the original name after retirement is *Joe*, the former Foss Launch and Tug Company towboat *Joe Foss*. *Carl Foss* was given the name *Sound* by new owners, this name harking back to the name given to the boat at launch christening. *Catherine Foss* is now *Kathadin*, the boat's original name. *Foss No. 15* has been renamed *Elf*, the name the tug had when launched more than 100 years ago for service with Olson Tug Boat Company at Tacoma.

Many of these retired towboats are present at the Harbor Days celebration that is held each Labor Day weekend in Olympia. The tugs begin arriving at Percival Landing early on the weekend, and most of them welcome visitors to go aboard and visit. On Sunday afternoon, the towboats participate in spirited race heats over a one mile course in Budd Inlet, with the finish line at Butler Cove. On the next page, the photos demonstrate the attraction these aging towboats have for visitors, as evidenced by the crowds of people walking the floats and visiting on board the boats.

Oswell Foss and other towboats during Harbor Days at Olympia, 2000. (From the author's collection)

In these photos, *Oswell Foss*, *Elf* (ex-*Foss No. 15*) and other towboats, most under private ownership and no longer in commercial towing now, welcome onlookers at Percival Landing for Olympia Harbor Days festivities. These elderly tugs get a lot of attention from visitors.

Elf and other tugs during Harbor Days at Olympia, 1992. (From the author's collection)

Tillicum and *Virginia V* backing out at Olympia, 1987. (From the author's collection)

In the photo above, *Virginia V* had just slipped her lines and was backing away from Percival Landing in Olympia with a full load of passengers who were visiting for the Harbor Days celebration. During Harbor Days, races are held by vintage towboats as shown in the photo below.

In the upper photo just to the left of *Virginia V*, the 87-foot-long *Tillicum* was backing out of Percival Landing. Formerly at work for American Tug Boat Company, but now privately owned, *Tillicum* was built of wood at Ballard in 1901. At right in the photo, a ship can be seen loading at Olympia's port pier, and at left in the distance on Olympia's West Side, the barn-like building is Reliable Steel, formerly Reliable Welding Works shipyard, no longer building ships.

Tug race at Olympia, mid 1990s. (From the author's collection)

The Delta V. Smyth Tugs and Barges fleet, 1930s.

In a kiosk at Percival Landing in Olympia, a splendid portrait of the Delta V. Smyth Tugs and Barges Company fleet of tugs by the Jeffers Studio, probably from the late 1930s, is on display. The picture above is a photo reproduction of that display. The boats are, left to right, *Eau Claire, Olympian, Oysterman, Sand Man, Alice, Lumberman,* and the steam powered tug *Flosie. Olympian* was 37 feet long and built at Bremerton in 1921. The other tugs have been described elsewhere. Eventually, the name *Olympian* was handed over to replace the name *Flosie* on the steam tug's bow. From then on, the largest tug in Delta Smyth's fleet, carrying the name *Olympian,* could be thought of as the flagship representing the home port of Olympia. The tug *Parthia,* which

was operated somewhat later on by Smyth, bore a close resemblance to *Olympian* as shown above. Still later, *Alice* became *Simon Foss,* and *Flosie* received the name *Adeline Foss* while under Foss Launch and Tug ownership.

Delta Smyth's boats received good care and, judging by their smart appearances, may have received some touchup in preparation for this portrait. In the background, two Capital City Tug Company boats are partially visible beyond *Sand Man* and *Alice*; a portion of *Edward A. Young*'s deckhouse is visible, and just above *Sand Man*'s deckhouse, part of *Virgo Young*'s deckhouse can be seen. The Washington Veneer sawmill's burner and sawdust conveyor are at left in the background. At center, far in the background, the tall stack at the Washington Veneer plywood plant is visible. At the extreme left, in the distance, the Port of Olympia's pier and warehouse are in view.

The illustration at left, from a plaque in the same display at Percival Landing as the tug fleet portrait shown above, is a brief biography of Delta V. Smyth, who passed on in 1972, and the Olympia area companies that he founded. Two of the towboats listed on this plaque as being owned by Smyth, *Hoonah* and *Nile,* were owned by him during a period later than the time of the tug portrait shown here.

DELTA V. SMYTH TUG AND BARGE

Born in 1891, Delta V. Smyth started his maritime career operating the tug *Oysterman* for Brenner Oyster Company and in 1920 started his own tugboat business in Olympia. Throughout his career he owned over 30 tugs, including the *Sandman, Lumberman, Olympian, Nile* and *Hoonah.* First headquartered at the Percival Dock, he later moved his business northward along the waterfront. Smyth's tugs moved lumber, pulp, oil, oysters and logs and at one time rafted logs off railroad cars from north of the 4th Street bridge. Besides tugs, Smyth was active in a number of other waterfront businesses in the wood and oil industries, including Hardel Plywood, Ordel Oil, Capitol Boom Company and Delson Lumber.

Delta Smyth sold his tugboat business to Foss Launch & Tug Co. in 1961 and is remembered in the yearly Labor Day Harbor Fair tugboat races in Olympia with the award of the Delta V. Smyth trophy to the winner.

**Delta V. Smyth memorial plaque
at Percival Landing in Olympia.**

As the old tugs were becoming fatigued and as they gradually found their way into retirement, new tugs were being built starting in the 1950s, as described previously in these pages. With welding technology having improved, particularly during World War II, the new tugs are being built of steel, this material having become less expensive than wood for use in ship construction. The new tugs coming along are beamier and have more displacement. The stern of a tug is no longer being built with a fantail, but instead, a broad stern that sits right down into the water is being designed to provide cover for the propeller, thus reducing the amount of air being drawn down into the wheel from the water surface.

As time went on and towing firms were absorbed by other towing companies or put out of business by the decline in the wood products industries, the towboats based at Puget Sound ports became fewer in number. But the power of the main engines in tugs has been increasing to the point where horsepower in the 1000s is being installed rather than horsepower in the 100s. Life is moving faster now, and so are the tugs with their tows. Today, towboats based on Puget Sound are in operation with up to 10,000 or more horsepower in the engine room.

More power is needed now to handle the bigger barges being built, as well as for handling the larger ships that are coming out of the yards and entering service. The new engines being installed are smaller in dimensions and of less weight, while putting out more horsepower at a higher rpm than the old heavy-duty, slow-speed engines. The fuel tanks are of a capacity far greater than the tanks were in the old days to permit long range and to feed these powerful engines.

All manner of electronic equipment is now being installed in the pilothouse, and a lead line is no longer needed for sounding water depth. Heat and sound insulation is being attached to the bulkheads and overhead. Crew accommodations have improved with the increase in space that is being provided, and crew comfort is much improved compared with conditions of years ago.

In the photo below, the classy looking tug *Norma H* was alongside the not-so-little barge *Little Boyer* while preparing to move out of Elliott Bay to make a run to Alaska for Boyer Alaska Barge Lines. *Norma H* is yacht-like in appearance just as *Georgeanne H*, operated by Halvorsen Towing Company and pictured earlier in the book, was in the old days. The 78-foot *Norma H* was built by the Nichols Brothers yard at Freeland on Whidbey Island in 1977. Boyer Alaska is operated by descendants of Boyer Halvorsen.

In this photo, Island Tug and Barge Company's *Patricia S* was assisting *Norma H* by pulling at the head end of the big barge. The size and mass of *Little Boyer* illustrates why modern towboats require more power than the earlier tugs needed for doing a job efficiently.

Norma H and *Little Boyer* in Elliott Bay, 1997. (From the author's collection)

Arctic Dawn with *Killer Whale* in tow and *Patricia S* in Elliott Bay, 1997. (From the author's collection)

Killer Whale in Elliott Bay, 1997. (From the author's collection)

The old and the new are shown in the top photo of World-War-II-era towboats handling a large, modern barge. At right in the background, a Washington State Ferries Jumbo Class auto/passenger ferry was entering Elliott Bay on the way into the landing on Seattle's waterfront.

In these photos, *Arctic Dawn* was entering Elliott Bay with *Killer Whale*, a 272-foot bulk-cement barge, in tow. The trip originated in the Fraser River in British Columbia, and the cargo was destined for Tilbury Cement Company located on the Duwamish Waterway in Seattle. *Patricia S* had just swung in alongside in preparation for assisting in handling the big barge when nearing the destination in the narrow channel of the Duwamish Waterway. *Arctic Dawn* and *Patricia S*, ex-U.S. Navy steel tugs of World War II vintage, were more than 50 years old at the time of the photo.

As a bulk cement carrier, *Killer Whale* is an example of a specialized barge. In recent times, many other barges have also been custom designed explicitly for transporting certain types of cargo. Like *Little Boyer*, pictured on the previous page, *Killer Whale* is large and requires a tug with a good deal of horsepower to handle it.

Arctic Dawn was being operated under a lease arrangement by Island Tug and Barge Company, also located on the Duwamish Waterway in Seattle. *Patricia S*, however, was owned by the towing firm. Island Tug and Barge was founded in the late 1970s with headquarters at Winslow in Eagle Harbor on Bainbridge Island, hence the origin of the name.

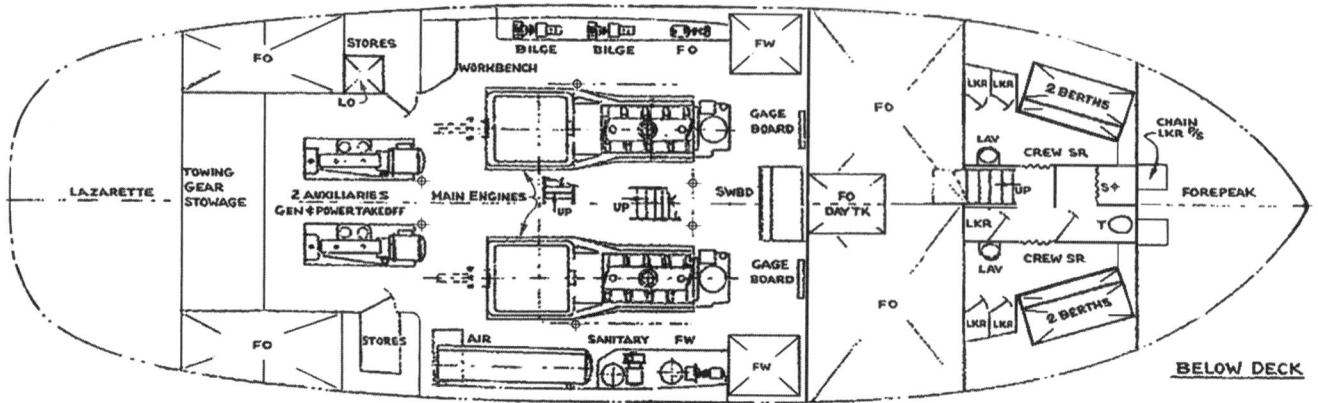

BELOW DECK

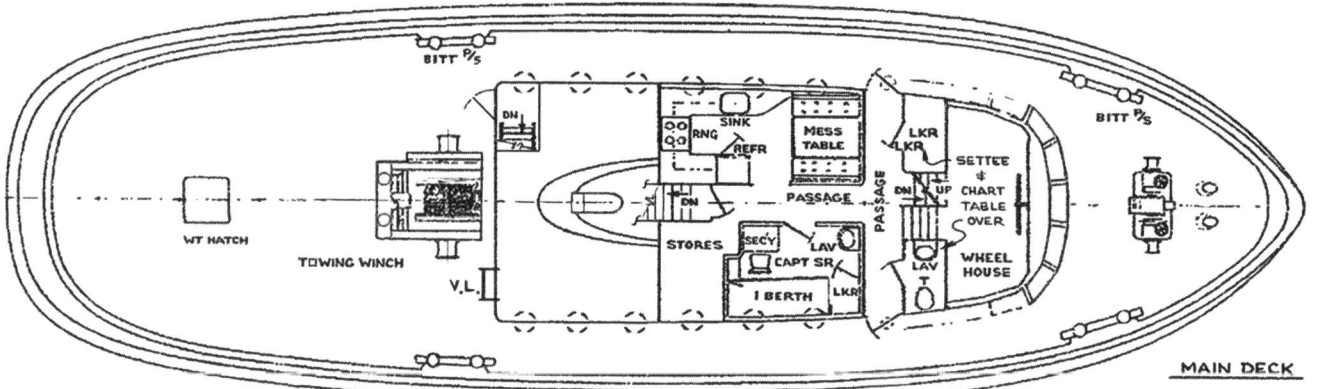

MAIN DECK

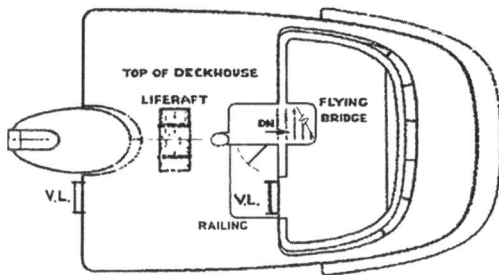

FLYING BRIDGE & HOUSE TOP

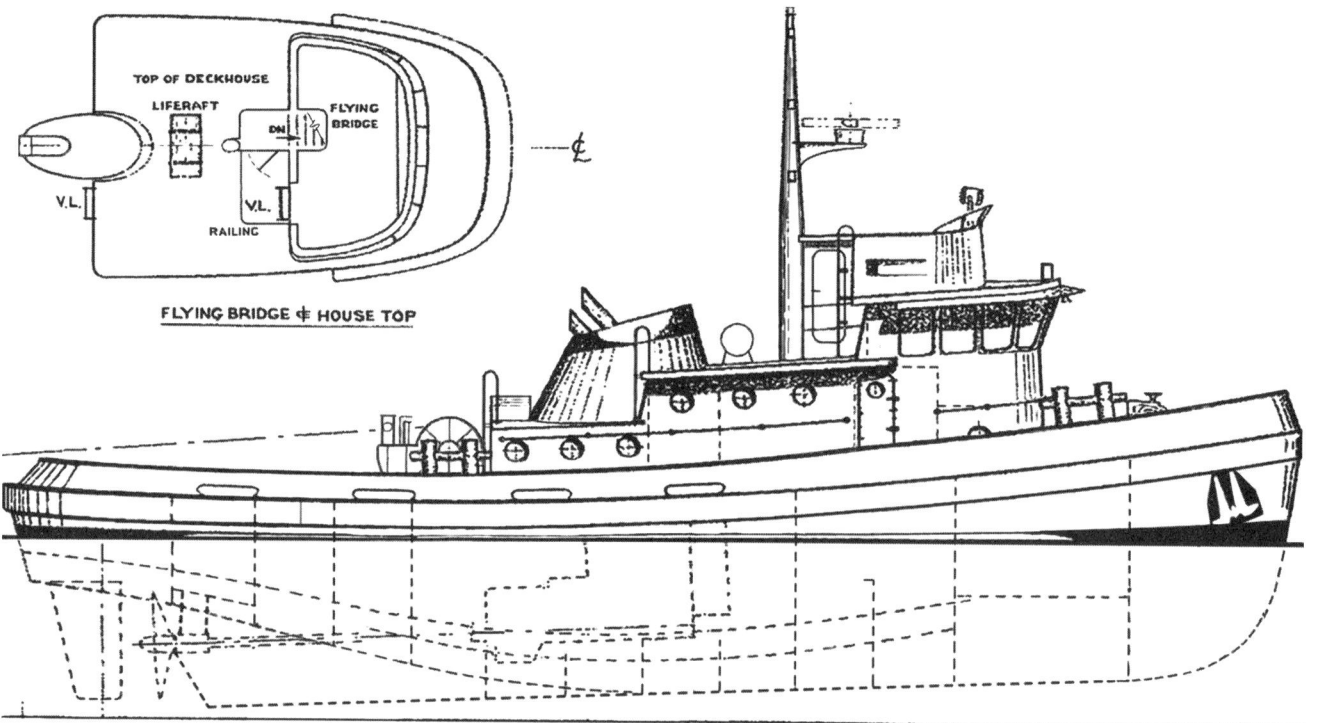

OUTBOARD PROFILE   N. KNUTSEN

A modern tug design with a split-level deckhouse and flying bridge.

Above and at the top of the next page are two drawings of a modern towboat. Both versions are assumed to be about 78 feet long overall and built of steel. These concept drawings are intended to show up-to-date arrangements as compared with the layout of the earlier tugs.

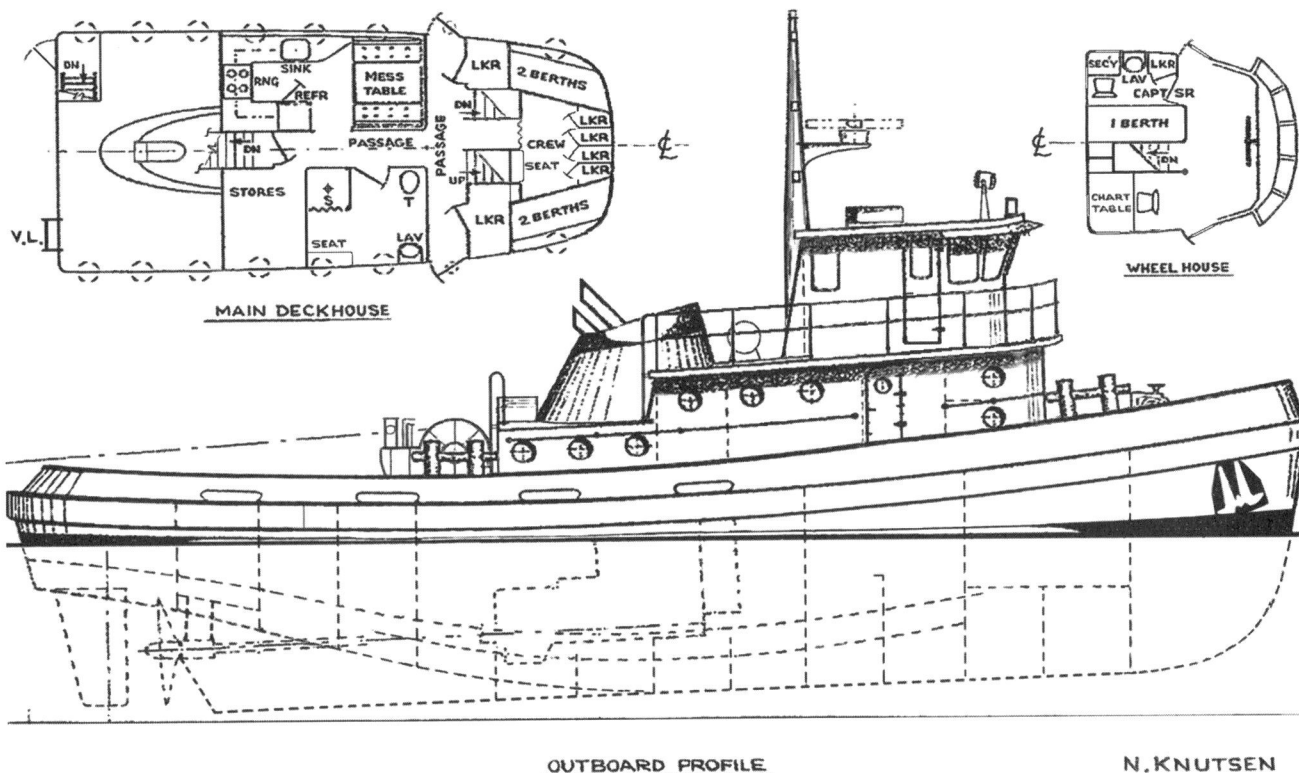

Main parts labeled in diagram:
- MAIN DECKHOUSE
- WHEEL HOUSE
- OUTBOARD PROFILE
- N. KNUTSEN

A modern tug design with a two-level deckhouse.

These two tug concepts are similar except that for the version shown above the pilothouse has been raised up to the bridge deck level. In this configuration, all crew accommodations are at the main deck or above, and space no longer occupied by crew quarters below deck, as in the version shown on the previous page, is available for additional stores and tanks. With modern engines, towboats of the size shown here can utilize in excess of 1500 horsepower, although the engine room is a bit crowded in that horsepower range.

In the photo below, the 100-foot, 3000-horsepower tug *Henry Foss*, of a design different from the more conventional towboats illustrated on this and the previous page, was maneuvering in the harbor at Olympia. This tug is the third to carry the name *Henry Foss*. The original towboat of that name, pictured earlier in the book, sank in British Columbia in 1959 with tragic loss of life. The second *Henry Foss* was in operation until 1979.

Equipped with what is referred to as a cycloidal propulsion system, the newest *Henry Foss*, built in the early 1980s, can maneuver in ways that a conventional tug with a propeller and rudder cannot. Vessels possessing characteristics similar to *Henry Foss* are sometimes known as "tractor tugs." In this photo, *Henry Foss* was moving sidewise, and on demand, the tug can move in longitudinal and lateral directions independently or simultaneously, as well as maintain position and rotate in place without travel.

The latest *Henry Foss* at Olympia, 1992. (From the author's collection)

At right are two views of a system that is used for converting power from the engine to thrust for ship propulsion. The illustration at left is an elevation of the system, and the illustration at right is a view looking up at the bottom of a ship hull showing the blades projecting downward. Produced by the German firm Voith-Schneider, the unit as shown is basically similar to the one installed in *Henry Foss*, but the configuration would vary somewhat depending upon the intended usage and amount of power applied.

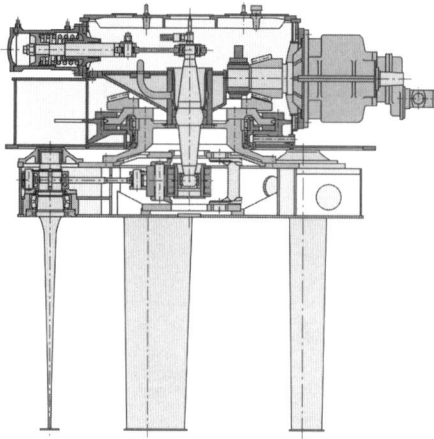

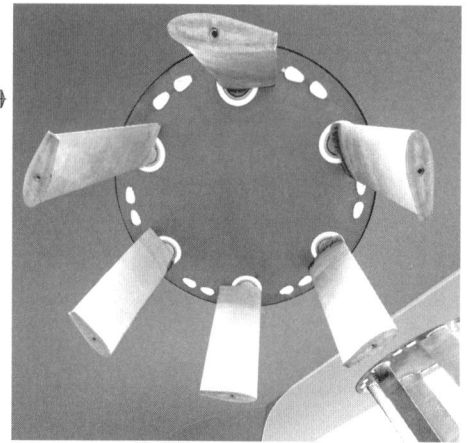

Two views of Voith-Schneider propeller.
(With permission of Voith-Schneider GmbH and Co.)

In the Voith-Schneider system, a rotor casing that fits flush with the ship's bottom rotates about a vertical axis and is fitted with a number of axially parallel blades. Each blade can also rotate about its own vertical axis, similar to a feathering airplane propeller blade. As the rotor turns, the blades are carried around with it in a circular motion, much like a merry-go-round. When generating thrust, each blade oscillates about its own axis, the angle of individual blade pitch changing throughout each rotor full rotation. Thus, the propulsion system can generate thrust in any direction in response to commands. In the photo of *Henry Foss* on the previous page, the tug was moving laterally to starboard in response to a pilothouse command that had directed propulsion thrust to port.

Shown at right is another versatile propulsion device, the Rudderpropeller, produced by the German firm Schottel. This unit projects down through the bottom of the hull and can rotate about the vertical axis to provide thrust in any direction. A hull-mounted engine supplies power to the propeller through the unit's right-angle shafts and gears.

Systems such as the Schottel unit, in various forms, have also been referred to as Z-drive, Z-peller, inboard/outboard drive,

Schottel Rudderpropeller.
(From Schottel literature)

and stern drive, the details varying with the application. This type of propulsion has been in existence for many years, and based in the Boston, Massachusetts area, Murray and Tregurtha were early pioneers in working with the concept.

During World War II, Murray and Tregurtha produced a great number of outboard drives for use on U.S. military barges. The Livonia, Michigan, firm Harbormaster Marine now produces these units. Years ago, one of the power scows that I decked aboard in Bristol Bay, Alaska, utilized such a device for propulsion. The engine was at deck level, and the transmission and propeller were mounted on the stern.

Washington State Ferries continued with the construction of new vessels to to meet the increasing demands of the traveling public. On the next page is the outboard profile for the Jumbo Class auto/passenger ferries as designed by Philip F. Spaulding and Associates and launched by the Todd Seattle yard in 1972. These new ferries were larger than any built previously.

Two vessels were built, *Spokane* and *Walla Walla*, each with an overall length of 440 feet and capacity for 2000 passengers and, with a double-car deck similar to the *Hyak* Class ferries, 206 vehicles. A diesel-electric propulsion plant of 11,500-horsepower gives the Jumbo Class ferries a service speed of 18 knots.

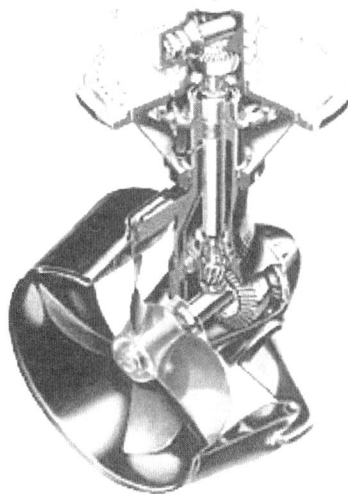

328

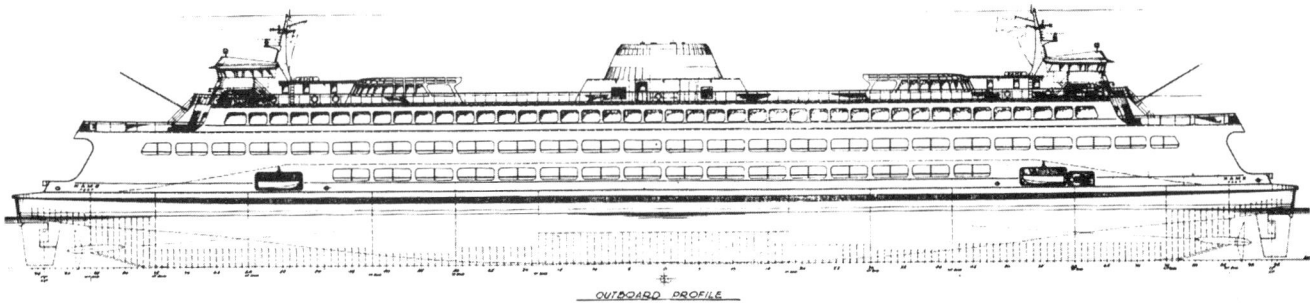

Jumbo Class auto/passenger ferry outboard profile, 1972.
(From a Philip F. Spaulding and Associates drawing)

Following construction of the Jumbo Class ferries, the need for additional new vessels continued. In 1981, design and construction was underway for a new group of ferries, known as the *Issaquah* Class, with capacity for 100 vehicles and 1200 passengers. This ferry series consists of *Cathlamet, Chelan, Issaquah, Kitsap,* and *Kittitas,* all later modified to carry 130 vehicles, plus *Sealth,* which remains as-built. All are 328 feet long overall with 5000 horsepower providing a 16 knot speed. The outward appearance of these ferries departs little from that of previous designs, except in some styling details such as, for example, the appearance of the pilothouse.

Marine Power and Equipment Company, located at the north end of Lake Union, was awarded the contract for the construction of the *Issaquah* Class ferries. Marine Power had been in the business of, primarily, ship repair for a number of years but had not been known as a yard that had a lot of experience in new-vessel construction, especially as related to building large and complex ferries.

The U.S. Gulf Coast shipyards have, for many decades, been able to build ships at lower cost than yards in other parts of the country, primarily due to lower labor cost. This difference in cost has traditionally been figured at 6 percent, a significant handicap that is difficult to overcome by yards elsewhere when bidding on a job. To keep the construction of the *Issaquah* Class ferries in the hands of a Washington State shipyard, the state legislature provided funds to cover this differential to Marine Power and Equipment.

By the time the *Issaquah* Class vessels were being built, both W. C. Nickum and Sons Company and Phillip F. Spaulding and Associates, after many years in business, were no longer in the profession of naval architecture and marine engineering. Hence, these design firms were not available to put their knowledge and experience to work for creating the new ferries.

In taking on the *Issaquah* Class ferry project, Marine Power embarked on a job that required skilled personnel with experience related to the work. These kinds of credentials are usually described to the client as part of the bid. If a firm does not already have these assets in place, then acquiring them is not an easy task.

Unfortunately, problems developed during and after construction of the *Issaquah* Class ferries, particularly regarding the decision to use a computer-aided controllable pitch propeller system for propulsion instead of the proven and successful diesel-electric system that uses a fixed pitch propeller. A controllable pitch propeller rotates in one direction only, and a vessel equipped with this type of propeller can move forward or back by changing the angle of pitch of the propeller blades, rather than changing the direction of propeller rotation as would be done with a fixed pitch propeller. Controllable pitch propellers have been used successfully, but introducing a computer into the system did not have a lot of precedent.

For many years, aircraft, both commercial and military, have been flying by means of a fly-by-wire system consisting of computers that function between the cockpit controls and the aero surfaces. However, to produce a successful operating system such as that requires a good deal of research, design, experience and testing. These intricacies are complex and are not easily modeled when writing the software and creating the hardware. Ship handling is involved and sometimes requires the kind of subtle touch on the controls that humans can deliver.

Problems can occur in the application of computers and in developing algorithms for use in software that can accurately replicate complex behavior. Computers do not make mistakes, but as the old saying goes, if the input is garbage then the output will also be garbage. Such, apparently, was the case with the *Issaquah* Class ferries.

For a number of years, considerable damage was done to landings because of malfunctions in the operating system aboard these ferries. On one shocking occasion, an automobile was dropped into the bay when a misbehaving *Issaquah* Class ferry began moving out of the landing slip while vehicles were being loaded. At times, response to pilothouse controls was unpredictable, and a vessel could not be steered on a desired course. *Issaquah* vessels broke down on many occasions and required tug assistance to a landing so that the passengers could disembark. The public became disgruntled and costs to the taxpayers grew large. Lawsuits between the state of Washington and Marine Power and Equipment abounded.

Expansion of the ferry fleet continued in the 1990s with the planning, by a design team assembled by Washington State Ferries, of the Jumbo Mark II Class auto/passenger ferries *Puyallup*, *Tacoma*, and *Wenatchee*, pictured below. These new vessels were built by the Todd yard at Seattle. With a length overall of 460 feet, these ferries carry 2500 passengers and 218 vehicles at 18 knots. For the new Jumbo Mark II Class ferries, the designers rejected the propulsion system as employed aboard the *Issaquah* Class ferries, with their attitude problem, and the more reliable diesel-electric system was again used.

While the new auto/passenger ferries were entering service, efforts were made to bring back passenger-only ferries on some of the routes traveled by the mosquito fleet of fast steamers in the old days. As described earlier in these pages, the mosquito-fleet vessels were done in by the increasing popularity of travel by automobile on the new highways that were being built. Attempts, which have even included trials with a hydrofoil, in recent years by the state of Washington to establish regular passenger-only service in various areas of Puget Sound have resulted in discouragement or, at best, mixed success.

The hydrofoil was invented by Enrico Forlanini in Italy in 1906. In 1919, Americans Alexander Bell and Casey Baldwin developed a hydrofoil called the Hydrodome that could reach a reported speed of 60 knots. A foil system was located near the bow and another at the stern, each foil installation consisting of multiple foils, or wings, grouped in an array much like a multiwing aircraft such as a biplane or triplane. As the power was increased, the boat climbed higher out of the water until the hull was above the water surface and only the lowest foils in the array were submerged. Such an array of surfaces was known as a "ladder" foil.

Later hydrofoils, in commercial service throughout the world, have utilized a single foil at each support. These boats have made use of surface-piercing foils; that is, each foil has dihedral like an airplane wing so that the lowest portion of a foil at vessel centerline is underwater at the design speed but the outer portion at the foil tips is above water. Hence, equipped with foils that are more or less skimming along at the water surface, a vessel would experience some rolling and pitching motion in rough water which could cause seasickness in the passengers.

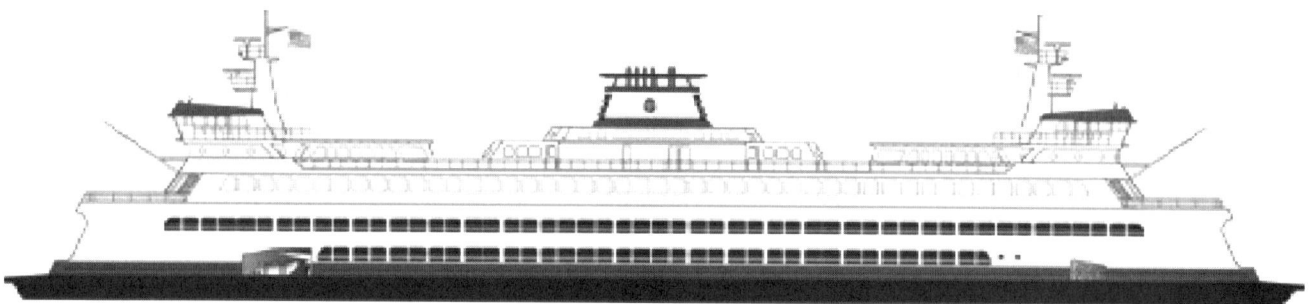

Jumbo Mark II Class ferry outboard profile, 1999.
(From Washington State Ferries literature)

In the late 1950s, the Boeing Company began development of a passenger-carrying hydrofoil featuring fully submerged foils. In this configuration, the foils did not pierce the water surface but were deep enough under water that, in moderate sea states, vessel motion would be negligible and ocean operation became feasible.

In the late 1970s, Washington State Ferries and the Boeing Company jointly operated a Boeing-built Jetfoil on Puget Sound for several weeks to explore the feasibility of high-speed passenger transportation. By the end of the trial period, Washington State Ferries determined that expenses were too great to permit further use of the Jetfoil.

In 1985, a company by the name of Island Jetfoil, headed by C. Stewart Vinnels of Victoria, British Columbia, was formed to provide Jetfoil passenger service between Seattle and the British Columbia cities of Victoria and Vancouver. The Jetfoil intended for this route had been operating in Argentine waters prior to acquisition by Island Jetfoil, but as it turned out, Island Jetfoil was unable to sustain itself, and operations ceased. At right is a reduced size reproduction of an Island Jetfoil advertising poster.

The Boeing Jetfoil hull and superstructure were built of aluminum, and the struts and foils were fabricated of stainless steel. The foil system consisted of a single strut forward supporting a foil and two struts aft, one on each side of the hull, with a foil, larger than the forward foil, supported between them. This arrangement is known as a canard configuration and can be seen in the illustration shown here.

Jetfoil was usually arranged to carry at least 250 passengers at a speed of well over 40 knots. Propulsion was provided by a pair of 3,800-horsepower Rolls Royce Allison gas turbines, located aft, that drove two Rocketdyne sea water pumps. The pumps discharged through nozzles at the stern; hence, water-jet propulsion and the name Jetfoil. The control system was a computer-operated, fly-by-wire arrangement, and the control surfaces on the foils automatically adjusted for any influence by waves, which in normal sea states produced a ride with little or no rolling and pitch-

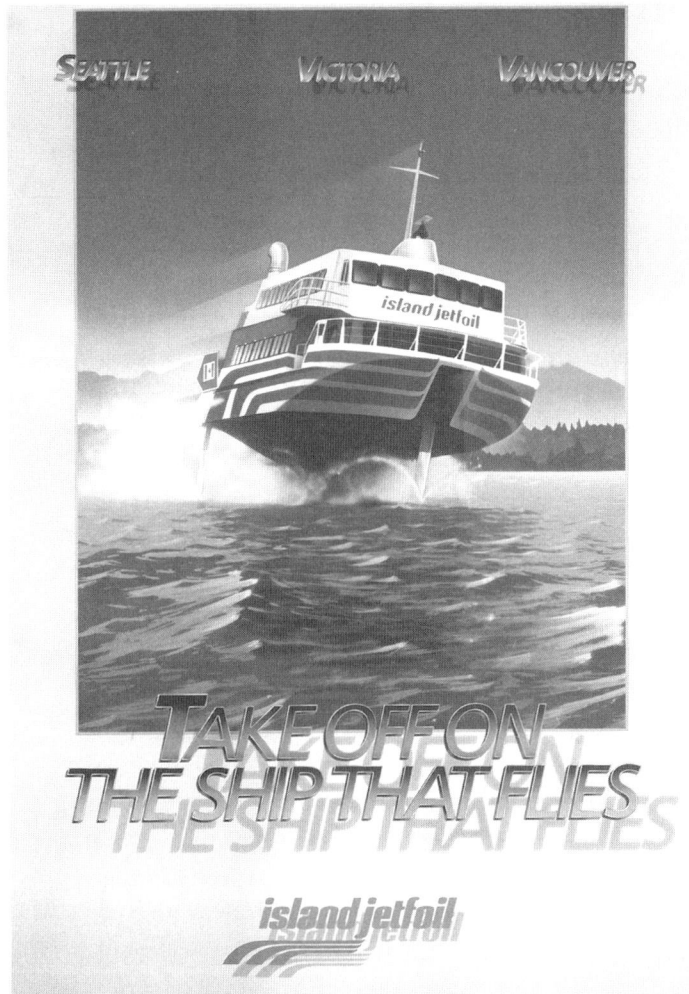

Island Jetfoil advertising poster, 1985.
(From the author's collection)

ing. Jetfoil was designed to provide coordinated turns; that is, the hydrofoil banked in a turn like an airplane.

Jetfoils were in use at various locations around the world. Some applications were successful for a time, but some routes presented difficulties. In certain areas, a potential hazard was striking a whale at high speed. In an Argentine incident, a Jetfoil struck a whale, which resulted in the tragic death of a stewardess when the sudden deceleration of the Jetfoil at impact threw her down a flight of stairs. Jetfoil service was initiated in the Hawaiian Islands but was eventually terminated. Although Jetfoil did well in most sea states, the waves in the area of the Hawaiian Islands were large enough that Jetfoil, even though the control system dampened a lot of the pitching motion, still did some contouring through the swells, which caused sea sickness in a number of passengers.

My experience aboard Jetfoil was one of comfort. The seats were of the airplane-type, and the ride was quiet and smooth. Takeoffs and landings were barely perceptible. Banking through turns reminded one of being aboard an airplane. But it all came to an end; the acquisition and maintenance costs of Jetfoil were high, and passenger revenues were insufficient to support service.

Even so, Washington State Ferries continued to pursue the establishment of passenger-only service on Puget Sound. In the late 1980s, WSF purchased a catamaran named *Express* that had been built by the Nichols Brothers yard on Whidbey Island. Renamed *Tyee*, this ferry carried 319 passengers at a speed of 23 knots. Then the fast ferries *Kalama* and *Skagit*, built by the Equitable yard in New Orleans, Louisiana, were added to the fleet. Of monohull design, *Kalama* and *Skagit* could carry 250 passengers at a 25 knot speed.

A contentious issue developed, though. Off and on, going back a long time before, the residents lining Rich Passage had complained about beach erosion caused by the wake sent out by some of the ferries. Although the speedy passenger-only vessels gave the appearance of slicing cleanly through the water, particularly the catamarans, appearance can sometimes be deceiving; wrath was felt as delivered by Rich Passage residents who claimed that the wake created by these fast ferries was causing damage on the shoreline.

A consultant was hired by Washington State Ferries to evaluate the situation, and the finding verified that wake damage indeed was occurring on the beaches of Rich Passage. The passenger-only ferries were then slowed to 12 knots when running Rich Passage. As a result, the trip time between Seattle and Bremerton increased from 40 minutes to more than 50 minutes, which was only a few minutes faster than the elapsed time auto-passenger ferries were making the run. The advantage that the passenger-only ferries had in reduced trip time compared with the auto-passenger ferries pretty much dwindled away.

While piloting a boat in deep water, I have crossed the wake of the speedy *Tyee*. The wake consisted of smooth swells of moderate height and long wave length. When crossing this wake, my small vessel responded with only a moderate pitching motion.

In mid-ocean, the waves that make up a seismic-generated tsunami have extremely low height compared with the wave length and travel at a high rate of speed. At sea, a tsunami wave may be only a few inches to a few feet in height with a length of 100 miles or more while moving at several hundred knots. Even at tsunami-speed, such a wave would require a number of minutes to pass under a ship, and because of the low height relative to the enormous length, those aboard a ship would likely not even realize that a tsunami had passed under the hull. Although a tsunami is undetectable at sea except by sensitive instruments, when the waves have traveled to the much shallower water near the beach, the length and speed decrease, and the height increases, resulting in tremendous devastation as they sweep ashore.

The size of the swell produced by *Tyee*, of course, was hardly a tiny ripple compared to the magnitude of a tsunami. Still, the fundamental behavior of waves is similar, regardless of size, and the wake produced by the high-speed passenger-only ferry could be thought of as a tsunami in miniature: a series of gentle swells of moderate height and long length in deep water that could pile up and produce a sizable surf at the shoreline.

At low tide, the water depth in Rich Passage averages about 12 fathoms, plenty deep enough that the wake produced by a passenger-only ferry at that location would be similar to the gentle swell that I have encountered in water of several times that in depth. However, considering that Rich Passage is narrow, the wake at mid-channel would not have had a great distance to travel before reaching shore. In such a case, the waves would have advanced to shallow water without losing much of their energy and, with increased wave height, hit the beach with considerable force.

In 1991, Washington State Ferries initiated a program to acquire additional passenger-only ferries and, as a part of that process, again asked a consultant to study the wake that would be produced by various designs. The conclusions were then used as criteria for selecting a design by the Australian firm Multi-Hull Designs, Ltd. The results of the study indicated that the wake produced by vessels conforming to this design and operating at rated speed, would not cause damage to the shoreline in Rich Passage.

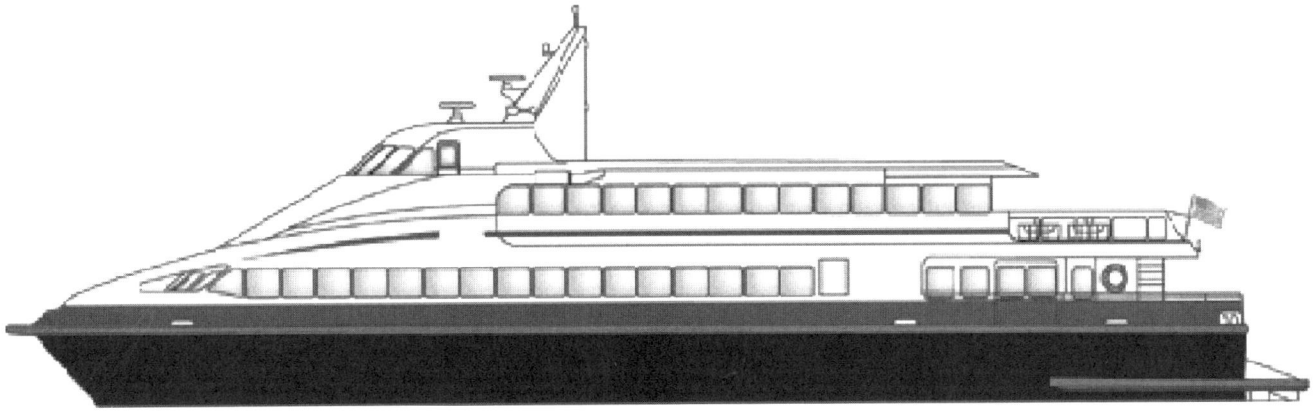

Chinook **Class passenger-only ferry, 1991. (From Washington State Ferries literature)**

WSF signed a contract with Dakota Creek Industries of Anacortes for the construction of the ferries, *Chinook* and *Snohomish*, shown above in outboard profile. Of catamaran configuration and more than 140 feet in length, the ferries built by Dakota Creek could carry 350 passengers in comfort at a speed of 38 knots. Power was supplied by four diesel engines that produced 7,200 total horsepower. These engines drove pumps that provided water-jet propulsion, a system similar to that of Jetfoil except for the use of diesel engines instead of gas turbines.

Getting there fast is expensive in fuel and maintenance, and the cost for acquiring and operating a high-speed vessel is high. Although the cost for operating a hull-borne ferry was less than would have been incurred with a foil-borne craft, attracting a ridership and maintaining a consistently high passenger load that could provide revenue to help offset the expense was still a challenge. What finally sank the passenger-only ferry operation between Seattle and Bremerton, though, was the same old problem involving the run through narrow Rich Passage. These new ferries were not expected to create a troublesome wake, but unfortunately, a damaging surf was created at the Rich Passage beaches by these new vessels, too, and the protests were heard again.

Since then, high-speed passenger-only service has been sporadic. Off and on, though, there have been proposals by Washington State Ferries and, also, by private operators to continue regularly scheduled passenger-only transportation on Seattle-Bremerton and Vashon-Southworth routes. Other service has been proposed that would include Seattle-Olympia and Seattle-Kingston runs.

Such a transportation system would replicate a few of the old mosquito-fleet routes. Trial runs of passenger-only ferries have been made on other routes, too, but for a variety of reasons, nothing substantial and long-lasting has emerged.

Meanwhile, the auto-passenger ferries that were built in recent years are still in operation. The majority of the ferries from long ago, though, succumbed to advanced age and went away, just as most of the old towboats disappeared from the sound. Four of the elderly steel-electric ferries, *Illahee*, *Klickitat*, *Nisqually*, and *Quinalt*, described earlier in the book, have finally deteriorated and were only recently pulled from service with Washington State Ferries. These were the 1927 San Francisco ferries that were displaced by new bridges in the Bay Area and brought north for Captain Peabody's Black Ball Line in the 1930s.

The 1947 ferry *Rhododendron*, towed to Puget Sound from Baltimore, Maryland, in 1953 by Puget Sound Tug and Barge's *Wando*, has needed much in the way of repairs and upgrades over the years but is still in operation. How much longer this elderly, hard-working vessel can keep going is questionable, though.

Evergreen State, *Klahowya*, and *Tillicum*, of the mid to late 1950s, are still in service on Puget Sound routes. The "Super Ferries" *Elwha*, *Hyak*, *Kaleetan*, and *Yakima*, as well as the smaller *Hiyu*, all of them new in the 1960s, are also still at work. These eight ferries, designed by W. C. Nickum and Sons Company, are not getting any younger, though, and, although they have given good service, are in an age group that needs increased maintenance and repairs to continue carrying autos and passengers.

A transportation system is made up of parts that need to be integrated to facilitate portal-to-portal movement of people. Most people need ground transportation to get to the beginning of a bus, rail, or ferry route and from the end of a bus, rail, or ferry route to the ultimate destination.

Many years ago, while living in the small town of Pitman, New Jersey, I commuted daily to a job as a naval architect at New York Shipbuilding Corporation in Camden. In Pitman, the distance from home to the local train station was an easy walking distance on level ground, and the distance to work by rail was about 15 miles, the train making a stop at the shipyard. The return trip in the afternoon was the reverse, and the commute was a relaxing and pleasant experience.

Most people do not live or work close to a bus, rail, or ferry stop. Then, too, a walk in the hilly terrain of western Washington would be too arduous for some. It may be, however, that if local transportation were available on schedule at the start and end points of a commute, a service such as a high-speed passenger-only ferry, for example, could become popular with the public; the substantial cost of acquiring, maintaining, and operating a high-speed ferry is intimidating, though.

Private investors have offered to operate passenger-only ferries, and in fact, with state approval, trial service was provided to evaluate passenger usage, and the results showed some promise. Recently, Washington State, King County, Kitsap County, and private interests have been working through the issues of who should be in the business of operating passenger-only ferry service and what routes might be put into operation.

The majority of employment opportunities are located on the east side of Puget Sound, but many people live in the relatively unpopulated west side of the sound. Anyone living west of Puget Sound but employed east of the sound must either ride a ferry or drive a long distance, frequently in heavy traffic either by way of the Narrows Bridge at Tacoma or around the southern end of the sound, to and from work. Most of the morning and early evening ferry riders on weekdays, then, are commuters who have chosen to go by water.

Less than two-thirds of the Washington State Ferry system cost is paid for through fares; the remainder is funded by public money through taxation. A fare paid by a ferry user is equivalent to a toll, and indeed, a ferry might be thought of as a form of bridge across the water. However, use of fixed bridges in the state of Washington does not require the payment of a toll (except, perhaps, a temporary toll to help pay for a new bridge) nor does traveling anywhere else on highways in the state. It would seem that there are inconsistencies in funding methods. In the Midwest and north eastern United States, many frequently-traveled roads, bridges, and tunnels carry a toll, but not in the West.

Today, the problems involved with moving people and goods in the increasingly populated Puget Sound region are among the biggest issues facing the public and government. The greatest portion of highway traffic moves in a north-south direction on the east side of Puget Sound. This corridor is bounded by water to the west and the Cascade foothills to the east, and much of the once undeveloped land between the water and mountains has by now been built on. Any expansion of these burdened highways would require a lot of time and money.

Recently, with growing population, the roads have frequently become so stuffed with slowly-moving cars and trucks containing frustrated drivers and passengers that additional integrated public transportation will probably be required. Americans have an affection for their cars and a feeling of independence that goes with using them, so enticing drivers out of their vehicles to use public transportation could be a challenge.

Western Washington is an area of numerous waterways, and in addition to bridges, ferries are needed to span them. The bridges and ferries are aging, but so are the ferry landings and terminals, as well as the roads. As might be imagined, a lot of ill-humor has been shown by ferry riders in reaction to fare increases. This is just one indicator that money to solve regional transportation problems could be hard to come by. Problems result if funds are not set aside over the years to take care of future equipment repairs and replacement. Establishing a fund for repair, replacement, and additions requires foresight and planning, and if the money is not there when needed, it takes a huge hard-to-swallow lump sum to make things right in the business of transportation.

If running the Washington State Ferry system, the largest such fleet in the United States, is a difficult task, perhaps managing the Pacific Northwest fisheries is equally challenging. The prime job of fisheries management is to look after the sea life while also dealing with the pressures that are applied by varied groups of people whose points of view and interests may be in competition. Fisheries management must use whatever is within their authority to prevent depletion of sea life that can occur due to pollution of the rivers and the sea, as well as from over-fishing.

On summer afternoons of 65 or 70 years ago, I swam with other children in Budd Inlet at Olympia. At the time, many waterfront homes simply emptied their sewers into the harbor, so occasionally undesirable objects floated by. Nonetheless, the author and the others survived in good shape, and apparently the sea life did too, since the fishing was good. But the number of people living in the area was only a fraction of the population of today, and presumably, the amount of pollution produced was much less than the contamination of today. By now, though, the increased pollution from industry, farms and households appears to be overwhelming the sea's healing power.

Today, fish are not found in the abundance that existed many years ago, and as a result, both commercial and sport fishing have had to be curtailed. Periods of time open for fishing have been shortened, and in addition, limits have been set on the number of fish caught. In some cases, fishing boats and licenses have been purchased by the government in buy-back programs. Ocean bottom trawling has been curtailed in some areas to prevent further damage to the sea floor; a bottom trawl scoops up everything in its path and some species of sea life are unintentionally destroyed in the process.

The issues mentioned above are only some of the problems that must be dealt with and are not unique to the Pacific Northwest but also exist in other areas of the United States and, indeed, the world. When problems caused by humankind are put together with natural cycles that occur in the ocean and atmosphere (many believe that global warming of the atmosphere is caused in large part by industrial and domestic pollution), the future of natural resources appears to be at risk.

In part as a result of the declining fish stocks and the restrictions placed on fishing, shipbuilding activity in the Puget Sound area has declined to a point where, of the many shipyards mentioned earlier in the book, only a few remain in business today. The latest casualty was Marine Construction and Design Company of Seattle. Marine Construction and Design built primarily commercial fish boats over a period spanning a half-century but recently ceased operations. For many years, the moorages at Fishermen's Terminal in Ballard were filled with commercial fishing vessels that were lying idle between seasons, but with the decline in the size of the fleet, some moorage space that would otherwise be unoccupied is now in use by pleasure craft.

Like the tugs, most of the earlier commercial fish boats are gone, too, but a few have survived. A fish boat that is still in operation after many years is the classic Pacific Northwest wooden troller *Duwam*, pictured in the photo at left while resting at Fishermen's Terminal in Ballard. The 33-foot *Duwam* was built at Seattle in 1940 and has since been outfitted with modern electronic equipment.

Duwam at Fishermen's Terminal in Ballard, 2006.
(From the author's collection)

The wooden purse-seiner *Antarctic*, another old timer still rigged for fishing, is pictured here while at Fishermen's Terminal in Ballard. The 59-foot *Antarctic* was built by the Martinolich shipyard at Dockton in 1927. Later additions are a pilothouse of modern appearance on top of the main deckhouse and a powered block hanging from the boom.

Antarctic at Fishermen's Terminal in Ballard, 2006.
(From the author's collection)

As described, the number of vessels in the Pacific Northwest fishing fleet is smaller than it was a number of years ago, and most of the boats built back in the earlier days have disappeared. Some of the boats currently operating on the North Pacific Coast were formerly at work on the East Coast or the Gulf of Mexico but wcrc surplused following the reduction of fishing in those areas. The size of the catch is restricted now by conservation measures that have been put in place. Then, too, the catching of wild fish has competition today from farms that cultivate fish in quiet salt water bays. In the earlier days, the catch was usually delivered to shoreside plants for processing, but today, much of the commercial fishing is being done by large vessels, usually owned by big companies that can both catch and process the fish.

In the photo at left, a monument to fishermen stands at Fishermen's Terminal. At the top of the column, the bronze statue depicts a lone fisherman hauling in a halibut caught on hook and line. At lower left in the photo, placed there are bronze plaques inscribed with the names of fishermen who have been lost at sea since the beginning of the last century while pursuing the ancient, and frequently dangerous, occupation of commercial fishing. The names are many.

This has been a glimpse of the present. There is still some commercial activity on the water and along the shore of Puget Sound, but nevertheless, everything looks so, well, modern-like. Most of the lumber and other wood-products industries that existed in the earlier days have departed, though, and the old-time freighters and other vessels that went about their business out on the saltwater, while capturing the imaginations of young and old, are no longer around, except for a few. Most of the folks who walked the decks of those hard-working vessels have passed on, too. For many people who were there in those days, it seemed as if things would always be that way, but it turned out to be sort of fleeting when placed in the greater context of time.

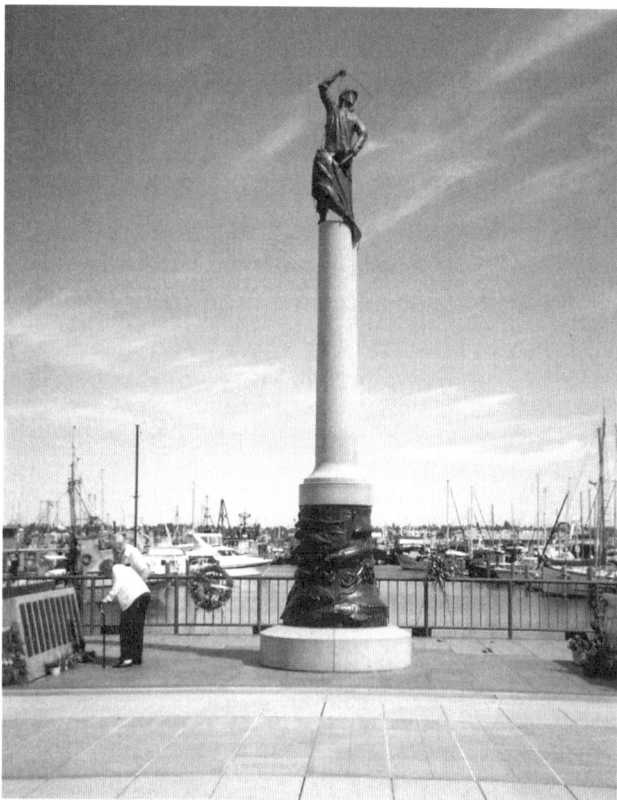

At Fishermen's Terminal in Ballard,
memorial to fishermen lost at sea, 2006.
(From the author's collection)

But that was the way it was, and this is the way it is. Things are still pretty good, and in many ways, life is better today. It is good to revisit the past, but maybe it is best that one not stay there too long because one should live in the present and look to the future, as well. There are occasions, though, when the past beckons and one cannot help but reflect upon a time when things moved along on a slow bell, as compared with the speed-of-light pace of today.

In the earlier days, people used whatever technology was available, but at least, they had not been supplanted by automation to a great degree. In these fast, and sometimes hectic, modern times, it is pleasant to remember an era when the sawmills and builders of wooden boats were busy, when the folks in town could set their clocks by listening to the steam whistles that blew at the sawmills, when a pleasant fragrance arose from the wood chips that surrounded a stout wooden boat under construction, when a ringing sound could be heard at each strike by a wooden mallet on a caulking iron, when a long line of railroad cars was being pulled by the brute force of a massive steam locomotive, when a vessel's engine room presented the elegance of a marine steam engine and was filled with the aroma of hot lube oil and the warmth of the firebox and boiler, when one could hear the sound of a whistle bouncing off the bank in a fog announcing a towboat finding a way through the obscurity, when the musical jingle-and-gong telegraph could be heard emanating from a towboat's engine room; when each of the tugs had a distinctive personality, and when the steam engines and the big slow-speed, direct-reversing diesel engines displayed a soothing rhythmic sound. These are pretty much gone, but they left vivid imprints on the mind and senses.

N. KNUTSEN

SELECTED BIBLIOGRAPHY OF RELATED READING

Books

Andrews, Ralph W. and Larssen, A. K. Fish and Ships, Seattle, Washington, 1959.

Andrews, Ralph W., *This Was Sawmilling*, Seattle, Washington, 1957.

Andrews, Ralph W. and Harry A. Kirwin, *This Was Seafaring*, Seattle, Washington, 1955.

Drushka, Ken, *Against Wind and Weather*, Vancouver, British Columbia., 1981.

Dumont, William H. and G. T. Sundstrom, "*Commercial Fishing Gear of the United States*, United States Department of the Interior, Washington, District of Columbia., 1961.

Faber, Jim, *Steamer's Wake*, with Foreword by Murray Morgan, Seattle, Washington, 1985.

Grainger, Martin Allerdale, *Woodsmen of the West*, First Edition, London, England, and Toronto, Canada, 1908. Reprint with Afterword by Murray Morgan, Seattle, Washington, 1988.

Hitchcock, Beulah and Helen Wingert, *The Island Remembers*, Shelton, Washington, 1979.

McCurdy, H. W. and Gordon R. Newell, *Marine History of the Pacific Northwest 1895–1965*, Seattle, Washington, 1966.

McCurdy, H. W. and Gordon R. Newell, *Marine History of the Pacific Northwest 1966–1976*, Seattle, Washington, 1977.

McDonald, Lucille, *Alaska Steam*, Anchorage, Alaska, 1984.

Munyan, May G., *DuPont—The Story of a Company Town*, Puyallup, Washington, 1972.

Neal, Carolyn and Thomas Kilday Janus, *Puget Sound Ferries: from Canoe to Catamaran*, Sun Valley, California, 2001.

Newell, Gordon R., *Pacific Steamboats*, Seattle, Washington, 1958.

Newell, Gordon R., *Ships of The Inland Sea*, Portland, Oregon, 1951.

Books (continued)

Newell, Gordon R. and Joe D. Williamson, *Pacific Tugboats*, Seattle, Washington, 1957.

Puget Sound Piling Busters, Yearbook, Seattle, Washington, 1950, 1951.

Skalley, Michael and James A. Cole, *FOSS: Ninety Years Of Towboating*, Seattle, Washington, 1981.

Stevenson, Shanna B., *Olympia, Tumwater And Lacey: A Pictorial History*, Norfolk/Virginia Beach, Virginia, 1985.

Thomas, Berwyn B. and Fredi Perry, *Shelton: The First Century Plus Ten*, Shelton, Washington, 1996.

United States Treasury Department, Bureau of Customs, *Merchant Vessels of the United States*, Washington, District of Columbia, 1868–Present.

Wick, Carl I., *Ocean Harvest*, Seattle, Washington 1946.

Wright, E. W., *Marine History of the Pacific Northwest*, Portland, Oregon.

Technical Papers

Hanson, H. C., "The Effect of Deadrise on Loadline Rules," The Society of Naval Architects and Marine Engineers, Seattle, Washington, mid 1960s.

Nickum, George C., "Puget Sound Automobile Ferries: Their Evolution and Design," The Society of Naval Architects and Marine Engineers, Seattle, Washington, 1965.

Periodicals

Pacific Motor Boat, Seattle, Washington.

Pacific Work Boat, Seattle, Washington.

Puget Sound Maritime Historical Society, *Sea Chest*, Seattle, Washington.

Seattle Times, Seattle, Washington.

News Tribune, Tacoma, Washington.

The Olympian, Olympia, Washington.

INDEX TO ILLUSTRATIONS

ACKNOWLEDGEMENTS

For generous assistance given, I am grateful to:

Sharon L. Knutsen, my wife and a good shipmate aboard our own little vessel, for believing that the time and expenditure of energy required to compose this book would be worth the effort and for being understanding of the occasional frustration endured in trying to piece together the past.

Susan M. Knutsen, my daughter, who holds a Bachelor of Arts Degree in English and is a teacher in the public high schools, for offering, from time to time, critiques of this book, as well as providing much appreciated encouragement.

Anna J. Knutsen, my mother, for providing a number of photographs that illustrate this book along with some background that helps to put those pictures into context.

Morris N. Knutsen Jr., my brother, for providing some of the photographs that are included in this book as well as for helping to provide information regarding who, what, when, where, and why.

Ralph Stroebel, Saginaw, Michigan, historian, whose enthusiasm for preserving records of local history must have eventually rubbed off on me.

Mary Jamieson, Betty Wolf, Randy Estvold, and John Hurst, tugboaters all, for contributing photos and sharing experiences from the days that were.

Jim Dunlap and Mike Harlan, of Dunlap Towing Company, for being giving of their time in contributing information regarding the history of that well-known La Conner firm.

Heine Dole, retired Naval Architect and Marine Engineer, for permission to reproduce a fishing boat drawing of his design, and for his accompanying anecdotes.

Billie Howard and Shirley Erhart at the Mason County Historical Society; the staff at the Tacoma Public Library, Northwest Room; Jack Carver, John Kelly, and Jim and Phyllis Kelly at the Puget Sound Maritime Historical Society; Nicolette Bromberg at the University of Washington, Special Collections; Eric Taylor at the Snohomish County Museum; Margaret Riddle at the Everett Public Library, Northwest Room; Terry Slotemaker at the Anacortes Museum; Jeff Jewell at the Whatcom Museum of History and Art; and Steve Davenport at the San Francisco Maritime National Historical Park.

Norm Knutsen